D0518855

THE GREAT CARUSO

Also by Michael Scott

THE RECORD OF SINGING, VOLUMES ONE AND TWO

THE GREAT CARUSO

by

MICHAEL SCOTT

HAMISH HAMILTON · LONDON

HAMISH HAMILTON LTD

Penguin Books Ltd, 27 Wrights Lane, London W8 5TZ (Publishing & Editorial)
and Harmondsworth, Middlesex, England (Distribution & Warehouse)
Viking Penguin Inc., 40 West 23rd Street, New York, New York 10010, U.S.A.
Penguin Books Australia Ltd, Ringwood, Victoria, Australia
Penguin Books Canada Limited, 2801 John Street, Markham, Ontario, Canada L3R 1B4
Penguin Books (N.Z.) Ltd, 182–190 Wairau Road, Auckland 10, New Zealand

First published in Great Britain 1988 by
Hamish Hamilton Ltd

British Library Cataloguing-in-Publication Data:

Scott, Michael
    Caruso.
    1. Caruso, Enrico   2. Singers—Biography
    I. Title
    782.1'092'4   ML420.C259

    ISBN 0-241-11954-5

Typeset in 11/13pt Sabon by The Spartan Press Ltd, Lymington, Hants
Printed and bound in Great Britain by
Butler & Tanner, Frome and London

For Nicholas J. Hamer

Contents

CONTENTS

PART TWO:
The Works

Acknowledgements

The genesis of this book goes back to 1983. I am especially grateful to Alexis Gregory, who first gave me the idea, and to the late Alfreda Huntington, to whom I owe my first contact with Knopf. To Robert Tuggle, Archivist at the Metropolitan, I am incalculably indebted, for he spent a seemingly endless amount of time making valuable contacts for me, lending me photographs, and providing me with a great deal of intriguing information – without him this book would never have seen the light of day.

It also gives me pleasure to thank a veritable host who graciously afforded me every kind of help: Richard Bebb, for loaning me the Caruso caricatures, as well as for countless acts of generosity; Kathleen Begley, of the Bank of England Library, for providing me with a list of various rates of exchange during Caruso's career; Gregor Benko, who furnished me with copies of Caruso's letters relating to his early Italian appearances; Erna Bennett, who was able to explain differing spellings of Irish-American names; Jack Buckley, who arranged with Dilys Soria, the Librarian of the British Council, Rome, for me to use their microfilm reader; Andrew Farkas, for waiving his *a priori* right to Tom Kaufman's chronology; Gerald Fitzgerald of *Opera News*, for giving me access to the Francis Robinson collection of Caruso memorabilia before it was despatched to the Vanderbilt University, Nashville, Tennessee; Syd Gray, who found me the appropriate quotations from the works of H. T. Parker and Landon Ronald; Michael Kendall of Guy's Hospital Library, London, who sent me a copy of *Surgery, Gynecology and Obstetrics* containing a medical account of Caruso's terminal illness; William R. Moran, who introduced me by mail to Dr John Bolig, the discographer, as well as providing innumerable pieces of valuable information; Luciano Pituello, of the Associazione Museo Enrico Caruso, Milan, for showing me his considerable collection of Carusiana; Edwin Quest, Librarian at the Peabody Institute, Baltimore, who made me photostats of Caruso's scrapbook; Mrs J. B. Ryan, for arranging for me to see the correspondence at the University of Princeton between her father, Otto Kahn, and Giulio Gatti-Casazza; and Dr Ruffo Titta Jnr, who provided me with a photograph of the painting of his father, Caruso and Chaliapin, as well as enabling me to examine Jean Pierre Mouchon's thesis on Caruso's life. Anyone else, whom I may have inadvertently omitted, I thank all the same.

I have to thank the kind offices of many friends who have come to my assistance in innumerable different ways: Stephen and Mary Banks; John Bird; Edward Bridgewater; Heather Edwards; John Freestone; Richard Gaddes; Michael Hartnall; Jack Henderson; Joel Honig; Pamela Jones; Karen Kristenfeld; the late Willy Lerner; Bert Luccarelli; Vivian Liff; Chris and Colin McLean; Liz Measures; Andy Miller; Joel Pritkin; Robert Roberts; Patric Schmid; John Scott; the late Martin Sokol; Professor L. J. Wathen; Don White; Michael Zaccaria; as well as my father, Reginald N. Scott.

To three I owe a special debt of gratitude: Randolph Mickelson of Venice; my sister, Edith Scott, who, when I needed to visit England, generously put her country home at my disposal; and Michael Aspinall (this book will, I hope, compensate him for the myriad problems with which I constantly beset him).

I should also like to thank Richard Simon; and Lavinia Griffiths for working so carefully and considerately through my typescript.

More than thirty years ago Claudia Cassidy wrote in the *Chicago Tribune*: 'Caruso is as urgent in communication as if he had closed the door of a room, not of life.' He last sang in London, where I come from, in 1914, a generation before I was born and I doubt whether there are many still living who will remember any of those performances.* It is his records that have sustained, even enhanced, his reputation. Now he has been dead sixty-five years, his fame has not diminished, rather it seems to grow. For the first time ever, all his records are available (see page 292); more in fact than there were even

---

*Mary Ellis (born 1900) can still recollect him. A noted singer and actress, who created Friml's *Rose Marie* as well as leading roles opposite Ivor Novello in his musicals. Mary Ellis began her career at the Metropolitan in 1918–22. She sang Giannetta to Caruso's Nemorino in *L'Elisir d'amore* and in her autobiography *Those Dancing Years* she remembers his singing 'was of such tangible beauty [it] put a seal on one's hearing'.

when he was still alive and his name a household word. In the process of trying to convey something of his unique greatness, I hope I have not been guilty of resorting to the language that conceals rather than communicates. When occasionally it has proved necessary to recourse to a particular foreign term – such as *verismo*, for example – I have endeavoured to explain precisely what the word means. And I have tried to keep the narrative strictly to Caruso; every time the path of another singer of consequence crosses his, I have done my best to resist the temptation to launch off obliquely on a vignette. My two-volume work, *The Record of Singing*, attempts to provide details of the careers of more than 400 other singers in the first quarter of this century, an appreciable quantity of whom sang with Caruso.

The title I have chosen for my book, *The Great Caruso*, was the ubique soubriquet used to describe the tenor in his day at the height of his career. But, as Stanley Jackson laments at the beginning of his biography, the cinema stole it and made it 'impossible to dissociate him from Mario Lanza'. Happily Jackson need not have worried, for time is the supreme rectifier: now that Lanza has been dead getting on for half as long a time as Caruso, it is apparent once again that there is, notwithstanding MGM, only one great Caruso. Accordingly, therefore, I have ventured to put the shoe back on the right foot.

Michael Scott, Rome, 1987.

List of Illustrations

Phonograph: Note for British Readers

Following American usage, the word phonograph is used throughout to describe the traditional record-player or gramophone.

Rates of Exchange

In the period 1895–1914 the following rates (roughly) pertained:
£1 = $4.875 = 25.5 French Francs = 20.75 German Marks = 26.75 Italian Lire = 30 Spanish Pesetas.

Preface

Enrico Caruso came from Naples, a city then renowned as much for its squalor as for its singers. His family was poor, but not as poor as some; he went to school, and it was while still a boy that he first revealed musical talent, singing alto in a church choir. Later, after his voice broke and he began to work, he started singing in earnest.

It was in 1895, and following a preliminary attempt, that he made his first operatic appearance, at the Teatro Nuovo, Naples. He did not create a sensation for, in spite of the beautiful quality of his voice, his art was crude and his technique incomplete. In particular he had difficulty with his upper notes, finding it hard to manage anything higher than a top A without its shattering. In the course of the next few years, singing throughout southern Italy, by dint of hard work and experiment in an increasingly more demanding repertory, much of it then still new, he began to forge his own technique. At first his reception was equivocal, partly because of vocal problems, and partly because the critics, accustomed to the old school, found it difficult to accept his vehement and frankly more vulgar style. By 1902, however – at the precise time his first records were published – the operas of the *verismo* school were triumphant. At the very beginning of that year, at the San Carlo, Naples, the critics and box-holders withheld their approbation, but Caruso appealed over their heads to the gallery. It was a new century and the age of the common man; from this time dates the beginning of his unrivalled progress throughout the operatic centers of the world.

By the end of 1903, Caruso reached New York and quickly established himself as the world's foremost tenor, notwithstanding a few initially dissenting opinions. Thereafter the Metropolitan became the center of his activities. Heinrich Conried, then its Director, had first heard Caruso's voice on a record, and so it can be said that the phonograph's role in his American career was significant. During the next seventeen years, he appeared at the Met more than six hundred times and in thirty-seven different roles. And here, as in so much else, his timing was perfection. The Met was ready for a new star. Until 1891 it had been a German theater. Then, in the 'nineties, under the sway of the de Reszke brothers, Jean Lassalle and Pol Plançon, it was the French repertory that predominated. From the turn of the century a new influence began to manifest itself, that of New York's half a million Italian immigrants. It was appropriate, therefore, that the new idol should have been one of their countrymen.

From his early years, like all opera singers of those days, Caruso had been an important performer of modern operas, and in New York for some time he continued to appear in new works, including roles such as Dick Johnson in Puccini's *La Fanciulla del West*, Julien in Charpentier's opera, Flammen in Mascagni's *Lodoletta* and Avito in Montemezzi's *L'Amore dei tre re*. The Charpentier was a flop and neither the Puccini nor the Mascagni made any lasting impression. The role of Avito was one of Caruso's rare failures; it stretched his technique to its limits and it was the last part from a new opera he ever undertook. It was almost as if he realized instinctively that there was nothing left for him in the contemporary repertory which, from a singer's point of view, had gone as far as it could.

So he began to switch his attention to revivals. At La Scala in 1901, he had already undertaken Nemorino in a revival of Donizetti's *L'Elisir d'amore* at Toscanini's suggestion, and, after the maestro came to the Met in 1910, Caruso appeared in one of his two only eighteenth century roles, Renaud in Gluck's *Armide*, in which he had precious little to sing. In 1913 he sang Riccardo in another Toscanini revival, Verdi's *Un Ballo in maschera*; then, during the later part of his career, he added Saint-Saëns's Samson, Jean in Meyerbeer's *Le Prophète*, Alvaro in Verdi's *La Forza del destino* and Eleazar in Halévy's *La Juive* (this was the last opera he sang).

All of these he created anew. His is the performing style still extant today, and by the end of his life the hegemony of his style was complete. It not only succeeded the 'bleating' vibrato-ridden tenor of the previous generation, which had never been popular outside the Italian operatic empire, but very soon the traditional French and Russian styles were also in retreat. No singers today are even faintly reminiscent of Alessandro Bonci, Edmond Clément and Dmitri Smirnov. Their elegant and refined manners could not survive when they came to New York, and they failed to make any headway with a public in love with Caruso's opulent voice.

PREFACE

More than half a century has elapsed since his death and every modern tenor right up to Luciano Pavarotti and Placido Domingo is a direct descendant of his, as his records make plain.

PART ONE

The Life

CHAPTER I

1873–1894

ENRICO CARUSO was born in Naples on February 25, 1873,[1] less than three years after the unification of Italy was finally accomplished and the outbreak of the Franco-Prussian War had caused the French garrison to be withdrawn from Rome. Until 1860 Italy had been simply a geographical expression, but in that year the kingdom of Italy was established. Before then, for centuries, it had been divided into states. Naples had been the capital city of the Two Sicilies, ruled over by a branch of the Spanish Bourbons. Although only a hundred and forty miles south-east of Rome, it retained its individual character; Neapolitan was spoken, and not only did it have its own particular architectural style, as every ancient city in Italy still does, but its inhabitants were different in appearance, being generally shorter, darker and more swarthy than their northern confrères.

It tells us something of Naples and its people that the apartment in which Caruso was born – situated today above a sweet shop in the crowded back streets, in Via San Giovanni e Paolo, popularly known in Caruso's day as Via San Giovaniello agli otto calli – looks now much as it must have done at the time of his birth. His family was poor but not poverty stricken. His mother, Anna Baldini Caruso, was then nearly thirty-five and, her first seventeen children all having died in infancy, it was not surprising that she had not the strength to nurse him herself. She passed him over to a Signora Baretti, who had recently had a child who had not survived. She was, by Caruso's own account, a lady of noble birth; and it was this woman's resilience, as well as 'putting into him some of her own big heartedness',[2] that enabled him to escape cholera and the other diseases then endemic in Naples. After Errico – as his name is styled in Neapolitan – his mother gave birth to three more children, two of whom, another son, Giovanni, and a daughter, Assunta, survived childhood. But by that time she was forty-four and she never regained her health.

Errico was eight when his father, Marcellino Caruso, who worked in the jute industry, became custodian of a warehouse of the Meuricoffre company and the family moved to a tied property at Sant'Anna alle paludi. By all accounts Marcellino seems to have been principally remarkable for his drinking habits. Apparently he was particularly fond of a wine that came from the slopes of Vesuvius. One day, as he was returning home with a cask of this, he was stopped by an exciseman and told he must pay a tax on it. 'What!' he exclaimed, 'me pay again for this wine?' And he sat down, up-ended the cask and drank it back. Then, staggering to his feet, he turned to the official and said: 'Now, I don't pay!'

It was his mother who took charge of Errico's education, and she gave him his first lessons in reading and writing, for at that time school had to be paid for. At the age of ten the young lad went out to earn his own living. At first, in the day-time, he worked as a mechanic at Salvatore de Luca's factory but, after demanding a pay rise which was not granted, he left and joined the establishment of Giuseppe Palmieri, a manufacturer of drinking fountains. In the evenings he became a member of a school that trained soloists for church choirs, and in such fashion he gained his first experience of singing in public. This choir was organized by Father Bronzetti and the choristers took part in services in Naples's churches. The basic experience he derived from this was to have a profound effect upon him. He studied *solfeggio* and learned to read music, and this enabled him to develop one of his first artistic skills – copying music. As he himself later told, the process assisted materially in impressing the words and notes of operatic roles upon his memory. It also had another effect that was to remain a talent for the rest of his life: he acquired a facility as a cartoonist and became skilful as a caricaturist.

Life in the cramped, squalid circumstances of Naples a century ago, with the high infant mortality rate and the epidemics of cholera, had a profound effect on the boy. From an early age he evinced a preoccupation with personal cleanliness that he never lost; his hair was always brushed, his clothes, no matter how worn, were always immaculately turned out. '[Yet the] future great artist was nevertheless a boy; pretty much all boy, and at [that] a capricious one.'[3]

Anna Caruso became increasingly unwell, and Dr Raffaele Niola came frequently to examine her. Since there was not sufficient money in the home to afford these visits, Errico was charged to take round to the doctor's house some *mozzarella*. After leaving the cheese in the kitchen, instead of departing, he would listen behind a closed door where he could hear the sound of scales, roulades and vocalises, for the doctor's sister, Amelia, gave singing lessons. He would then try to imitate these exercises. Eventually Signorina Niola heard him and she became interested in him. When she agreed to give him some free lessons, he rushed home and proudly told his father. But she was shocked by his excitable gesticulations and his provincial accent. She forbade him to pronounce in front of her a word of Neapolitan and decided to concentrate at first on his Italian. So he did, for a time, but Errico wanted singing lessons, not Italian lessons, and he soon began to stay away. It was not until some time later, when the doctor asked Marcellino what had become of Errico, that his father first learned of his truancy. Furiously he ordered his son to start work immediately at the Meuricoffre factory.

The boy was, however, not particularly successful weaving jute. He preferred to scrawl designs for rugs on rough sheets of wrapping paper, thinking them better than any of the ancient patterns used. But his father quashed any aspirations he may have had to art and gave him a mighty box on the ears as his only reward. Nevertheless Errico persisted and when another worker accepted one of his patterns, and was only too delighted to give him 20 Lire for it, his father refrained from boxing his ears a second time. And he did not entirely relinquish his singing. During those years he might be called upon, for a lira or two, crouched beneath a balcony, to raise his voice in song, and deputise for some mute Romeo apparently serenading his Juliet. He was barely a teenager and already, we may believe, the possibility of a singing career must have preoccupied him. In 1887 he made his first appearance in an operetta, when he sang the part of the comic Janitor Don Tommaso in *I Briganti nel giardino di Don Raffaele* by Campanelli and Fasanaro. And there were a number of other musical events in which he took part.

One would always remain in his memory – June 1, 1888, when he sang at the Church of San Severino. He had gone there reluctantly, for his mother was seriously ill, and it was while he was in church that a neighbor came looking for him with news of her death. This was a traumatic event for the boy, although by November of the same year Marcellino Caruso had married again. Errico's father's second wife, Maria Castaldi, an intensely religious woman, proved the opposite of the traditional stepmother, for she worshipped him and they remained on good terms throughout his life.

It was at the time of his mother's death, as he later himself related, that he felt justified in altering his career while there was yet time, and he thereupon announced his intention of abandoning the jute business to devote himself entirely to music. His father, when he heard this resolution, gave him the choice of learning to be a mechanic or starving. Preferring starvation, he became that day a wanderer on the face of the earth, with a strong physique, his voice, and an unfailing optimism.[4]

So it was that he managed to pick up a poor living singing at church festivals and private entertainments. By the autumn of 1889, and after his voice had broken, he began to appear in the evenings at various *caffès* singing Neapolitan *canzoni*. At one of these he was accosted by a man who urged him to protect his voice and to learn to use it correctly, and who offered to take him to meet his brother, a singing teacher. 'At seventeen, I faced the problem – was I a baritone or a tenor?' Caruso recalled in after years. 'I went to this teacher but I left after only eleven lessons because he could not tell me which class of singer I belonged to.'[5] But he continued singing wherever he could. On another occasion we catch a glimpse of him in an impromptu concert given at the Caffè dei Mannesi.[6] Out of a crowd stepped a man with a hazlenut colored bowler perched over his right eye; pushing people out of the way, he pointed to a slim youth and said, 'Let Errico sing!' The musicians looked at each other disdainfully, and one of them turning to the young lad said: 'Too many cooks spoil the broth.' 'I want him to sing,' the man insisted, and he led him among the orchestral players saying, 'Tune up! The boy will sing a song by Denza.' The music struck up and the voice of the youth, luscious, passionate and resonant, combined with those deep, almost African eyes of his, conquered all hearts; the crowd was untiring in its demands for an encore.

In 1891 Errico met Eduardo Missiano, a young baritone from a good family. (Years later, in 1908, he would bring Missiano, then destitute, over to New York to sing *comprimario* roles at the Metropolitan; he remained there for the last four years of his life.) Missiano was greatly impressed with Errico's voice, and, waving aside objections that he had no money, he at once took him to meet his maestro, Guglielmo Vergine. But Vergine said Errico was too young and that his voice was not yet sufficiently mature. ' "It is," he claimed, "like the wind whistling through a chimney." '[7] However, when Missiano insisted on Vergine's giving the young man a second trial, he agreed to accept him for regular lessons, and Errico, not having any money, signed a contract obliging him to pay, at such time in the future that he might be earning, a quarter of his salary to Vergine over a period of five years. (When the young singer's reputation was burgeoning, Vergine sought to interpret these terms in a rather extraordinary manner and this led to a law suit, as will be seen later.)

It was Vergine's practice to hold his lessons for all his pupils together in a large room, and he would call upon each of them to sing arias or deliver exercises. He would then approve or admonish and ask for comments from other members of the class. At first Errico was not surprised at being ignored, for he considered it valuable for him to hear and observe. In such a fashion did Vergine prevent his students developing any overweening self-confidence. When Errico was eventually called upon to sing, he did not use his full voice. He had listened to the other singers, some with stronger voices than his own, and thought then, as he admitted in later years, only slightingly of his own chances. It was Vergine who impressed upon him the need to sing naturally – the public should never become aware of how much effort a singer uses. Errico took this dictum to heart, and it was only gradually that he came to develop his full powers so as to reveal all the distinguishing characteristics of his voice. This slow development accounts for much of the criticism that he was then subjected to. For some years he continued to crack on high B flats and B naturals, even after the natural beauty of his voice had already established for him considerable recognition on the operatic stage. It was only later that he learned the art of supporting the high notes.

It should not be forgotten that Caruso's art came to maturity at the same time as *verismo* opera, and there was the inevitable delay between the growth in the style, as evinced in the increasingly dramatic demands of works then being composed, and the adaptation made to it by the singers of the day. This continuous development, as *verismo* opera came to the pinnacle of its popularity and the phonograph was rapidly introducing opera to vast new audiences, led to Caruso's perennial preoccupation with the production and scale of his high notes; it remained a constant dynamic element of his art.

While young Errico was taking singing lessons from Vergine, he was scraping a living, earning perhaps ten Lire an engagement, singing at church festivals in Naples and its environs. Once, at Maiori, some thirty-five miles down the coast, after the service was done and he was anxious to get back home again, a summons came for him to sing at the home of the mayor, Baron Zezza. He could not but comply. He sang there all night and it was not until dawn broke that he was free to leave. The morning air proved so intemperate, however, that the Baron insisted on giving the tenor one of his old shooting jackets to keep him warm and as a souvenir of the occasion. Years afterwards, in 1913, Caruso was reminded of that night in a letter from the Baron, who wanted to know why, if he was the same Caruso who had sung at his house all those years ago, he had never returned the jacket. Caruso replied that he had no idea what had become of it, but if the Baron wanted another he must first send the money that he should have been paid. His fee was by then $2,000, and that was only for three hours work, whereas he had sung on that occasion for eight hours – and there was twenty years' interest too! Baron Zezza hastily responded that he had no intention of annoying Caruso about the coat. He merely wished to find out if the young man who had sung at his house was indeed the world-famous tenor. He was content to secure his autograph. With typical generosity Caruso despatched the Baron a framed photograph and a silver hunting flask.

Errico continued his studies and then, in accordance with the laws of conscription, he enlisted in the army and became a soldier. There was no escape from this, and for the next few months he served with the Thirteenth Artillery at Rieti. But even as he was trying on his first uniform he swore that Naples should one day acclaim him its favorite tenor. This was like whistling in the dark, for he was not sure how he was to become a singer, but at any rate it strengthened his resolve. One morning, as he was busy at his bench polishing his buttons on his uniform and singing away at the top of his voice, an officer, Major Nagliati, chanced by. 'What is your profession?' he demanded. Errico stammered, 'I have none but I want to become an opera singer.'[8] The Major did not reply but strode out of the room; Errico fancied he was laughing at him. Great was his surprise, therefore, when that evening he was summoned to the Major's office and told that a singing teacher had been found who would give him lessons for the rest of his service. After the first few weeks he had learned the role of Turiddu in Mascagni's new *verismo* opera, *Cavalleria rusticana*, then only three years old. By this time the whole regiment knew what was happening. Some days, during his free time, he would sing for the men in the drill hall. After a few such appearances the Major came and stopped him. 'How many times must I tell you not to annoy me with your singing?'[9]

he demanded. The Major then called Errico to his office again. He told him that it was impossible for him to be a singer and a soldier at the same time, and that, therefore, providing his brother came in his stead, he would be demobilised. One may imagine the intense gratitude that overwhelmed the young man.

Back in Naples again, Vergine decided to draw Errico to the attention of Nicola Daspuro. We get some idea of the close inter-relationships in opera in those days from Daspuro, for he was the representative for southern Italy of a leading music publisher, Casa Sonzogno, as well as being a successful journalist, impresario and librettist. In 1893, when Daspuro had secured from the municipality of Naples the exclusive management of the Teatro Mercadante, he arranged for Sonzogno to supply him with the music of a variety of operas. His company was made up of several prominent singers including Roberto Stagno and Gemma Bellincioni, Francesco Tamagno, Adelina Stehle and Angelo Masini.

Years later, Daspuro remembered how Vergine had come to him raving ecstatically over some young tenor, a possessor, so he claimed, of a voice of exceptional beauty and angelic sweetness. Vergine wanted Daspuro to engage him at the Mercadante, but this was not possible, for the company was complete. Vergine was not deterred, however, and he went on to describe in detail, with infinite fervor and expression, all the qualities of his exceptional pupil; he went on begging and beseeching Daspuro, in the way peculiar to Neapolitans, at least to give the young man a hearing. To get rid of him, Daspuro agreed: 'All right,' he said, 'bring him over with you and I'll hear this miraculous voice!'[10] So next day, Vergine was back at Daspuro's office, and this time with Errico. After hearing him, Daspuro congratulated him on the beauty of his voice, his clear enunciation and the warmth of his delivery. He promised that he would do everything in his power to secure him his first engagement. He kept his promise; when his conductor arrived he called Errico back, and they all heard him, and it was agreed that he should make his debut as Guglielmo in Thomas's *Mignon*, a lyric role. The day of the first rehearsal arrived. But, alas, what a different Errico was there then. The extreme sensitivity of his temperament, the nervous excitement occasioned by the other professional singers and the conductor, his uncertain execution of the music, all of these things succeeded only in paralysing his nerves. He mixed up the words, he began or finished a phrase out of time and, worst of all, his voice cracked on every high note. At length

9

the conductor lost his temper and told Daspuro it would be utterly impossible to keep him. Vergine took Errico away, almost in tears, and that was the last Daspuro heard of him for some time.

It was typical of Caruso's superstition that he never did sing the role of Guglielmo, which would have ideally suited him.

We may easily imagine the kind of nervousness that beset the young singer when he found himself required to raise his voice at the opera for the first time. Even in Naples, then a center of vocal culture, he could not have had much idea of the prevailing standards in his art. He did not have, as singers would in the next generation, any clues from records. Indeed it seems doubtful that he had ever been inside an opera house before he made an attempt to sing in one. Nowadays, in a world surrounded by a blather of artificial noises, it is extremely difficult to get even a faint impression of what life was like before electric amplification. Today, as often as not, opera singers are discovered at televised singing competitions. But in Caruso's day all of them had, perforce, to acquire the art not simply of producing an ingratiating sound but of projecting that sound through the spaces of an auditorium and out over the ever-larger orchestras. It was in such a fashion that they gained their reputations.

The triumph of the tenor is a comparatively modern one. Before the invention of the phonograph, opera was still a dynamic art form, and opera singing was in a constant state of development, dictated by the ever more elaborate works then being composed. In baroque days it had been the castratos who stalked the scene – male sopranos who were decked out as Julius Caesar, Hercules or Aeneas. There was nothing preposterous about them, given that these mighty warriors burst into song in the first place. We should remember that without artificial amplification brilliant voices are by their very nature more affecting. With the advent of the romantic style and the invasion of the theaters by a bourgeois audience, these male sopranos were inevitably succeeded by prima donnas, whose voices could contrive similar effects. It was not until Napoleon's day that a revolution in the production of the tenor voice came about. The problem lay in the management of the falsetto register which would bring into play more than a fifth of an octave in range and enable the tenor to vie with the soprano. The history of singing throughout the nineteenth century deals with the fashion in which these notes were produced so as to sound out over the increasingly strenuous accompaniments and appeal to the singer's masculine ego. Initially, the tenor's upper range did not extend far; by Rossini's day, however, it encompassed the high C, sometimes C sharp and even D. These notes were still produced in falsetto, not the coarse, white and open tone that the term may suggest today, but in a blending of the registers – the *voce mista* – in which the head voice predominated. In the next generation came Giovanni Battista Rubini, one of the legendary names from the age of *bel canto*. His influence was to have a profound effect on singing even up to the time of Caruso. His was a vaunting virtuosity; the tale of his singing an F instead of a D flat during a run-through of Bellini's *I Puritani* in 1835, and of the composer's decision thereupon to mark it in the score, much to the embarrassment of every Arturo since, has become a legend. But for certain the F would have been completely in falsetto; physiologically it could not have been otherwise.

It is said that Rubini introduced the vibrato, perhaps as an expressive device but, more probably, as a kind of sleight-of-the-voice – as a way of papering over the crack between the chest and head register. His method was widely copied and for a time, at least, proved successful. But by the 1850s, when Verdi had written *Rigoletto*, *Il Trovatore* and *La Traviata*, the steady growth of the orchestra led to singers, in their efforts to hold their own, being forced to resort to an excess of vibrato. In what we may call the Italian operatic empire – which stretched via Spain and Portugal to South America, and across Europe to Poland and Russia – it became the *modus operandi*. In the Anglo-Saxon world, however, its use became so obtrusive that 'Italian' tenors sang, as Shaw describes, 'so horribly that they were classed as "Goatbleaters".'[11] He particularly railed against Enrico Tamberlik and Julian Gayarré; although: 'I admit the right of anybody to prefer [the vibrato] to the round pure tone and unforced production without which no singing is beautiful to my ears.'[12] We can hear something of it in recordings of Bonci, Fiorello Giraud, Fernando Valero and Fernando de Lucia. In the recordings left by the last named, the suspicion lurks that it also facilitated his skill in fioritura, enabling him, as it were, to run up and down the vibrato, so making florid music relatively easy to accomplish. It is indicative too that the trill was not a part of De Lucia's technique.

In the third quarter of the nineteenth century there gradually came about a definite separation between the lighter and heavier types of tenor voice, a part of that process of classification which was such a feature of the history of singing until recent times. Throughout the 1850s and 1860s Italian tenors, such as Mario, had sung everything from Ottavio, Almaviva and Nemorino, to Raoul in Meyerbeer's *Gli Ugonotti*, Giovanni in *Il Profeta*, Manrico in *Il Trovatore* and Riccardo in *Un Ballo in maschera*. In the succeeding generation Masini undertook a similar repertory and also added the tenor part in Verdi's *Requiem* and Radames in *Aida* on European tours under the composer's direction. But, though he continued to venture both of these for some years, by the end of his career in the first part of this century, he was resorting once again, as befitted a vocal virtuoso, to Almaviva and the *bel canto* repertory. On the other hand Tamagno, six years younger than Masini, did not become an international artist until his voice had developed sufficiently and he began to essay the heroic repertory, culminating in his creation of Otello in 1887 (even though in 1900 at Monte Carlo he could still manage Alfredo in *La Traviata*, which he sang for the only time in his career). In the nineties Otello became his most famous impersonation all the way from Buenos Aires to Moscow by way of New York. It was not until after the establishment of the *verismo* – true to life – style, that the categorization of the tenor repertory, as we know it today, was effected.

Gino Monaldi claims *La Traviata* as the first verismo opera. Till then, like Donizetti, Verdi had treated historical dramas – those of Shakespeare, Byron, Schiller and Hugo. With Dumas fils's *La Dame aux camélias* he abruptly shifted to the 'real' world, or at any rate to the contemporary world, to subject matter that had so scandalised bourgeois morality that, at first, it was found necessary to cloak it in the decency of period costume.* Though it quickly became one of his most popular works, and has remained so ever since, it was an experiment he did not choose to repeat. Similar claims have been put forward on behalf of Boito's *Mefistofele*, composed some fifteen years later in 1868. Here it is not so much the subject matter as the musical style that is prophetic: the strenuous vocal writing, in particular the inept setting of words in high-flying climactic phrases and the heavy orchestration, all prominent features of the operas of Mascagni, Giordano and Leoncavallo. In Margherita's Mad Scene, one of the last in Italian opera, the outbursts of coloratura are written in the

*However, recent research suggests that this was necessary at that time when Italian choristers were largely part-timers. They looked awkward in fashionable evening clothes, and it was thought better to attire them in fancy dress.

traditional modes, but to make their proper effect they should be expressed in a more anguished and dramatic style than would be appropriate for, say, Lucia or Elvira in *I Puritani*. Boito was the author of the libretto of another precursor of the verismo: Ponchielli's *La Gioconda*. With *Aida*, it is the most successful Italian adaptation of the French Grand Opéra, of Scribe's recipe. But if the architecture looks backwards – one show-stopping number after another – the impassioned style keeps going at full tilt all evening: Mascagni, as it were, out of Meyerbeer. Listening to, for example, La Cieca's 'Voce di donna', Enzo's 'Cielo e mar!' or Gioconda's 'Suicidio', we hardly need to be told that Puccini was a pupil of Ponchielli.

It was not until 1890 that all the ingredients of verismo were finally brought together under one act in Mascagni's *Cavalleria rusticana*. Here was a realistic subject, a contemporary setting, stark passions expressed in appropriately perfervid vocal writing, and a scenario moving swiftly and inexorably to a climax through a series of instantly appealing arias and duets. Hardly surprisingly, it created a sensation and became a model upon which were based a whole series of successors. However, as Franco Onorati has pointed out,[13] though Verga's short story from which the opera originally derives is nothing if not the quintessential piece of verismo, Verga himself watered down its effect for the stage version, and by the time Mascagni's three librettists got going on it, they could only manage a tepid and old-fashioned drama – it was left to the music to make the verismo impact. In the wake of *Cavalleria*, Franchetti, Giordano, Cilea and Catalani all brought out pieces in the same mould. It was with the appearance of *Pagliacci* in 1892, for which Leoncavallo had written words and music, that both libretto and opera could be said to be archetypically verismo.

There was the inevitable delay while singers hastened to adapt their techniques, for the high degree of realism demanded an appropriate singing style. In the course of the next few years this would become apparent in a shift away from those elegant, albeit tremulous tenors of the post-Rubini tradition, to tenors with less charm and more decibels. It was their concern to contrive a more manly sounding timbre, so as to match the heroes of verismo opera. Producing an altitudinous range was no longer regarded as so important, especially when this depended upon the use of a marked vibrato which became, with the increasing power of the orchestra, more bleat-like. It seems likely that Masini, although he never made any records, had a smooth round tone without the 'goat-bleat', and Francesco Marconi too; his records confirm this. So Caruso was not the first tenor to abandon it, yet he was the first to achieve a complete success in so doing – as his records were to show.

CHAPTER II

1895–1897

CARUSO'S CAREER may be said to have begun on January 2, 1895, when he sang the 'Tantum ergo' in the Vespers at Caserta Cathedral. A double-bass player heard him and was sufficiently impressed to recommend him to a wealthy dilettante who was planning to present an opera of his own composition in Naples during the following three months. So it was that Caruso came to make his operatic debut on March 15, 1895, at the Teatro Nuovo in Domenico Morelli's *L'Amico Francesco*. He took the leading tenor role in this *commedia lirica*, which the composer presented before an invited audience. It is difficult to get much idea of the effect Caruso created from reading the reviews today, for his contribution did not receive more than a line or two; indeed, whether all the journalists who wrote about it were actually in the audience seems doubtful. *Il Pungolo parlamentare* carries a cursory notice which refers to 'scintillating lights', 'bouquets of flowers' and 'applause which frequently interrupted the singers'.[1] It does at least mention Caruso, as well as the baritone Ciabò and the soprano Belvetti, and they are all praised for 'their accomplished interpretation of the composer's thoughts'. It is interesting to compare this review, which tells of some verses by a Signor Martorelli that were given in the form of an address by the Duca di Caccari before the performance, with another review in the *Don Marzio*, which writes of the address as if Martorelli had spoken it himself. Nor is this the only difference. There seems to be some confusion as to who was conducting, or at any rate, how the conductor spelled his name – was it Salvadore or Sansone? The *Don Marzio* concludes, 'Morelli is a young *appassionato di musica* who, in this opera, has given evidence of his considerable talents as a composer. Remarkable are the many melodic passages, and the orchestration is exquisite.'[2] There is no mention of Caruso at all, nor of any of the other singers. Judging from these critical panegyrics, which were written after the fashion of the day –

perhaps with a little silver inducement from the composer – it seems hard to explain the cancellation of the second two of the four originally planned performances. Reading between the lines, it was unlikely that this opera ever enjoyed any kind of real success. But Caruso did. He had been engaged at twenty Lire a night and, whatever Morelli felt about the fate of his own work, he was sufficiently grateful to pay him not only eighty Lire for the four scheduled performances but a bonus of fifty Lire as well. At the second, and as it transpired, the last, *L'Amico Francesco* on March 20, two attentive spectators were present at the theater: Francesco Zucchi, an agent, and Carlo Ferrara, an impresario who was organising a season at the Cimarosa, Caserta. In a little over a week, on March 28, Ferrara had secured Caruso to sing Faust, and it is a review of this assumption in *Il Vespero* which gives us the first description of Caruso's art: 'He is vocally charming. His voice is sweet and vibrant, mellow and melodious (as is his face) and most of all it is fresh. But he is, if I may say so, a Faust only a little in love. However, he is quite young and will certainly do honor to Neapolitan art.'[3]

The Caserta company was a typically precarious financial venture. Ferrara had got together a group of operas, including not only *Faust*, but two contemporary works, the inevitable *Cavalleria rusticana* and Pietro Musone's *Camoëns*, about the Portuguese poet, and for them he had contrived an all-purpose company with his wife, Ferrara Moscati, the contralto Molinari, Caruso and the baritone Enrico Pignataro, the only other singer whose art survives, for he made a few recordings in 1906. Perhaps inevitably, Turiddu, a Sicilian peasant, was, for Caruso, a sympathetic character and he received an even more enthusiastic reception than he had done for Faust. His voice, artistry, effortless emission and sentiment were all much praised. His phrasing too was commended, and one critic finished off prophetically: 'Caruso is a young man of great promise and the most splendid horizons have opened for him. A round of applause brought the endearing Turiddu to the footlights.'[4] In spite of his participation, however, *Camoëns*, was a failure and seems to have hastened the collapse of the season. Ferrara found it difficult to meet his obligations and after a month events came to a halt.

At that time, in the heyday of verismo, there were more than three hundred opera seasons going on throughout Italy each year; even small provincial towns such as Caserta managed one. In a large metropolis such as Naples several companies flourished: alongside the

San Carlo, which today is the only opera house, the *Teatri* Bellini, Nuovo and Mercadante all offered equally busy programs. Zucchi and Ferrara, like Daspuro and Sonzogno, were both agents as well as impresarios – to be one almost invariably meant the other. But where Daspuro and Sonzogno were important figures in the world of opera in those days, Zucchi and Ferrara were grabbing a living as best they could. It was now Zucchi's turn to play a role in Caruso's career. He had been a singer and knew something of the art from the inside. He is described as having a burly bulldog-like physique, henna-colored hair and a mustache in the style of Napoleon III. He kept an office, *al fresco*, at the bar of the Caffè de'fiori in the Via del municipio, one of Naples's busiest thoroughfares. From there he would combat the incursions of the Milanese agents into Neapolitan affairs, and organize his entire business with a veritable bandwagon of singers all ready, at the drop of a hat, to work for him.

It did not take Zucchi long to realise some of Caruso's potential and he soon arranged the young singer's next engagement in Naples. This came about when the Faust at the Bellini became indisposed. Pignataro, the Valentino, told Zucchi, and Caruso was at once pressed into service. Though performing in Naples was more demanding than singing at a provincial theater like Caserta, critical opinion of Caruso was enthusiastic. He remained there for the rest of the season, adding to his repertory the Duke in *Rigoletto* and Alfredo in *La Traviata*.

Afterwards, at the end of that summer, came his first international engagement, in an opera season held in Egypt. On the voyage out it soon became generally known that there was a singer on board. Basking in this new-found popularity, it happened one day, as Caruso was on the point of leaving the bar, that he was surrounded by a group of young British army officers who insisted on his rendering a few numbers. At first he showed some signs of reluctance but when they let him know that if he didn't oblige they would throw him into the Suez Canal he assented with alacrity and ended up singing all night. At length, towards dawn, one of the young men passed a hat around. When Caruso finally got back to his cabin and could count the money he found he was almost £100 richer – such a sum then seemed to him a staggering amount. After his death, in 1921, a report of this occasion appeared in *The New York Times* written by a Scotsman who claimed to have been present. But to judge from his account, for he remembered 'an Italian waiter in the officers' mess in Cairo'[5] who was urged to have his voice trained and given some help to do so, Caruso's own recollection of the occasion, as he told it to Pierre Key, is not only fuller but also more accurate.

In those Imperial days at the end of the last century the Italian influence was strong in North Africa; in Egypt, notwithstanding the British hegemony, Italian immigrants had settled in large numbers. At that time, in the golden age of opera, it was not surprising to find a considerable interest in it had spread as far as Egypt. Adolfo Bracale, the Egyptian impresario, was an Italian who had been a cellist in the Khedive's orchestra before embarking on an operatic venture of his own. Arthur Rubinstein remembers him as 'small . . . clean-shaven, [with] vivid blue eyes that never looked straight at you.'[6] The company appeared at an open-air auditorium in the Ezbekieh Gardens, and Caruso stayed at the Hotel Venuti in the Rossetti Gardens. The atmosphere of Egypt worked a particular charm on Caruso, away from his home environment for the first time. Various stories survive. With Enrico Santini, Bracale's nephew, he made a visit out to the Pyramids. As they were returning on the Nile, their boat capsized and they were precipitated into the muddy waters. Since no driver would take them back to their hotel, for fear of spoiling the fittings in his carriage, they were forced to ride a donkey, tandem. Another incident involved the baritone Vittorio Ferraguti. The two men, fancying themselves great lovers, became enamoured of a couple of Egyptian vaudeville artists, who spoke not a word of Italian and understood nothing of Italian opera, preferring the costumes to the singing. At the same time Caruso began to eat more and also to drink too much. Bracale recalls a splendiferous luncheon party held the day of one of the performances of *Cavalleria*. Caruso was a guest of honor, but unfortunately the wine proved too potent for him and, though Bracale did manage to haul him away, it was not soon enough to leave no effect on his singing that night. In the *Brindisi* he came to grief on the top C, and the audience was quick to express its displeasure. When he reached Turiddu's farewell, 'Addio alla madre', where he had to manage a top B flat, he cracked again and pandemonium broke loose – it was just as well it was only a one-act piece.

The next night, his sobriety having been restored, he enjoyed a big success as Enzo in *La Gioconda*; this was the first time he undertook the role. Another new part was des Grieux in the Egyptian premiere of Puccini's *Manon Lescaut*, then not yet three years old. Caruso spent five days closeted with Sarmiento, the conductor, trying to learn the part, but he had not mastered it sufficiently, as the Manon of that occasion, Elena Bianchini Cappelli, recalls.[7] She reveals something of the rough and ready circumstances in provincial touring companies of those days; in the last act, when Caruso had gone off-stage, she was suddenly surprised to hear him calling from the wings, *sotto voce*, telling her not to move because he was going to put the score behind her back, for otherwise he could not go on. She describes how embarrassed she felt before the public, for she was supposed to be dying, and she had appropriate gestures to make. But with the score propped up against her she was helpless to do more than just hold as still as possible, serving as a music stand for Caruso. Great was her fury when she realized that he was longing to laugh. Finally, when the curtain came down, she pursued him, hurling after him the score, which he had dropped in his flight. But no one in the audience was any the wiser and after the last performance Caruso created such a furore that Bracale made him a gratuity of £20.

Upon his return to Naples he found news of his success in Egypt had preceded him. The ship was barely in the harbor when a small boat came out to meet it with Zucchi on board bringing him an offer, and so on November 29 he made his Mercadante debut as Alfredo, only a little more than a year after his abortive attempt at Guglielmo in *Mignon* at the same theater (although by this time the management had changed).

The company – although relatively new – included two other singers whose careers were to become notable: the soprano Emma Carelli and the baritone Francesco Bonini. Caruso appeared in *La Traviata*, *Rigoletto* and *Faust* and, a comparative novelty at that time, Bellini's *I Capuleti ed i Montecchi*, in which Caruso's Tebaldo found much favor. The *Corriere di Napoli* acclaimed 'his sensitive moving performance, endowed with the most exquisite resources'.[8] Although he did not sing in the rest of the prodigious repertory – Cimarosa's *Il Matrimonio segreto* and *Giannina e Bernardone*, Auber's *Fra Diavolo*, Donizetti's *La Favorita*, Meyerbeer's *Gli Ugonotti* and Verdi's *Il Trovatore* and *La Forza del destino* – his performance schedule was extremely tight (and much tougher for the singers than anything one might come across these days). In Christmas week he actually sang no fewer than twelve performances!

Wednesday, December 25, 1895: *Rigoletto*,

Thursday, December 26, 1895: Matinée, *Rigoletto*,
Evening, *I Capuleti*,
Friday, December 27, 1895: Matinée, *La Traviata*,
Evening, *Rigoletto*,
Saturday, December 28, 1895: *La Traviata*,
Sunday, December 29, 1895: Matinée, *Rigoletto*,
Evening, *La Traviata*,
Monday, December 30, 1895: Matinée, *I Capuleti*,
Evening, *Rigoletto*,
Wednesday, January 1, 1896: Matinée, *La Traviata*,
Evening, *Rigoletto*.

By the time Caruso reached the Mercadante he had already begun to attract attention. Emma Calvé, the most famous Carmen of her day, heard him. She was overcome with astonishment. 'What a marvellous – what an extraordinary – voice. It is a miracle! . . . a diamond of the first water!'[9] Caruso himself later came to admit that these performances were his first significant essays in opera. On January 11, 1896, he appeared as Faust, and before the end of the month he had sung it ten times. On January 30 his *serata d'onore* produced a sizeable audience at the Mercadante and he was warmly acclaimed and loaded down with bunches of flowers. '*Faust* was staged and the opera gave ample opportunity to display his formidable technique, as well as the grace and charm of his appealing voice. He sang with great sensitivity and persuasion and finally complying with the audience's demand he gave an encore, "Fiorellin d'aprile" by Galassi.'[10]

Early in February Zucchi arranged for Caruso to return to Caserta to sing Faust. '"But the peasants," as Zucchi puts it, "are always peasants. They are unaccustomed to *bel canto*,"'[11] and after a fairly tumultuous second act the opera ended abruptly. The season did not resume and Caruso returned once again to Naples.

At the same time his younger brother was leaving for Massawa, where Italy had become involved in its first attempt to gain control of Abyssinia. No doubt this war, in which Giovanni deputised for him, would be one of the many reasons for his liberal generosity towards his brother in the years to come. Only a week later his next engagement, a Sicilian tour, began at the Garibaldi, Trapani, on February 15, where he undertook for the first time Edgardo in *Lucia di Lammermoor*. A couple of days previously, at the dress rehearsal, he had been involved in another vinous incident, possibly out of feelings of guilt over his brother's departure for Abyssinia. He would relate this story of intemperance on many occasions during his maturity. Apparently he had drunk more than he should have at a luncheon, and then gone to sleep off the effects, but he had not woken again by the time the dress rehearsal was under way. He was hauled out of bed, washed, costumed and then thrust on stage. He had only just made his first entry when he confused the words, singing 'le volpi della Scozia' (the foxes of Scotland) for 'le sorti della Scozia' (the fate of Scotland). Howls of derision greeted this, the curtain was rung down and, when the rehearsal was finally resumed, it was conspicuously without Edgardo. At the premiere the audience greeted him with shouts of 'le volpi della Scozia!', and, though he was no longer under the influence of any libation, by the end of the opera he had practially lost his voice – or maybe nerve. The enraged impresario peremptorily dismissed him. But before Caruso had been able to rustle up the money to undertake the trip back to Naples, his replacement lost his nerve, too. The public insisted, there and then, on the return of 'le volpi della Scozia'. So at least everything ended satisfactorily and next morning, amid the clamor, the press were round at his hotel. They took a snap of him, apparently draped in a Roman toga, but in fact it was only a bedspread – his one shirt was out on the line drying.

Caruso remained with the same company in Sicily for another three months, eventually giving his last performance at Marsala. As well as Edgardo, Turiddu and the Duke, he appeared as Elvino in Bellini's *La Sonnambula*, which he only ever undertook once again, and he sang in the Sicilian composer Paolo Frontini's *Malia*, which he did not repeat. Upon his return from Sicily at the end of May, again at the behest of Zucchi, he was invited back to Naples for a brief sojourn at the Bellini, where he sang the Duke, Alfredo, Faust and Piero in Bucceri's *Mariedda*.* He then went to Salerno, a port some thirty-five miles south-east of Naples. This engagement was to prove most significant and from the beginning he was challenged by the demands made of him. He appeared on September 10 as Arturo in Bellini's *I Puritani* under the direction of Vincenzo Lombardi. This is a notoriously high role. *I Puritani* was then more than sixty years old; and Rubini, the

* The conductor here was Gaetano Scognamiglio, who later moved to New York where he plays accompaniments for many of Caruso's records (see page 280). He is not to be confused with another Neapolitan, Enrico Scognamillo who organized the birthday party for Caruso in 1917 (see page 151), as well as journeying with him on his United States concert tours. In the summer of 1921, he came back to Naples to spend some time with Caruso. He died there too, only a few weeks after the tenor. He is buried opposite Caruso at the Cimitero del pianto in an identical sarcophagus carved with a frieze featuring theatrical masks and musical instruments.

tenor for whom Arturo had been composed, produced his top notes with a greater proportion of falsetto than would have been considered tolerable by Caruso's day. So it had become necessary to delete or alter much of the tenor's music: for example, the passage 'Credeasi misera', in which Bellini has written an F above high C for Rubini, was usually cut, while the aria 'A te, o cara' was transposed down, sometimes a semitone, but often a whole tone.

At this stage of Caruso's career a good deal of what constitutes today's popular operatic repertory was still being written – the works of Puccini, Mascagni, Leoncavallo and Giordano, for example. It is not surprising that the management of his top notes and his ability to combat the ever-increasing size and importance of the orchestra should have been the key to his success. Lombardi, as was common at that time when opera was still a vital art form, was an important singing teacher as well as conductor: his pupils included De Lucia and Pasquale Amato. It was he who offered to assist Caruso suit this music to his voice. It was not his concern that Caruso should seek to emulate tenors in the Rubini tradition, rather that he should come to terms with *I Puritani* in the verismo style: all the music would be sung in that fashion, and what could not be managed must be either transposed or cut. Nothing was to be allowed to affect the natural quality of his voice. His problem was putting out the exacting tessitura with sufficient power, masculine sounding, but not shouting; opening the throat sufficiently, supporting the voice fully. '"I will make 'longer' [your] voice," Lombardi promised, "because you do not know *how* to sing."'[12] As well as concentrating on his voice Lombardi also recognized the importance of the development of Caruso the artist and accordingly he made himself responsible for the singer's introduction to the wider world. One day, instead of lessons, he took him out by carriage to the ancient ruins of Pæstum. In those years began Caruso's gradual awakening to the beauties of the world. It was then that he would wander through the museums and galleries in Naples making sketches of the bronzes and statues. This interest was to grow with the passage of years when later he would begin to acquire many works of art himself.

Notwithstanding the greater confidence that Lombardi imparted to him, he only ever undertook Arturo, like the other Bellini roles he assumed, on a handful of occasions. *L'Eco* writes of his fluency, grace and of a voice 'which has been well trained', but that his uppermost notes were not faultlessly produced is evident, for 'he was visibly indisposed and could not display all the vocal means with which he is endowed.'[13] After one of the performances of *I Puritani*, at the instigation of Lombardi, De Lucia came to meet Caruso. Since all the transpositions in the world could not have lowered Arturo sufficiently for De Lucia, there was no hint of competition and this was a role that he never attempted. He congratulated Caruso, only emphasising the need to study.

In the next part Caruso undertook, Turiddu, he was entirely at home: 'His sweet voice, that of a real tenor . . . proved capable of stirring the entire auditorium'.[14] It was in this more vociferous work that the greater tension in his technique he had imbibed from Lombardi now enabled his high notes to come forth more easily and with increased power. He developed a characteristic gesture when producing them which he did not change thereafter. As we can still see in photographs of him singing, he would hold his head back so as to let out the tone to the highest reaches of the auditorium (see front cover).

These performances of *Cavalleria rusticana* brought his first season at Salerno to a conclusion, but this proved to be no more than a brief hiatus in Caruso's engagements there. *La Frusta*, a local newspaper, was owned by Giuseppe Grassi. He had not been present at Caruso's debut, and it was as a result of Lombardi's enthusiasm that he went to a performance of *I Puritani* and heard the young tenor. He was profoundly impressed by the beauty of his voice and he took his daughter along to hear him; in no time she had fallen madly in love with Caruso. Caruso was the toast of the town. No other singer at Salerno had ever enjoyed such acclaim, and Grassi lost no time in engaging the tenor himself and organizing a special season of 'Carusiana' that was to begin that October.

On November 22 Caruso added a new role to his repertory, Fernando in *La Favorita*, and the press went wild in its enthusiasm. The effect he created was electric. 'His performance was a revelation . . . a triumph in the full sense of the word,' wrote *L'Eco*. 'He lavished on every piece the emotion and sensitivity of the true artist. His portrayal of Fernando is by no means inferior to the greatest celebrities of our day . . . and to think that in just three days he was able to assimilate a whole opera that he had never seen before and perform it so impeccably!'[15] Grassi's newspaper, *La Frusta*, even went so far as to challenge the San Carlo or La Scala to find anyone his equal, extolling his 'timbre', 'perfect intonation' and 'consummate skill even in the most difficult passages'. In the last phrases of his part he interpolated a high C which 'was of a silvery timbre, unwavering tone [and] the effect was truly astonishing.'[16] It is interesting that when he recorded 'Spiruto gentil' from *La Favorita*, almost ten years later, the high C in it causes him no difficulty, and one can hear the same silvery timbre alluded to by *La Frusta*. On the other hand, in the next part he sang for the first time in Salerno, Don José in *Carmen*, he cracked on the high B flat, a tone lower. The reason for this is explained by the change in style between *La Favorita* composed in 1840 and *Carmen* in 1875; the difference between producing a head note only supported by the orchestra, and contriving a chest note so as not to be obliterated by the more strenuous accompaniment.

That season at Salerno he was also booked to appear as Torre Pazzia in Sebastiani's *A San Francisco*. This was the first part of a double-bill which included Leoncavallo's new opera *Pagliacci*, for which Caruso had not been engaged. However, from the beginning there was some doubt whether Pagani, who had been cast in the role of Canio in *Pagliacci*, would prove well enough to undertake it. Grassi, anticipating problems, had advised Caruso that it might be necessary for him to sing it too, so it would be as well if he learned it. For the first two performances Pagani did manage to get through it somehow and it was not until the third performance, when Caruso was already embarked on a substantial meal – a plate of spaghetti, a couple of pork chops and almost a litre of wine – that it became obvious, as the opera proceeded, that Pagani was losing his voice. Despite Caruso's protests – 'You must be crazy!' – he managed to sing for the first time what was to become his most famous impersonation, and even then it was 'frantically applauded'.[17]

There was a considerable amount of coming and going in those early years of his career, for he left Salerno and returned to Naples to start another season at the Mercadante on December 16, when he appeared as Alfredo and Fernando and then, for the first time in Italy, he was Enzo in *La Gioconda*. In this he was commended for his magnificent singing of the aria 'Cielo e mar!' from the second act, and a bright future was predicted for him because of the qualities of lyricism that marked his art and vocal skill. In February and March he was in leading roles in two further pieces of ephemera: Fornari's *Un Dramma in vendemmia* and the world premiere of Lamonica and Biondi's *Celeste*. Only a couple of days after his Neapolitan engagement was done he was on his way back to Salerno. Undoubtedly the feeling of being a big fish, even if the pond was as small as Salerno, very much appealed to Caruso. He had responded to the amorous advances of Giuseppina Grassi and the two became engaged to be married – much to her father's satisfaction. Caruso was undoubtedly flattered by the attentions of a family seemingly so grand and influential. The whole of Salerno became like a second home for him. Although he only received twenty Lire a performance, 'I sing wherever I am asked, and in return I am given luncheons, dinners and sometimes presents.'[18] On this visit he also appeared as des Grieux in *Manon Lescaut* (his Italian debut in the role), Azim in Napolitano's *Il Profeta velato* and Enzo in *La Gioconda*.

Though he could not have realized it then, his frontiers were widening. After *I Puritani*, at the beginning of his Salerno stint, an offer had come from La Scala, Milan, inviting him to create Eraste in Franchetti's *Il Signor Pourceaugnac*, but his engagements had not permitted him to undertake it. Rumors of his successes had reached Daspuro and encouraged him to hear Caruso again. Daspuro came down to Salerno but, in view of the nervous crisis that had effectively put paid to Caruso's engagement in 1894 at the Mercadante, he did not advise the tenor beforehand of his presence. He sat at the back of a box throughout the performance and only went round and revealed himself after it was over. He took Caruso out to supper, telling him how much he admired his singing and promising to secure an engagement for him from Sonzogno in Milan. Almost immediately after this there came a telegram from a Milanese agent offering him a contract to appear in thirteen performances of *La Gioconda* at Palermo at 2,750 Lire for a period of forty-five days.

So it was that he left Salerno, and, with the prospect of such an emolument, he left Giuseppina Grassi too, taking with him instead a ballerina out of the 'Dance of the Hours'.

CHAPTER III

1897–1898

CARUSO HIMSELF later felt that his performances at Palermo marked the end of the first part of his career. Until then he had sung only in southern Italy and Egypt. He had been engaged on a tour of Sicily on one occasion previously, but not at Palermo. This was the inaugural season at the Teatro Massimo which, as the name suggests, is a big theater. The opening productions were of Verdi's *Falstaff* and Puccini's *La Bohème*, and after these came *La Gioconda*.

At the rehearsals the conductor, Leopoldo Mugnone, seems to have had mixed feelings about Caruso, whether because of the young singer's unreliable top notes or because of his success with the ballerina, whom Mugnone had also had an eye on, is difficult to say – maybe it was a bit of both. Caruso had an undoubted success when he made his debut on May 29, 1897, but there were qualifications. The critics seem to have been generally sharper than those at Salerno. They praised the freshness and appealing quality of his voice and commended the eloquence and grace of his style; but although his *mezza voce* was admired, his high notes were still considered somewhat defective. It was thought that the warmth of his voice made it ideally suited to roles of *mezzo carattere* but not to the dramatic repertory; it was in lyric music he excelled and it was in that that he would surely come to the fore. The *Gazzetta dei teatri* made some precise musical observations: 'The *romanza* in the second act ["Cielo e mar!"], thanks to the farsightedness of Mugnone, was transposed down a semitone, and the high notes in the duet ["Deh! non turbare"] following it were also lowered. But for the rest, when he sang in the middle range or at the bottom of his voice, he was bewitching.'[1]

Caruso's substantial fee at the Massimo effected a series of sartorial transformations and brought out the fancy dresser in him. He acquired a Derby hat and Prince Albert-style suit for the first time. The mustache he had worn until recently had been shaved off (it was to come and go fairly often in later years, making its final reappearance at the Metropolitan in 1916 for *Les Pêcheurs de perles*). His Salerno engagement in *Manon Lescaut* had prompted this – for was not, he reasoned, the Comte des Grieux a French nobleman who could never have looked like a Neapolitan ice-cream vendor? At that time photographs still show him looking slim, if not elegant, and although his hair-line was beginning to recede it was not for another two decades that it could be said to have retreated irretrievably. Until he reached Palermo, his name on posters was still often spelled after the Neapolitan fashion – Errico – but afterwards he would always remain Enrico Caruso.

Just as his career had expanded southwards so now, as a result of Daspuro's visit to Salerno, he was to journey northwards for the first time and appear in Milan. News of his success at Palermo once again travelled ahead of him and an offer came to stop off en route for some performances at the Goldoni, Leghorn. There he was engaged to sing Alfredo in *La Traviata*. Although this was Mascagni country – the composer had been born in Leghorn – Lisciarelli, the impresario, was anxious to mount for the first time another new work, Puccini's fourth opera, *La Bohème*, with Caruso as Rodolfo. *La Bohème* had had its premiere in Turin only eighteen months before and it was already proving such a success as to make Puccini incontrovertibly the greatest Italian composer after Verdi. Caruso had been disappointed when he had not been engaged to sing it at Palermo and it was Mugnone who thereupon recommended him to undertake it at Leghorn. Lisciarelli was a wily operator, however, and, taking advantage of Caruso's desire to sing Rodolfo, he booked him for a trifling fifteen Lire a performance – 'no one here cares about your acclaim in Palermo,' he declared. He did add, somewhat vaguely, that if Puccini liked him then he would up his fee to 1,000 Lire a performance.

Caruso, finding out that Puccini lived nearby, decided one day to pay a call on him. Accordingly he made the trip out to Torre del Lago, some twenty-five miles from Leghorn, to meet the composer at his villa. 'After hearing [the] ebullient young Neapolitan sing several measures of "Che gelida manina" from *La Bohème*, Puccini . . . exclaimed "Who sent you? God?" '[2] He later told how 'apprehensive Caruso had been, but he did not confide it to me then; only years afterwards did he tell me that he would have liked to have it transposed down a semitone. I told him that if it was a little high for him, then he might leave out the top C, for it was only an *oppure*.'[3] But since other tenors had quickly accustomed the public to it, Caruso found it more convenient to transpose the aria down a semitone and sing a top B instead of C. He returned to Leghorn with the composer's compliments ringing in his ears, and he went straight round to Lisciarelli to demand a bigger fee. The impresario prevaricated. 'Your contract, you have put your signature to it,' he insisted, 'calls for 15 Lire a performance' – and that was all he received.

Meanwhile Caruso was in love with the soprano, the Violetta and Mimì of the Leghorn performances, Ada Giachetti. She was some few years older than Caruso, a mature woman who was already married, and, although there was divorce in Italy in those days, their relationship was never legalised. She was, photographs suggest, a comely woman with a voluptuous figure. From the beginning their 'marriage' was to have a profound effect on Caruso. As his inept dealings with Lisciarelli had demonstrated, he needed someone with a firm hand on the reins of his career, and this she could certainly provide. She was strong minded, assertive, and even though her voice may have been only a run-of-the-mill soprano she was a good musician who could play the piano capably. She had come up the hard way and had developed considerable histrionic skill which, in particular, made an impression on the inexperienced young man from the start of their relationship. This is apparent from the *Gazzetta Livornese* after his first Rodolfo: 'he demonstrated his talent both as a singer and a dramatic actor . . . the strength, clarity and freshness of his voice are so well attuned to the role it is hard to believe that Rodolfo is not expressly created for him . . . The part demands exceptional acting ability and this is far from lacking in Caruso. One can predict a great future for him.'[4]

As with Canio in *Pagliacci*, Caruso's style and the role of Rodolfo in *La Bohème* were perfectly in tune.

His next engagement was at the Lirico, formerly the Canobbiana, Milan, then under the direction of Eduardo Sonzogno who, with Ricordi, was one of the leading music publishers in Italy. And it is not surprising that the operatic repertory there should have consisted of works published by Casa Sonzogno – works by Mascagni, Giordano, Cilea and Leoncavallo, and Bizet and Massenet, as well as such forgotten composers as Ferdinand le Borne. At that time opera was still a vital as well as, potentially at least, a profitable business, and the influence of the music publishers (for they represented the composers) was then at its height. One may imagine the jockeying for position and the various internecine feuds that went on behind the scenes; for these business dramas were quite as impassioned, though not perhaps as newsworthy, as the quarrels of warring divas. Sonzogno had been too much occupied at first even to hear Caruso, and it was only after a variety of disquieting rumors reached him that he wrote to Daspuro: "'I thank you for the present you have made me by engaging a baritone instead of a tenor!" Daspuro hastily responded: "Wait . . . do not lend your ears to jealous and wicked tongues." "Before judging it is essential to hear and see. Anyhow, if Caruso is a baritone De Lucia* is a *basso profundo!*"'[5]

It was not until November 3, 1897 – by which time Caruso had been waiting so long that he was obliged to secure an advance against his salary – that Sonzogno rescued him from the miserable state of improvidence that he had been left in after Leghorn, and at last he was engaged to sing Aracchillo in Massenet's *La Navarrese*. This role is in a one-act work written after the enormous vogue created by *Cavalleria rusticana*. He was expected to master it in only a few days. It proved difficult for him to do so and he became increasingly apprehensive. The rehearsals did not go well, yet the more mistakes Caruso made, the more the lady from Navarre insisted on his singing it (actually she was from the Opéra-Comique, Paris, a Belgian soprano by the name of Zinah de Nuovina). She did not fancy any competition and she felt sure that Caruso's success would be negligible. And so indeed it seemed to be, at first, for when he came on stage at the beginning he was greeted by ominous mutterings. But after he had sung his aria these were replaced by roars of approval. The *Gazzetta dei teatri* wrote: 'a revelation was the young tenor Caruso, who is destined for a great career. He had to repeat his aria after a thunderous ovation.'[6]

This concentrated attention on Caruso and led to his creating two further new operas that season. On November 10 he undertook Vito Amante in the first performance of Giordano's *Il Voto*, a reworking of *Mala vita*, which had had its premiere in 1892. After appearing in a double-bill singing Turiddu and Aracchillo on the same evening, he created Federico in Cilea's *L'Arlesiana*. Cilea had heard him and lost

---

* This is perhaps less remarkable than it may sound, for by the time De Lucia came to make his first records in 1902 he needed so many transpositions that he was increasingly unable to accommodate his voice to those of other singers. Although he continued to make records until 1920, of solos, duets and ensembles, these too would often be transposed.

no time engaging him. From this triumph his success in Milan was assured. 'His voice is wonderfully perfumed, his accents always touching and often irresistible, and his technique is praiseworthy indeed. He is at the very beginning of his career and still has some study ahead of him. Experience will help a great deal, of course, and before long he will be a star.'[7] At one of these performances Tamagno had been present. As he was leaving the theater, in the lobby, he ran into the Editor of *Il Secolo* – 'Did you ever hear anyone like him?' he exclaimed. 'He will be greater than any of us!'[8]

Following *L'Arlesiana* Caruso interrupted his stay in Milan, albeit briefly, for Sonzogno had been quick to contract him for a further period, and went down to Genoa, to the Carlo Felice, where he remained until the end of February. Here he added two new roles: Marcello in Leoncavallo's *La Bohème* and Nadir in Bizet's *I Pescatori di perle*. As his reputation grew, so he began to appear with more distinguished singers; in Milan, *Il Voto* had included Rosina Storchio as Cristina. In Genoa she sang Mimì Pinson in Leoncavallo's *La Bohème*, while Colline was Giuseppe De Luca, who was also Zurga in *I Pescatori*. This was the prelude to a duet between Caruso and De Luca that they would resume on a regular basis in later years. According to Giovanni Martinelli,[9] De Luca was always careful with his money. Even after Caruso's death he remembered vividly that, in Genoa, Caruso earned 5,000 Lire for the entire season (that is, in Milan as well as Genoa), whereas he had only earned 750 Lire. Caruso lived like a swell, for he had a spacious two-room apartment while De Luca had to make do with a cramped bedroom. Nevertheless, their friendship developed and Caruso would frequently hire a carriage on a fine day and take De Luca out with him for a ride in the Ligurian hills. There, captivated by the beauty of the vistas, he would stand up and sing wherever they happened to be. After the performances at the Carlo Felice he would invite De Luca out to dine with him at a *caffè* in the Galleria. Here he might be recognized and on one such occasion, when the proprietor begged him to sing something, Caruso got up and rendered the Flower Song from *Carmen*. Then, with De Luca, he sang 'Del tempio' from *I Pescatori*.

On March 8, 1898, in his second season at the Lirico, Milan, he was Marcello in *La Bohème* again. Although the characters in Leoncavallo's opera are the same as in Puccini's the libretto treats different scenes out of Mürger's autobiographical *La Vie de bohème*. Leoncavallo's score is after the operetta style, much beloved by him and in which many of his works are written. During the next year Caruso would appear in it twenty-nine times in all and even by 1911 he had not quite forgotten it, for in that year he recorded two of Marcello's arias. From the first time he had undertaken it in Genoa his teacher Vergine had warned him against it, and when he sang it in Milan newspaper opinion was also divided as to Marcello's suitability to his voice. The *Rivista teatrale melodrammatica* spent a considerable amount of space on his performance. 'His is one of the most beautiful tenor voices of today, but he should sing the old *bel canto* repertory, like *La Favorita*, *La Traviata*, *Lucia* and *Rigoletto*, instead of expending it on the invective of the third act of *La Bohème*, in which the exacting demands of the most dramatic declamation, one in which Caruso gives his all, can cost him his career if he does not accept my advice and abandon this opera and others like it.'[10] Years later in *The World* Caruso recalled the effect he made. 'I had been told that the music was not suited to my voice. But Sonzogno insisted on my studying it. Accordingly I sang it and to my amazement made such a hit that I pleased the composer and "notched" for myself, I am happy to say, the first step in such reputation as may be mine today.'[11]

In his next opera, *Carmen*, on March 16, the *Rivista* again praised his eloquent singing, particularly of the Flower Song, which he was obliged to encore, but lamented that in the third and fourth acts he seemed determined to outsing Tamagno. The season ended with another world premiere, Ferdinand le Borne's *Hedda*. As with *La Navarrese* by Massenet (whose pupil le Borne was), this was another attempt by Sonzogno to cash in on the popularity of the French repertory. But the work was thought too ponderous and it gave Caruso no opportunity to shine, though he did 'manage the terrible tessitura'[12] to advantage. From Milan Caruso travelled eastwards to Fiume.* Here, in company once again with Giachetti, he appeared in Puccini's *La Bohème*, *La Traviata* and Boito's *Mefistofele*, in which he sang Faust for the first time. On his way back to Milan, now the center of his activities, he stopped off at Trento and on June 4 he appeared as Gianni in the Italian premiere of Massenet's *Saffo*. The composer wrote a letter to the Trentine thanking them for having

---

* At this time and until the end of the First World War Fiume was in Austro-Hungary. In 1919 it was seized by Gabriele d'Annunzio at the head of a collection of fanatics. During the next five years it was an independent state but in 1924 it passed to Italy. After the Second World War, however, it was ceded to Yugoslavia and renamed Rijeka.

chosen to premiere one of his operas; from this we see how Sonzogno was doing his best to identify Caruso with works of the Casa Sonzogno.

It was during that summer, on July 2, that Ada gave birth to a son, Rodolfo. He was so named to commemorate their first meeting at Leghorn the previous year when Caruso had been singing in *La Bohème*.

By a coincidence Caruso was back in Leghorn for his next engagement, but this time at the Politeama Livornese. He sang there on separate evenings in *Pagliacci* and *Cavalleria rusticana*. In October, following a couple of months' break, Caruso came again to the Lirico, Milan, where he took part in revivals of two of the previous season's novelties: he was Federico in Cilea's *L'Arlesiana* – the composer had made some changes since the premiere – and Marcello in Leoncavallo's *La Bohème*. By this time his reputation had been well established and after Marcello on November 8 the *Gazzetta dei teatri* waxed eloquent in its praises: 'Caruso is always Caruso, but all the more so for his fabulous voice, his effective phrasing and his natural stage presence.'[13]

Sonzogno was doing his best to insert these operas into the standard repertory, and at the same time he was anxiously looking round for novelties. That season he was intent on producing a sequel to *Andrea Chénier*. So, on November 17, he introduced another Giordano opera, *Fedora*, with Caruso in the role of Loris. The occasion was well-organized and for the first time journalists from outside Italy heard Caruso. His success was complete and overwhelming. This must have been gratifying for Sonzogno, yet it was of such a magnitude as to leave the work, which, after all, was his first concern, in second place to the performance of it.

Caruso and *Fedora* were not instantly happily married. Originally Sonzogno had conceived the opera as a vehicle, as *Cavalleria rusticana* had been, for Bellincioni and Stagno. But Stagno, who was sixty, had died suddenly before Giordano had completed the opera. Sonzogno's first problem therefore was to find a tenor who would satisfy the composer as well as the public. Giordano had heard Caruso in his *Il Voto* only the previous year, and he thought the part too heavy for him. But after his attempts to secure De Lucia and the French tenor Charles Delmas proved abortive – the one was too expensive and the other too busy – he begged Bellincioni to make the decision for him and go and hear Caruso. She went to Leghorn and there heard him as Canio. She wrote back extolling the beauty and spontaneity of his singing though, as she notes, in a very different part from that of Loris. She concluded: 'Caruso's vocal gifts already make his success practically assured, and moreover as an actor he has dramatic temperament.'[14] Such a testimonial from Bellincioni was no mean compliment, for she was the 'Duse of Song' and one of Italy's leading sopranos in the last decade of the nineteenth century. It is interesting to note here the development in Caruso's dramatic art. Undoubtedly this was in part the result of the direct encouragement he had received from Giachetti but, indirectly as well, she was responsible for his increasing self-confidence that was becoming commented on from this time. She had, in fact, made a man out of him.

At the premiere of *Fedora*, Bellincioni failed to move the public as was her wont. Even in her appeal to the cross, 'Su questa santa croce', she was overshadowed by Caruso's achievement. Yet, in her autobiography, she does not fail to accord his performance its just worth: 'His triumph was a revelation and from the *romanza* in act two, "Amor ti vieta", began the fantastic good fortune that always accompanied the *divo* throughout his career.'[15] With this aria the opera reached its apogee and it brought the house down, as Giordano, who was himself conducting, recalls.

> The applause was not mere hand clapping, but it seemed to be explosions of passion. The cheers became overwhelming. Caruso gave an encore, as soon as I, surprised by that insistent, intoxicating storm, was able to calm down and start conducting again. The delirium was ecstatic and then there was a second encore and then another. The third act was a crescendo of enthusiasm . . . *Fedora* had been consecrated with the new star. Caruso's voice had conquered everyone's heart.[16]

For, notwithstanding Giordano, it was Caruso who enjoyed the real success.

In its first years following that premiere, *Fedora* was heard throughout Italy. In 1905, when it was given in Paris, Caruso would sing Loris with Lina Cavalieri and Titta Ruffo. The next year at the Metropolitan, New York, he repeated it with Cavalieri and Scotti and in 1907, again with Scotti, he appeared in it at Covent Garden, London. Since those days it has been mounted fairly often in Italy, but usually as a soprano vehicle, with Giuseppina Cobelli, Gilda Dalla

Rizza and Maria Caniglia, the last two of whom both left complete recordings, and more recently it has been revived with Renata Tebaldi and Maria Meneghini Callas. 'It was with the part of Loris that Caruso made his reputation and proved his individuality. Before this revelation, on going to the opera one was happy to know that Caruso was singing; now one goes expressly because it is he who is singing.'[17] Another aspect of Caruso's Loris was indicative: Giordano, later Artistic Director of Fonotipia, an Italian record company, actually made some recordings of himself at the piano in various selections of the tenor's music out of *Fedora* so that Caruso might work on the music on his own. This was the very first influence the phonograph would ever have on a singer's art.

Years later Caruso told Pierre Key: 'After that night the contracts descended on me like a heavy rainstorm.'[18] Carlo d'Ormeville, a librettist and noted critic as well as agent, lost no time signing him up for a season the following year in Buenos Aires, but before this he had still to fulfil his obligations at the Lirico, Milan, where he was to sing Gianni, this time to Bellincioni's Saffo, and then he would depart for his first engagement at St Petersburg, at the Grand Théâtre du Conservatoire. Suddenly it seemed the whole world was opening up.

CHAPTER IV

1898–1900

FOR THE first three years of his career Caruso's singing had been an Italian phenomenon. When he journeyed to Imperial Russia for the first time in 1898 it took on an international perspective.

At that time, in the generation before the Russian Revolution, the last years of the old regime were set in splendid chaos. Notwithstanding deep social unrest or, perhaps, because of it, this was a golden age of the arts. In the theater came Chekhov, Stanislavsky and Gorky. With the choreography of Fokine, the dancing of Pavlova, Nijinsky and Karsavina, and the decor and costumes of Benois and Bakst, Russian ballet revitalised its cultural counterparts in Western Europe. Russian opera, too, had been virtually unknown outside Russia prior to the advent of Diaghilev's company and Chaliapin in Paris after 1908, with the music dramas of Moussorgsky, Borodin and Rimsky-Korsakov. The terrible inequalities in wealth that enabled the aristocratic society to patronise Italian opera in the palmy days of Imperial Russia also enabled Russian singers, in the age immediately before the phonograph's invention, to acquire their technical expertise from Italians, both from teachers and from examples set down in front of them – like Caruso. To St Petersburg and Moscow impresarios would bring Italian companies to appear at leading theaters while the regular Russian troupe was on holiday. In the winter of 1898/9 Antonio Ughetti, an Italian who had been organizing groups of stellar names in Russia for many years, brought over Sigrid Arnoldson, Luisa Tetrazzini, Guerrina Fabbri, Masini, Marconi, Mattia Battistini and Caruso.

That first visit to Russia, only to St Petersburg, lasted about a month and Caruso appeared in four operas. He made his bow as Alfredo in *La Traviata*. There may have been a good dramatic excuse for the Germont of that occasion, Battistini being seventeen years older than his son, but the fact that the Violetta, Arnoldson, was also a dozen years Caruso's senior must have made him acutely aware that for the first time he was singing with two world famous artists whose careers stretched back to the beginning of the previous decade. The cast of the next opera, *La Bohème*, included not only Arnoldson and Battistini but Tetrazzini, the most brilliant 'coloratura' of her day, as Musetta. At that time she was still an immature artist and the best part of a decade away from the days of her great renown. Apart from that winter and the next in Russia, and a solitary *Rigoletto* at the Metropolitan, New York in 1912, they never sang together in opera again, although they always remained the best of friends. Years later she describes how Caruso's art developed:

> I remember Enrico as a youth of twenty years, before his voice was yet rounded and the different registers smoothed out. I recall the difficulty he had even with such ordinary notes as G or A. He always stumbled over these, and it annoyed him so that he even threatened to change over to . . . baritone [voice] . . . In those early days I did not run across him very often, and it was some years later, when during an opera season in St Petersburg I sang with him for the first time, that I saw what progress he had made and realized what a remarkable voice he had. The opera was *La Bohème*, the year 1897 (sic). I can hear that velvet voice now, and the *impertinenza* with which he lavishly poured forth those rich, round notes. It was the open *voce napolitana*, yet it had the soft caress of the *voce della campagna toscana*. There was never a doubt in my mind. I placed him there and then as an extraordinary and unique tenor. From top to bottom his register[s] [were] without defect.[1]

We may imagine Caruso's feelings in that cold, northern clime for the first time. In February, St Petersburg lay blanketed by darkness and the snow lay thick upon the ground. On the streets one heard only the muffled sound of sledges coming and going. Indoors the world came alive again in buildings carefully insulated against plummeting temperatures which frequently descended far below zero. Nowhere could have been less like Naples, even in the worst winter there – inside as well as outside, as Caruso discovered when he was summoned to take part in a concert at the Imperial palace at Tsarskoe Selo. The occasion remained in his memory for years after. 'The scene was brilliant. Such color, together with the beauty of the women and the bearing of the men. . . . I could feel people staring as I was received by the Tsar, [who was] a small, almost insignificant looking man with an anxious face.'[2] For Caruso's last engagement that season he appeared in both parts of a double-bill: as Turiddu in *Cavalleria rusticana* and

Edgardo in *Lucia*. Tetrazzini was to sing Lucia; as was then often the case, such a custom-staled work was revived solely for the benefit of a fabled *soprano leggiero*, and as soon as the Mad Scene was done the opera was too, so Caruso never got the opportunity of singing Edgardo's last act *scena*. Instead it was felt necessary to begin the evening with some contemporary piece and *Cavalleria rusticana* – then very much a novelty in Russia – was given. Caruso was to sing Turiddu opposite Ada's Santuzza. One may easily imagine how demanding it was to sing both these works on the same evening. Turiddu is a typical verismo part, while Edgardo is an old-fashioned lyric role with a comparatively high tessitura. It was not surprising that Caruso barely managed to get through the two performances.*

Bad news travels fast and, before he had got back to Italy, the air was thick with rumours of his voicelessness. The South American *impresaria*, Armida Pasi Ferrara, who had booked Caruso next after some performances at the Lirico, Milan, was very apprehensive. She rushed there to hear him as Loris in *Fedora* and was infinitely relieved to find him singing, if anything, even better than he had done the previous year. Undoubtedly his Russian experience had taught him the importance of pacing himself and, after finishing his Italian engagement, he continued his journey south-westwards across the Atlantic to Buenos Aires. It was the largest city in the southern hemisphere, and fast becoming one of the most important cosmopolitan centres in the New World. Newspapers there were published daily in Italian, French and English, as well as Spanish. This was the age of extensive immigration from Italy, mirrored in the growth of Argentinian opera houses at Córdoba, La Plata, Rosario and Tucumán, as well as Buenos Aires. There in 1908 would open the Teatro Colón, one of the largest theaters in the world. Its seasons were basically Italian and organised by Italian impresarios; even when the occasional French or German opera was given, it was always heard in Italian – such as *Lohengrin*, which Caruso was to sing in the 1901 season. In 1899, as usual, the company affected a predilection for 'Italian' singers, including Bellincioni, Regina Pinkert, Bonci and Adamo Didur.

* One story seems not to realize that Caruso sang both parts on the same evening. This was enough to explain his vocal difficulties without recoursing to a fancy tale of his having encored Turiddu's opening off-stage aria, the *Siciliana*, no less than three times and before he has even entered! This story goes on to tell of Leonid Sobinoff, the Russian lyric tenor, jumping up on stage, in mufti, and at once replacing him. The fact is Sobinoff never sang the role of Turiddu.

Caruso made his debut at the Teatro de la Opera in *Fedora* on May 14, after which he sang Alfredo, Gianni in *Saffo*, Enzo in *La Gioconda* and then he undertook Osaka in the first performance of the revised edition of Mascagni's *Iris*. His 'voice was acclaimed the most beautiful tenor of today',[3] and he was obliged to repeat the *Serenata*, 'which he sang wonderfully, like the rest of the performance'.[4] As Assad in Goldmark's *La Regina di Saba*, the aria 'Magiche note', with its delicate ascending conclusion to a piano high C sung in head voice, earned him such a reception that it seemed to be as much Caruso's as Goldmark's opera. Even in the long-forgotten Italo-Argentine composer Berutti's *Yupanki*, his singing of the aria 'Dea soave e pallida' made a delightful effect. His season eventually drew to a conclusion with Turiddu in *Cavalleria rusticana*. After the *Brindisi* such bedlam broke loose that he was obliged to repeat it three times. All the Argentine critics seem to have lost their heads amidst the raptures and when another tenor became indisposed and he was unable to attempt Sigmondo in Wagner's *La Walchiria*, Caruso was urged to undertake it instead – needless to say, he did not comply. By the end of that season the *impresaria* could count herself fortunate at having secured Caruso's signature on contracts for another two years, though she did agree to increase his salary for each occasion: that year he received 12,000 Lire a month, in 1900 this was to increase to 25,000 Lire and in 1902 to 35,000 Lire.

That summer back in Italy he returned to the scenes of his childhood. In Naples again, he visited his family. He bought his stepmother and sister lavish gifts, and took the whole family out for drives in the countryside. His father and he reversed roles they had once played; the old man sat silent now and listened to the tales told by his son. On other days Caruso was content to stroll through the streets of his home town acknowledging old acquaintances, and perhaps stopping for a moment at the fountain by the Ponte di Cerra, which he had once adjusted as a boy. During the brief interim before his next engagement he decided to secure the services of his first secretary. He remembered a promise he had made in Salerno at the time of his appearances there more than two years before, to a young enthusiast, Enrico Lorello, who had rushed back stage prophesying that 'you will one day be the greatest of the greatest!'[5] It was typical of Caruso that he should have at once responded by assuring Lorello that if he did become so successful then he would offer him the job of his secretary – the question of whether the boy might be suitable for the work was another matter. At all events, he did not forget him. It was this ebullient naïvety that made Caruso an easy victim of almost every kind of chicanery.

There was his contract with Vergine, which he had signed years ago in lieu of money for the lessons he received. He had promised to pay Vergine, at such time in the future when he might be earning, twenty-five per cent of his salary over a period of five years. But now that Caruso's reputation was expanding vigorously, Vergine claimed the contract did not mean fees from only the total number of engagements Caruso managed to secure during the first five years of his career, but a quarter of the total he had earned on 1,825 occasions, i.e. five times 365 performances! If this looks rapacious it might be remembered in Vergine's defence that his other pupils, even had they been on similar contracts, would scarcely have produced much, and there was no guarantee that even a majority of them would have provided him with much of a living. Caruso would have discussed the matter with Ada, and perhaps it was she who told him to refuse to pay. Vergine then took him to court and finally, after another three years had passed, a settlement was reached and Caruso paid over 20,000 Lire in lieu of the contract, but by that time Vergine's costs must have pretty well swallowed that up. In after years, Caruso's attitude to Vergine was ambiguous; in 1902 he denied that his success was due to any vocal tuition he had received, but by 1915 he would speak glowingly of Vergine's 'kindly sympathy and unfailing pains, he was the best of teachers and I always feel that I owe him the deepest debt of gratitude.'[6]

Caruso's engagements resumed the next season at the Costanzi, Rome, on November 4, 1899, as Osaka in Mascagni's *Iris*, and his success was widely commented upon by the press. 'He let loose a hymn of praise which can only be reported pallidly, it was such an overwhelming success,'[7] wrote *Il Popolo romano*. *Il Messaggero* thought that 'he possesses a truly exceptional *mezza voce*, his singing is so wonderful, it has passion, color and flexibility,'[8] while *La Voce della verità* dedicated most of its article on the opera to him, analysing his interpretation, and comparing him with other tenors – 'He has all the grace of De Lucia plus the voice of Tamagno.'[9] The remaining critics carried on in the same vein. A week after *Iris*, Caruso undertook Enzo in *La Gioconda*. And to this performance critical reaction was similar; 'There was such enthusiastic anticipation for the tenor Caruso that it was only equalled by the public's impatience. When the time drew near for the famous *romanza* "Cielo e mar!" there was a deadly hush. . . . He then sang so exquisitely, with such purity of tone and such uncommonly sensitive phrasing, that the public, electrified, broke into applause and clamored for an encore. . . . Thus, this accomplished artist received his second baptism of fire from Rome.'[10] By the end of 1899 he had been singing more than four years, yet the Romans still treated him as if they had been invited to give him the official seal of approval. All the performances were under the direction of Mugnone; this was the first time he had conducted Caruso since they had met seventeen and a half months before. Augusto Carelli, brother of Emma, who sang Iris at the Costanzi, tells how hard Mugnone had been on Caruso at Palermo.[11] When Lombardi, incensed, had wagged a warning finger at him – 'You'll see. This young man will soon be earning 1,000 Lire a night!' Mugnone had laughingly replied, 'When I'm Pope!' They met again at the Costanzi, and immediately Lombardi started genuflecting before Mugnone. 'I'm only doing my duty,' he announced. 'Now, you've become Pope.'

Caruso had become a focus of interest everywhere. The tenor Marconi, then at the end of his distinguished career, had no sooner arrived from Warsaw than he went to a performance of *La Gioconda*. And after Caruso's final opera that season, *Mefistofele*, in which he was Faust, the composer Arrigo Boito came backstage and was fulsome in his praises, congratulating Caruso warmly. Shortly before his farewell at the Costanzi he found time to sing at a press reception organized by the editor of *La Tribuna*, at which he enjoyed such an ovation that he had to repeat the 'Lamento di Federico' from Cilea's *L'Arlesiana* three times.

On January 17, 1900, the world premiere of Puccini's *Tosca* took place at the Costanzi. But by then Caruso had already left Rome. It is clear from an autograph letter of Caruso's in the Museo Teatrale alla Scala, Milan, written on board ship en route to Buenos Aires the previous year, that he had been definitely offered the role of Cavaradossi at the premiere, by the composer himself. However, it seems that the first Tosca, Hariclea Darclée, insisted that her lover, the tenor Emilio De Marchi, sing it with her. Caruso was, no doubt, disappointed. Yet that same July in Buenos Aires he would deputise for De Marchi in a performance of Massenet's *Manon* and then the following year, again at Buenos Aires, he sang Cavaradossi opposite Darclée's *Tosca*. That Puccini came to accept de Marchi seems to have been but one of the many machinations of Ricordi. For it was typical of him to penalise a singer who had been associated with so many successful operas published and staged by his rival Sonzogno. It was not until 1910, by which time Puccini was indisputably the leading Italian composer of the day, that he sought the services of the leading tenor of the day to create the hero in his latest opera, and Caruso came to introduce Dick Johnson in *La Fanciulla del West*. But by then, ironically, the opera did not enjoy anything like the acclaim that he did.

Caruso undertook Alfredo in *La Traviata* in St Petersburg again on December 28, 1899. His next part, on January 3, was Radames in *Aida*, which he was undertaking for the first time. The cast included not only Salomea Kruszelnicka but also Battistini as Amonasro and Vittorio Arimondi as Ramfis. Caruso's mastery of Radames, which was to become, after Canio, his most popular assumption, was gradual, and much of the opera's subsequent popularity dates from his great success in the role. Until then it had been undertaken by a variety of tenors from the stentorian-toned Tamagno and the perfect matinée idol of the nineties, de Reszke, to interpreters of Rossini, Bellini and Donizetti, including Gayarré, Masini and Marconi, all of whom today would be thought to have voices too lyric for such music.

'At first, the notion of Caruso [too] seems somewhat strange, for his outstanding qualities have been his incomparable lyricism and grace. One should bear in mind, however, that Caruso means to dramatise, and that his voice, with its strength, range and fullness, does lend itself extremely well to such an interpretation. Moreover, where is it written that the part of Radames can only be sung by a *tenore di forza*? Masini was never considered as such, and yet he was one of its most widely acclaimed exponents. And what effects he could produce with that beautiful, manly voice that he colored with such enchanting nuances! Such effects are within Caruso's means as well. He endows Radames with that sensitivity and vulnerability, along with the heroic aspects of the warrior. *Est modus in rebus*, and we can well imagine what Caruso does with his magic throat in 'Celeste Aida', in the third-act duet and the final scene of the opera. Caruso earns the praise of the most demanding, even in dramatic passages, which call for that vibrant voice that he has the good fortune to possess.[12]

Arimondi describes the performances as a great triumph for Caruso; at the beginning of 'Celeste Aida' he was a little nervous but his fresh voice and admirable method made the public go crazy about him. It was in these performances that Caruso sang for the first time 'a satisfactory high B flat'.[13]

In St Petersburg that season he also added another Verdi part for the first time, Riccardo in *Un Ballo in maschera*, with Kruszelnicka and Battistini. Tetrazzini took the travesty part of Oscar. He appeared with the same casts as the previous year in *La Bohème* and *Lucia di Lammermoor*, but this time, and notwithstanding Tetrazzini, the final scene was given so that he might finish the opera. The last role he undertook that season was in a revival of Donizetti's *Maria di Rohan*, a *cheval de bataille* of Battistini – nevertheless Caruso enjoyed a signal triumph in it. He also took the tenor parts in a double-bill of Lorenzo Perosi's oratorio: *La Resurrezione di Lazaro* and Rossini's *Stabat Mater*.

On January 22, 1900, he was Faust in the Russian premiere of Boito's *Mefistofele* with Arimondi in the title-role. It was on the morning before the last performance of this that Ada Giachetti and Maria Arimondi, the basso's wife, were expected from Italy. Lorello, Caruso's secretary, was despatched to the station to meet them. However, after waiting some hours in the arctic cold he returned alone to the hotel; without being able to speak any Russian or read Cyrillic he could not discover what had happened to them. Caruso and Arimondi were frantic, but at length a telegram arrived from Maria Arimondi; it had been transmitted in Russian, although she spoke not a word of it. They rushed down to the desk clerk but all attempts to decipher it proved unsuccessful. At length, braving the elements and altogether unsuitably clad, for the temperature was thirty degrees below zero, Caruso himself went round to the station. There, he managed to find out that the delay had been caused by a derailment, although there were no serious casualties. Eventually both ladies arrived by relief train and, except that they were suffering from exposure, they were well enough. The next day, and after *Mefistofele*, it was Caruso who was suffering from exposure and he developed bronchial pneumonia. He was obliged to take to his bed for two weeks while Ada ministered to his every need.

This year he travelled from St Petersburg to Moscow where he appeared in a shorter season and in works drawn from the same repertory, except that he sang a solitary Faust in Gounod's opera. It was more than four years since he had last sung it in Naples. Before the opera began, Caruso and Arimondi, the Mefistofele, were discussing the stage business – the precise manner in which he would pull the cord in his dressing gown to reveal the costume of the young metamorphosed Faust – when, suddenly, in the middle of their conversation, without warning, the curtain rose. No sooner had the public clapped eyes on the tenor, half in and half out of his costume, than everyone burst into laughter. And the reason for this sudden and unexpected curtain call was Maria Arimondi, who had been trying to find a place in the wings from which to watch her husband. She found what she thought was an undisturbed spot; what she did not realize was that she was standing right on top of the curtain release. So curious was she to find out what all the laughter was about that she stood on it again, and so to the great diversion of the public, down came the curtain as abruptly as it had gone up.

It was hardly surprising – being shuttled to and fro, back and forth across Europe and the Atlantic, from Russia to South America – that Caruso did not sing well on the first night of his second season at Buenos Aires on May 10, when he sang Faust in *Mefistofele*. The cool reception made him unsure of himself, plunging him into a typical depression, and he was on the point of quitting the Teatro de la Opera when, only a couple of nights later, at the second performance, he created his customary sensation. With the sun shining again, the season proceeded as it had done in the previous year; *Iris* followed and the Serenade was greeted by an hysterical public. Though the opera was a *succès de scandale*, it caused a number of protests and various religious organizations attempted to boycott it, 'for there were too many nudes but, as always happens on such occasions, the house was filled to the eaves at each performance.'[14] A string of successes followed: Assad in Goldmark's *La Regina di Saba*, Rodolfo in *La Bohème*, Turiddu and Massenet's des Grieux, in which he must have derived a sense of satisfaction at being asked to replace De Marchi, even though it was not as Cavaradossi. At the end of the season he took part in Verdi's *Requiem*, in a performance given as a memorial for Humbert I of Italy, who had been assassinated by an anarchist at Monza. On August 12, he appeared at the Progress Club in a charity concert, in which he sang a group of Italian songs and an aria from Massenet's *Il Re di Lahore*.

From South America Caruso returned to Italy and Ada Giachetti. After some weeks spent relaxing he resumed his engagements at

Treviso, and there, for the first time, he undertook Cavaradossi in *Tosca*, his performances drawing accolades 'for his marvellous voice, spontaneous, mellow yet powerful throughout its entire range.'[15] And here reviews suggest once again a notable improvement in his dramatic form. This may have been at least in part the result of Giachetti's presence as Tosca, but in all probability it had more to do with the fact that this was another new verismo opera; he was portraying Cavaradossi, a painter, as Rodolfo was a poet, and he was not required to play at being a king, duke or other noble, and this was not such a step away from his own circumstances. After a dozen performances at Treviso he went on to repeat these at Bologna, and here he was accompanied not only by Giachetti, but also by Eugenio Giraldoni, who had created Scarpia. The opera was conducted, as had been the Roman world premiere, by Mugnone, and here too Caruso earned superlatives. He then sang Osaka before departing for his next engagement that winter, in December, which would take him to Italy's leading theater, La Scala, Milan.

CHAPTER V

1900–1902

LA SCALA, Milan, marked another milestone in Caruso's path. Though he had already sung in South America and Russia, it was not until after his debut there that his career became truly cosmopolitan and took him within a few short years to Monte Carlo, London, Paris, Berlin and New York.

The date of his first appearance, December 26, 1900, was undoubtedly propitious. The sudden indisposition of Giuseppe Borgatti, the Tristano in La Scala's first production of Wagner's music drama, obliged the administration to switch operas for the opening night of the season and give *La Bohème* with Caruso instead. He was lucky, and turned this unexpected opportunity to advantage, although at first circumstances seemed compromised by his having a bad attack of nerves. It was not only the glory of the theater which intimidated him, but also Arturo Toscanini's prodigious reputation. The importance of conductors had increased steadily since the second quarter of the nineteenth century. Orchestral music had grown more elaborate and sophisticated and composers gradually ceased to be able to direct their own works, either from the keyboard or by conducting themselves. Toscanini may not yet have been the foremost conductor but, even at the age of thirty-three, he had built up a formidable reputation. The atmosphere of intense discipline which he created no doubt seemed strange, if not shocking, to a singer who had hitherto sung mostly in the provinces and, save for Mugnone, had not known many conscientious maestri before. The rehearsals for *La Bohème* had gone on a great length of time and Toscanini and Caruso had had not unfriendly discussions as to whether he should or should not sing out the high notes in full voice. Though, as we have seen, Caruso had already secured Puccini's explicit permission to omit the high C, he was too proud, or perhaps nervous, to ask such a thing of Toscanini. The *prova generale* commenced in the morning and continued all day with only a short interval prior to the open rehearsal which was held that evening. At break time Caruso at once took himself off and, ravenously hungry, availed himself of a much needed repast. So, when he returned to the theater he was quite unable, notwithstanding an urgent request from Giulio Gatti-Casazza, the Director General of La Scala, to manage more than half voice. Toscanini indignantly halted the rehearsal and would not have continued had not the Chairman of the Board of Governors, Guido Visconti, made peace.

The whole atmosphere of La Scala was so radically different from anything Caruso had experienced hitherto it was hardly surprising that he did not give a full demonstration of his capabilities until well after the first night. L'Alba ran the following account of his performance at the premiere:

> Caruso was a disappointment. The public had been expecting wonders untold from his golden throat and was instead left disconcerted, mortified at having been so poorly recompensed. [He] was obviously either in poor form or petrified with stage fright, his *mezza voce* is admittedly incomparable, but this, along with the occasional brilliant finale, hardly suffices to constitute success on La Scala's stage. . . . His best is yet to come, for with an artist of Caruso's talent we can well expect the opposite of what he gave.[1]

From the second performance onwards, however, everything changed as if by a miracle. The public, who were filling the house to overflow, were in ecstasies over his voice and his phrasing.[2] Yet even at later performances his acclaim was far from overwhelming. One obdurate critic, on January 5, 1901, still harbored reservations. He wrote that Caruso had recovered from his initial indisposition and produced a few persuasive tones with his marvellous instrument, but, though he was obliged to encore 'Quest'è Mimì' in Act II, his performance was still felt to be a far cry from the outstanding vocal and dramatic interpretation that his reputation might have led one to expect. Nevertheless throughout that month his reputation grew gradually and effectively. On the 27th, Verdi died and, in lieu of a lavish funeral, which he had explicitly forbidden, a special commemorative performance was given at La Scala five days later. According to Augusto Carelli's account, it was his sister who secured from Toscanini the opportunity for Caruso, rather than Borgatti, to sing in the quartet from *Rigoletto*. The choice was a fortuitous one in view of Caruso's success. 'All the artists were acclaimed in their respective roles but where the triumph attained a degree of climax and where the emotion was real was in the *Rigoletto* quartet. Each time that Enrico Caruso with his golden voice . . . attacked the phrase "Bella figlia dell'amore" an electric charge passed through the spectators, which certainly they had never felt before.'[3]

The next opera Caruso appeared in at La Scala was Mascagni's *Le Maschere* and he was to sing Florindo. The work was inspired by the *commedia dell'arte*, and this was the first time that Mascagni had attempted a vein of comedy. Sonzogno had fixed six different premieres of it all over Italy on the same night, but it was a success only in Rome, where the composer was conducting. At La Scala it survived just three performances, entirely owing to Caruso, for he was the sole positive element in the reviews – his singing 'like a ray of sunshine'.[4] The flop sent Gatti and Toscanini into a huddle. The orderly progress of the season was abruptly broken. What they needed was to find 'a practical substitute . . . something [else] of a comic nature'.[5] It was then that with Toscanini's agreement, Gatti decided to produce Donizetti's *L'Elisir d'amore*. Nowadays it may seem surprising to believe that it could ever have been out of the repertory and comparatively unknown, at least in Milan. Indeed it was still performed at provincial theaters in Italy throughout the last century, but not at La Scala, which prided itself on the modernity of its repertory. Nothing else in the 1900–01 season was older than *Tristano e Isotta*, which had had its premiere in 1865. Gatti lost no time in approaching Caruso, between acts of *La Bohème*, to sing the role of Nemorino. 'I know only "Una furtiva lagrima",' the tenor replied, 'but if [you wish] I will begin tomorrow to study it.'[6]

There was a considerable amount of apprehension before the premiere. Gatti received many letters from irate subscribers plainly telling him that he was turning La Scala into a provincial theater and that he would be punished with a fiasco even more decisive than he had had with *Le Maschere*. Quite possibly these exhortations were fathered by the music publishers, for no one owned the rights to a Donizetti opera any longer; he had been dead fifty-two years.

It was not until Caruso had begun the passage 'Chiedi al rio perchè gemente', his voice and art in a perfect balance, that at length the audience gave in. He had hardly finished the last note of the cadenza when an explosion, a tempest of cheers greeted the youthful conqueror. So uproariously and so imperatively did the house demand a repetition that Toscanini, notwithstanding his aversion to encores, was compelled to grant one. When the curtain fell Nemorino was called out again and again, and during the interval Caruso alone was talked about. His critical reception was unanimous: the *Gazzetta dei teatri* almost passed out in pirouettes of hysteria.

> What can one say of Caruso? This irresistible charmer, who from the beginning of the season until today has marked a triumphal ascent which has brought him to the pinnacle of success. . . . One can go no further than that. He is not just a *tenorino* but a flesh-and-blood Nemorino, recreating the composer's intentions like a true artist. In the two duets with Adina it is hardly possible to imagine greater powers of expression or greater vocal control. Never is his phrasing vulgar, never is there any strain in his delivery. He is spontaneity personified. Privileged by nature, Caruso is born to sing and bewitch. The culminating point of his success that evening was, naturally, "Una furtiva lagrima", which is one precious gem of divine Italian melody. Oh! how that tear makes us cry! Some impressions one cannot relate, one simply has to experience them. The audience sprang up acclaiming him, and then reacclaiming his encore. Triumphal honors were awarded this fascinating artist.[7]

Caruso concluded his first La Scala season as Faust in *Mefistofele*. The performances began on March 16, 1901, and introduced into Western Europe the Russian bass Feodor Chaliapin, who, like Caruso, was born in February 1873. Chaliapin ranks along with Caruso as one of the greatest singers of his day. Indeed, in one respect, Chaliapin's achievement was even greater. The naturally affecting quality of high voices, as we have already noted, gave sopranos and tenors the ascendancy in opera. Up till then even the best basses had been used to singing supporting roles. Chaliapin changed all that, transforming the bass from a character and secondary player into the protagonist. And it was inevitable after he had undertaken the title role in *Mefistofele* with success at La Scala that it should have become established in the international repertory. After seeing Chaliapin in the part, Boito wrote: 'Only now do I realize that I never had up to this time, any but poor devils!'[8] Chaliapin's first appearances in Western Europe almost eclipsed Caruso; the *Gazzetta dei teatri*, for example, found only space for two or three lines about his Faust: 'His heavenly voice vibrates in the air and in our hearts like the echo of a fascinating enchantment, and applause broke out whenever he stopped singing.'[9] Perhaps it was to their mutual advantage that they only appeared together in two seasons in their careers, for few impresarios would have cared to pay out both their fees at the same performance. After Caruso's death Chaliapin recalled those rare occasions:

I met him first in the rehearsal rooms at La Scala before undertaking Mefistofele. Caruso and Carelli were singing in half voice and I must say that I was very greatly relieved; it had been a strenuous journey from St Petersburg, so when I had to sing I did as they did and just hummed. Toscanini hesitated a moment but he did not say anything. After a minute or two, however, he went to speak to Gatti, who thereupon told me to employ my full voice, as was the custom at La Scala with someone they did not know. I did so at once and was sincerely congratulated, but I was a little nervous of Toscanini, at the way he acted. Caruso explained that Toscanini was like a dog that barked a lot but did not bite; he knew the other singer's voices, but I was another matter. . . . I gained the most delightful impression of Caruso, he had the face of goodness. And his voice – it was the perfect tenor. What a treat it was to sing with him! I met him on the working stage only once again, that was in New York at the Metropolitan in 1908, when we were both singing Faust in French for the first time. [In fact Caruso had already sung Faust in the original at the Metropolitan in 1906.] I remember how scared we were, and we agreed that we should care more about the emission of notes rather than the pronunciation of words. But everything went well and we even managed to pronounce the text correctly![10]

Records confirm that their enunciation was clear even if their accents were foreign, and certainly Chaliapin created a mesmeric effect, to which almost every succeeding interpretation has been indebted. For Caruso, his Faust in Mefistofele was a timely engagement. Since his first appearances in southern Italy, he had worked a considerable improvement on his dramatic abilities. As reviews suggest and photographs show, he had become altogether surer and more relaxed after his first La Scala season. Without even remotely attempting to emulate the Russian's histrionics, Caruso was nevertheless encouraged by the dramatic element at work in Chaliapin's art.

Caruso's next engagement was again at the Teatro de la Opera, Buenos Aires. That year Toscanini was to conduct there for the first time and Caruso's season commenced on May 16 when he sang Cavaradossi with the original protagonists: Darclée as Tosca and Giraldoni as Scarpia. At first, memories of last season's cast at the same theater, Carelli and De Marchi, caused some dissension and the audience was unresponsive until the second act had begun. But at Cavaradossi's outburst "'Vittoria! Vittoria!" with his heavenly voice'[11] Caruso swept all recollections aside and the public hostility vanished. His triumph was such that the next act could not proceed until he was permitted to encore 'E lucevan le stelle', despite Toscanini's objections. Subsequently he repeated Assad in *La Regina di Saba*, Osaka in *Iris*, and for the first time in Buenos Aires he was the Duke, Nemorino and Alfredo. He also undertook three performances of *Lohengrin*, the only time he ever appeared in a Wagner role. He sang in Italian. It was not until 1922 that Wagner's operas were first given in the original at the Colón. Undoubtedly *Lohengrin* was the best suited to Italian taste, being the most lyrical of Wagner's mature works. Toscanini had directed it at La Scala in 1900 and it was perhaps inevitable that he should have conducted it again in Buenos Aires the following year. In 1906, in New York, by which time Wagner's works were heard at the Metropolitan in German, Caruso told the *Morning Telegraph* that he would still like to sing Tristano and Walther in *I Maestri cantori*, for 'it was not the strain of the vocalisation but the strain of the German consonants upon the vocal cords'[12] that particularly bothered him.

On July 29 he sang in a concert at the Teatro de la Opera 'Cujus animam' from Rossini's *Stabat Mater* and on August 17 the season ended, as it had begun, with a performance of *Tosca*. In South America that year photographs show him looking much as Geraldine Farrar described him when she first met him: 'Clad in shrieking checks, topped by a grey fedora, yellow gloves grasping a gold-headed cane, he jauntily walked onto the stage.'[13] Although his sartorial taste ran amok, he was always scrupulous in matters of personal hygiene. His general dislike of physical exercise was causing him to put on an increasing amount of weight and he would often be seen smoking, usually Balkan Sobranies, and any suggestion that this might harm his voice would be lightly brushed aside.

During the next two months he remained in Italy with Ada Giachetti, and then resumed his career, travelling once again to Imperial Russia, but this time only as far as Warsaw, Poland. Here he was to undertake five operas: *Rigoletto*, *Carmen*, *Aida*, *Un Ballo in maschera* and *La Traviata*, but his success was so great that he was obliged to add *La Bohème* and *Mefistofele*. The company included a number of artists with whom Caruso had previously appeared in St Petersburg and Moscow, including Kruszelnicka, who was once again Aida, Amelia in *Un Ballo in maschera* and Margherita in *Mefistofele*, as well as Janina Korolewicz-Wayda, who remembers him in her autobiography. His Italian season began again at Bologna, when he sang the Duke. Newspaper critics were again enthusiastic, commenting on his inclusion of the aria 'Parmi veder le lagrime' which at that time it seems to have been the custom to 'generally omit'.[14] After this he went on a trip to Trieste, where he undertook a couple of charity performances of *L'Elisir d'amore*. This was the first time that his new-found affluence had enabled him to donate his services. Trieste was then still in Austro-Hungary and after the second evening he was brought back before the curtain to a cheering house to be presented with a special souvenir: a tie-pin, a pearl surrounded by emeralds, diamonds and rubies – the Italian tricolor.

These events were succeeded by a debut which held special significance for Caruso personally. This was at the San Carlo, Naples – a theater second in importance in Italy only to La Scala, Milan – where he sang Nemorino on December 30, 1901. He had, of course, appeared in Naples before, but only at lesser theaters which had not the prestige to compare with the city's leading opera house. Caruso looked forward to singing there for, not unnaturally, an enthusiastic reception from his townspeople meant more to him than one in Buenos Aires, St Petersburg or even Milan. When he had last sung in Naples he had not yet secured his high notes and, though the quality of his voice attracted attention, it did not come forth effortlessly or spontaneously. But he had already been away nearly five years, and in the interim he had worked a considerable improvement on his form. He was returning home confident that a great success awaited him – for surely, he reasoned, everyone in Naples would want him to have one. It was at La Scala, Milan, that he had revived *L'Elisir d'amore*, and with his accomplished manner and modern approach he had succeeded in restoring it to the front rank of the operatic repertory. It was only natural that he should expect that Naples would grant him a similar – even a more enthusiastic – reception. As Daspuro recalls:

He was young, inexpert, nonchalant and full of vigour, sure of himself and of his beautiful voice, and not in the least inebriated with his memorable success at La Scala. He was convinced, as any young man would be too, that his fellow citizens would be proud and very anxious to have him sing in Naples again, and bring him home like some Masaniello of the arts. Because of his confidence, he did not think it important to pay homage to anyone. He did not care to be introduced to any of the clique of self-appointed seers, nor did he send visiting cards out to any of the critics, and I myself did not know of his presence in Naples. Which was a pity, for I was not able to warn him of the dangers of his self-confidence.[15]

When Caruso first came forth and delivered the aria 'Quanto è bella, quanto è cara' he was, according to surviving accounts, greeted by a round of applause, but this was immediately interrupted by hissing and cries of 'Wait! Let us judge him.' As Key tells, he was 'stricken momentarily dumb by this reception, [he] stood hesitant . . . the malcontents who sat shoulder to shoulder [were] ready *en masse* to squelch any further efforts to encourage an artist who would lightly pass them . . . by.'[16] In the face of this, he determined to win the public over and so set forth his best voice and in such fashion he triumphed. But that there was ever anything more than a small phalanx of interjectors seems highly unlikely. Many critics wrote admiringly of his voice. Of the dress rehearsal the *Don Marzio* had written: 'He promises for tomorrow night a spectacle of grace and charm.'[17] It was not until after the premiere that Procida, the critic of *Il Pungolo*, although assuring his readers that 'Caruso's voice was beautiful, very beautiful indeed', found it, nevertheless, 'not at all suited to the idyllic character of Nemorino [since] for "Una furtiva lagrima" a more tenor-like rather than baritone-like timbre is called for.'[18] Perhaps he was cavilling about Caruso's style, and not complaining about the quality of his voice, for there can be little doubt that the role had never been essayed before by any singer commanding Caruso's prodigious vocal resources; audiences in 1902 might well have been puzzled to hear Nemorino interpreted with the wealth of tone and dramatic power of a successful Radames and Canio. Whereas in the provinces of southern Italy *L'Elisir d'amore* might still have been quite well known, at La Scala Milan at the beginning of this century the repertory was contemporary, and no one knew – still less, cared much – about an historic work's performing style; the last time *L'Elisir* had been heard there was a solitary performance in 1865 with Antonio Giuglini. No doubt Caruso's failure to bribe the claque at the San Carlo did not improve matters, for there was a distinct hostility in a country only recently united to any artist coming back home brandishing spurs he had won in Milan, fast overtaking Naples in population and importance to become Italy's second city.

It would be easier to feel that Procida in *Il Pungolo* had not merely been giving way to chauvinism, had there been anything consistent about his reviews. By the second performance of *L'Elisir*, on January 2, 1902, there can be little doubt that Caruso had completely won over the Neapolitan public – the *Corriere di Napoli* finished off its laudatory epistle: 'Caruso came, sang and conquered all the differing tastes of a public that could still recall Gayarré, Masini and Stagno.'[19] And Procida seemed too to have changed his mind, for he tells of 'Caruso's marvellous singing of that pathetic melody of Donizetti ["Una furtiva lagrima"], how he . . . achieved positively miraculous effects of resonance, accent and color.'[20] However, two weeks later, when Caruso undertook des Grieux in Massenet's *Manon*, Procida led off again on a lengthy diatribe.

> A beautiful voice, without a doubt, with notes of sonorous power, of clear timbre and tonal color with an easy extension. It is a beautiful voice in every way, fully equalized and warm throughout its range. But that is not enough. He lacks the charm of an accomplished singer, the elegance of an actor, which come only from study. . . . The voice is too throaty, with not sufficient head register, and passages of *mezza voce* are too often sung loudly and without polish. The ear is surprised, taken aback, by crude sounds, yet in the midst of these are some of the most limpid tones that I have ever heard. Des Grieux is too exquisite a character to be adapted conveniently to match Caruso's opulent costuming and his athletic figure. To the character he should give more elegant gestures, a more gentlemanly manner and more vivacious expression. He thunders out the notes in a Tamagno-like fashion. . . . In the Dream, for example, he makes too much of a *gruppetto* that a finer artist would merely suggest, but Caruso seems more concerned to secure the utmost applause and give an encore. The *romanza* in the third act is well sung with fervor and sentiment . . . [and] his triumph, earned at that moment from the public, merits their assent . . . [but] he still needs discipline, refinement and self-criticism. [Nevertheless] I see in him a force for good in opera, with a truly precious voice.[21]

Although the *Corriere* may again have praised Caruso, it was his failure to secure the unambiguous approval of *Il Pungolo* that affected him profoundly and he never forgot that season. As Daspuro recalls Caruso told him: 'I shall not sing in Naples again! I will only come back to see my dear mother and eat *vermicelli alle vongole*.'[22]

At the end of January Caruso quit Naples and proceeded to Monte Carlo for his first visit there. The Salle Garnier was another product of Charles Garnier, who had designed the Paris Opéra, and it too was in

Second Empire style, though here much smaller, seating only six hundred. It was opened in 1879 but it was not until the beginning of its fifteenth season that Raoul Gunsbourg was appointed Director. Save for a brief interruption during World War II he remained there for the next fifty-nine years, by far the longest reign of any operatic impresario; and during those years he presented almost every famous singer from Adelina Patti to Régine Crespin. Gunsbourg was one of the originals of his day; he could never have been anything else but an impresario. As well as producing many new operas for the first time, he composed a whole gallery himself, some of his own and some contrived from works not conceived for the stage, such as Rimsky-Korsakov's *Schéhérazade*. In 1902 he cast Caruso as Rodolfo in *La Bohème* and the Duke in *Rigoletto*, and de Reszke, king of tenors at the turn of the century, as Faust in Berlioz's *La Damnation de Faust*, Lohengrin and Roméo in Gounod's opera; this was the only season in which the two ever appeared together in the same theater – a veritable coup.

Sticklers for historical accuracy are not likely to care much for Gunsbourg's autobiography, *Cent Ans de souvenirs . . . ou presque*. Unfortunately, as the title suggests, this was not written until the very end of his long life, after he was forcibly retired, and perhaps hardly surprisingly his memories are vague. Through the years he added so many embellishments to his stories it is extremely hard for us, as it probably was for him too, to work out the truth. He tells a fabulous tale of how Caruso was first engaged at Monte Carlo. He claims that he met the young tenor at a night club in Milan where he was singing Neapolitan *canzoni* at only ten Francs a show. Gunsbourg promptly contracted him for the Monte Carlo opera at 1,500 Francs the season, but after Caruso had a sensational success at the premier, he ostentatiously tore up the contract and made him out a new one at 1,500 Francs a performance. However, by the time Gunsbourg had written his autobiography he had forgotten that he had actually engaged Caruso, for the whole season, at 3,000 Francs a night!

Caruso's debut took place on February 1, as Rodolfo. The critic of the *Journal de Monaco* wrote ecstatically of 'the charm of his enchanting voice.'[23] He sang two further performances and then appeared as the Duke to similar acclaim: 'This marvellous tenor, who in the preceding performances of *La Bohème* was admired for his superb voice, attained in the role of the Duke something even more remarkable. He had only to open his mouth to be applauded. His art of singing, his musical style and the clarity of his diction are all exemplary qualities. After the ballad, "Questa o quella", an enthusiastic ovation came from each side of the theater, and the interpretation which he gave was all perfection.'[24] The Mimì and Gilda of these performances was the great Melba. After Patti's, Melba's voice was the most perfect and her career the most remarkable. In her autobiography, *Melodies and Memories* – ghosted by Beverley Nichols, an English journalist – she tells of her partnership with Caruso 'which was never clouded for an instant, and of which I have the happiest memories'. She claimed then (and it is worth remembering that she did not publish this until four years after Caruso's untimely death) that she found him irrepressible. '[It was] difficult . . . to stop laughing . . . he was so full of practical jokes.' But whether she was so amused is open to doubt, for she was the quintessential prima donna, a congenitally disputatious personality; and something of the real Melba can be detected in her analysis of Caruso's singing. 'Though [by 1902] his singing was spontaneous and natural, I do not think that in those days he was so fine an artist as later on, when perhaps his voice was not so wonderful. It makes me sad to think that the culmination of his art should not have coincided with the greatest years of his voice.'[25] Whether we accept her opinion or not there is no doubt that the culmination of her art – and her career lasted almost forty years – certainly did not coincide with the greatest years of her voice, although it may have been remarkably well preserved.

In March Caruso was back in Milan at La Scala, where he embarked on another creation; this was the world premiere of Franchetti's *Germania* on the 11th. It ran fourteen performances and enjoyed a more appreciable success than the only other new work he had attempted there – Mascagni's *Le Maschere*.

CHAPTER VI

1902–1903

IT WAS during the run of performances of *Germania* at La Scala that Fred Gaisberg, one of the pioneers of the recording industry, heard Caruso for the first time.

In his memoirs he tells how he was on his second trip to Italy and had arrived in Milan, where he had gone hoping to make some recordings of opera. He was staying at the Grand Hotel Spatz, then well known as a residence for singers and other musicians: Giordano, the composer of *Andrea Chénier* and *Fedora*, was the son-in-law of the hotel proprietor. Verdi had stayed there regularly when he came to Milan, and it was while he was occupying a suite there that he had died only the previous year. The day following Gaisberg's arrival, the local representative of the Gramophone Company, Alfred Michaelis, came round to the hotel full of the news created by two of La Scala's leading tenors, Bonci and Caruso. So it was that Gaisberg arranged to attend a performance of *Germania*.

'I cannot describe my transports or the wild enthusiasm of the audience when Federico Loewe [Caruso] urged the students to revolt against the invader, Napoleon – "Studenti! Udite!"' Gaisberg recalls. 'The impassioned appeal ends with a burst from the crowd singing Weber's "Lützov's Wilde Jagd". In the first act there was a wonderful love duet with Ricke [Amelia Pinto] rich in opportunities for both tenor and soprano, that held the audience spellbound . . . is it to be wondered at that I lost my head?'[1] On the spot he determined to get Caruso into the recording studio and in spite of the tenor's demand for £100 for ten 'songs', and in defiance of head office, which was in no mind to shell out that kind of money on a singer who had not yet been to London or New York, Gaisberg went ahead. For they would need a profit of only a shilling on each of two thousand records to cover the fee. The die was cast.

One sunny afternoon Caruso, looking fresh and debonair, sauntered into Gaisberg's hotel room, adapted for the occasion into a studio, and there in exactly two hours he sang the following ten arias to the piano accompaniment of Salvatore Cottone:

'Studenti! Udite!' from Franchetti's *Germania*,
'Questa o quella' from Verdi's *Rigoletto*,
'Celeste Aida' from Verdi's *Aida*,
'O dolce incanto' from Massenet's *Manon*,
'Una furtiva lagrima' from Donizetti's *L'Elisir d'amore*,
'Giunto sul passo estremo' from Boito's *Mefistofele*,
'Ah, vieni qui . . No, non chiuder gli occhi vaghi' from *Germania*,
'Dai campi, dai prati' from *Mefistofele*,
'E lucevan le stelle' from Puccini's *Tosca* and
'Apri la tua finestra' from Mascagni's *Iris*.

Caruso earned his £100 on the spot, and Gaisberg was amazed, even appalled, at the ease with which, it seemed to him, such a prodigious sum could be earned. He did not foresee that these ten records would be only the first steps in a recording career which would eventually net Caruso more than two million dollars during his lifetime and the industry twice that amount. From that day, April 11, 1902, when he committed to wax those ten operatic arias, the very first recordings he ever made, his success has left its mark indelibly on all his many successors.[2]

Until 1902 there were many different singing styles but in the course of the next generation almost all Italian-type tenors began obviously to ape Caruso. As Sydney Homer puts it, 'Before Caruso came I never heard a voice that even remotely resembled his. Since he came I have heard voice after voice, big and small, high and low, that suggested his, reminded me of it at times even forcibly.'[3] Although certain aspects of his style have been ignored or become modified – we shall touch on some of these later – he has remained, thanks to the phonograph's influence, the archetypal tenor, not only in Italy, but also in the fullness of time in the United States, Scandinavia, Great Britain, Spain and eventually even in Russia. In the early years of this century Caruso, like every tenor of his day, was predominantly a singer of contemporary music. Although he did undertake, with varying degrees of success, Bellini and Donizetti roles, the bulk of his repertory, from the Duke in *Rigoletto* onwards, had been composed in the previous sixty years.

None of it then was as old as the newest popular Italian opera in today's international repertory, *Turandot*, while most of it was still contemporary. It was not until after Caruso and Puccini were dead, that there came an end to verismo opera and the drying-up of that well of instantly appealing melody that for so long had sustained Italian opera. Henceforth, save for a gesture or two by Montemezzi and Zandonai, it was exhausted.

As we can hear if we compare Caruso's records made at various times in the course of his career, his art was in a constant state of change and development. His technique, though firmly based, was continually developing: it shifted in response to the demands made of it by the repertory he essayed. It was not until the last years of his career, when he abandoned contemporary opera – or it abandoned him – that he came to undertake an ever-increasing number of dramatic roles. Some changes become easily apparent if we compare various pieces that he recorded on different occasions. He left no fewer than six accounts of 'Celeste Aida' between 1902 and 1911. The first of these is unlike all the others for he treats the aria in a light lyric fashion, so as to minimise the inevitable dosage of falsetto on the soft high B flat which he finishes it with, and which Verdi wrote. By the time he recorded it next, seven and a half months later, his more dramatic approach presents him with a quandary: whether to emit the note lightly as before, although this would produce too abrupt a change in quality, or risk a fortissimo yell. He safely compromises by simply omitting the final phrase altogether. By 1904, when he recorded it for Victor the first time, and still with piano accompaniment, his manner has become altogether more assured and he brings it to a typically full-throated conclusion. A long unpublished version made in 1906 is taken at too slow a pace, causing him to breathe obtrusively and sometimes in the wrong places. He recorded it again in 1908 – and, incidentally, prior to his performance in Toscanini's famous revival at the Met – and this is well sung. But by 1911, when he adds the recitative 'Se quel guerrier io fossi', the whole performance benefits from his characteristically noble repose. It is not surprising that it has always been considered one of his finest recordings.

It is a similar story with his three accounts of 'Cielo e mar!', recorded in 1902, 1905 and 1910. It is the third performance that has the advantage of maturity. The phrasing is more surely composed, and his use of portamento on the first word, 'Cielo', as marked in the score linking the E flat to B flat, is not only stylish but consummately executed; well supported by the breath and with no suggestion of sliding. This makes an interesting comparison with a 1918 record by Gigli, in which every marking is interpreted with the exaggerated temperament of the mature verismo style. Nor is Jussi Björling's 1937 recording as stylishly accomplished, for his voice is too vibratory – although the recording is almost certainly exaggerating this – and not sufficiently suave. Moreover, he ignores most of the grace notes and generally marks the portamento too discreetly, as if it were simply an ornament rather than an essential part of the shaping of the phrase. It is this aria that W. J. Henderson, one of the most perceptive critics, singles out in his eloquent obituary, when assessing Caruso's achievement. 'When the years have made the perspective clearer the most sensitive among music lovers will recall [his] delivery of the great aria 'Cielo e mar!' as one of the loftiest flights of his lyric genius . . . [It] was the high-water mark of his vocal art and one of the supreme pieces of singing of our time.'⁴

As we have seen, it took Caruso some years to accomplish his high notes stylishly according to the age of the different operatic music he sang. The session of February 11, 1906, provides an excellent opportunity to compare arias requiring different technical and stylistic approaches. 'Che gelida manina' from *La Bohème* he transposes down a semitone as he always did, from A flat into G, which enables him to take the climactic high note, now a top B, fortissimo and in full verismo style. This is appropriate in *La Bohème*, where the note should be attacked in full voice. But not in 'Salut demeure' from *Faust*, which he sings next in the original key, for here he manages the high C, taking the note in the head register, and then increasing the resonance as he sustains the note. This is only possible when the voice is limpidly produced. Lastly, in 'Spirito gentil' from *La Favorita* there is another top C, which again he executes after the correct style – lyrically and in a *voce mista* throughout.

Unfortunately, there are comparatively few examples of his having recorded the same solo aria both in the earlier and in the later part of his career. 'M'apparì' from *Marta* is an exception, for he made this twice, the first time in 1906 and then again in 1917. The voice has changed color relatively little in more than a decade but the second version is altogether more assured and at the end 'he does not have to pave the way for the B flat, he just lands on it right in the middle'.⁵ In the first recording there is no gainsaying its youthful freshness, but the secret of Caruso's unique success, for the man in the street as much as for the most exacting critic, lies not solely in the quality of his instrument but also in the way he invariably uses it to its best advantage. It was his intense seriousness about his singing, even in comedies, that makes his later recordings demonstrably superior, and for other reasons than any technical improvement in the phonograph. They reveal, as well as an increase in the size and amplitude of his voice, a growing security, one could almost say discipline, in his technique, which enables him to make effects without any of those tiny tell-tale flaws that are noticeable from time to time on his early records.

The concerted items provide the best opportunities for comparisons across the years: the *Lucia* sextet, for example, made in 1908, 1912 and 1917. If we compare his execution of an ornament he introduces in each version when he joins Lucia on the high B flats (an octave lower, of course), we hear that, whereas with Marcella Sembrich he merely sustains these notes, with Tetrazzini and Amelita Galli-Curci a greater sureness enables him to reattack the B flat three times on each occasion, precisely as they do. This freedom of attack became one of the most striking and original features of his art; a testament to the effortless limpidity of his singing. A similar progress may be traced through the series of recordings he made of the quartet from *Rigoletto*; he made the first in 1906 and the others on the same occasions as the *Lucia* sextet. The Duke was one of his most popular assumptions and it always lay comfortably within his range. What strikes the listener most on hearing these, in the order they were made, is that just as his singing becomes more opulent, so it becomes surer and more relaxed. By 1917 his voice has grown bigger and he makes a tremendous burst of fortissimo immediately before the recapitulation of 'Bella figlia dell'amore', so seemingly defying one of the limitations of pre-electric recordings. This version has an altogether greater breadth of delivery and grandeur of manner; yet he sings the opening phrases more exactly and nimbly than he had done previously and without trace of aspirates. Notable too are the *marcato* notes, mordents – and at the end of the introduction he interpolates a graceful flourish. Altogether this performance has a monumental dignity and effortless elegance: no art could be described as more Verdian – it was appropriate that he should have sung in this at a special La Scala commemorative concert following the composer's death. Every tenor today worth his salt attempts to sing the Duke after Caruso's style – the phonograph has seen to that – and considering that his interpretation is well on the way to being three-quarters of a century old, it is the definition of a classic rendering.

It was as the Duke that Caruso made his Covent Garden debut on May 14, 1902 with Melba and the French baritone Maurice Renaud. He left Milan at the end of April for London, having signed the contract three years previously, but not without some reservations, given the relatively unattractive financial terms, and it was Scotti who finally persuaded him to go. The Chairman of the Opera Syndicate at Covent Garden, Harry V. Higgins, was 'noted for his wit in making *bon mots* and *obiter dicta*, always sharp as a needle and possibly Rabelaisian'.[6] His business acumen was sharp as well, for he persuaded Caruso to sing in London for the first time for a fee of 2,000 Lire a performance, which was 500 Lire less than he had been earning at La Scala. However, this was accompanied by another contract which, contingent upon his initial success, would guarantee him an increase of 500 Lire a night annually over a period of five years. After the first night the *Daily Telegraph* praised him in the highest terms: 'He has an ample voice, round and resonant, and he employs it with the skill that only an experienced artist can claim. Well suited by the music, though he began nervously, he quickly won his audience's approval.'[7] And other critics were no less enthusiastic. The *Illustrated London News* wrote at length of his powerful and melodious voice, the *Sunday Times* thought him 'the most gifted vocalist that London has heard for sometime past,'[8] but probably the most revealing account of his art appeared in the *Daily News* by Percy Betts, who noted that though Caruso

> may have his vocal limitations, especially when he has any florid passages to sing, the music of the Duke . . . happily contains comparatively few examples. He has a delightful *mezza voce*, and he has neither the nasal quality nor the 'bleat' which are the bane of so many of his compatriots: the voice being of the soft, velvety timbre which old opera-goers will associate with Giuseppe Fancelli, and still older men with Giuglini, although combined, when its owner chooses, with the full power of Tamagno in his best days. It is, in fact, that heaven-sent rarity, a pure tenor voice of the old Italian type, a voice which, if subsequent tests in more exacting characters show that its owner possesses real musical feeling and intelligence, will indisputably make him a power in operatic life.[9]

Caruso's first visit to London took place at the beginning of the Edwardian era; and opera seasons were held regularly at Covent Garden from late April or early May, through June and July. That year he appeared not only with Melba but with two other celebrated divas, and each for the first time: Calvé and Lillian Nordica. The rest of the company was made up of a bevy of cosmopolitan talent, including Félia Litvinne, Suzanne Adams, Regina Pacini and Louise Kirkby-Lunn. Among the baritones as well as Renaud there was Scotti, with two basses, Pol Plançon and Marcel Journet, and an outstanding buffo, Antonio Pini-Corsi. All Caruso's operas were under the direction of Luigi Mancinelli,* one of Italy's foremost composer/conductors in the generation before Toscanini, a complete musician whose operas had been performed at the Metropolitan, La Scala and Covent Garden.

Caruso also accomplished a number of his usual parts, including Rodolfo, Edgardo, Radames, Nemorino, Turiddu and Alfredo, and he added one of his two eighteenth-century roles: Ottavio in Mozart's *Don Giovanni*, which he only ever sang at Covent Garden. Thirty years later, in her autobiography, Litvinne, the Donna Anna of those performances, enthused ecstatically over his 'incomparable Ottavio with his luminous voice. . . . When he came on stage for the masked trio, his arms about Donna Elvira [Adams] and Donna Anna [it was perhaps not surprising, for she was of Russian birth, that she should have remembered], how he made me laugh saying "I am a samovar!"'[10] The London season was a great event for Caruso and he reaped encomiums. On May 24 he appeared in a command performance of *La Bohème* with Melba in the presence of Edward VII and Queen Alexandra. Suddenly he was famous everywhere. It took him some weeks to become accustomed to the pressure of social engagements, and in a relatively

*Albeit unknowingly, Mancinelli made a number of primitive cylinder recordings at the beginning of this century. These fragments are from actual performances at the Metropolitan, New York. They were contrived by the house librarian, Lionel Mapleson, a nephew of the impresario. At first he installed his apparatus in the prompt box, but after complaints about its noisy company he took it up to the paint bridge. Among these souvenirs are two minute snatches from a variety of works directed by Mancinelli, including excerpts from Act II of *Tosca* with Emma Eames, De Marchi and Scotti; a performance given within three years of the opera's premiere. There can have been few other conductors who give such a vital rendering of *Tosca* and yet at the same time are so considerate of the singers. Equally remarkable is part of the great ensemble 'O sommo Carlo' from *Ernani*: a performance notable for its grand manner and lavish use of rubato; the company, led by Scotti and also including De Marchi with Sembrich, are completely at their ease and not reduced to a regimented strait-jacket. The direction leads the singers in perfect harmony and gives to the music the fullest dramatic expression. See the Mapleson Cylinders, 1900–4, Complete Edition – R and H 100.

short while he was inundated with invitations to dinner, at which it was hoped that he might be prevailed upon to sing a song. If the mood took him, he would eagerly open the piano and once comfortably ensconced he would sing away for hours on end, accompanying himself, but he soon learned to be canny. At one stately home he was received by the butler and ushered into a drawing room and there left to cool his heels. He had the time, however, to spy the piano, and turning the lock he quickly pocketed the key before at last his hostess made her appearance. Great was the anticipation when he acceded to her gracious request and agreed to sing a song, but greater still was her chagrin when all attempts to open the piano failed; as he was leaving he contrived to drop the key into an ashtray.

At that time he spoke little English and Scotti acted as his interpreter. He took him round to his Savile Row tailor, but photographs suggest it took him an unconscionable length of time not to look as if the noisy dresser would not occasionally break loose. Tosti and Denza, the two most popular Italian song composers, summoned Caruso to luncheon parties. A photograph of the occasion at Denza's survives, taken out in a sunlit arbor of the garden at his Hampstead home. Richard Barthélemy, a song composer and later Caruso's accompanist for many years, tells of a luncheon at Tosti's. 'Princess [Alice] of Monaco was also present [and] ask[ed] me to perform my latest songs. I complied with pleasure. Caruso came and sat down near the piano, asking to sing some of [them] . . . I hastened to tell Caruso that not only was I going to send him my *mélodies* but that I should be delighted to compose some for him . . .'[11] And from that time until 1917 Barthélemy provided accompaniments for Caruso at many of his concerts, as well as composing several songs which Caruso often sang, including 'Triste ritorno' and 'Pesca d'amore', both of which are dedicated to him. As we shall see, Barthélemy was Caruso's most ambitious accompanist, for he induced him to undertake a number of 'French' *mélodies*, which may seem surprising bearing in mind the song repertory he recorded. On other occasions in London, Caruso 'would descend on Tosti's house in Mandeville Place, embrace his "Ciccio" fervently, pour out all his troubles, joys, business arrangements and confidences . . . [and] then before Tosti could answer a question or give him a word of advice [he would], still talking volubly . . . sweep him off to Pagani's restaurant.'[12] Pagani, the proprietor, had been chef to Mario, the most successful Italian tenor in the middle of the nineteenth century.

It was on one of his first London visits that Caruso came to create some of his earliest caricatures. Henceforth this art would become a favourite form of relaxation for him, and it could have become quite profitable. In later years he chanced upon one that had found its way on to a dealer's list; the price seemed rather high and his eyebrows shot up – 'That's good pay for ten minutes work,' he said. 'Better we stop singing and start drawing.'[13]

The Covent Garden season drew to a conclusion on July 28, with a performance of *Rigoletto*. No sooner was it over than his thoughts turned to Italy and Ada, and he rushed round to Burlington Arcade and purchased a magnificent ring for her. The rest of the summer and autumn they spent with their son in Milan and at the Terme di Salsomaggiore. It was not until November 6 that he resumed his career, at the Lirico, Milan, as Maurizio in the world premiere of Cilea's *Adriana Lecouvreur*. By this time Caruso's reputation was spreading rapidly. But it was typical of him that he should have waived his fee and it was only when Sonzogno insisted on paying him something that he agreed to accept 3,000 Lire for the six performances – such a sum did not even pay for half his costumes which, as was then the custom, were made at the singer's expense, for they remained his and not the opera house's property. The press was glowing, at least about Caruso's performance, if not the opera, and there was regulation approval for the Adriana, Angelica Pandolfini, and the Michonnet, De Luca. The *Gazzetta dei teatri* opined 'that the magician Caruso gave us new proof of his supreme value. When one hears that voice so much his own, so warm, so mellow, so full of charm and so insinuating, one feels so much well-being one wishes one could jump on stage and embrace him.'[14] There was a new-found confidence in his delivery. But though he could afford to be generous to Sonzogno – it did not cost his pride anything – he was at pains to deny Vergine or Lombardi any share of his success. 'Instead of following all the suggestions of my teachers, I did just the opposite,'[15] he stated. It may have seemed churlish for him to have claimed all the recognition for his success himself yet, as we can hear over the next eighteen years on his records, it was unquestionably through his own ceaseless activity that his art developed. After his performances of Maurizio he departed for another charity performance, this time as the Duke in *Rigoletto*, on December 10, at Trieste, in aid of the Benevolent Association. The *Indipendente* joined in the general acclaim: 'We can understand how all the composers of modern opera yearn for Caruso and want to write for him alone. He is one of the rare examples of a modern singer who does not brandish his virtuosity as if it were a weapon at a tournament.'[16]

His next engagement was at the Costanzi, Rome, where he returned after an interval of three years. Perhaps he had recovered from the disappointment in the aftermath of his last visit, when he was not offered the role of Cavaradossi at the world premiere of *Tosca*. At any rate, there was no time for bitter memories, for he was greeted by a hurricane of applause. The press went wild over his Duke and des Grieux. The effect he created at one of the rehearsals of *Manon Lescaut* was recalled nearly seventy years later by Vittorio Gui, who later became a leading opera conductor but at that time was still a student at the Accademia di Santa Cecilia.

I recall him singing in half voice without, seemingly, being much involved. Then something remarkable, almost miraculous, happened. It was at the end of the third act, when Manon is about to embark on the boat that will take her and the other poor prostitutes to exile in America. When all of a sudden des Grieux resolves to follow the woman of his heart in the hard life of exile and he falls before the feet of the captain and begs that he may be allowed to go too, even as a cabin boy. . . . Caruso had thrown his hat and stick into the wings; it was no longer the tenor but des Grieux who burst out with this cry of desperate supplication. An immense wave of emotion swept over us all, principals, chorus and conductor, and we students wiped our eyes in the dark. Finally the rehearsal was interrupted; the old *comprimario* Gironi, who had to ask: 'Ah! young man you want to go to populate America', could not utter the word 'populate' before bursting into tears. Maestro Vitale, a good father to us all, took a great white handkerchief from his pocket, and pretending to wipe away the perspiration, instead wiped his eyes.[17]

Whether he repeated a part, such as Faust in *Mefistofele*, or whether he took a role for the first time in Italy, such as Radames in *Aida*, the critics penned their eulogies. 'He sang the music of Radames with marvellous intensity, letting loose the total enthusiasm of the public. No other tenor today possesses the power and skill to sing with passionate emphasis and with the vocal strength of Enrico Caruso in the third and fourth acts of this grand opera. . . . He gave us an encore ("Celeste Aida"), but why did he not encore the entire role?'[18]

From Rome he departed for Lisbon to make his bow at the São Carlos on February 14, 1903, as Loris in *Fedora*. Lisbon, like Barcelona and Madrid, lay in the Italian sphere of influence and the operas there were all from that repertory. Caruso was to sing a half a dozen roles, including five he had undertaken before: Loris, Radames, Cavaradossi, Maurizio in *Adriana Lecouvreur* and the Duke, and he added Gennaro in Donizetti's *Lucrezia Borgia*, a vehicle for Darclée. And it was the same story here too: on the last night, after a performance of *Rigoletto*, he was recalled eight times and Carlos I, King of Portugal, awarded him the Cross of the Order of St John. Towards the end of March he was back in Milan with Ada for a few days prior to his departure for the second of his visits to Monte Carlo. This year he sang but one role, Cavaradossi in the local premiere of *Tosca*, on March 28, opposite Darclée with Renaud as Scarpia and Pini-Corsi as the Sacristan. This was the most stellar *Tosca* Caruso had yet appeared in and the *Journal de Monaco* seemed to have been only telling the truth when it wrote that this was 'an event not only for Monte Carlo but for the entire world'.[19]

Between his Monte Carlo appearances and his departure for Buenos Aires he found time to purchase his first estate, the Villa alle Panche at Castello near Florence. He paid 250,000 Lire for it, but there was no time then to enjoy it, for he was obliged to leave to undertake his most extensive South American tour yet; he would be away five months and would sing not only in Buenos Aires but also at Montevideo and Rio de Janeiro. That year the company was led again by Toscanini and a number of other reputable artists would appear with Caruso, including Carelli, Maria Farneti, Arimondi and Medea Mei-Figner. His first appearance was at the Teatro de la Opera, Buenos Aires, as Cavaradossi opposite Mei-Figner's Tosca on May 19. 'In the second act, after the torture scene, when Scarpia learns that Napoleon has won the Battle of Marengo, the "Vittoria! Vittoria!" that Mario hurls out, Caruso delivered with a vibrant strength of voice reminiscent of Tamagno. His *romanza* in the last act, "E lucevan le stelle", moved the entire theater from the boxes to the gallery, which made no attempt to contain its enthusiasm. The end of the piece was greeted with a volley of applause.'[20] He went on to sing Federico Loewe in *Germania*, in which he was thought to have arrived at the summit of his career. His other roles included Nemorino, Osaka in *Iris*, Faust in *Mefistofele*, Maurizio, and des Grieux in *Manon Lescaut*. Save for Faust and Federico Loewe, he repeated these in Montevideo and then travelled northwards to Rio de Janeiro, where he appeared in *Rigoletto*, *Tosca*,

Manon Lescaut and *Iris*. It was at a performance of *Manon Lescaut*, according to Augusto Carelli, in his biography of his sister, that there was something of a crisis when Emma declined to undertake the title-role. 'It was therefore necessary to produce another distinguished artist, but she did not have the repute of the rest of the company and, notwithstanding the presence of Caruso that evening, the theater was almost empty.'[21] He goes on to describe Caruso at lunch the next day with Camillo Bonetti, the impresario. He was so chagrined at the size of the audience that, by Carelli's account, he insisted on singing it again for nothing. There were certainly two performances of *Manon Lescaut*, but so there were of every opera. And Bice Adami, who sang both Manon Lescauts, was a reputable artist, for she made a number of records. (She married Ferruccio Corradetti, a well-known buffo singer; their daughter was also a successful soprano, Iris Adami-Corradetti.) The whole story sounds as if it were prima donna's pique and an invention of Carelli's, Emma's perhaps rather than her brother's.

CHAPTER VII

1903–1904

THE MECCA of every opera singer at the turn of the century was – as, indeed, it still is – the Metropolitan, New York. The theater was opened in 1883 and, after the next seven years when it was given over exclusively to a German company, it quickly became the world's leading opera house. In the 'nineties it was the French repertory that charmed the Diamond Horseshoe and the exclusive society of old New York epitomised in the novels of Edith Wharton. In those years the reigning tenor had been de Reszke who, in his last season in 1900–01, ran the gamut undertaking Rodrigue in Massenet's *Le Cid* (which role he had created), Siegfried in *Götterdämmerung*, Walther in *Die Meistersinger*, Tristan, Roméo, Lohengrin, Faust, Vasco in Meyerbeer's *L'Africaine*, Raoul in *Les Huguenots* and Radames.

Two and a half years later Caruso arrived, ushering in a new period of Italian predominance: although at one stage or another of his career he did come to undertake the last five of these roles, all of them (save for Faust) he sang in Italian and inevitably his emphasis was quite different. Whereas de Reszke's Raoul had been the consummation of courtly nobility, Caruso's was a typical Italian *borghese*; and whereas de Reszke had sung Radames only a half-dozen times in New York and, as often as not, according to his biographer, Clara Leiser, omitted 'Celeste Aida',[1] the tenor role in *Aida* was Caruso's most popular assumption after Canio.

The first negotiations with Caruso had begun in 1899, but it was not until Maurice Grau, then the Met's Managing Director, had heard him at a performance of *Rigoletto* in his debut season at Covent Garden that he decided to secure his services. They exchanged contracts for the tenor to appear forty times in the 1903/4 season, but then Grau retired and Heinrich Conried succeeded him. It was one of the many anomalies at the Met in those days that whither the Managing Director went so went the artists' contracts; Caruso's was, as a result, not worth the paper it was printed on unless it should be taken up by Conried. Conried was a manipulator, although something of a musical ignoramus, for he had no experience of opera, and had been the Director of the Irving Place Theater, a German drama company. Nevertheless, he fancied himself a shrewd businessman: when rumours began to reach him of the success of Bonci, he decided that so large a number of performances from Caruso, a then unknown tenor, was altogether excessive and he determined on what he felt was a more sagacious policy. He offered Caruso twenty instead of the original forty performances. Caruso, perhaps apprehensive that he might not get to New York at all, agreed on twenty-five, and the matter was settled. It was not until contracts had been exchanged that Conried took the trouble to enquire among the *cognoscenti* as to who was superior – was it Bonci or Caruso? By his biographer Moses's account, he interrogated practically everyone he came in contact with, from clubland musical connoisseurs to sidewalk bootblacks, and they all came back with the same story: 'Caruso, of course.'[2] Eventually Conried first heard Caruso's voice on a phonograph record, and he made no attempt to conceal his disappointment at not having engaged the tenor for the forty performances, as the contract had originally specified. He immediately sent Caruso a wire to that effect to Buenos Aires, where the tenor was then appearing, but by then it was too late, for Gunsbourg had lost no time in engaging him for a season at Monte Carlo in March 1904.

Caruso's Metropolitan debut took place on the opening night of the 1903/4 season, on November 23, as the Duke in *Rigoletto* with Scotti and Sembrich, the Polish soprano who had sung Lucia there on the second night of the inaugural season in 1883. She was considered by Henderson of the *Sun* to be 'one of the immortals of song, [and] the greatest Lieder singer among women ever heard in New York,'[3] and Richard Aldrich (although he spent the best part of a paragraph on Caruso) in the *Times* thought 'the central point of the performance was still Sembrich but he made a highly favorable impression and he went far to substantiate the reputation that had preceded him. . . . He is an Italian in all his fibre, and his singing and acting are characteristic of what Italy now affords in those arts. His voice is purely a tenor in its quality, of high range and of large power, but [it is] inclined to take on the "white" quality in its upper range when he lets it forth. In *mezza voce* it has expressiveness and flexibility, and when so used its beauty is most apparent. Caruso appeared last evening capable of giving intelligence and passion in both his singing and acting and gave reason to believe in his value as an acquisition to the company.'[4] Henderson, the sagest vocal critic of the day, wrote that 'Caruso, the new tenor, made a thoroughly favorable impression, and will probably grow into the firm favor of the public. He has a pure tenor voice and [it] is without the typical Italian bleat. Caruso has a natural and free delivery and his voice carries well without forcing. He phrased his music tastefully and showed considerable refinement of style. His clear and pealing high notes set the bravos wild with delight, but connoisseurs of singing saw more promise for the season in his *mezza voce* and his manliness. He is a good-looking man and acts with dignity, if with no great distinction. But the Duke gives little opportunity for the exhibition of histrionic powers.'[5] Henry Krehbiel, on the *New York Tribune*, joined Aldrich and Henderson in a trinity of opinion. 'Caruso is generally a manly singer, with a voice which is true, of fine quality and marvellous endurance, that "La donna è mobile" was permitted to pass with but a single repetition was due to the apathy of the audience, but [he] has however many of the tiresome vocal affectations, and when he neglects to cover his tones, as he always does when he becomes strenuous, his voice becomes pallid. He had a gratifying reception in the first act; [but] the honors of the evening went in good measure to Sembrich and Scotti.'[6]

Critical opinion was generally complimentary but not overwhelming; memories of de Reszke, doubtless, especially to non-Italians, made Caruso seem inept dramatically and a little crude vocally, though not precisely vulgar. That first New York season was the only time it was possible to secure complimentary tickets for Caruso performances. In the week following his debut he was stricken with tonsillitis and he did not undertake either a scheduled *La Bohème* or another *Rigoletto* before he was well enough for his second performance, as Radames in *Aida*, on November 30. For the first time, direct comparisons could be made with de Reszke. It was to become one of Caruso's outstanding roles at the Met and he was inextricably involved in the increasing popularity of the opera. Johanna Gadski headed the cast. Edyth Walker, at that stage still a mezzo-soprano, was Amneris, while Scotti and Plançon were Amonasro and Ramfis. For Aldrich in the *Times*

the greatest interest was felt in Caruso's assumption of the part of Radames, and though he evidently had not fully recovered from the troubles that put so sudden a check upon his career here after his first appearance, he materially deepened the favorable impression he then made. He was clearly singing with circumspection and care, especially in the first acts of the opera, and the skill of his vocal technique, the manifold resources he possesses to make every effect count, tell even against the most unfavorable influences. He sang with some evidences of effort when he did sing with his full power. With all his reserve, however, the quality, the flexibility and the expressive capacity of his voice beautified everything he did. His action was forceful and authoritative, so far as force and authority came into the purview of Radames's experience. There was passion and conviction in his interpretation of the fated lover, and everywhere the marks of the adept in stagecraft. It was an admirable performance and commanded not only the enthusiastic plaudits of the cooler portions of the audience, but also the frenzied 'bravos' of his compatriots who were present in large numbers.[7]

Henderson, too, noted the way 'he saved himself a good deal in the early part of the opera [but] he confirmed the good impression he made at his debut.'[8] If anything, however, it was Krehbiel who was the most enthusiastic – 'his skill in overcoming the drawbacks [at the beginning of the evening] helped to a keener appreciation of his knowledge of the art of singing, and involved still further admiration for the superb beauty of his voice. The pleasure which his singing gives is exquisite, scarcely leaving room for certain questionings touching his limitations. He is to be accepted for what he is, with gratitude, and no man who loves the art of singing ought to miss the opportunities which his presence at the Metropolitan offers.'[9]

It was on December 2 that he undertook his third role, Cavaradossi. Milka Ternina sang Tosca and Scotti was Scarpia. It is not surprising, bearing in mind both Ternina's and Scotti's considerable histrionic skill, that Caruso's dramatic abilities did not show up particularly well. His failure to create anything like the right effect in this piece of dramatic verisimilitude was much commented upon. Henry Finck in the *Post* complained that 'there was nothing new about his conception. It lacked altogether aristocratic flavor, and therefore seemed to be out of the picture.'[10] Krehbiel, in the *Tribune*, after commenting upon 'his musical instincts [which] are as perfect as his voice is luscious,' went on to affirm that 'neither his instinct nor his voice is at the service of dramatic characterisation.'[11] And Aldrich in the *Times* lamented 'his bourgeois air, [and] little distinction of bearing.'[12] But Henderson was probably the most condescending; not only was his

Cavaradossi 'bourgeois [but] it was difficult to believe in the ardent passion of the aristocratic Tosca [which the character certainly is not, even if Ternina gave that impression] for this painter of hack portraits at job prices.'[13] It was curious that the New York critics in an egalitarian society should have complained so strenuously over his seeming vulgarity.

Nevertheless, increasing waves of enthusiastic praise greeted Caruso's remaining appearances that season. In *La Bohème*, which he sang three days after *Tosca*, Aldrich commended 'the supreme beauty of his voice, and the perfection of his style',[14] and for Henderson, too, 'all the lovely qualities of his uncommonly beautiful voice are brought into prominence'.[15] In *Pagliacci* Finck confirmed that 'he is the best Italian tenor New York has heard since Italo Campanini retired from the stage'.[16] By this time his nervousness had begun to wear off and his voice rang out, fuller and richer than before. Even as Alfredo in *La Traviata* with Sembrich, a diva's opera if ever there was one, he managed to make an effect. And it was the same thing, too, when Sembrich sang Lucia to his Edgardo, for 'his manliness, vigor, passion and withal beauty of tone and vocal style left nothing to be desired'.[17] *Lucia* had been last heard in New York three years previously, when Melba undertook it, and the opera had ended with the Mad Scene.

Probably his greatest triumph in a triumphant season was as Nemorino in *L'Elisir d'amore*. 'Caruso's part [represents] one of the futile, subdued despairing class of operatic lovers who cut a very poor figure on the stage, but there is music for him to sing, in which he revelled with all the graces of the Italian tenor superimposed upon the truly beautiful voice and style . . . that he can command. What could be more captivating, more melting, more flowery in its old-fashioned rhetorical passion than his singing of the famous air "Una furtiva lagrima" in the last act? Rapture is no fitting expression for the state of mind into which it threw the audience, and he was instantly called upon to unfold that tale of amorous longing again.'[18] It was after one of his final appearances that season that the house went crazy, yelling, stamping and shrieking. At length, one young woman managed to force her way up on to the stage and as he emerged for a bow, she tore a button from his coat and then – to his evident amazement – burst into tears. Caruso had caught fire. After that, the house looked back to the days of complimentary seats with wistful longing, while Conried looked forward to a five-year contract with great enthusiasm.

Conried's previous experience with an ensemble theater company had persuaded him that stars had no place in the operatic firmament at the Metropolitan and that they were outmoded. Yet, ironically, it was on his own first night as Managing Director that he was responsible for the introduction of the most brilliant star in its entire history. It was at Caruso's third appearance of the season, during *Tosca*, that Conried rushed into the press office at the beginning of the third act ordering all the critics back to their seats so that they might hear Caruso sing 'E lucevan le stelle' and instructing them on how best they should listen to the performance. One may imagine that critics such as Henderson, Aldrich and Krehbiel, among the most eloquent practitioners of their art ever, were affronted, and that it was Conried who needed to do more listening. On another occasion, during a performance of *La Traviata*, he came backstage after Caruso's extraordinary success with 'Dei miei bollenti' to suggest that he should introduce some ballads into the third act, at Flora's party, as a kind of good measure. It was typical of Conried that no sooner had he realized what had so providentially fallen into his lap than he, and not the Metropolitan, immediately offered Caruso an exclusive world-wide contract on a rising scale that would eventually, over the next five years, secure him $2,000 a performance. But Caruso, no doubt with recollections of his ordeal with Vergine, was too astute to accept. Even so, Conried was still able to avail himself of Caruso's exclusive Metropolitan contract and, when he sang that season at the homes of Mrs W. Payne Whitney and Mrs Orme Wilson, Conried, on behalf of the Metropolitan Realty Company, pocketed the difference, only paying Caruso his regulation fee.

On February 14, 1904, he quit New York and embarked for France. With him was Arturo Vigna, who had conducted all his Metropolitan appearances and was to appear with him again at Monte Carlo, and 'Mrs' Caruso, as Giachetti had become, for her own career was virtually over now and it was her relationship with Caruso that was all important. From Le Havre they undertook the rest of the journey to Monte Carlo by train. By this time his reputation, like his fee, had appreciated prodigiously. News of his American successes preceded him and everyone in the principality was eager to hear him again. He made his first appearance that season as the Duke – 'You ask about his welcome?' declared Fernand Platy of *Le Journal de Monaco*. 'It was as follows: frenzied applause, recalls, ovations, nothing had been spared,'[19] and *Il Trovatore* went on at length about 'his truly exceptional vocal qualities'.[20] A week later he appeared in *La Bohème* with Farrar for the first time; years later she tells how her 'emotions got all tangled up in the golden tones of Caruso's voice. I forgot all about the theater, the action, everything. I sat there sobbing like a child. When my cue came, I didn't hear it. The orchestra hesitated. My mother in the wings waved dramatically at me. I did not see her, I was having a most beautiful old-fashioned cry. Then the prompt rose from his seat and started whispering: "Well, Miss Farrar, are you going to sing or not?"'[21] That year he also starred in performances of *L'Elisir d'amore* and *Aida*.

While in Monte Carlo he received a letter from Leoncavallo begging him to create Henning in the Italian premiere of his *Rolando* (the opera was to be given first in German in Berlin before Kaiser Wilhelm II). Caruso's appearance in it might have shown the piece off in its best light, for 'you have . . . done [the same thing] for Giordano and Cilea.'[22] The cast – so the composer claimed – would include Carelli and Battistini (though neither of them did in fact appear in it), but unfortunately Caruso had to forego the pleasure, for he was already committed to the Metropolitan. Even at this stage of his career, there were no longer any more *Fedora*s or *Adriana Lecouvreur*s to interest him and he began to turn increasingly to the kind of charitable event which was to introduce him to Paris on April 14, as the Duke in *Rigoletto*. On this occasion he appeared at the Théâtre Sarah Bernhardt (in aid of a hospital train for the Russo–Japanese War which had broken out three months previously). The cast was headed by Renaud and included Lina Cavalieri as Gilda. 'Caruso's triumph surpassed anything seen in Paris before. When he sang, seated on a corner of a table, the famous aria "La donna è mobile", holding in his hands a pack of playing cards that he threw into the air, there was a veritable frenzy in the audience. For Paris, Caruso was unquestionably the greatest tenor heard there in years. His reputation had already preceded him. One day at the box-office there was an elderly peasant in blue overalls with a 100 Franc note in his hands, asking for a place anywhere just to hear the famous tenor, for so great was his name that it had already spread to the farthest corners of France.'[23] And it was while in Paris that year that he was able to start to satisfy an ambition that he had had back in his Neapolitan days: he began to acquire a collection of gold coins, going back to the Egyptian princess Arsinoë.

(By 1916,his coin collection contained some two thousand examples, worth in excess of 800,000 Lire.)

From Paris Caruso travelled to Barcelona for what were to be his only two appearances in Spain. He sang the Duke there but he was not a success and, as was the case in Naples, he was never to appear there again. At least a couple of differing accounts survive of what took place. Key relates the authorised version, as told by Luis Piera Figueras, a patron of the Liceo, Barcelona. According to him, at the first performance of *Rigoletto*, Caruso's singing captured the public at once and he was obliged to repeat 'Questa o quella', but then in the duet 'E il sol dell' anima', some hissing broke out because, so Figueras claims, the Gilda, the Cuban coloratura Esperanza Clasenti, sang out of tune. Caruso was much put out at this, and notwithstanding a tremendous demonstration of enthusiasm after 'La donna è mobile', he adamantly refused to sing an encore, and so the opera just came to a tame conclusion. Since the public felt short-changed without the inevitable encore, Bernis, the impresario at the Liceo, told Caruso that he ought to take no more than half his fee of 7,000 Pesetas for the performance. But this the tenor indignantly refused to do, vowing that he would sing the second performance, for which he was contracted and then leave Barcelona. *Il Trovatore*, however, gives a modified version.[24] By its account, at the first performance Caruso in fact not only encored 'Questa o quella' but sang 'La donna è mobile' no less than three times, and this is confirmed in *La Publicidad*;[25] it was not until the second performance that he declined to repeat 'La donna è mobile'. Years later Bernis confirmed this when he told Andrès de Segurola that it was at the second performance that Caruso had sung flat in the duet and the public's reaction was justifiable, and he felt sure that, had he responded to the clamor and repeated 'La donna è mobile', then the whole incident might well have been quickly forgotten. But he did not appear in Barcelona again, nor in any other Spanish city.

Notwithstanding this slight hiccough in his progress, the Duke remained his most popular role, and he undertook it again when he made his debut in Prague on May 4. In those days Prague was in Bohemia, a province of the Austro-Hungarian Empire, and the German language prevailed. The impresario, Angelo Neumann, whose memory stretched back to the 1870s, evoked spirits long departed when he inscribed Caruso's autograph book – 'After Graziani and Calzolari, I have never heard a voice or an artist as superb and complete as you are.'[26] Two days later he sang Nemorino and then travelled on to Dresden, where he appeared yet again as the Duke. According to Ludwig Hartmann, 'singing gives him, so far forward on his lips does his voice lie, almost less effort than speaking does the rest of us. His breathing is inaudible, his phrasing full of taste and his technique positively phenomenal.'[27]

Caruso then proceeded to London and sang at Covent Garden again, after an interval of two years, on May 17, 1904 – in 1903 Bonci had appeared in London in his stead, as Edgardo, Rodolfo, the Duke and Ottavio in *Don Giovanni*, and he also undertook Almaviva, which Caruso did not venture. On the first night Caruso was again the Duke opposite Melba's Gilda. *The Manchester Guardian* confirmed his inevitable triumph: 'His voice has grown even fuller and richer than it was and he has gained as an actor, and that "La donna è mobile" was rapturously encored goes without saying.'[28] 'He sang to perfection and he is the embodiment of the finest epoch of Italian *bel canto*. His ringing tones were marked by an essential gift of music, and by a fineness of timbre you will not easily find surpassed.'[29] The audience was led by a glittering clutch of celebrities, headed by Edward VII and Queen Alexandra, Princess Victoria and the Duke and Duchess of Connaught. Not everything came up roses, however, for when he tried out one of his typical practical jokes on the Maddalena, Kirkby-Lunn, she was quick to slap him down. He invited Barthélemy to a performance of *Pagliacci*, and though he did not care for the opera much, 'Canio was a real revelation to me of [Caruso's] incomparable talent. I did not hide my admiration from him [and] he attempted to calm my enthusiasm [and] asked me to share his simple breakfast at Pagani's restaurant.'[30] That spring Caruso again sang in *La Bohème* and *La Traviata* with Melba; and in *Aida* and *Un Ballo in maschera* he was joined by Giannina Russ, a leading Italian soprano, but though 'her dramatic gifts were appreciated . . . her voice did not possess the necessary suavity that Amelia's music requires'.[31]

CHAPTER VIII

1904–1905

IN THE summer of 1904 Caruso returned to Italy, but not to sing. Instead he confirmed his new-found eminence, literally, when he purchased from Baron Pucci the Villa Campi, which lay situated on top of a hill near the village of Lastra a Signa, some seven miles west of Florence. He paid 300,000 Lire for it, and in the course of the next dozen years he was to spend more than ten times that amount on the villa itself, as well as beautifying the gardens and developing the acreage that formed the estate. He renamed it, appropriately, the Villa Bellosguardo – beautiful view. From its upper windows

> there is a magnificent prospect of a landscape of eternal youth and bewitching beauty. We gaze out into the open country, the luxuriant fruitfulness of which delights the eye, while its charm of color grows iridescent under the combined influence of clean air and burning sun . . . [T]he eye may travel without interruption to a magnificent scenic picture – the lofty peaks of the Apennines disappearing into the blue haze. Heavily wooded, these noble mountains form a romantic frame for the soft curving plain, lush with vegetation, a picture varied at every point of the compass.[1]

On the estate surrounding the villa lived some twenty-five peasant farmers who held it by a centuries-old system of tenure. By this, the tenant was given a house and land which he cultivated. He would then keep half the proceeds and the other half he would pay over to the owner – this was known as *mezzadria*. It worked well – at least, until the First World War – and on the estate there grew a relative abundance of flowers, vegetables and fruit, and from the grapes came a wine of the Chianti style. The villa was situated in its own parklands.

> Proudly crowning a noble elevation is an imposing facade, in the shape of a splendid colonnade . . . [this has] a faint blue gleam, a peculiarity of the valuable hard stone quarried in the vicinity. And in keeping with this . . . is

77

a magnificent Italian garden. With its glorious exotic plants, its picturesque parterres, in which flowers are represented in all their variety, in great vases, and poetic nooks and crannies. . . . [A]nd then begins the park, wonderfully romantic and though giving an impression of having been left to its own free and unhindered development, it is carefully laid out and maintained. Paths ray out and extend downwards along every slope of the hill, and the entire propery is enclosed behind a high and massive stone wall.[2]

Within the villa was a great central hall that ran the entire breadth of the building, and into which rooms on all storeys opened out. Even during the hottest summer days it was cool and agreeable, and open windows ventilated the property. Off it ran a whole series of salons, dining, drawing and billiard rooms, as well as more than fifteen bedrooms. There were also two central rooms adjacent to either side of the great entrance hall. One of these was Caruso's music room, and here it was that he would practise while the staff and guests tip-toed about.

The summer of 1904 was a particularly happy one for Caruso. Not only was he busy with Villa Bellosguardo but his relationship with Ada had never been warmer. In August they retired to the Villa alle Panche to await the birth of their second child. This proved to be another son. Enrico Junior was born on September 7. Here it was that only a few days later the tenor received a visit from Henry Russell, the colorful impresario, afterwards Director of the Boston Opera, and a son of the composer of 'A life on the ocean wave' and 'Woodman spare that tree'. At that time Russell was planning to bring an ensemble from the San Carlo, Naples, to Covent Garden in October of that year. He had written to Caruso asking if he might visit him, for he wanted him to head the company. Russell's description of the interior of the villa suggests that Caruso had yet to earn his spurs interior decorating.

> He welcomed me in his usual hearty way, and no sooner had I arrived than he dragged me off on a tour of inspection. . . . It may be unfortunate, but it is nevertheless true, that . . . Italian singers often show an extraordinary lack of discrimination in furnishing and decorating their houses. . . . Caruso's villa was no exception to the rule. Externally it was a hideous modern pile, and the interior would have made an admirable. . . cinema. Modern furniture, covered with fiery plush, gilt trimmings, fringes, loops, porcelain souvenirs, in fact every conceivable kind of garniture had been gathered for the mansion. Caruso seemed particularly pleased with the

decoration of a ball room that had just been finished. On the ceiling were atrociously bad and elaborately painted portraits of himself in the costumes of various operatic roles. It seemed curious that a man with so keen a sense of humor could not see the ridiculous side of these frescoes.[3]

Needless to say Russell did not express these opinions publicly until he wrote his memoirs long after Caruso's death, and he departed having secured the tenor's services. Caruso had but one engagement to undertake before his return to London. He began his travels in the 1904/5 season by journeying for the first time to Berlin. He made his debut there as the Duke at the Theater des Westens. This was not an opera house and it was chosen most likely for its large seating capacity; which accounts for Frieda Hempel noting in *Mein Leben dem Gesang* that much to her, and presumably Giachetti's, surprise, for Hempel caught a glimpse of her in the audience that night, the theater was only half full. Save for Caruso, the cast was ordinary. There was only one other performance, *La Traviata*. When he came again the next year it was to the Königliches Opernhaus, where he would appear with Farrar and Emmy Destinn.

He was back in England, for Russell's autumn season at Covent Garden, on October 17, and he made his bow opposite Rina Giachetti, Ada's sister, as des Grieux in *Manon Lescaut*. *The Pall Mall Gazette* sought to make a comparison between him and de Reszke. 'One would say that de Reszke had the finer temperament, and far and away the more carefully conceived outlook upon the parts which he had sung; still, Caruso is an absolute wonder, and there is an end of such discussion.'[4] Indeed, comparisons are vain, for de Reszke's repertory was different. He never undertook des Grieux in *Manon Lescaut* nor Rodolfo, nor, indeed, any Puccini role, and though he did sing two of Caruso's other parts in Russell's season, Don José and Canio, he only appeared in *Pagliacci* a handful of times at the Paris Opéra in 1902, when he was on the brink of retirement. Clara Leiser, his biographer, tells us that in this 'the pain, humiliation and rage . . . were portrayed with intensity and truth, and the impersonation was called a triumph by some [yet] the general feeling was that the role was unworthy of the great de Reszke'[5] for he was too much the gentleman to make the right effect in this music. After de Reszke's death in 1925 Lord Wittenham, in a letter to *The Times*, compared Tamagno, de Reszke and Caruso.[6] Tamagno he found a tremendous *tenore robusto*, who literally made one jump in one's seat in *Otello*; de Reszke did all the wonders he did without a great natural voice but by the illuminating magic of his genius; while Caruso was a golden tenor, who comes only once or twice in a century.

Although these singers were all tenors and had several roles in common, a century ago much of their repertory was still being written and there were marked stylistic differences in their interpretations – as we can hear when we listen to records made in later life by Tamagno, De Lucia and Marconi. In the period before the phonograph had established Caruso's style – B.C., we may call it – it was inevitable that tenors who sang the same repertory should have radically differed from one another. But since Caruso's day the phonograph has not only established his style internationally, but at the same time the 'mummification' of Italian opera has effectively frozen it. Even non-Italians have taken Caruso as their example. Among the earliest to become enchanted by him was the Irish tenor John McCormack. McCormack was not more than twenty and only a student when he came to the gallery at Covent Garden one evening in 1904 during Russell's season and heard Caruso sing Rodolfo. He fell under his spell; forty years later he would write: 'That voice still rings in my ears, the memory of it will never die.'[7] Fired with enthusiasm to succeed in Italian opera, McCormack went off to Italy for instruction. At the beginning of his career his singing was, as Henry Wood recalls, 'in the true Italian tradition'.[8] By the time he made his first appearance in New York in 1909 a clamorous delegation of his countrymen secured for him the success that was denied other lyric tenors, such as Clément, Florencio Constantino, Smirnov and Hermann Jadlowker, none of whom made much impression on audiences infatuated with Caruso's magnificent outpourings. It was not until the early twenties and after Caruso was dead that McCormack, by then an American citizen, ceased to appear in opera and the Irishman reasserted himself in his singing of songs.

Caruso returned to New York for his second Metropolitan season in the autumn of 1904. The grandiosity of *Aida* made it appropriate material for opening night, on November 21. Caruso was to sing it there again on three more such occasions. The cast was a typical one, led by the diva Eames, an American, a rival of Melba and a classical beauty with a cold personality. Of her Aida, James Huneker once wrote: 'Last night there was skating on the Nile.'[9] Nor does her behavior seem to have been much warmer on this occasion, 'for when

Caruso came up behind her, [and] slapped her lightly on the shoulder and dodged behind a piece of scenery. . . . Quick as a flash the prima donna looked round, and seeing some "supers" nearby, nearly froze them with her glance.'[10] At this performance Caruso's Radames had matured and Aldrich writes expansively of 'its resonant purity, its lyrical beauty and full-throatedness'.[11] His repertory was still, however, fundamentally lyric, save for Canio, and he undertook seven such roles before the end of the year, including Edgardo, Alfredo, Rodolfo, the Duke and Nemorino, which he had sung last season, as well as Enzo in *La Gioconda*, which was to become another of his calling cards, and a solitary Gennaro in *Lucrezia Borgia*, which was the second and last time he would ever undertake it. 'Caruso seems to have little interest in the proceedings which fell to his share in the opera till the last act and, indeed, he was at first far from being in his best voice. But his aria "Come soave", he had to repeat.[12] During the rest of the season he added Cavaradossi, Raoul in Meyerbeer's *Gli Ugonotti* and Riccardo in *Un Ballo in maschera*. He also sang in three concerts in New York, two at the Waldorf Astoria: the first was one of Mr Bagby's matinées and the second a benefit arranged by Miss Leary with Nordica and Victor Herbert and his orchestra, for the large number of Italian immigrants who were then pouring into America. On January 12, 1905, he took part in an entertainment organized by Mr James Henry Smith at his new residence, 871 Fifth Avenue. This was a kind of house-warming and Caruso was engaged to undertake a group of songs. It tells us something of the tenor's schedule that the same day he had been invited to a tea-party at the Lew Fields Theater. He had gone there first and then, begging to be excused a while, he was sped uptown in an automobile to Mr Smith's residence, where he sang 'Ideale' and 'La mia canzone' of Tosti, 'Di te' of Tirindelli and 'Non t'amo più' of Denza, and for these he received $3,000. He had no sooner pocketed the proceeds, Mr Smith giving him an envelope containing six $500 bills, than he was chauffeured back to the theater again. He had been away less than an hour, with such alacrity had the motor accomplished the trip, and he was in time to escort the Fields, Albert Saléza and Giraldoni to a celebratory supper at the York Hotel, his residence that season.

Caruso's last appearance in New York that year took place at a gala in which he sang the fourth act of *La Gioconda* and then finished the evening with the first act of *Pagliacci*. He then undertook his first journey through the United States, travelling via Boston, Pittsburgh,

Cincinnati, Chicago, Minneapolis, Omaha, Kansas City, San Francisco and Los Angeles. He sang Edgardo, Canio, Enzo and the Duke, either all four or a permutation of any two or three of them. On March 20 he reached Chicago as Edgardo.

> It is casting no reflection on any of the other singers engaged in *Lucia* last evening to say that interest centred almost wholly on Caruso's Edgardo. [This makes an interesting contrast with the critical reception accorded his Duke at his Met debut at the beginning of the previous season, and Sembrich was again singing with him.] The performance showed him to be a man not particularly prepossessing in face or form, being too short in stature and too heavily built to be an ideal operatic hero. But there is a certain suggestion of good nature and bonhomie about him which wins him the liking of the audience, and as he bears himself with ease and a fair amount of grace and acts with no inconsiderable intensity and power, he quickly gains approval. And when he begins to sing all about him is forgotten save for his voice. It is a true tenor of exceptional resonance and power . . . it is a voice even throughout every section. There are no weak spots in it, and every tone is produced with a freedom and ease of emission which tells of 'natural placing'. His voice blended finely with the other singers, and when a phrase needed accentuation it rang out clear and distinct, [and] musical proportion and artistic values are carefully observed.[13]

As we shall have several occasions to note, Caruso loved to find an excuse to take over some of the music of another singer when he was appearing the same evening. At one performance in Chicago he was down to sing Canio, and before the *Pagliacci* there was the inevitable *Cavalleria rusticana*. Andreas Dippel had been announced as Turiddu, and he was a remarkably versatile tenor. That season in New York his repertory had embraced sixteen roles, all the way from Almaviva and Ernesto to Rodolfo, Cavaradossi, and even Parsifal, Siegfried and Tristan. It was not that he could have sung them all so well; but that he managed them in a company that could boast artists of the calibre of Caruso speaks eloquent testimony to his adaptability – or at the least to his prodigious musical memory. On this occasion, however, he was unwell; since the Met was away from home, and the question of securing a replacement difficult, he agreed to undertake Turiddu, so long as someone could be found to manage the opening off-stage serenade on his behalf. Caruso volunteered straight away. Since no one in the audience in Chicago had ever heard Caruso before, perhaps it was not so remarkable that when he sang the serenade, unannounced, he was greeted by only the usual regulation applause. Nevertheless, throughout the tour, he was the toast of the towns. In Kansas City shades of Campanini and Tamagno were evoked: 'They had the trick of literally assailing their audiences . . . and Caruso has it too.'[14] And, in San Francisco, the *Chronicle* acclaimed him 'the greatest tenor we have heard here, at least, during the period of grand opera since Colonel Mapleson first came out twenty-one years ago'.[15] Mapleson, an intrepid impresario, first organized seasons in London, and then soldiered back and forth across the United States in the 1880s with Patti and company in the vanguard and the bailiffs never far behind. After Caruso's vociferous greeting in Los Angeles it must have been interesting to see the face of the manager who had written to Conried in New York, before the season began, begging him to 'substitute Dippel for Caruso. I am sure Dippel would attract a larger audience; he is far better known here than Caruso.'[16]

He made his way back across the States to New York by train and then sailed for Europe again. On May 13 he appeared in Paris at the Théâtre Sarah Bernhardt as Loris in *Fedora* with Cavalieri and Titta Ruffo, who was known as the Caruso of baritones – though as Howard Greenfeld notes Caruso was never styled the Ruffo of tenors. The music publisher Sonzogno had approached Caruso in January that year to sing these performances in a season he was giving to advertise his wares. (The repertory also included Giordano's *Siberia* and *Andrea Chénier*, Leoncavallo's *Zazà*, Cilea's *Adriana Lecouvreur*, Mascagni's *L'Amico Fritz*, Orefice's *Chopin* and Rossini's *Il Barbiere*, in which Masini bade 'farewell' to the stage as Almaviva. But there were no Verdi or Puccini operas and Sonzogno was at something of a disadvantage.) It had originally been planned that Caruso would appear only four times, but so complete was his success that Sonzogno entreated him to add more performances. So it was that he appeared six times in eight days, and one would have to go back to his early years in Naples to find anything like so strenuous a schedule. 'His voice, and the realism of the anguish and horror he put into the phrases were as lightning in a terrible storm. The breathing of that assemblage seemed to me to be the breathing of Caruso; the life of each person appeared to be controlled by the singer's lips.'[17] The audience was not only made up of Parisian society but also present was a plethora of leading French musicians, including Massenet, Ravel, Fauré, Debussy, Leroux, Saint-Saëns and Bruneau. Even the usually waspish Saint-Saëns was complimentary about the opera and he wrote a congratulatory letter to Giordano quoting some measures from it from memory. Bruneau, another leading opera composer and critic, writes in *Le Matin* of 'Caruso's singing, so easy and natural, and at the same time he showed no tendency to shout or become insipid.'[18]

Later that month Caruso again returned to Covent Garden. This was his third visit to London. Opera was the grandest of entertainments; in those days, before electric amplification, its sheer scale was appreciated by the prosperous bourgeois audiences of the Edwardian era, whether or not they understood a word of the Italian text. Caruso made his debut that year on May 22, in *La Bohème* with Melba.

'The opera in London is really more of a pageant than a musical function. The front of the house frequently claims more attention than the stage. On Caruso and Melba nights it blazes. Tiers and tiers of boxes race round in a semi-circle. If you are early, you see them as black gaping holes. But very soon they are filled. The stalls begin to leap with light for everybody who is not anybody, but would like to be somebody, drags out everything she possesses in the way of personal adornment and sticks it on her person, so that all the world may wonder. At each box is a bunch of lights, and with the arrival of the silks and jewellery, they are whipped to a thousand scintillations. The blaze of dancing light becomes painful; the house, especially upstairs, is spitefully hot. Then the orchestra begins to tumble in; their gracefully gleaming lights are adjusted, and the monotonous 'A' surges over the house – the fiddles whine it, the golden horns softly blare it, and the woodwind plays with it. But now there is a stir, a sudden outburst of clapping. Campanini is up. Slowly the lights dissolve into themselves.* There is a subdued rustle as we settle ourselves. A few peremptory *Sh-sh-sh* from the ardent galleryites. Campanini taps. His baton rises ... and suddenly the band mumbles those swift bars that send the curtain rushing up on the garret scene. ... [It] is low-pitched, with a sloping roof ending abruptly in a window looking over Paris. ... Down stage, almost on the footlights, is an easel, at which an artist sits. The artist is Scotti, the baritone, as Marcello. The orchestra shudders with a few chords. The man at the window turns. He is a dumpy little man in black wearing a golden wig. What a figure it is! What a make-up! ... The yellow wig, the white ... mustache, the broken collar. ... But a few more brusque bars are tossed from Campanini's baton, and the funny little man throws off,

---

* This may be a little literary confusion, but it could be that at that time the house lights were not dimmed until after the conductor had taken his place.

cursorily, over his shoulder, a short passage, explaining how cold he is. The house thrills. That short passage, throbbing with tears and laughter, has rushed, like a stream of molten gold, to the utmost reaches of the auditorium, and not an ear that has not jumped for joy of it. For he is Rodolfo, the poet; in private life, Enrico Caruso, Knight of the Order of San Giovanni . . . Chevalier of the Order of Santa Maria, and many other things. As the opera proceeds, so does the marvel grow. You think that he can have nothing more to give you than he has just given; the next moment he deceives you. Toward the end of the First Act Melba enters. You hear her voice, fragile and firm as fluted china, before she enters. Then comes 'Che gelida manina' for Caruso and 'Mi chiamano Mimì' for Melba, and then the wonderful love duet 'O soave fanciulla'. Gold swathed in velvet is his voice. Like all true geniuses he is prodigal of his powers; he flings his lyrical fury over the house. He gives it all, yet somehow conveys that thrilling suggestion of great things in reserve. Again and again he recaptures his first fine careless rapture. . . . There never was such warmth and profusion and display. Not only is it a voice of incomparable magnificence; it has that intangible quality that smites you with its own mood; just like something that marks the difference between an artist and a genius. There are those who sniff at him. 'No artist,' they say, 'look what he sings.' They would like him better if he were not popular; if he concerned himself, not with Puccini or Leoncavallo . . . but with the pretentious subtle triflers. . . . But true beauty is never remote. The art which demands transcendentalism for its appreciation stamps itself at once as inferior. True art, like love, asks nothing and gives everything. The simplest people can understand and enjoy Puccini and Caruso and Melba, because the simplest people are artists. And clearly, if beauty cannot speak to us in our own language, and still retain its dignity, it is not beauty at all.'[19]

The Covent Garden season also featured Caruso as the Duke, Raoul in *Gli Ugonotti*, Radames, Riccardo in *Un Ballo in maschera* and he again sang Ottavio in *Don Giovanni*. On this occasion Bernard Shaw, though he had long ceased to be a music critic, complained about Caruso's performance in a letter to *The Times*. 'My language was fairly moderate considering the number and nature of the improvements volunteered by Caruso.'[20] And certainly these 'improvements' are unlikely to have been stylish 'Mozartian' embellishments we might find in eighteenth-century manuals, but probably more like the kind of pulling-about of the time which can be heard in recordings of Ottavio's arias left by De Lucia. But no one else seems to have been much bothered by the changes he made. The view seems to have been, as one newspaper had it: 'A great tenor is needed to sing Ottavio. It is rare that one hears "Il mio tesoro", save for its lovely opening measures, made extremely interesting. . . . Caruso showed how it should be sung and achieved a very great success.'[21]

He sang at Covent Garden for the last time that year in the London premiere of Puccini's *Madama Butterfly* with Destinn. Ricordi had been in London the previous winter to arrange the performances, and he had written to Caruso in New York to tell him that as he would be singing Pinkerton, 'it would seem an opportune thing for you to have your costumes made while you are in America. The uniforms are two; a dark blue one for the first act and another for the last act in white. Mind, however, that both of them are simple uniforms of a Lieutenant of the navy.'[22]

On July 26, after having bade farewell to opera in London, he was engaged as guest artist to provide the entertainment at a banquet given by an American, George H. Kessler, in the central courtyard of London's Savoy Hotel, which had been flooded and transformed for the occasion into a Venetian lagoon. The dinner guests were seated at a long table in a gondola. Then, on one of his last days in England, he drove out, in company with Scotti and Tosti, to take lunch at Windsor with Patti and her husband Baron Cederström. Afterwards, the diva lined up the trio and she photographed them, bowing deferentially, hats in hand. His final engagements that season took place at the Belgian coastal resort, Ostend. There he appeared to a polyglot audience, headed by the King and Queen of the Belgians, the Duke of Abruzzi and the Shah and Empress of Persia, in a polyglot performance of *Rigoletto* – Caruso sang in Italian and the rest of cast in French. *Le Carillon* acclaimed 'Caruso's voice, for it defies the most eulogistic praises: one is taken aback by its brilliance and tenderness.'[23] On August 6, in company with the Bohemian violinist Jan Kubelik, a prodigious virtuoso, he sang in a concert at the Kursaal. *Le Saison d'Ostende* wrote of 'his voice of incomparable splendor; [and] he possesses to an unparalleled extent the art of enslaving musical expression through the whole gamut of sentiment.'[24]

For this occasion he earned 10,000 Francs and received an enormous palm tree for the gardens at the Villa Bellosguardo.

CHAPTER IX

1905–1906

BY 1905 Caruso had been singing a decade and he was entering his golden days. He had appeared throughout Europe; in Russia and Poland, France, Germany, Austro-Hungary, England, Spain and Portugal, as well as Italy. He had journeyed to South America and travelled across the United States from New York to San Francisco. At the same time he was aggrandising his reputation – albeit unconsciously – through the phonograph, which was spreading his name internationally and even to places where he would never appear. Curiosity was such as to make him a figure of growing interest throughout the Western world; as his photographs were starting to be reproduced in newspapers and magazines, so he was fast becoming a public personality. His daily routine, diet, exercise, what he liked, and what he did not, all got into print. Not infrequently he was the victim of newspaper reporters whose imagination was often quicker than his English. Even the most fantastic tale would enlist the support of some enterprising editor. And there was nothing he could do to assuage feelings of latent hostility and jealousy arising from the ever-increasing number of Italians coming to the New World – as we shall see.

At the Metropolitan during his third season he sang fourteen different parts, including the Duke, Nemorino, Rodolfo, Cavaradossi, Radames, Edgardo, Alfredo, the inevitable Canio, and two French roles for the first time in the original, Faust and Don José – he had sung them elsewhere before but always in Italian translations. For the first time too, he was Lionello in Flotow's *Marta*, one of his most celebrated impersonations, which he would sing until 1920, Fernando in *La Favorita*, which he had not undertaken in the United States before and would not again, and Elvino in *La Sonnambula*, which he had sung only once, in Trapani, Sicily, at the beginning of his career. That season in New York he appeared as often as three times a week and in different operas. On opening night, November 20, 1905, he

87

was Enzo in *La Gioconda*, in a cast headed by Nordica. Henderson was conservative in his praises of Caruso:

> The audience, which quite filled the house, had assembled for the laudable purpose of listening to Caruso. Now, this is at all times an interesting occupation, but unless one has made up his mind in advance that the king can do no wrong there are moments when doubt will intrude itself. It does not make the slightest difference how many people shout 'bravo' or how many bruise the palm of their hands, the white voice is not a grace of song when it is overused, nor is a throaty quality of tone at any time desirable. Caruso is guilty of much whiteness and occasional throatiness. On the other hand, the beauties of his style are so many and the glory of his voice is so dazzling that his offences are condoned by an adoring public, and deplored by a few lonely critics who love him for his virtues and not his faults.[1]

Save for a parenthetical caveat, the *Philadelphia Inquirer* was in a more laudatory frame of mind when, on December 5, at the Academy of Music, the Metropolitan company appeared in a performance of *La Favorita*.

> Caruso sang with a beauty and volume of voice and acted with an authority and intelligence which rendered his impersonation to the highest degree satisfying and impressive. [He] never spares himself (sometimes it would be better if he did) but last night he seemed more than ever to throw his whole heart into his work. He made his Fernando an extremely noble, moving and sympathetic figure and went far by the sincerity of emotion with which he vitalised the character to impart a serious significance to the extremely artificial story of the opera. Under all the circumstances it is not easy to make a real, human hero out of Fernando, but by his earnestness Caruso succeeded in making the improbable scene which forms the climax of the third act momentarily convincing.[2]

In this we see how, in those days, an operatic libretto was still supposed to derive from a telling drama, as new works, like *Tosca*, for example, still were. After four further performances in New York *La Favorita* lapsed from the repertory.* At the matinée of *L'Elisir d'amore* on December 9 two accidents overtook Caruso and he was lucky that he did not leave the theater in an ambulance rather than an automobile. The first happened toward the end of the first act; he and Sembrich had just finished their duet when the curtain descended suddenly and it was only in the nick of time that he stepped back and

* It had to wait until 1978 for its next performance at the Met, with Luciano Pavarotti.

88

saved himself from being felled. During the second act he was waving the bottle of elixir about when he accidentally broke it over his head and the house physician had to bandage him.

The third 'antique' opera he undertook that season was *La Sonnambula* and he sang Elvino. Aldrich was very scathing:

> It cannot be denied that he has recently done much to give his discriminating admirers uneasiness. He has been prone to let his voice fall into a throaty quality; his tones have sometimes sounded pinched. There has been more than a suspicion of 'bleat' that is generally associated with the idea of the Italian tenor of the older sort. In seeking for those exaggerated effects of pathos and tears and superhuman passion, he has not infrequently, and more frequently than he used to, cast to the winds all thought of tonal beauty, of that smoothness, purity, translucent clearness that are truly the distinguishing marks of his wonderful voice. In the few appearances he has made this season, this fact has impressed itself upon many of his listeners – the listeners who listen and do not strain themselves to get in a "bravo" before he has finished the phrase of an aria. In *La Gioconda*, in *Rigoletto*, in *La Favorita*, there have been too many evidences of a straining for effects that he has no need to strain for.[3]

On January 3, 1906, when Caruso sang Faust for the first time, the opera was given without a chorus. The singers had gone on strike demanding $25 a week. Conried equivocated; he admitted they needed more pay but he would not, he said, deal with any union, for the Metropolitan had not engaged one, and he was only prepared to treat each singer individually. Two days later, for a performance of *Tristan*, he secured a sailors' chorus by using principals who were not singing that night. Even Caruso volunteered his services, but it was decided that his German was not good enough, and he never appeared in any work in German in the theater. In Hamburg, on one occasion, he declined the brief role of the Italian tenor in Strauss's *Der Rosenkavalier*. Since all his music is sung in Italian we may assume the deterrent was not the problem of language but the altitudinous tessitura, for many German singers, including Tauber, transpose his aria down – although Caruso is on record as having stated that he used to parody the Prize Song from *Die Meistersinger* to a stream of German-sounding words, bits of 'menuese' and usually ending up with 'sehr schön'. His wife tells of finding several German arias amongst his music after his death.

During that winter he moved his apartment from the York Hotel to 54 West 57th Street, so that he could cook Italian food when he wished. Between Met performances, on January 18, he sang at the home of Mr

Smith, where he had been engaged the previous year, offering 'Salut, demeure' from *Faust* and a group of Tosti songs. Four days later he appeared at the Waldorf Astoria in one of the Bagby musical matinées in which he again shared the program with Victor Herbert and his orchestra. On the 24th he was driven down to Washington in a hired car to take part in a reception at the Perry Belmont home, with Bessie Abott and Jean Gérardy, the cellist. He contributed a song of Buzzi-Peccia, 'Una furtiva lagrima' from *L'Elisir d'amore*, and he was joined by Abott in the duet 'O soave fanciulla' from *La Bohème*. In New York on February 27th he sang at a reception at Mrs Orme Wilson's. His last concert appearance, once again at the Waldorf, took place on March 17, in another benefit for Italian immigrants, and this year he was joined by Scotti.

In the spring of 1906, when the New York season was done, Conried again arranged the Metropolitan tour with Caruso. The program was more expansive this year, and he sang Lionello in *Marta*, Faust, Edgardo, Canio, Don José and Rodolfo. The company stopped at first at Baltimore, where the *Sun* wrote that 'he is without doubt one of the greatest living tenors, and perhaps the greatest heard in this country in many years'.[4] In Washington one performance was given before President Theodore Roosevelt and during the interval he came backstage. But when the tenor was told of this sudden and unexpected visit he immediately assumed his leg was being pulled and he remained in his dressing room. It was only when he made to return to the stage that he found himself, to his infinite embarrassment, face to face with Roosevelt. The President warmly congratulated him, however, and presented him with a signed photograph of himself as a souvenir – it was to prove unexpectedly valuable. From Washington Caruso proceeded to Pittsburgh where he was reported to be suffering from a cold, but if so 'his voice showed no sign of indisposition'.[5] At his next stop in Chicago, in the opinion of the *Tribune*, 'he sang with more artistic finish and closer attention to detail than he did at any performance in which he was heard last year. . . . The music of the first act from *Faust* is perhaps the most trying for a tenor. It lies uncomfortably low, and not infrequently it places the voice in a condition where the singing of the music of the later acts becomes peculiarly difficult. Caruso sang it with the remarkable ease and fluency which distinguish all his work. . . . 'Salut, demeure' was sung in a manner truly exquisite . . . even the use of falsetto at the close (on the high C) was so skilfully accomplished that it proved the artist.'[6]

After three more performances, two at Saint Louis and one in Kansas City, at length the troupe reached the West Coast.

The Met's San Francisco sojourn began on April 16 at the Grand Opera with a performance of Goldmark's *Die Königin von Saba*. Caruso was not in this, though he had undertaken Assad some years previously in South America, but in Italian. The next evening he made what was to be his last appearance in San Francisco, as Don José opposite the Carmen of Olive Fremstad. Many years later she told her biographer 'that she [had] sensed something, [and] felt an odd depression and lethargy. She said that she had had to lash herself into her work and found it very hard to sing.'[7] Caruso, however, seems to have gone to bed that night quite easily and he was fast asleep when the first shock came, and he felt the room quiver; instantly he jumped out of bed and made for the windows. He realised what was happening, having had some experience of earthquake shocks near Naples.

All the way down the California coast in a matter of minutes the San Andreas fault had caused a cataclysmic tremor. In San Francisco much of the town was wiped out. Thirty thousand buildings were razed, including the opera house, and more than two hundred thousand were rendered homeless. Later, back in New York, Caruso gave Herman Klein a vivid word picture of events that night. 'It seemed an eternity, but I fancied that, so long as I remained under the beam at the top of the frame [of the doorway], I should be protected from the bits of loose masonry which I saw falling . . . below.'[8] 'I remained speechless, thinking I was having some dreadful nightmare, and for something like forty seconds I stood there while the buildings fell and my room rocked like a boat at sea. . . . During that time [my] whole life passed in front of me, and I remembered trivial and unimportant things. . . . Then I gathered my faculties and called for my valet. He came in . . . quite cool and without a tremor in his voice he said, "It is nothing". But he advised me all the same to dress quickly.'[9] Undoubtedly earthquake tales do not produce the soberest kind of journalism and reports of Caruso were subject to many different interpretations. A number of them, however, do seem to coincide, and so it is possible to chart his approximate progress, as well as record his state of mind. Scotti tells of meeting 'Caruso . . . fully dressed [as] he came out of his [hotel] room . . . I begged him to wait, but he seemed half-crazed and only continued on his way downstairs.'[10] A few minutes later Abott provides another glimpse of him. 'I heard a shout that sounded like an Indian war-whoop, and then above the heads of the crowd of men nearly a block away I saw, as if in a dream, the face of Theodore Roosevelt. In my nervous condition the effect was peculiarly startling, but after the first shock I realised that it was only a big photograph I was looking at and that the photograph was being waved high in the air by Caruso. In all his excitement he had not forgotten his treasure.'[11]

Later on Scotti and Caruso met again and they decided to quit town as quickly as was possible. Eventually they came upon a man with a horse and cart and managed to arrange a price with him to get them away with all their belongings as soon as possible. They passed out of the danger zone and managed to reach the address of an opera lover who was pleased to help them. Nevertheless Caruso was not anxious to spend another night indoors and he managed a cat-nap wrapped up against the cold under a tree in the garden. At any rate, the next day, things did not look so bad, and he determined to go back to his hotel to rescue many of his valuable costumes. Scotti continued the journey and it was not until much later, when he had finally secured places on a boat to Oakland, that Caruso reappeared; he had become involved in a heated altercation in broken English with members of the crew and it was necessary to wave 'President Roosevelt' about frantically. At length, he was allowed to rejoin Scotti and he left San Francisco for ever. Caruso reached New York in safety, but his losses were considerable. All attempts to retrieve his costumes proved abortive and he spent $2,000 replacing them, not only those for *Carmen* but also – and before either of them could be staged – those for *Faust* and *Marta*, which had perished too.

From New York he departed for Europe, arriving in England to take part in the Covent Garden season to commence on May 15, once again as the Duke. 'The house was crowded and he received a prolonged ovation. [It was just possible that part of this reception was the result of the San Francisco earthquake, for London newspapers were full of stories of his experiences there.] Caruso certainly deserved, for his own merits, a great deal of superlative appreciation. Vocally he was tremendous. It is no wonder that his success was so great, because the absolutely pure pleasure of listening to his voice will be as memorable to this generation as was, probably, the pure pleasure of the last generation in listening to Sims Reeves.'[12] That year he also sang Rodolfo, Canio, Pinkerton, Cavaradossi and Radames, the last two again opposite Rina Giachetti. The season culminated with two of the most stellar casts: *La Traviata* with Melba, Caruso and Battistini under Cleofonte Campanini (brother of the tenor, and later Director of the Chicago opera) and a *Don Giovanni* with Battistini, Caruso, Journet, Destinn, Agnes Nicholls and Pauline Donalda under Messager (renowned as a composer of operettas, some of which are still occasionally played even today). While in London he took part in a charity concert organized at the French embassy, as well as singing some Neapolitan songs of Tosti, to his accompaniment, in front of a stream of celebrities at the Golden Jubilee celebrations of the great English actress Ellen Terry at Drury Lane on June 12.

From London he departed for Ostend where he appeared at eight summer concerts at the Kursaal with a number of distinguished supporting artists, including Marguerite Carré, Cavalieri, Marthe Chenal, Kirkby-Lunn, Selma Kurz, Jean Noté, Elza Szamosi and Alice Verlet. In between concerts, needless to say, he went into the casino. There on one occasion he met Elena Gerhardt, who was then at the beginning of her career as a Lieder singer. She remembers that he demanded to know her age; she was twenty-two, so he put all his money down on that number and great was his thrill when it came up.

Once again Caruso spent the summer months in Italy with Ada and their two sons. At length, on October 6, he commenced the new season making his first appearance at the Hofoper, Vienna as the Duke in *Rigoletto* with Ruffo and Kurz. Needless to say, such a cast was 'crowned by the most immense ovation'.[13] He proceeded to Berlin and on October 9 he repeated the Duke, with Farrar undertaking Gilda for the only time in her career, and then he was Don José and Radames. From there he travelled on to Hamburg, making his debut as the Duke on October 16 and following it with Don José. On the 25th he made a solitary appearance in Paris at the Trocadéro in a concert which also included Calvé and Noté. He sang Barthélemy's 'Serenata napolitana', an air from Charles Pons's *Laura*, 'La donna è mobile' and he also joined in the quartet from *Rigoletto*. On November 2 he embarked for New York.

Caruso had only been back in New York a matter of days when, on November 17, eleven days before his first engagement that season at the Metropolitan, his name was splashed across the newspapers. He had been arrested the previous afternoon at the Monkey House in the

Central Park Zoo, and he was arraigned on a charge of disorderly conduct.

The arrest had been made by a Patrolman James J. Kane, or Cain, as his name was sometimes – perhaps more appropriately – spelled. The name is a common Irish one, and it is not unusual to find it spelled, or maybe misspelled, in a variety of different ways. By his account Caruso was guilty of harassing a woman, Mrs Hannah Graham, three times; he was taken to the Arsenal Station at Central Park, where he was charged, after which, accommodation there being insufficient, he was escorted through the streets to the East 67th Street police station and there incarcerated. His knowledge of English being then rudimentary, he scribbled a note to Barthélemy, who was residing with him that year at the Savoy Hotel, begging him to contact Conried. So it was that the Manager of the Met duly hurried over to the police station, arriving within the hour, and paid over the requisite bail so that Caruso might be freed. As soon as Conried properly understood the details of Caruso's arrest, he issued the following statement to the press.

> Ridiculous, absolutely ridiculous! Who would believe such a story? I have known Caruso for many years and he is a man of honor and dignity. Such conduct is beneath him; he would not be capable of it. Would a man of his distinction go to Central Park to flirt? No, no he could have almost any woman at his heels if he gave them the least encouragement. The occurrence was a great misfortune and Caruso has been done an enormous injustice. He tells me he intends to sue the woman for making false statements and causing his arrest. He is perfectly right in so doing and I have no doubt that he will be able to punish her, if he takes the affair to court. As I understand it, she simply says that Caruso touched her on the hip. Well, what of it? Maybe he did. That happens thousands of time every day in public places. If he touched her on the hip it was an accident pure and simple.[14]

The next day the trial commenced at Yorkville Police Court. But Caruso did not appear; he sent in a doctor's certificate stating that he was suffering from sciatica. Nor did the complainant appear, either. When the judge asked for her, Kane had to admit that she had given a false address. Yet he was allowed to continue his case. He then made a statement which seems more revelatory of himself than of Caruso, claiming that he had seen Caruso before 'on December 20, 1905, when a woman complained to me that [he] had annoyed her, and I kicked him out of the Monkey House. [But Caruso had sung the Duke on the night of December 20, and it was his habit never to go out on such days before leaving for the Metropolitan.] I did not know who he was then, but I recognised him the minute he entered this time. I never make mistakes in these cases. I can spot any one of them as soon as he enters the door. I have arrested lots of them. They say he could not be guilty of such a thing because he is a foreign gentleman! Why I grab a count or baron in the Monkey House every once in a while and boot him out of the park, because I cannot get the woman to complain of him.'[15] The case was resumed on November 21, when Caruso was subpoenaed. All attempts to locate Mrs Graham had failed; instead a veiled woman in white was brought in who accused Caruso of having annoyed her at a performance of *Parsifal* at the Met the previous February. And several other such accusations were levelled against him, even though the police did not introduce any witnesses; they had all refused to leave their names and addresses because of the notoriety that would ensue, or so at least the police claimed. At length, on the afternoon of the second day of the trial, the Magistrate found Caruso guilty and he had to pay the minimum fine of $10, and after he made an unsuccessful appeal there was an end to the matter.

What, we may ask, really happened? Caruso was an ebullient Italian, not a hide-bound Puritan, and the notion of his making an amorous advance to a lady does not seem so unlikely, but that there was anything sordid or indecent about it does seem highly improbable. It might be remembered that in Europe in 1906, though not perhaps in America, any lady found wandering around a zoo without a gentleman escort could hardly have belonged to the respectable classes. And Kane was a typical *agent provocateur*. It later transpired that he had contrived eight similar charges against less celebrated persons, all in the Monkey House, and in the same period as the Caruso case. Afterwards, in December that year, 'he was accused in a Harlem court of making a false affidavit in order to secure the release of a prisoner.'[16] It seems likely that Kane had secured Mrs Graham as his accomplice; she would start a seemingly innocent conversation – the Monkey House was an obvious place – and then he could be there on the spot. It is possible that at first neither of them recognised Caruso. But when she discovered who he was she determined on vanishing, for she did not relish the prospect of what all the attendant publicity would bring. At any rate, this fits in with what she claimed when she did finally reappear after the case was closed. It also might explain why she had left a false name, and not a very original one either. She was in fact the sister-in-law of a Mrs Graham. She was the wife of an unsuccessful ball-game player named Stanhope, and at the Stanhope marriage – by the strangest coincidence – Kane had been best man.

What seems particularly reprehensible was the court's decision and the behavior of the New York Police. A former Chief was moved to describe the conviction as an outrage, based on no evidence at all; while the Deputy Police Commissioner, who had prosecuted Caruso, later admitted in a statement 'that clergymen, bankers and others were guilty of the same offences charged against the tenor, but that the cases never come to light because they were handled by the police'.[17] To judge from many of the trial press notices Caruso was a focus for the considerable antipathy then shown to Italians. Inevitably Italians' knowledge of English was limited – as in Caruso's case. This was a period when the Italian immigration into New York was expanding rapidly; between 1900 and 1910 the number of Italians increased from 145,000 to 340,000, and, if we include first generation Italians born in America, the grand total amounted to 523,000. The New York Police on the other hand, as Kane's name suggests, were largely of Irish stock.

CHAPTER X

1906–1908

WHILE THE hullabaloo was still going on in the press, the Metropolitan season commenced with Gounod's *Roméo et Juliette*, which served to introduce Farrar to New York. This was the only opening night in eighteen years when Caruso did not appear. It was typical of the man's modesty and generosity, for he could certainly have essayed the role of Roméo but he preferred to let Farrar have the evening to herself. He appeared on the next night, on November 28, 1906, as Rodolfo and he was by all accounts in excellent voice; the strain of recent happenings in New York seemed to have left no effect on his singing.

It must have been a moment of excruciating suspense. He could not [see] his jurors to read their verdict on their smiling faces, it was his part simply to wait and in silence he peered through the painted window, listening for sounds that must either confirm him as the idol of the opera-going public or shatter that idol in obloquy or shame. Would it be cheers or hisses that would greet his ears? Caruso was not left long in doubt. . . . One long shout of greeting rose simultaneously from every portion of the house. It welled from pit to dome. It came surging down from the crowded galleries away up under the roof and it rolled in continuous volume alike from the parterre boxes of the fashionable world . . . from the "Cranks alley", where battalions of Caruso's compatriots from Italy punctured the din with staccato shouts of 'Bravo Caruso!' and from the topmost tiers of the family circle, where a regiment of admiring Frenchmen shouted 'Vive Caruso!' until the electric lights seemed to vibrate visibly.[1]

Caruso and Sembrich finally had the stage to themselves at the end of the first act with their duet, and it seemed they had seldom sung it more beautifully. Three or four times the audience interrupted them with frantic applause, and at the end there were repeated curtain calls, until at last Caruso, without Sembrich, stood before the curtain to take the

97

applause alone. By all the signs he might have kept on taking curtain calls for the rest of the evening.[2]

Conried was soon to realise just how much he relied on Caruso, for not only was he beginning to suffer from the fatal illness that would lead inexorably to his retirement and early death, but that season would mark the first appearance in New York of the Manhattan Opera with Oscar Hammerstein. In its great days, opera was full of impresarios who mirrored in themselves something of the hyperbolic scale of their art. In that tradition we may include Domenico Barbaja (sometime scullion and waiter, highly intelligent but almost illiterate, who during a period of thirty years was at various times in charge of the San Carlo, Naples, while Rossini was penning his *chefs d'oeuvre*, La Scala, Milan and the Theater an der Wien, Vienna), Mapleson and Gunsbourg. Whereas these three were also involved in operatic adventures fairly consistently and for periods of at least a quarter century, Hammerstein blazed a comet-like trail that lasted less than four years. As John Cone tells: 'He accomplished this without stockholders, advisers, partners, a board of directors, or the patronage of the rich. He announced his intention to compete against New York's Metropolitan Opera Company in the fall by presenting opera on an unprecedented scale and with international stars at his new theater.'[3] Although this was not Hammerstein's first operatic venture, it was not until the first decade of this century, when New York's population was growing rapidly, that at last he felt able to take on the Metropolitan. Notwithstanding various ham-fisted attempts by Conried to thwart his endeavors, Hammerstein went to Paris and succeeded in marshalling an impressive list of singers, led by Melba, Bonci and Renaud.

The lists were drawn and the battle began on December 3, six days after the Metropolitan had opened, when Hammerstein introduced Bonci to New York as Arturo in Bellini's *I Puritani*. Aldrich in *The New York Times* thought:

> His qualities are not quite such as will fire the . . . heart as Caruso's have done. His is a much subtler art than the tenor at the Metropolitan possesses. The gifts of voice that nature has endowed him with are less opulent. . . it is a small voice, a delicately and exquisitely modulated one. Bonci is not provided with that enormous lung capacity that stands Caruso in such good stead in giving him power and as well an unfailing command of the long and finished phrase. His voice has occasionally shown a tendency to take on the pallid color that is known in the slang of the

vocalists as 'white', the quality that is called 'open'. But this was only occasional, as was also the tendency towards a nasal tone that he showed. . . . In richness and fullness of color his voice cannot be compared with Caruso's. It is inferior to the sensuous charm of that wonderful organ, whether in *mezza voce* or in the intoxicating fullness of the fortissimos which so delight the demonstrative portion of the Met audiences. But, on the other hand, so far as can now be judged, Bonci is not likely to fall into those deplorable errors of taste and . . . feeling that afflict the most judicious of Caruso's listeners – the forcing of his tones beyond even the superb fullness that needs no forcing, the exaggeration of phrasing, the pumping-up of sentiment, the opening of the lachrymose floodgates, and the aspiration of vowels.[4]

It is doubtful if there was ever any real animosity between Bonci and Caruso, for their voices, like much of their repertories, were markedly different, increasingly so with the passage of time. Bonci was a lyric tenor and remained so throughout his career, even in the late twenties when he was approaching sixty. But although, as we saw when comparing their Covent Garden repertories, Caruso too started out a lyric tenor, by the last years of his career he came to undertake a more dramatic repertory albeit still continuing to sing certain lyric roles, such as Nemorino and Lionello in *Marta*. If there was ever any conflict between the two it was of reputation rather than repertory, a fact that became self-evident by the end of that season when Hammerstein, realising that Bonci – for all his fine art and top Cs – was no answer to Caruso, switched his attention first to Giovanni Zenatello then to McCormack. The following season when Bonci defected to Conried at the Metropolitan, Hammerstein put up no obstacles, as he might well have done, bearing in mind his fondness for litigation.

Caruso's repertory in the 1906/7 season included Alfredo, Lionello, Loris, Edgardo, Radames, Cavaradossi, Canio, des Grieux in *Manon Lescaut*, Pinkerton, the Duke and Vasco in Meyerbeer's *L'Africana*, which he was singing for the first time. That year in Philadelphia, the *Inquirer* complained that 'Caruso's expression of passionate emotion in *Pagliacci* had degenerated into vociferation,'[5] though it had to concede that in *La Bohème* 'his part in the duets with Mimì was singularly eloquent and entirely convincing and the presentation of the character in its entirety was vital [and] consistent'.[6] The tour began in 1907 in Baltimore and then the company proceeded via Washington to Boston and Chicago. There William Hubbard of the *Tribune* praised 'the perfect ease with which he emitted every tone, and the surety and smoothness with which he gave utterance to every phrase. The great aria "O paradiso!" from *L'Africana* was faultless, both as regards tonal splendor and musical phrasing.'[7] His Radames followed next and '[he] did some of the most beautiful work he has ever done here in the Tomb Scene.'[8] The Met then journeyed on to Cincinnati, Saint Louis and Kansas City, where the *Times* again praised 'the unique beauty of his voice'.[9] It was the same story at Omaha, Saint Paul, Minneapolis and Milwaukee, wherever he stopped. 'The voice is like a moving personality itself, individual, impressive and ever changing, preserving its essential quality, and the highest register is capable of infinite power and great intensity. So assured is his control and so perfect his technique it is almost as if he possesses none. Personality, color, vital meaning and true impersonation are found instead of conscious intellectual analysis. Passion and feeling obscure technique.'[10] This kind of panegyric greeted him at every city and it was not surprising that, at the end of the season, Conried should have felt obliged to put his fee up to $2,000 a performance, for Hammerstein was all ready to poach on his preserves.

That spring Caruso left America bound for Europe on the *Deutschland*. We catch a glimpse of him on board the first morning, when he had come on deck in the hope of securing some solitude for a few moments, but 'he was easily recognised from his photographs, and in another instant he was surrounded by a flock of women asking him whether he was really the great tenor. He laughingly replied that he was the "bestia feroce" and doubling up his fists like a lion's paws, growled some untenorlike tones. He was always approachable all day long even during the roughest weather, and he was always surrounded by questioning admirers.'[11] At length the boat docked at Plymouth and Caruso proceeded to London, making his bow at Covent Garden on May 15 as Rodolfo in *La Bohème*. We get some idea of the exacting schedule he set himself when we note that after the second performance that season, a Pinkerton opposite Destinn's Butterfly on the 17th, he took the packet across the Channel the next morning at an early hour, and appeared that evening in Paris at a concert at the Trocadéro for the benefit of Belgian charities under the patronage of the Ambassador and the Comtesse Greffuhle. He returned to London the next day, and during the following couple of months undertook his usual gallery of roles, including Alfredo, Radames, Don José, Cavaradossi, Riccardo in *Un Ballo in maschera* and Canio. On June 11 he appeared in a 'gala night at the opera, [and this] was perhaps the most brilliant event in English society. . . . [T]he crowded house was ablaze with jewels and gorgeous uniforms, beautiful dresses and court costumes.'[12] Seat prices ranged from two shillings and sixpence in the gallery to £50 for a grand tier box. After the event the King conferred on Caruso 'a decoration in the fourth class of the Royal Victorian Order, which entitles the holder to write the letters M.V.O. after his name'.[13] He also undertook two operas by Giordano: on July 3 he made his London bow as Loris in *Fedora*, and then on the 20th, for the only time in his career, he sang Andrea Chénier. He was announced for this part at the Metropolitan in February 1921, but after the commencement of his fatal illness, and so Gigli sang it instead.

That year Covent Garden provided an opportunity, as the Metropolitan and Hammerstein had done in New York, for a direct comparison to be made between Caruso and Bonci, for Bonci succeeded Caruso in performances of *La Bohème*. According to the *Musical Courier*, 'One can say, whereas Caruso carries his audiences away by his irresistible crescendos, it is the delicious decrescendos that are the great strength of Bonci.'[14] Bonci, however, did not prove to be any more competition for Caruso in London than he had been in New York. Even at this stage of Caruso's career, reporters had already begun to harry him, and he often felt obliged to give telling responses even to the most vapid queries. When a journalist demanded to know whether it was true that he was planning his retirement, Caruso hesitated before replying: 'Let me give you some good advice. When you hear an artist attempts to retire, don't you believe it, for as long as he keeps his voice he will sing. You may depend upon that.'[15] There was something endearingly honest about the man, which deeply impressed the brother of the famous Jean, the bass Edouard de Reszke:

I am so sorry I could not manage to come and bid you good-bye before leaving London, and tell you again *viva voce* all the pleasure I had from hearing you sing. I never heard a more beautiful voice. . . . You sang like a god. You are an actor and a sincere artist, and above all, you are modest and without exaggerations. You are able to draw from my eyes many tears. I was very much touched, and this happens to me. . . seldom. You have heart, feeling, poetry and truth, and with these qualities you will be the master of the world. Please do accept these few words from an old artist who admires you not only as an artist but as a very dear man. May God keep you in good health for many years. *Au revoir*, until next year.[16]

That summer Caruso again retired to Italy, and travelled to Milan to undergo an operation for the removal of some nodules from his vocal cords. Bearing in mind the exacting schedule of engagements he had been setting himself, there is nothing especially remarkable about this. In all probability his condition was exacerbated by his excessive cigarette smoking, though listening to his records today does not reveal any sign of its having had much effect on his singing.

On October 2 he resumed his career and began his usual 'German' tour at the Budapest Kiralyi Operaház with a solitary performance of Radames in *Aida*. His reception here, as in Naples and Barcelona, was unfavorable. Probably this had to do with the fact that it was in Budapest that the singer was earning, for the first time in his career, his new American fee of $2,000, the largest sum he had yet earned anywhere, and not only was this reflected in a rise in the seat prices, but it seems that the rest of the cast were barely up to scratch. The Aida was a last-minute replacement and only one of the other principals, Mihály Takáts, the Amonasro, made even a very few records. After the barrage of publicity organized by his German manager, Emil Ledner, the people of Budapest were expecting a fabulous vocal treat. But Caruso had not sung for more than two months; after the operation on his vocal cords he was still, not surprisingly, unsure of himself and there being only one performance – unlike Naples or Barcelona – he never got the opportunity to relax and gain confidence, so the public remained disappointed. But only two nights later he repeated Radames in Vienna, and this time the cast included Lucie Weidt, Madame Charles-Cahier and Wilhelm Hesch. Mahler was conducting, and, in spite of that plenitude of magnificence, the *Neues Wiener Tagblatt* noted that 'in contrast [to Budapest], our public applauded [him] unanimously, frantically, for a long time, one might almost say demonstratively.'[17] He then added Rodolfo and the Duke, and by this time there was no doubt he was in charge of his resources once again. Bruno Walter heard him and remembers the 'sense of beauty expressed in his tone coloring [and] his portamento and rubato'.[18] At his next port of call, Leipzig, he was again Radames and the *Neueste Nachtrichten* spent several columns waxing almost as lyrical as Caruso's singing over 'the wonderful quality of his marvellous voice', 'his mastery of his art', 'his perfectly pure intonation',[19] etc. Thereafter he visited Hamburg, Berlin and Frankfurt. At the Königliches Opernhaus, Berlin, he added the Duke and Edgardo, and these were opposite the Gilda and Lucia of Frieda Hempel, who writes of the 'exceptional quality of his voice which was so beautiful that one cannot describe it to those who have never heard it'.[20] Ledner singles out a Berlin Radames opposite Destinn's Aida as one of Caruso's finest performances:

> He sang 'Celeste Aida' so brilliantly that the applause stopped the show. The third act was truly . . . an experience. . . his Radames reached such heights that those lucky enough to have been present will remember the occasion. . . for the rest of their lives. Both singers emitted tones of unearthly beauty in the great duet. It was the epitome of perfection, a unique and unparalleled occasion. What happened at the end of this duet was not merely applause, but an uproar, a cry of jubilation. The audience clapped, yelled and stamped their feet . . . The end was greeted by a repetition of the furore that had followed the third act. In the course of many years I witnessed many triumphant Caruso nights but none . . . quite like that . . . Aida.[21]

Before Caruso returned to America that autumn, the New York press was full of speculation over whether his conviction in the Monkey House case might not ban him from re-entering the United States. A lawyer, however, denied that there was any question of extending the prohibition on entry to those convicted merely of a misdemeanor. And so it proved, for when Caruso disembarked there was no trouble with Immigration.

On opening night, November 18, 1907, he introduced to the Metropolitan a role he had created five years previously, Maurizio in Cilea's *Adriana Lecouvreur*, but the opera survived only one other performance that season. As the London *World* had written after the Covent Garden premiere of *Fedora*: 'Opera-goers prefer that which they know, and take only a languid interest in that which is unfamiliar even when the cast contains the brightest stars.'[22] Later, he introduced another novelty, again a part that he had been connected with from its earliest days, Osaka in Mascagni's *Iris*; but then, in New York, coming after *Butterfly*, though it had been written eight years previously, it served only to emphasise the paucity of Mascagni's ideas rather than Puccini's plagiarism of many of Mascagni's musical clichés.

That season Caruso made his customary round of roles including Radames, Rodolfo, Pinkerton, Loris, Cavaradossi, Faust, des Grieux in *Manon Lescaut* and Canio, and, for the first time, he undertook Manrico in *Il Trovatore*. According to Henderson

It was a foregone conclusion that Caruso would deal more mercifully than most Manricos do with the lyric passages of the part. With all the robustness that he has of late cultivated he has not thrown aside his skill in the delivery of cantabile music. It was therefore to be expected that he would sing agreeably such numbers as 'Ah sì, ben mio'. On the other hand no one who is familiar with his doings entertained any doubt that he would fire the true Italian heart with the high C in 'Di quella pira'. It could not have been curiosity to hear him sing this much-prized note, without which Manrico simply does not count in the Italian mind, that assembled last night's audience, for he habitually sings the upper C in the *racconto* in *La Bohème*. [In fact, to judge from his 1906 recording of this aria, he would transpose it down a semitone. In such fashion the upper note became a B rather than C, see page 59.] He also sang it in 'quel amor' outside the window in *La Traviata* and it is nothing new for him to be a celebrated high C tenor. But perhaps *Il Trovatore* for many persons gives the C a local habitation and a name, and this much is gained. At any rate there was a considerable howdydo over it last night. And it sounded somewhat low for a C too, did it not?[23]

Indeed it probably did, for he recorded 'Di quella pira' in 1906 in the key of B major, i.e. transposed down a semitone.

Meanwhile Hammerstein was giving Conried a good run for his money; he made a profit that year of $250,000 while the Met lost close on $100,000. During the autumn Hammerstein introduced a constellation of luminaries, including Mary Garden and Zenatello, as well as bringing back to New York Renaud and Ancona. But the most sensational of his debutantes was Tetrazzini, whom he introduced on January 15, 1908, as the perfect complement of Melba the previous year – if it was hardly a compliment to her. Though the press adopted a condescending tone towards a 'coloratura' soprano: 'It is useless to discuss the phenomenon [of her success]. The whims of the populace are as unquestioning and irresponsible as the fury of the elements,'[24] yet it 'would be difficult to find a parallel for it in the operatic annals of New York.'[25] It was only one of Conried's mistakes that he had passed up an option on her services and so missed the chance of a lifetime. He did, however, secure Chaliapin, who made his Met debut that season. Unfortunately, amid all the critical cerebration over his controversial stagecraft, only one critic, Henry Finck, recognized his true genius. Even the usually perceptive Henderson rated his art 'cheap claptrap'.[26] Chaliapin dissolved into what Farrar calls a 'huge pout'[27] and vowed that he would never return to New York; nor did he until after the Russian Revolution when his world had crumbled about him.

In order to combat the competition Conried increased Caruso's total number of performances. That year he made a stream of appearances for the Metropolitan company, including sixty-eight in the United States, fifteen in Europe, as well as seven concerts and two New York musicales, and from these he earned $187,500. As Key puts it: 'The New World was assuredly an El Dorado for this Neapolitan.'[28] But what to do with the money? A newspaper columnist asked him whether he ever speculated. 'No, never in my life. Although a friend did make me several hundred dollars in the street, even [after] that I was never tempted. I said to myself: "What's the use? Money easily earned is money easily spent . . ." You want to know what I do with all my money? Three quarters of it I spend and the rest I invest in securities and bonds.'[29]

In view of the quite heroic losses sustained by the Metropolitan that season, there was, doubtless, a considerable amount of relief when Conried's illness obliged him to announce his intention of quitting. On March 24 a benefit was held for him. As well as Beethoven's Overture Leonore No. 3 under Mahler's direction, there were six substantial operatic scenes and Caruso sang in three of them: Act IV, Scene I of *Il Trovatore*, Act II of *Faust* and he finished the evening with Act I of *Pagliacci*. That spring he went on tour with the company to Boston, Baltimore, Washington, Chicago and Pittsburgh, after which he undertook his first concert tour, appearing in Columbus, Toronto, Detroit, Buffalo, Cleveland, Rochester and Montreal. A performance was arranged at Scranton, but upon his arrival there the house had not sold sufficiently to meet his guaranteed fee, which was always paid in advance. When Caruso learned this, he refused to be paid, and cancelled the contract, returning to New York. It was typical of him not to oblige his manager to sustain the loss. The program was made up of a variety of operatic excerpts, among them 'Celeste Aida', 'Vesti la giubba', 'Salut, demeure' and the quartet from *Rigoletto*, and he also gave a number of songs by way of encores, including Fatuo's 'Sento ch'io t'amo', Gastaldon's 'Musica proibita' and Buzzi-Peccia's 'Lolita'.

At length, on May 21, Caruso left New York for Europe on the *Kaiserin Augusta Victoria*. He had been on the voyage three days when the first piece of bad news was telegraphed out to him: his father had died. Although they had never been close, and there had been a considerable amount of friction between them in those early years when Caruso had determined on becoming an opera singer, that was long ago now and he was genuinely distressed.

No sooner had the boat docked at Plymouth than news reached him of Ada Giachetti's elopement with his chauffeur. His immediate reaction was to cancel his engagement in London and a solitary *Rigoletto* he was committed to in Paris, and rush after them. But eventually he was persuaded to appear at the Royal Albert Hall concert, since this was to be held in the presence of royalty, and also to undertake his Paris Opéra debut, since this was a charitable occasion. For the London concert amongst his selections was 'Vesti la giubba' and we may imagine with what feeling he invested the phrases 'E se Arlecchin t'invola Colombina, Ridì Pagliaccio, e ognun applaudirà' (And if Harlequin steals your Colombine, Laugh Pagliaccio and everyone will applaud you). Certainly Edward VII and Queen Alexandra applauded, and they had only heard of the loss of his father. In Paris at the Opéra his Duke, with Melba's Gilda and Renaud's Rigoletto, was acclaimed both 'for the amplitude and equality of his voice from top to bottom, as well as for the tenderness and expression shown in his singing'.[30] No trace of his personal tragedy showed up in this melodrama.

Truth to tell, the elopement was not so unexpected. The superintendent at Caruso's villa near Florence had become aware the previous year of the relationship which already existed between the handsome chauffeur and Caruso's 'wife' and decided to remedy matters. He decided the best way to accomplish this would be to fire the chauffeur and so nip scandal in the bud and spare Caruso much grief. Apparently blows were struck between the two men and the superintendent had the chauffeur summoned before a magistrate. But, although he was found guilty, he obtained a pardon. As soon as Caruso returned he was informed of the affair, but Ada let him think that the fault had all been on the superintendent's side, and, although several jealous *scenas* took place, finally he was content that the chauffeur should remain in his employment.

Straight after the Paris *Rigoletto* he rushed back home in search of Ada. He went to Florence, Milan and other cities, but without finding trace of her. He was so distressed that he even appealed to his 'wife's' legitimate husband in an attempt to locate the pair. He went so far as to invite him to a meeting, which was to take place at Florence, 'but the husband never kept the appointment – he simply sent a couple of friends along, and into their ears Caruso was obliged to pour out all the bitterness of his soul.'[31] In August he journeyed to Paris and spent a couple of days at the Grand Hotel before returning to Florence. But no sooner was he back home again than 'he had a strong idea that Ada was in England and he left Italy for London.'[32] There, an American music lover, Albert J. Weber, met him at the Star and Garter Hotel, Richmond, Surrey. By this time he appeared to have begun to recover for, as Weber tells, 'he sang for me several times, a selection from new roles which he is to sing in New York this winter and I was especially impressed by those from Tchaikovsky's *La Dama di picche* which is to be given at the Metropolitan.'[33] (In fact *The Queen of Spades* was not given in Italian but German and it was held over for another season, when Hermann was sung by Leo Slezak.)

Perhaps now resigned to the loss of Ada, at length Caruso returned to Naples to spend some time with his recently bereaved stepmother. He created a minor sensation on the streets of his native city when he returned from a jaunt to Tunisia fitted out in Arab costume. When he landed there was a considerable amount of curiosity shown in his bulky figure, clad in a white caftan with a gorgeous turban on his head, and followed by what appeared to be a numerous European suite. The rumor soon spread that he was a Turkish potentate and great was the respect shown him. He accepted it all with splendid condescension until, just as he was getting into his carriage, he turned round and smilingly broke into broad Neapolitan, confessing himself flattered that he could deceive even his own people.

On October 1, he resumed his career and began a round of performances, singing the Duke, Rodolfo or Canio at Wiesbaden, Frankfurt, Bremen, Hamburg and Leipzig. On October 20 he reached Berlin and it was claimed that he enjoyed triumphs there that had not been known since the days of Pauline Lucca, a contemporary of Patti's and a celebrated Viennese soprano who had died earlier that year. At the Königliches Opernhaus he appeared in *Pagliacci*, *Aida* and *La Bohème* with Metropolitan casts including Farrar, returning once again to the scene of her first triumphs, and Scotti, making his Berlin debut. But all the artists were overshadowed by Caruso, for 'everyone bows down to the brilliancy of this wonderful southern star and acknowledges there is no voice like his'.[34] Although prices had escalated and were three times the ordinary, the house was sold out each evening.

In the middle of the season came a summons from Potsdam for Caruso to dine privately with the Kaiser. He was much alarmed at the prospect of such exalted company and he sent a letter begging that he might be allowed to bring his own valet to serve behind his chair. The Kaiser agreed, and at the dinner as he raised his glass and toasted Caruso he observed: 'If I were not Emperor of Germany, I should have liked to be your valet.'

CHAPTER XI

1908–1910

FROM GERMANY, Caruso proceeded to New York, and this year he moved to the Hotel Knickerbocker, which was to remain his residence until 1920. That season a new Director of the Metropolitan was appointed, Gatti-Casazza, whom Caruso had worked with at La Scala, Milan. And on November 16, 1908, *Aida* served to introduce the New York public to the other half of the new management, Toscanini. In the newspapers next day it was his contribution that was noted first rather than last, the place accorded to most conductors at that time. Aldrich in *The New York Times* acclaimed him:

> a strenuous force, a dominating power, a man of potent authority, a musician of infinite resource ... [he] insists on clear-cut outline, on abundant detail, on the strongest contrasts, on vivid color.... The orchestra sounded of greater richness and fullness in this fine score, and seldom have many of the finer details of it been so well brought out.... That it was from time to time too powerful and covered the voices of the singers was a part of the ... character of the performance. The prevailing spirit influenced every member of the cast, apparently to strive for the strenuous in a similar degree. It needed nothing so potent to loosen the vocal cords of Caruso, who reappeared in the part of Radames, and sang with probably more power, with more insistent dwelling on the highest tones, with more prodigal expenditure of resources than ever before.[1]

Here, with the emergence of the star conductor and the orchestra now shifted into top gear, singers had to learn to combat the new-found energy of the orchestra by concentrating increasingly on developing the size of their voices – as we noted in Caruso's successive recordings of 'Celeste Aida'. After the furore created by Toscanini and Gatti in those first few weeks of the season, rumors quickly spread that their original one-year contracts were to be replaced by options covering a further two-year period. 'It is amusing to note that Caruso and Scotti were the most agitated over the control allowed their compatriots.'² A letter of objection, duly signed by Caruso, Farrar, Scotti, Eames and Sembrich, was despatched to the board. As Farrar remembered years later: 'Gatti could never quite forget this first sign of rebellion, but Caruso and Scotti offered persuasive and soothing extenuation of their part to their irritated countrymen.'³

Notwithstanding these opening skirmishes, Caruso was to remain loyal to the Metropolitan, while Hammerstein was offering him every conceivable blandishment. Arthur Hammerstein, the impresario's son, took Caruso a proposal. The terms the Hammersteins were ready to offer were startling: $5,000 a performance, three times a week for twenty weeks, if Caruso so wished. At the Metropolitan he was earning $2,000 and that season he sang there forty-two times, plus seven performances outside New York at $2,500 each. This was the highest fee then paid to any singer, but Hammerstein would have doubled it. At this time the impresario had reached the pinnacle of his eminence. On the night after the commencement of the season at the Met he opened a completely new opera house in Philadelphia, and it seems a strong likelihood that had he had Caruso singing for him then, it would have been the Met and not the Manhattan that folded. Caruso must have been tempted but in the end he refused, and the reason he gave was that he felt he would lose his voice if he ever abandoned the Met. As Vincent Sheean observes: 'He is known to have been superstitious, but it seems that other reasons besides a superstition must have operated in the matter.'⁴

As with Conried, so with Gatti; and that season the Met was notable for Caruso's prodigal expenditure of resources. Two days before opening night, on a Saturday, he was Faust in a special pre-season performance at the newly-built Academy of Music, Brooklyn. The day after *Aida*, on Tuesday, he was Rodolfo in *La Bohème* in Philadelphia (the same night incidentally that Hammerstein's Philadelphia Opera House opened with *Carmen*, with Maria Labia, Charles Dalmorès and de Segurola). On Thursday, back in New York again, he sang Pinkerton to Farrar's Butterfly, with Toscanini conducting. Then on Friday, at the last minute, he deputised for an indisposed Bonci as Alfredo in *La Traviata* with Sembrich, 'to the immense satisfaction of the public',⁵ and on Saturday, again under Toscanini, he appeared as Cavaradossi opposite Eames's Tosca. He sang six times in eight days – 'truly a remarkable feat!'⁶ In the course of the rest of that season he also undertook Don José, the Duke and Canio, and he sang Turiddu and Massenet's des Grieux for the first time in America, as well as appearing in Brooklyn and Philadelphia as Manrico in *Il Trovatore*. That the rigorous demands he should have set himself at the beginning of that season led again to vocal problems was not surprising. In December he sang twelve performances; in January this was reduced to nine; in February to four; and in March and April to only a couple each.

He must have been made to feel a lot more unwell when Giachetti unexpectedly arrived in New York at the end of January. She lost no time in coming round to the Knickerbocker in person. Evidently she had been tipped off, for she had no difficulty in finding Caruso's room. His valet was on guard, and ran to warn his master, but too late, for she had followed him through the door he had left open. The tenor was taking a bath and unable to stop her. 'He knew her to be a strong-minded, assertive woman and one not be thwarted by subterfuge, so he shiveringly gathered the robe about him and greeted the fair but fickle Ada.'[7] 'A minute or so later the corridors echoed to their spirited debate. Suddenly the door was flung open and out stalked the Signora, her face flaming and her eyes blazing with anger.'[8] She thereupon drove off to the Hotel Navarre and before leaving on *La Lorraine* for Europe, she had extorted from Caruso a promise that he would continue to pay her monthly emolument.

It was at his penultimate performance that season, on April 3, 1909, that Caruso took part in the first experimental broadcast of an opera. As Dr Lee De Forest recalls,

I received permission to install a radio telephone transmitter at the Metropolitan, as well as microphones on the stage. In order to pick up music and voices at a distance I had to use the acousticon microphones, such as are employed by the deaf. These were operated by a battery, and their output led to a receiver in the attic, pressed against the microphone of the radio telephone transmitter. We did not have the audio amplifier in those days. Our transmitter microphone was placed in the ground lead of the sending apparatus, carrying the full force of our transmitted energy. Our long-sought opportunity to attain the heights of airshowmanship came when Caruso sang the *Siciliana*, the prologue to *Cavalleria rusticana*. This is sung before the rise of the curtain, making it peculiarly effective for the audience out the front and even more so for audiences out back! We were permitted to move our microphones close up to Caruso as he sang behind the scenes, and to remove the apparatus just as the curtain went up. Technically, we could say that we broadcast from the stage; actually we picked up the song under almost studio conditions [and] a few listeners, mostly wireless operators on shipboard, heard Caruso broadcasting.[9]

Unfortunately, as Dr De Forest states, the microphones were unable to pick up and transmit sounds unless they were right on top of the source, and it was not until more than a dozen years had passed and more sensitive means had been developed that larger audiences could be reached.

No doubt problems with Ada had encouraged Caruso to occupy himself single-mindedly with his career. But vocal indisposition brought his season to a premature conclusion after his next perform-ance, as Radames on April 7. It also obliged him to relinquish any possibility of being able to undertake the Met tour that year; for this, happily, Gatti was able to announce that Hammerstein had agreed to release Zenatello. It must have been galling, to say the least, for Caruso to have read all the newspaper speculation this occasioned. He quit New York and the next news of him was from Milan at the end of April when he entered the clinic of Professor della Vedova. During that summer, after a period of recuperation spent at Villa Bellosguardo, he went to the medical spas at Salsomaggiore and Montecatini. By this time, however, the increased clamor for news of him at almost any cost was doubtless responsible for della Vedova telling all in an interview he gave the *Corriere della sera*;[10] the tenor had had to submit once again to an operation for removal of nodules from his vocal cords – or so della Vedova claimed. Caruso became incensed when he read it and would have declined to settle the specialist's fee had he not been persuaded to pay up and avoid the even greater publicity that would have been surely set off by any legal wrangle.

It was not until the beginning of August that he travelled to Ostend for three concerts at the Kursaal. Of his vocal indisposition there was now no trace.

His voice was still beautiful and lovely. There was far more sweetness in its quality than was contained in it last spring, and its control was admirable. The miles and miles of affirmation and denial that Caruso's voice 'had gone where the woodbine twineth' had naturally aroused the greatest curiosity here. The audience accordingly was on tenterhooks when Caruso entered to start the air vibrating to the opening bars of 'O paradiso!'. The great tenor has evidently not spent his retirement in vain, and he sang with more delicacy and taste than has been displayed for some seasons past.[11]

That year he did not return to Covent Garden and instead undertook a concert tour of the British Isles, beginning in Dublin on August 20 at the Theatre Royal, then proceeding to Plymouth, Blackpool, Glasgow, Edinburgh, Newcastle, Manchester, Belfast, London and Liverpool. In Dublin he vied with the Horse Show,

> but it could not be complained that he short-changed Dubliners. Besides a duet, 'Solenne in quest' ora' from *La Forza del destino* with Armand Lecomte [Count Scalzi, with whom he often sang], two items were placed in the program against his name, 'O paradiso!' and 'Celeste Aida', but as he responded to the increasing enthusiasm his list of solos extended to seven. His first encore, sung in French, was Tosti's 'Pour un baiser'; the second also was Tosti's, 'L'alba separa dalla luce l'ombra', sung with intense emotional force. . . . Then, by way of contrast, he gave an appealing little encore piece, all tenderness and trembling love; tones that quivered with the sweetness of a precious sigh. It was Tosti's 'Ideale'. With his next encore the climax of his efforts was reached. It was 'Vesti la giubba', in which the heavy-hearted Pagliaccio laughs bitterly at the mockery of fate, [then] yielding to the remarkable enthusiasm which followed it, he sang another song, 'Sento che t'amo' by Fatuo.[12]

Landon Ronald remembers the Blackpool concert; he was accompanist to Patti and Melba, brother of Russell, and later conductor of the London Philharmonic Orchestra, as well as being a highly successful composer of songs, more than one of which Caruso sang.

> The methods he employed were both original and interesting. He would allow himself only to be announced for one solo in the first part of the program and one solo in the second half. He arranged with the accompanist to have five encores ready after his first appearance and five more after his second appearance. The result was he never came on and bowed: he simply sang the item on the program, walked off the platform amidst a hurricane of applause, promptly returned with an encore, and repeated this performance until the five numbers had been sung. After this, wild horses would not have dragged from him anything more. He had given his audience twelve songs and that sufficed. I remember him bowing at Blackpool with a big coat on, hat and stick in hand and smoking a large cigar. The audience took the hint, and eventually stopped applauding.[13]

At the end of September Caruso left England for Germany, where he began his tour in Frankfurt on September 29, afterwards stopping in Nuremberg, Hamburg and Berlin. There, as Lotte Lehmann relates in her autobiography, she first heard him as Don José [in *Carmen*]. Thrilling as an actor, quite apart from his singing, he was a revelation to me. . . . His complete abandonment to his part communicated itself to his audiences . . . and I am sure that many who had only come 'because one must have been there' forgot about sensation and remembered only Caruso. I had studied Eurydice . . . and had the great joy of having to sing it on a Caruso evening [for he sang Canio straight after *Orpheus*]. What a thrill it was when he came up to me in the wings after the performance and cried, wringing my hand: 'Ah brava, brava! Che bella magnifica voce! Una voce Italiana!'[14]

From Berlin he travelled to Bremen. That year his repertory in Germany also included Cavaradossi and Edgardo in *Lucia*.

His first American engagement that season was at Camden, New Jersey, when he resumed his recording career after more than a year and a half. He chose to begin the sessions with Tosti's 'Pour un baiser', which he had included in his British tour. It proves conclusively, as Aida Favia-Artsay states, '[though] nodules on his vocal cords may be the result of any type of vocal abuse . . . their removal is in no way detrimental to the voice.'[15] After a brief stopover in Philadelphia for a couple of performances of *Aida* with the Met company, the New York season began on November 15, 1909, when Caruso sang Enzo in *La Gioconda* with Destinn, Homer and Amato under Toscanini. In the reviews the next day Toscanini's contribution again took pride of place; according to Henderson, his conducting was 'worthy of a great theater',[16] and Caruso too created his usual fine impression, 'Cielo e mar!' being notable for his 'beautiful cantilena'.[17] In contrast to his schedule the previous year, there was no longer the urge to prove himself, to take up everything in the book and all in one week, night after night and without a break. He sang only another eight roles: Alfredo, Pinkerton (in Brooklyn), Canio, Cavaradossi, Faust, Rodolfo and the Duke, and Federico Loewe in Franchetti's *Germania*, which part Caruso had created at La Scala eight years before. Two reasons may account for his restraint: the need not to compromise his health again by acquiring another vocal nodule, and Gatti's having secured a number of other reputable tenors to share the work load (as well as Bonci and Riccardo Martin, that season the company also engaged Jadlowker, Clément and Slezak).

It was on the morning of March 3, 1910, that Caruso received a menacing note demanding payment of $15,000 from 'The Black

Hand', a Mafia-like organisation. It was written in Italian. He was required to walk along Forty-second Street and pass the money to a man who would accost him with a strange sign.

Upon receipt of the blackmail note, Caruso immediately went down to the desk clerk to ask him to find a policeman. Inspector McCluskey was passing the Knickerbocker at the time, and he urged Caruso to walk along the street as he was told and he would then follow him. The tenor obeyed, but no one approached him. The next morning, March 4, Caruso found a second letter from the same writer. This said that Caruso had been under surveillance the previous day and the police bodyguard had been detected but that such precautions could avail him nothing. 'The Black Hand' would 'get' the singer, in his room, on the street or at the opera house, and there could be no escape. The letter closed with a repeated demand, which directed Caruso to leave the money outside an address in Brooklyn. The police then took charge and they arranged that Martino, Caruso's valet, should take the package of money. They had placed a banknote on the top and bottom of the bundles, otherwise it only consisted of strips of paper cut so as to look like the real thing. Martino made his way to the Brooklyn address, while the entire block around the house was surrounded by detectives. He then placed the package on the steps of the house, as demanded. For a while nothing happened and it was not for another quarter of an hour that three men appeared. They passed the step where the money lay, returned, passed it again and then picked it up. Instantly detectives swarmed upon them; one of the three men escaped but the other two were arrested. At the trial they were convicted and imprisoned. The publicity of the affair may have served as a lesson to anyone else with similar ideas – at least, it would have done were it not that, when a petition was organized for the men's pardon, Caruso's signature headed it. As with the Monkey House incident, newspapers lost no time in having a field day at the expense of Italians. One story had it that Caruso's cowardice had encouraged him to do a deal and settle up with 'The Black Hand'. This was but one piece of unsubstantiated propaganda directed against him by a patronising press.

Meanwhile the competition between the vying opera houses was reaching a climax. Hammerstein's grandiosity – as well as the Manhattan and his new theater in Philadelphia he was planning yet another in Chicago – was bringing his affairs to a ruinous climax, while the Met had been encouraged to undertake a futile gamble by opening the New Theater. This was conceived as a riposte to Hammerstein – a house for more intimate opera – but it was never a success and it survived only a year after the Manhattan was closed. Eventually an agreement had to be reached which cost the Metropolitan – or should one rather say, its President and Chairman, Otto Kahn[18] – a million and a quarter dollars; for this was what Hammerstein was paid so that he should not undertake, in New York, or other east-coast North American cities, any further operatic adventures for the next decade. The signatures on the contract were hardly dry before Hammerstein rushed off to London to open a new opera house there, and so the Met was able, once again, to concentrate exclusively upon its own affairs.

That season Caruso was to relinquish two of his more secondary roles in New York: Alfredo in *La Traviata* and Pinkerton in *Madama Butterfly*. He also made his customary appearances in Philadelphia as well as Brooklyn, and journeyed to Baltimore and Boston. The tour afterwards took him to Chicago, Cleveland, Milwaukee, Saint Paul and Saint Louis, as well as Atlanta for the first time.

At the beginning of May, Caruso quit America for France. Gabriel Astruc, the most celebrated French impresario of his day, the Founder of the Société Musicale, tells the story of Caruso's visit to Paris with the Met that spring:

> The apogee of Caruso's French career came in the season organized by the Metropolitan and me. I worked with Kahn, the financial brain of the visit. I told him that "if we have Caruso, and if Caruso sings in *Aida*, *Pagliacci* and *Manon Lescaut*, success is assured. The financial guarantee will not be broken and it will not be necessary to touch it. Subscriptions will be sufficient to meet all expectations.' I wanted the great artist to confirm that he would indeed be taking part, and I received from him the following letter: 'My dear Astruc. I shall finish my season in America in a few days, and I dream with joy of the moment I shall come to Paris to sing at the Théâtre du Châtelet three favorite roles of mine for the Parisian public. With warmest wishes: Caruso.' The operas – with soloists, the chorus, decors and costumes – were all rehearsed in New York. The repertory was made up of six works: the three that Caruso was appearing in, plus *Cavalleria*, *Otello* and *Falstaff*. Two weeks before the first performance the box-office was opened, and immediately it was besieged; subscriptions for all six operas were taken up. As I guessed, the public had a predilection for the Caruso performances. I was careful enough to announce beforehand that it would not be possible to subscribe to *Aida* without buying a ticket for *Otello*, nor could one hear *Pagliacci* without hearing *Falstaff*.

Everyone accepted this, and in this way the finances of the trip were saved. So it was that by May 21 all the subscriptions for the season were taken up by some of the most illustrious members of French society, and they had paid more than 600,000 Francs for the privilege. At the premiere Caruso sang Radames in *Aida* with Destinn under Toscanini's direction. Thereafter he was Canio in *Pagliacci* with Amato and Maestro Podesti, and des Grieux in the French premiere of Puccini's *Manon Lescaut* also under Toscanini, with Lucrezia Bori, an outstanding lyric soprano, who was making her debut with the company. And Caruso's heart was as generous as his voice. Three days before the first night, in a concert at the Trocadéro, he raised 150,000 Francs for various good causes, and after it he returned to the organizers the check for his fee of 10,000 Francs. On June 19, this time at the Opéra, he appeared in a gala benefit including the third act of *La Bohème* with Farrar and Scotti and the final scene of *Faust* with Farrar and de Segurola, and this brought in 185,000 Francs for a number of charities. It may be noticed that during the last six days of that season Caruso actually sang on five occasions![19]

That autumn he resumed his busy schedule with *La Bohème* on September 24, 1910, at the Monnaie, Brussels. 'All the seats were sold out days before the performance,' as Frances Alda recalls. 'Would we, the directors begged, give a second, repeat performance on the next evening? We would.'[20] The Belgian press was more than a little preoccupied by his fee, details of which had escaped into the public domain, and the newspapers seemed relieved that he lived up to his reputation. 'An accident is always possible even to the most finished artist, and there are circumstances where such a thing is unpardonable. . . . Thanks be to heaven, however, everything passed off well and Caruso's high C [as we have seen, it was more likely a B] came out triumphantly.'[21]

In October he began his German rounds again at Frankfurt singing in *Aida* and *Carmen* – 'Caruso came, sang and conquered . . . the effect his art created was so prodigious and so immense that one might have cried out: "For nothing in the world would I have missed hearing Caruso!" His Don José is the most remarkable I have seen on any German stage in a quarter of a century.'[22] At Munich, he repeated Don José, this time to Margarete Matzenauer's Carmen, then added a Rodolfo. He travelled on to Hamburg and sang Don José again, after a Duke and Lionello in *Marta*. These performances were all directed by Otto Klemperer who, more than half a century later, remembered that 'Caruso was an exceedingly musical singer who adapted himself perfectly to the ensemble without showing a trace of soloist's temperament.'[23]

That year upon reaching Berlin he appeared at a private gala at the Imperial Palace, Potsdam, on the occasion of the fifty-second birthday of the Empress. The season in Berlin took place at the Neues Operntheater, and Caruso himself remembered:

'After I made my first appearance that year in *Aida*, I was told by a friend of a conversation he had overheard between two women, how one [had] remarked, "why he isn't a tenor, his voice is a baritone!" At my next effort, three nights afterwards, in *Carmen*, their discussion continued. The ladies agreed that they might possibly be mistaken during that performance: and when *L'Elisir d'amore* was presented, my critics no longer questioned that I was a tenor. In explanation of this seeming misunderstanding, I can say that I always use a different character of voice for music that is strictly lyric or dramatic; Radames is a role that demands a dark, heavier quality of tone, while Nemorino is just the opposite.'[24]

It was while in Berlin that year that another chapter in his love life, which had begun in Milan the previous summer, reopened.[25] He had met a nineteen-year-old assistant in a glove store. He immediately became enamoured of her, for she was by all accounts a very pretty young woman. He even spoke of marriage and offered her a trip that autumn to Germany. She agreed to come – providing she was accompanied by her father. They arrived in Berlin and the daughter's good looks soon attracted attention. The father was elderly and rather stout, and both of them were wearing new clothes. Signorina Elisa Ganelli seemed at ease, while Signor Ganelli, arrayed in borrowed feathers, looked uncomfortable, as if he were not used to them. They took rooms at the Hotel Bristol. Secluded mostly in their apartment, they saw Caruso only in the theater, the drawing room, or when he went out for a stroll with them. He behaved in public in a very correct, upright manner, treating Signorina Ganelli as if she were a great lady, and acting as if he were very much in love. He entertained them in princely style, introducing them as his prospective bride and father-in-law at a Press Club banquet given in his honor. He spoke freely of his plans for the future. Father and daughter spent about ten days in Berlin.

When the Ganellis left, the parting from Caruso was most moving, the tenor weeping copiously. He embraced his fiancée and future father-in-law repeatedly, exclaiming between sobs: 'We shall be united always.' Only a couple of days after they had parted, however, he cabled Elisa from Bremen: 'Am leaving, full of grief. New and grave circumstances have arisen which force me to revoke our not yet publicly announced engagement. Please maintain a scrupulous silence.' Although his fame might now make it possible for him to indulge every passing whim, in the course of the next year, as he was soon to discover, he would find it a lot more costly than a mere telegram to bring his engagement to Signorina Ganelli to a conclusion.

His lack of success in his romantic liaisons was not mirrored in any lack of courtesy to other artists. As we saw, four years previously at the Met, Caruso had been content to leave the opening night to Farrar, so that she might make her debut unencumbered by established stars, and in 1910, when Toscanini was co-director and wished to launch the season, on November 14, with the first American performance of Gluck's *Armide*, Caruso agreed to undertake Renaud. As he told the *World*: 'There were three acts in the opera in which I did not appear, and I never knew what to do to kill time.'[26] This opera marks the first eighteenth-century Met revival to open a season, part of an earlier repertory which gradually came to compensate for the lack of enduring popularity of contemporary works of Giordano, Cilea, Mascagni, Leoncavallo and even Puccini, after the addition of *Butterfly* to the repertory. It marks, too, a significant step forward in the ascendancy of the conductor; for this revival of *Armide* at the Met was at the direct instigation of a new type of virtuoso conductor, Toscanini. This was Caruso's only venture at the Metropolitan into the classical repertory, and though Fremstad, as Henderson wrote in the *Sun*, 'splendidly rose to its realization, he did not look happy with the declamatory style of the recitatives.'[27]

Caruso was ... too fat ... to impersonate successfully a romantic Crusader, [and] he wore a most unbecoming wig which produced in him a disturbing resemblance to Benjamin Franklin. His supposed charms spared him the stroke of Armide's dagger, but nothing could prevent that embarrassing ordeal when the rose-strewn couch, bearing both his considerable weight and Armide's, must be wafted through the air. The caresses of the lovers at this point had a tense and frantic quality, their smiles frozen on stiff faces as they braced themselves for a series of jerks and bouncings which lifted them, by a sort of hydraulic elevator, four or five feet from the stage. Here they usually stuck fast and the trailing vines and garlands which were designed to mask the mechanism swung so violently with the shock that the footlights revealed all, including the elevator man, unless the curtain fell swiftly.[28]

After some performances of *Aida*, *La Gioconda* and *Pagliacci*, on December 10, he created a leading role in a world premiere for the last time: Dick Johnson in Puccini's *La Fanciulla del West*.

This created an enormous sensation; seat prices were doubled, and the daily newspapers produced lengthy reviews. Puccini came from Italy to superintend the rehearsals and to assure the realization of his intentions in the music. David Belasco, a master of stagecraft – upon whose drama, *The Girl of the Golden West*, the opera is based – spent days and nights directing the stage management and securing the co-operation and interplay of all the factors that would count for a perfect ensemble. The opera house itself provided the finest talent that it had then at its service to interpret the work – Toscanini conducted it; Destinn, Caruso and Amato sang it. It was the first time that a new work written by the most distinguished and popular operatic com-poser of the day had its premiere in New York. Aldrich in the *Times* considered it

> unlikely that any finer or more authoritative presentation of this most difficult opera will be given on the other side of the water. . . . It will have occurred to many who heard *La Fanciulla del West* last evening that the new work shows considerably less fecundity of melodic inspiration, or even call it invention, than Puccini's earlier ones. There is certainly far less of the clearly defined melodic luster, outline, point and fluency, far less of what is tangibly thematic than there is in his earlier works. There is, in fact, little of it; and what there is has not more distinction than the tune the miners set themselves to waltzing to in the first act. . . . It is a tune of very commonplace character for the important role it had to play. There are various snatches of syncopated rhythm known as "rag time" now supposed to be typically "American", that are used repeatedly; but they are of astonishingly little melodic value and, indeed, seem intended to have only a rhythmic one. . . . There are scraps of melody that are common-place, impotent to express what they are associated with and frankly dull. There is little of the Puccini of earlier years. . . . Dick Johnson is a part in which Caruso appears on the stage to better advantage than he does in many of the others. He was successful in representing the rough energy, the dare-devil audacity of the outlaw and his stoicism in the presence of death. And his singing was of his best; such phrases of expression as he had to deliver were given with beautiful voice and art, and he refrained from the overaccentuation that must be accepted with the better things he does in his other parts.[29]

Caruso appeared as Dick Johnson during a total of four seasons at the Metropolitan, as well as on visits to Philadelphia, Chicago and Boston, and he also undertook it in its premieres in Paris and Hamburg. We may wonder why he never recorded the aria from it, 'Ch'ella mi creda'. Recently Robert Tuggle, in his *The Golden Age of Opera*, has revealed yet another of Ricordi's machinations.[30] It would appear, according to *Musical America* of December 17, 1910, that Tito Ricordi forbade the recording of any excerpts from *La Fanciulla del West* because he had got it into his head that these would interfere with the sales of vocal scores!

On January 3, 1911, after a performance of Canio at Brooklyn, *Musical America* wrote jubilantly that '[Caruso] was in his best voice, his "Ridi Pagliaccio" had caused a veritable demonstration, and he had sung the aria with all his old-time fervor and passion.'[31] On the 14th, he repeated this part in a guest performance with the Chicago Opera, and he had the same reception there too: 'Seldom has "The Lament" been carried with more impassioned power or with more thrilling or tenderer tone. It would be difficult to distinguish one episode as more impressive than another; for the growth and admirable consistency of his characterisation and the unrivalled quality and sonority of Caruso's singing still stands supreme.'[32] Until the end of that month he was making his customary number of appearances. On the 27th he was Dick Johnson; on the 30th he took part in one of Mr Bagby's musical matinées at the Waldorf Astoria; on February 1st he sang Federico in *Germania*; on the 4th another Dick Johnson; then a couple of nights later he was Federico again – after which some cancellations and then silence. At once newspapers were alive with speculative gossip – that he was leaving to sing at Monte Carlo, that he was 'temporarily voiceless', that 'a fortune teller had frightened him',[33] and so on.

Although he did not sing at the Met again that season, he did not leave America until the season was over and this was because he wished to prove his good faith with the public, by remaining within call, so that if his condition did improve sufficiently, as it was believed it would, he would be able to take his place in the cast. Until April 5 it was still hoped he would sing and then go with the company on tour, but this hope was dashed when Gatti received the following letter signed by Drs H. Holbrook Curtis and Frank H. Millar: 'This is to certify that we have examined Enrico Caruso and find that he is still suffering from the effects of his recent attack of grippe and laryngitis and that, in our opinion, it would be advisable for him not to attempt to sing again this season, but to seek a change of climate.'[34] Accordingly, on April 18, he left New York for England.

In London he went immediately to Clarendon Court, Maida Vale, where his younger son was ensconced with his governess, Miss Saer. At this time the Tax Inspector of the Inland Revenue had judged Caruso a resident domiciled in England, and assessed him accordingly. The tenor was outraged and immediately set about selling off the apartment, including all its furnishings. His son and governess thereupon moved up the Edgware Road to Cricklewood, to the family home of the Saers, where they would remain until 1914 and the outbreak of the First World War.

CHAPTER XII

1911–1913

BY THIS time Caruso's name was becoming a household word, and now that he had been untypically silent for nearly three of the busiest operatic months of the year, it was only to be expected that it would seem something a lot more serious than grippe or laryngitis. Italian newspapers were particularly interested and spread stories that Caruso had been back to Professor della Vedova for more surgery, and reports began to appear that he might not sing again. He was in London when news of these stories reached him and at length he felt obliged to make a statement to the press:

> The canard that my vocal cords are giving me trouble is pure invention. The Italian doctor who is said to have started the rumor did so merely to advertise himself; and the story he gave to a reporter, about a corn having made its appearance in my throat is absolutely without foundation. Indeed this Italian doctor has not examined me for two years. For the rest, my voice is in good condition as ever and I will duly keep my continental and other engagements. Dr William Lloyd, under whose care I have been since my return to London, assures me that my vocal cords are perfectly healthy and normal.[1]

If his art was public property, there was also his private life for newspapers to turn to. Since the end of his 'marriage' to Giachetti – and full particulars of that relationship would make headlines in the Milan newspapers during the following year – he had become a matrimonial objective for many ambitious young women, such as Lillian Berbours, who 'represented herself as a beautiful young American girl with a lot of money. "I am young, proud, and as far as money goes, there is nothing lacking to make the marriage desirable, especially since I sympathise so deeply with your solitude."'[2] It seems they never met, though he admitted that after receiving this letter he did ask the Metropolitan what could be found out about her. But there were those whom he did come to know, such as Louise Grenville, a

Canadian soprano, whom he had met that season in Chicago; she sang Mimì, Tosca, Marguerite in *Faust* and Antonia in *Les Contes d'Hoffmann*. When a report appeared in the press that they 'had become secretly engaged, he denied it, and a laugh and a shrug accompanied his refusal of this honor'.[3] And there were others who quite shamefacedly attempted to jump on his bandwagon. The glamorous soubrette Emma Trentini had sung an occasional Oscar in *Un Ballo* for Hammerstein, but was more often Berta in *Il Barbiere* and other secondary roles. When the Manhattan folded she moved over to undertake Victor Herbert's *Naughty Marietta*, also for Hammerstein, and she needed all the publicity she could get, so she announced their engagement. Caruso was accosted by a reporter demanding to know what truth there was in it, and he scoffed: 'Why, none at all. She is too leetle!'[4] At that the flak began to fly and the air was soon thick with recriminations and counter-recriminations – it looked more as if a divorce rather than a marriage was in the air.

That summer Elisa Ganelli's name arose once more. Having failed to receive any response to her endless letters, she – or, more probably, her father – took Caruso to court. She sued him, in Milan, for breach of promise, demanding $60,000 in redress. She lost, but at least had the satisfaction of seeing excerpts of his love letters published throughout the world after they were read out in court by her attorneys: '"Dear sweet thing . . .", "My little sugar doll . . .", "My little treasure" and "You shall be my little queen, my mistress and I your faithful and devoted slave," etc. etc.'[5] In English they sound quaint if not risible, but in Italian, no doubt, they seemed little different from any of the opera librettos he was so busy with. Years after his death, in 1956, there was a postscript to their romance when she endeavored to get all his correspondence published.

It is small wonder that he remained unable to sing that summer, and the conflict between Caruso the world-famous tenor and Caruso the man was to continue for at least another seven years, until he was safely married.

Seven months' silence had elapsed before he felt able to resume his career, in Vienna, on September 20, 1911, as Canio in *Pagliacci*. The tremendous enthusiasm generated by this appearance seemed to have been only augmented at two succeeding performances: as the Duke and Don José.

His voice positively contradicts all rumors of its impairment, having still the incomparable Caruso timbre, and his art is wholly perfect – hyperbole, if not applied to him. In *Rigoletto* as a matter of course, he had to repeat the famous ditty of woman's fickleness, together with the cadenza and high B and the soulful quartet . . . likewise. Joseph Schwarz [the greatest German baritone of that time] as Rigoletto did surprisingly well, characteristic in acting, passionate in singing and supplying temperament in which Hedwig Francillo-Kaufmann as Gilda, though otherwise excellent, was lacking.[6]

In *Carmen*, although Marie Gutheil-Schoder, histrionically an impressive artist, did her best, there was little doubt from the notices that it would have been more appropriate had the opera been styled *Don José*. After the Flower Song was greeted by an uproarious ovation, storms of applause prevented the opera continuing until an encore was wrested from him, in which he sang as evocatively as before.

Throughout that autumn Caruso remained busy with his German engagements. He travelled to Munich, Frankfurt, Hanover and Hamburg, at which he repeated Canio, Don José and the Duke and he was also heard as Radames, Rodolfo and Riccardo in *Un Ballo in maschera*. He finished the tour in Berlin where he sang Nemorino in *L'Elisir d'amore* as well as a Duke and Canio. The Kaiser and Empress of Germany with members of the Imperial family attended each performance, and the monarch called the singer to his box, congratulating him and making him promise to return to Berlin each year. The Königliches Opernhaus was sold out quickly despite box-office prices which were three times that of seats for regular performances, yet ticket speculators still reaped a rich harvest. Perhaps, if those anxious to obtain tickets at almost any price had known how near they came to losing their money, they might not have made such a headlong rush. For Caruso was suffering from a nervous indisposition and when he arrived in Berlin his three physicians, the impresario and intimate friends all advised him to cancel his performances. But he persisted with his strenuous schedule although he suffered continuously from neuralgic headaches and his throat showed signs of inflammation. He felt it would never do to disappoint the Imperial family and the hundreds of people who had bought tickets at such extortionate prices, and so he forced himself to appear. On the day following his final engagement a luncheon was given in his honor, which was attended by a phalanx of musical and other artistic dignitaries. But on this occasion the tenor had a complete collapse, and his condition was considered so serious by his physicians that he was advised to cancel his journey to America. But Caruso would not hear of this and no sooner was he rested than he left for Bremen, where he boarded the *Krönprinzessin Cäcilie* bound for New York and a fresh season at the Metropolitan.

In the meantime Italian opinion was expressing its dissatisfaction, for more than eight years had passed since he had sung in his home country, and the success of the Met's Paris *tournée* had encouraged rumors that the company would appear in Rome in the spring of 1911. But Caruso's indisposition had militated against this. It was not surprising, therefore, to find *Orfeo* writing in commending tones of Bonci for 'reappearing in Rome, where he will have a baptism of glory for his golden voice, while Caruso is an exile who feels no longing for home'.[7] Though it may have been true that Caruso had not sung in Italy he had, nevertheless, been at his Florence home for almost as long as he had been in New York. Before reaching American waters he was obliged 'to wireless that his health was "arcimentevolissimevolmentebene", which being translated means, more or less, arch-hyper-superlatively-excellently-well'.[8]

The Metropolitan commenced on November 13, 1911, with Caruso and Toscanini in *Aida* again, shades of opening night three years before. But on this occasion, as well as Destinn, Matzenauer was making her Metropolitan debut, and Amato replaced Scotti. That season Caruso undertook a perambulation through his usual repertory of roles, including Canio, Enzo, Cavaradossi, Turiddu, Rodolfo, des Grieux in Massenet's *Manon*, and he repeated Dick Johnson in *La Fanciulla del West* and Renaud in *Armide*. On February 6, 1912, he was the Duke in a *Rigoletto* which contained two valedictory tributes to the recent demise of Hammerstein's Manhattan Opera – Renaud and Tetrazzini. 'No [one] could remember . . . when a line of standees began to form at half past one in the afternoon, and patience finally exceeded bounds when the doors were opened at seven o'clock. The line dissolved into a milling throng at the box-office, the attending police wielded sticks, some standees were nursing bruised ribs as well as sore feet when the day ended [and] it was estimated that two thousand more persons than the house could hold were turned away.'[9] This was the last of the comparatively few occasions on which he sang with Tetrazzini, though they were to remain good friends and appeared together again in a concert in 1920.*

---

* In 1932, when Tetrazzini was over sixty, a snippet of film of her was made at the HMV shop in Oxford Street, London. She is seated beside a phonograph which is playing Caruso's newly released rerecording of 'M' appari'. At one point, wiping her eyes, the diva takes up the melody sustaining a long tone with the lamented tenor, and it is interesting to note that as she does so her jaw, with its many sets of chins, starts wagging away, yet her tone remains as limpid and steady as it was even at the height of her fame.

That year the tour took him to Boston, Philadelphia and Atlanta, where he gave a handful of performances as well as taking part in a special benefit at the Met on April 29 for the families of those who had perished on the *Titanic*. On this occasion, he sang Sullivan's 'The Lost Chord' just after having recorded it in Camden, New Jersey. Immediately before departing for Europe again he received a cablegram from Boito inviting him to create the title-role in his opera *Nerone* at La Scala, Milan, the premiere of which, so he said, had been arranged to take place the next season. But in fact another eleven years were to elapse before it was performed, by which time both Boito and Caruso were dead, and Nerone was undertaken by Aureliano Pertile.

His first European engagement that year was in France, where he proceeded to Paris to join a brilliant ensemble at the Opéra, organized by Gunsbourg with members of the Monte Carlo Opera. Since Caruso had always found it impossible to get time off from the Met and the Monte Carlo season was in February and March, Gunsbourg decided to go to Paris in May; if Mahomet could not come, then he would get the mountain to go to him – or at least part of the way. With one eye on the Met's visit two years before, which had Caruso in casts including Bori, Destinn, Amato and Scotti – Astruc had styled it the 'apogee of Caruso's French career' – Gunsbourg determined to go one better, and engaged not only Caruso but also Chaliapin, Ruffo and Tetrazzini. It is a measure of his prodigious skill that though, so he claimed, Tetrazzini welshed on him, he instantly managed to persuade another well-known 'coloratura' soprano, whose records have always been much admired, Antonina Nezhdanova, to take her place and sing outside Russia for the first time. And this was the only time in their careers that Caruso, Chaliapin and Ruffo all appeared in the same season (the occasion is perpetuated in a fine painting of the three singers by the Polish artist Tadé Styka). Gunsbourg paid Caruso and Chaliapin 12,000 Francs a night and Ruffo 7,000. The repertory included *Il Barbiere di Siviglia*, *Mefistofele*, *Rigoletto* and the Paris premiere of *La Fanciulla del West*, for which the impresario had succeeded in getting Puccini to come to Paris. He obtained Caruso for the last of these two works alone. Notwithstanding all his eloquence and all his blandishments, the tenor declined to undertake Almaviva, so he never did manage to engage all three *divos* together in the same opera. Chaliapin sang Basilio and Mefistofele, and Ruffo sang Figaro, Rance in *La Fanciulla* and Rigoletto.

Henri de Curzon, a noted critic of his day, thought 'a comparison between the voices of Caruso and Ruffo is very interesting. They are justifiably considered amongst the most beautiful of our time. But if Ruffo's, in the fullness of his powers, is of a flexibility and astonishing brilliance, then Caruso's, though he seems hardly to have as much voice, remains to the last even more beautiful, of a more penetrating charm and seductive grace, even if it is more covered, more nasal and of a less moving timbre.'[10] The rest of the casts included Nezhdanova as Gilda and Elvira de Hidalgo as Rosina; Smirnov undertook Almaviva and Faust in *Mefistofele* opposite Adelina Agostinelli's Margherita; while Carmen Melis and Tina Poli-Randaccio, two leading verismo sopranos, 'alternated as Minnie, vying with each other in their expressions of vocal brilliance'.[11]

Following his familiar summer vacation in Italy Caruso re-emerged at the Hofoper, Vienna, on September 14, and then travelled via Munich and Stuttgart to Berlin and Hamburg. His repertory included Don José, Riccardo in *Un Ballo in maschera*, Cavaradossi, the Duke, Canio, Rodolfo and Alfredo in *La Traviata*. On October 22, once again, on the occasion of the Empress's birthday, he appeared at the Imperial Palace, Potsdam.

Before returning to New York he stopped in Milan for yet another chapter in his long litigatory struggles with Giachetti. More than three years had passed since their affair had come to an end, but if Caruso hoped that there would be an end to her demands he was to learn better. In a Milan court she stated that she had not started to live with the chauffeur, Romati, until her relationship with Caruso was over. She further charged him with aiding and abetting the proprietress of a Milan pensione in stealing some jewellery and certain letters from her, as well as a contract with Hammerstein to appear with the Manhattan Opera in New York. She also claimed that the tenor had sworn falsely before an official at the time their sons were born that she was unmarried. The court, however, dismissed her suit and at the same time remanded her for trial on countercharges brought by Caruso. But by then Giachetti had flitted off to South America, ostensibly to undertake an engagement there. Caruso denied that there had been any termination in their relationship before her affair with the chauffeur had begun. He also refuted her suggestion that he had stolen any of her jewellery; on the contrary, it was he who had originally given it to her, and he produced a letter from her confirming that she had, of her own volition, returned it to him three years previously. As to her story of a contract with the Manhattan, Hammerstein wrote to Advocate Ceola, who was acting for Caruso, 'that he had never even thought of engaging Signorina Giachetti'.[12] It was hardly surprising that she remained in South America and never returned to Italy. The considerable amount of dirty linen that she washed publicly had a traumatic effect on Caruso, especially when one of the witnesses stated that 'she had never loved him, not even during the first years of their living together, while Caruso still loves her.'[13] But though he may never have forgiven her, he could not forget her; years later it is his wife who tells how even after they had been married he would send her to his 'bank with instructions to pay the mother of [his] boys her monthly allowance.'[14]

Back in New York again the Metropolitan opened on November 11, 1912, when Bori made her house debut as Manon Lescaut and Caruso was des Grieux. It proved a taxing role for Bori; like Caruso she developed nodules on her vocal cords, and after 1915 she was obliged to withdraw and not to sing for a period of almost four years. When she resumed her career she did not undertake Manon Lescaut again for more than a decade. Although Krehbiel was impressed by her 'fine vocal skill, [nonetheless] in the first act she was distinctly disappointing and her voice seemed pallid and infantile when mixed with the rich organ tones of Caruso [despite the fact that he] seemed purposely to have modified his own glorious [voice] for her sake.'[15]

That season Caruso undertook his usual repertory, including Enzo, Canio, Dick Johnson, Rodolfo, Radames, Cavaradossi, des Grieux in *Manon*, Turiddu and Raoul in *Gli Ugonotti*, which part he was singing again in New York for the first time for nearly eight years. Henderson thought that though 'Caruso sang his music better than he did when he was last heard in [this] opera, he can hardly be regarded as an ideal Raoul. His training has been in roles wholly different from it in style and his sympathies have never been enchained by the methods of French grand opera.'[16] That year he appeared in Philadelphia and Brooklyn and went on tour to Atlanta. He also paid a solitary visit to Boston to sing with Russell's company. Here H. T. Parker wrote eloquently of his Canio:

The voice is still there, not a mite of its glory is missing; but with it is a treasure too rarely combined with such a voice – mind and imagination – Caruso has not gone back in vocal power, he has gone forward in art. . . .

Five years ago he sang his Canio with the same supreme mastery of phrase and vocal color. His Canio of last evening dazzled as it did then . . . but he has learned other means of communicating the thrill than with unexpected outbursts of volume at the end of phrases already longer than any other singer could sustain. Caruso's Canio . . . is finished now in the utmost minutiae. His delivery of every phrase has the air of finality, the calm assurance that none but he can suggest a better. Once he loved to dominate every ensemble with weight of sound. Now he can dispense with his old-time fury. His Canio suffers the more poignantly, the more believably, because the old exaggeration of grief, the overstatement of suffering, is gone, and a greater sincerity that is quietly sure of carrying conviction, takes its place.[17]

In Atlanta, following a des Grieux on April 23 he journeyed out with Bori to the Federal Penitentiary and there, accompanied by the prison orchestra, and in front of eight hundred and thirty inmates, he sang 'O paradiso!' from *L'Africana*, Tosti's 'Ideale' and 'Vesti la giubba' from *Pagliacci*. For creating a memorable oasis in their otherwise desert-like existence, the prison newspaper, *Good Words*, printed a poem written in his honor.

From Atlanta he returned to New York and then embarked for Europe. Arriving in London he made his first appearance as Canio at Covent Garden after six years, on May 20. The subscriptions were all taken up within three quarters of an hour. Orchestra seats, normally a guinea, were doubled in price. A queue began to form at six in the morning of the day before the performance for the unreserved gallery and the price for these had also risen from two shillings and sixpence to five shillings. Caruso's fee had risen too to £500 a performance (this was now more even than he was earning at the Met).

So completely was it Caruso's evening that at the end of the first act he alone came before the curtain . . . for at that moment, with the sound of his wonderful voice in 'Vesti la giubba' still filling our ears, the song to which everyone had been looking forward all evening, it was scarcely possible to think of anything else . . . his capacity for combining unrestrained and intense emotion with absolute ease of vocalisation shone out in its full power as it could not do before, and it was sufficient to carry the audience away.[18]

But the emotional nature of his first operatic appearance in London in six years much taxed Caruso's strength and, following the curtain calls, he collapsed and had to be assisted back to his dressing room.

Chaliapin, who was then making his London debut as Boris Godounov in Diaghilev's triumphant season of Russian ballet and opera at the Theatre Royal, Drury Lane, came backstage cautioning Caruso against undertaking too strenuous a schedule 'that would . . . undermine his health'.[19] This was, in fact, though they could not have known it then, the last time they would meet.

Caruso's other roles that year included Radames and Cavaradossi opposite Destinn's Aida and Tosca, and then Rodolfo in *La Bohème*; and it was at the second of these performances, on June 23, in the presence of His Majesty George V and Queen Mary, that Melba first joined him that year. He was then forty and she fifty-two and it may have needed a conscious effort to see much in either of them of the youthful, starving and, no doubt, skeletal lovers of Murger's Paris, yet, as their incomparable record of the love duet confirms, they set standards of vocalism in this music that have never been equalled. Osbert Sitwell recalls: 'As fat as two elderly thrushes, they trilled at each other over the tiaras, summing up in themselves the age, no less than Sargent netted it for others'.[20]

While in London that year Caruso toyed with the idea of entering his elder son, Rodolfo, at the Charterhouse School but, eventually, he sent him instead to Badia di Fiesole near Florence and that summer, as usual, he retired to the Villa Bellosguardo.

In the autumn he commenced his customary 'German' tour at the Hofoper, Vienna, on September 15, as Don José in *Carmen*. Thereafter he passed through Munich – 'where he displayed the profound beauty of his voice more convincingly and clearly than ever'[21]–Stuttgart, Berlin and Hamburg, repeating a typical repertory: Rodolfo, the Duke, Canio, Cavaradossi, Radames and Dick Johnson in *La Fanciulla del West*. In fact, this proved to be his German farewell, for before he could return the following year the First World War had broken out. The Minnie on that occasion was Florence Easton, and the next time she would sing with him would be at the farewell performance of his career in *La Juive* at the Met in 1920. Even after 1919 Caruso did not re-appear in Germany. The Weimar Republic was going through a period of unparalleled inflation and money was reduced to mere paper. Caruso remembered how nervous he had been made that October in Berlin by the incessant military parades going on in the street outside his hotel. 'From my windows I watched soldiers marching with cannons and then more soldiers, and it went on for hours.'[22] He became so worried that he asked Ledner, his German manager, to cash in all his securities – he had saved more than a million marks. But Ledner made light of his fears and eventually Caruso allowed himself to be persuaded. So he left Germany for the last time with a mere 80,000 Marks and he never saw the million again.

The Metropolitan season resumed on November 17, 1913, with *La Gioconda*. The rest of the cast included Destinn, Matzenauer and Amato, and Toscanini conducted. 'Another wondrous thing about Caruso is his remarkable influence on other singers when they are singing with him. This was particularly noticeable on the first night. Destinn, at the beginning, had been singing finely as she always does, but her tone appeared at times somewhat forced. Later, when she sang with Caruso, his influence seemed to impart something to her which made her sing beautifully, nobly; her phrasing was delightful, her emphases correctly placed.'[23] As we shall note when considering his many duet records, Caruso always serves to show off the other singers to their best advantage; and his influence on himself, as Toscanini remembers of the same performance of *La Gioconda*, was no less remarkable:

A little while before the curtain was due to go up I went, as was my habit, to visit Caruso in his dressing room. As I approached I heard the voice of the theater doctor exclaiming, 'But Commendatore, you absolutely cannot sing with a throat like that.' And then Caruso's voice answering, 'Dottò, give me a brushing with tincture of iodine and glycerine and don't worry yourself about it!' I went in, the doctor, when he saw me, said 'Maestro, look at that throat and tell me if he can sing in that state.' I drew near and the doctor lit Caruso's throat for me. What a mess! I myself, who understood very little about the throat, was beside myself. Only think the uvula was so enlarged and inflamed that it covered the entire opening of the throat, an astonishing thing! I said, 'But Enrico, you cannot sing in this condition.' Without answering he looked at me and then, turning to the doctor, said 'Brush me here and then you'll hear.' The doctor, seeing Caruso's insistence, went ahead brushing. I returned to my dressing room very worried. Well, when he opened his mouth and pronounced the first phrase: 'Assassini! quel crin venerando rispettate!' his voice issued forth more beautifully and more ringing than ever: they were little diamond beads that issued forth from his mouth![24]

The remainder of his repertory included Riccardo, both des Grieux, Canio, Radames, Cavaradossi and Dick Johnson, and he also sang Rodolfo, for the first time that season, at the Academy of Music, Philadelphia on December 23. 'On that evening,' as Caruso himself recalled, the theater was full and had taken $15,000. The bass, de Segurola, who was singing the role of Colline had been ill and had not yet properly recovered his voice. Throughout the performance he managed to declaim the part. But the poor man was very apprehensive as the fourth act approached, for he had a celebrated aria to sing, 'Vecchia zimarra' [the Coat song]. Just before it I whispered to him: 'How are you feeling?' 'Pretty bad,' he replied. 'Give me the coat,' I said underneath my breath, 'and I'll sing it for you.' To his surprise – and to the amazement of Maestro Polacco – I sang it.[25]

Caruso's singing of this aria has been much written about, and spoken about too. Over thirty years later Alda, the Mimì of that occasion, tells the tale on the other side of a hitherto unpublished record which had eventually turned up that Caruso made of the Coat Song a couple of years later. It gives us an opportunity of hearing the full extent of his compass. Although the aria does not descend lower than the first C sharp below middle C, nevertheless he manages the tessitura comfortably, and not as one might have expected of a tenor whose upper range extends to an unequivocal high B. It was a curious quirk of the great man to possess himself at the drop of a hat, as it seems, of another singer's music in any performance he might be appearing in. There were several such occasions such as the one we have already noted on March 22, 1905, when the Met was in Chicago and he deputized for an ailing Dippel in Turiddu's *Siciliana*. Rose Heylbut and Aimé Gerber in their *Backstage at the Opera* tell of another Chicago *Cav* and *Pag*, on April 23, 1908, when he stepped in for Albert Reiss in Beppe's Serenade. Apparently this too created no effect. Nor did it on October 20, the same year, at the Berlin Königliches Opernhaus, when he sang it again in lieu of Walter Kirchhoff. And then there was the concert at the Colón, Buenos Aires, on June 18, 1915, which he was finishing with Act I of *Pagliacci*. As he was in mufti, he agreed to undertake Tonio's Prologue as well, in place of Giuseppe Danise, although he transposed it upwards. This occasion is mentioned in Zirato's draft biography and by Horatio Sanguinetti in a letter he wrote the day after, which was eventually published in the Argentinian journal *Ayer y Hoy de la Opera* in the issue of September/October 1979. There were doubtless other occasions too. At the beginning of the second act of *La Bohème*, in a performance at the Met, he once made an *ad hoc* appearance singing with the chorus in the Café Momus scene. Nevertheless there are comparatively few references to any of these events, although, in a lengthy interview on his 1917 South American tour, which appeared in the *Musical Courier*,[26] he tells how in *Pagliacci* he was often mistaken for a baritone, yet he makes no mention of his having sung the Prologue there on his previous visit.

As a young singer he was frequently described as sounding baritonal but this had less to do with the color of his voice than the fact that his high notes did not always come forth effortlessly. As we have noted above, Key's biography cites him recalling an occasion in Berlin in 1910 when members of the audience were confused as to what type of voice he actually possessed.[27] By the time he went on his last concert tour in 1920, as we shall see, its color had become almost unambiguously baritonal, yet his later recordings show his high notes coming forth with certitude, greater, indeed, than they had ever done before. That Caruso's upper register became more reliable and skilfully produced with the passage of time may have been a response to the dramatic development of the verismo style or perhaps, especially after the invention of the phonograph, it was his method of voice production that became the model upon which the increasing demands of verismo were based. Whatever the reason, even if it was only a result of his excessive smoking, as his voice developed and became more secure so its color became darker.

It was this baritone-like quality, the remarkable similarity between Caruso's voice and that of, say, Ruffo, Amato, Ancona, Scotti or De Luca, which accounts in great measure for the peculiar success of much of his duet singing that survives on record. There is something almost chameleon-like in his ability to effect changes in his vocal quality depending on whom he is singing with. Perhaps this was not so remarkable with another stellar instrument, such as Ruffo's, in 'Sì, pel ciel' from *Otello*, which is noteworthy for its balance and fine blend. But with Amato, in a scene from *La Forza del destino*, Caruso's eloquence seems to suppress the other singer's very obvious vibrato. And even more telling are any of the five duets with Scotti, from *La Bohème*, *Madama Butterfly*, *La Forza del destino* and *Don Carlo*. In all of these their voices blend perfectly, yet Scotti's idiosyncratic method could hardly have been less like Caruso's opulent tone, fresh and spontaneous sounding. This skill in concerted art never left him, though his early records are very different from those he made later with De Luca, in excerpts from *L'Elisir d'amore* and *La Forza del destino*, and notwithstanding that singer's grey, wooden tone. There is the same kind of alchemy when Caruso manages to blend with Emilio de Gogorza's throaty voice in a Spanish song, 'A la luz de la luna'. In all his duets one can say that the whole is greater than the sum of the parts – which is what duet singing should be.

The blend of voices in his recordings with baritones may not seem so remarkable, but there was also his ability to suit his voice to that of almost any singer – soprano, mezzo-soprano or bass – however different that singer's style may have been, and without compromising the music, as we saw at the beginning of the 1913 Met season in *La Gioconda* with Destinn. In part this had to with the wondrous limpidity of his voice production, and to an instinctive artistic modesty. This is nowhere more apparent than in the famous 1907 recording of the duet 'O soave fanciulla' from *La Bohème* with Melba. Her vocal style is manifestly different from his and it seems outdated for it antedates *La Bohème*; she studied with Mathilde Marchesi, a pupil of Garcia, one of the most successful teachers of her day, and she made her debut eleven years before the opera was written. Caruso perfectly complements her, his voice flowing effortlessly, although his broad tonal palette is better suited to verismo than Melba's. She may have been an imperious prima donna who loved the sound of her own voice – whether speaking or singing – yet she well knew, through almost forty years, that the glory of her singing was dependent on its exquisite perfection. Like many soprano voices it was unfortunately less than perfectly captured by the acoustic phonograph. It had been conceived for a world before the existence of recording and at close quarters the column of sound she produced was too penetrating for the equipment; her voice had a bejewelled brilliance which was calculated to make its effect best in a large auditorium. An attempt was made to compensate for this by having her situated far back from the recording horn.* It is indicative that her voice sounds at its most beautiful in this duet towards the end, in the long sustained notes culminating in a perfect piano high C. She was a dozen years older than Caruso and incapable of adjusting her voice to suit the phonograph, yet her singing is faultlessly projected. Notwithstanding these differences in style, the beauty of both singers' art in duet, their matching quality and steadiness of tone have never been equalled since.

It was perhaps not surprising that Caruso should have taken a fancy

---

* In May 1910 Melba recorded some phrases from the *Hamlet* Mad Scene at various distances from the recording horn (HMV RLS 719: HLM 7086).

to much in *Pagliacci*, for although he did not create Canio it was this role which he undertook more than any other and with which his memory is inextricably involved. In New York he sang it more than eighty times and of all his interpretations it was the most popular. Unfortunately he recorded only two excerpts from it; 'Vesti la giubba' and 'No! Pagliaccio non son!', and neither of these was made after 1910. In 'Vesti la giubba' the grandeur of his every utterance, his controlled sweep of the downward portamento in the phrase 'ridi del duol', could hardly have better realized the marking in the score, *con grande espressione*. In 'No! Pagliaccio non son!' he does not allow his emotion to distort the line, as Gigli and di Stefano both do. He communicates the strongest feeling by purely musical means. For example, on the phrase 'Sperai, tanto il delizio accecato m'aveva', he underlines the shift in key from E flat minor to major exactly as the score directs and without sliding and other self-indulgences. Nor, on the other hand, does he leave out written portamento, as Jussi Björling does, excellent singer though he be, and so fail to make the full impact of the verismo style. Photographs of Caruso in this role have always been revealing, such as the one of him standing astride the drum and holding above it a stick ready to beat it with – a pose copied by many other tenors, up to Pavarotti. His face is wreathed in a broad grin and yet it is impossible not to feel that tragedy seems to lurk only a little below the surface; in such fashion does he hold for all time the quintessence of the drama. H. T. Parker, the distinguished Boston critic, whom we have already quoted on Caruso's Pagliaccio, after his death left a description so as to leave no doubt as to the truth of his characterisation.

In *Pagliacci* Caruso had a clear notion of his personage that he wrought into a workable and cumulating histrionic design. From year to year, he amplified it with much illuminating and defining detail. Recall, for instance, the exaggerated whimsies of a strolling player with which his matured Canio cozene the crowd at the beginning of the play; the wiping of the powder from his face as of a player resuming relievedly his own person; the intensity, brooding or ominous, that he threw into his declamation in the play while in action he was but doing the part; the fashion in which he went emotionally dead when he struck down Nedda; how he returned a little to himself, dragged out of his throat 'la commedia è finita' and huddled away, distraught, blind, blank again. Always, too, Caruso's song was the speech of Canio, as elemental in all his moods, as direct and full-voiced in his emotions, as simple or savage as the character really is. He made tellingly but untheatrically the swift change from playful banter over the lightness of women to the amorous and vindictive words about a wife he already suspects; he did not overdo the celebrated soliloquy ['Vesti la giubba'] as a Canio might utter it; he sang in the final scene with accents of pain and the passion that rent the clown amid the ironies of make-believe and the reality. The music of Canio suited the best compass and best quality of his mature voice. Hackneyed, 'popular' and all the rest of the damning adjectives of superior righteousness his Canio may have become. But it remains one of the most remarkable operatic impersonations of our time.[28]

CHAPTER XIII

1914–1916

THE LAST part he undertook at the Met in the 1913/14 season was Julien, the title-role in Charpentier's ill-fated sequel to *Louise*, on February 26, 1914. Henderson declared that 'Caruso deserves hearty praise for what he has accomplished. Julien is one of the most difficult roles offered to a tenor at any period in opera. . . . [But] the part is out of his territory. It is a profoundly reflective study, and it would be hard to find any singer who could meet its demands. Caruso . . . sings it with beauty of tone and with sympathy [and] he acts it with sincerity and devotion, but it would be idle to say that he realizes all its possibilities. To fill the role a tenor should be an actor of great imagination, of extraordinary skill in the nuances of face, gesture and pose, of inborn understanding of the niceties of French diction.'[1] Farrar (who sang five roles – Louise, Beauty, a young girl, a grandmother and a street girl) found 'no merit in it for the singers'.[2] It ran just five performances and was never heard again; but Caruso did sport a costume from it the first evening he went to dine at his future father-in-law's. He wore it in order that, so he later confided to Dorothy, 'You would remember me.'[3]

There was a short postscript to the Metropolitan season at Atlanta, where Caruso appeared in *Manon*, *Un Ballo in maschera* and *Pagliacci*. A few days before leaving New York he was required to make a settlement in another of his amorous disputes. This was with Mildred Meffert, whom he had met after a performance of *Tosca* at the Met in 1908. In court she claimed that his attentions had immediately become ardent and that he had asked her to marry him. She further claimed that once at a matinée of *La Bohème* he had said to her: 'My adored one, I sang to you all the time. Did you not hear me? Instead of Mimì I sang again and again Millie!'[4] At the time of the action it was alleged that Caruso had given her $10,000 worth of jewellery and had allowed her $7,000 a year. Her rapacious lawyer had at first demanded $100,000 for the return of Caruso's letters but Miss Meffert, in an out-of-court settlement, eventually relinquished them for a mere $3,000.

Less than two weeks after leaving America he made his first appearance that year at Covent Garden on May 14 as Radames. 'His voice has a little more baritone quality than it had before, but it is, if anything, better than ever. There is no dramatic tenor like him. He is able to accomplish, with apparent ease, effects which cost his rivals visible effort. In short, he is still supreme in Italian opera and, judging by last night's performance, promises to remain so.'5

While in London, one day he journeyed out to Hendon Airport and made a flight in a biplane with Mr Grahame-White, the first Englishman to gain a pilot's license. 'C'est magnifique,' the famous tenor exclaimed rather breathlessly when the machine came to ground after a circuit of the aerodrome. Caruso seemed delighted with his experience. He said he had tried a note or two while in the air, but the conditions were not favorable for singing.

After including Pinkerton, Riccardo and Rodolfo in that season's repertory, he sang Cavaradossi at Covent Garden on June 29. 'So eager were all in the crowded audience to make the very most of their opportunities in the way of paying tributes to the "hero" . . . of the occasion that it might also have been Caruso's farewell to public life, and not merely his last appearance that season.'6 Yet it did transpire to be his London farewell, for only the previous day, at Sarajevo, Bosnia, a Serbian anarchist had assassinated Archduke Franz Ferdinand, the Austro-Hungarian heir apparent; the inevitable consequence was the conflagration which set all Europe alight. Opera was reduced to the side-lines and henceforth, save for charity galas in Italy and a short season at Monte Carlo, Caruso did not sing in Europe again and was obliged to reorientate his career in the Western Hemisphere.

That summer Madame Meyerheim, a reputable London singing teacher, secured an injunction against the John Church Company, publishers, prohibiting them from selling a book entitled How to Sing, allegedly by Caruso but in fact a copy of her book, L'Art du chant. The Church Company pleaded that they had bought the rights from another concern, and had had no dealings with Caruso personally, so they were innocent parties to the infringement as well as victims. It seems probable that Caruso was also a victim, for he was singularly free in giving his name to song writers and *literati* who were anxious to make a few coins by putting his name at the top of their unsaleable compositions. At any rate, Caruso did not defend the case and let it go by default.

The outbreak of hostilities having led to the cancellation of his German and Eastern European tour, he finally reappeared once again in Italy, after more than eleven years, for a special benefit at the Costanzi, Rome on October 19, to assist Italian workmen in Germany obliged to return home. The program included the Overture to *Guglielmo Tell*, the ensemble 'O sommo Carlo' from Act III of *Ernani*, led by Battistini, both of which were conducted by Mancinelli; and Act II of *Butterfly* with Bori, who was also Nedda in Act I of *Pagliacci* with Caruso. These excerpts were both under Toscanini's direction. The very next day he set sail from Naples on the *Canopic* for Boston. A photograph shows a large contingent of artists from the Met roster on board, including Toscanini and Bori, with Hempel, Farrar and Elisabeth Schumann.

The Metropolitan opened on November 16, 1914, and Caruso, back in New York again, sang Riccardo in *Un Ballo in maschera*, conducted by Toscanini, with Hempel as Oscar, Destinn as Amelia, Matzenauer as Ulrica and Amato as Renato. This was to be Toscanini's final first night at the Met. By the spring of 1915, it was claimed that he had become irritated and depressed with its routine, the basis of that theater. Yet Harvey Sachs, his biographer, considers the real reason for his departure more probably to have 'come in the form of an ultimatum from Farrar [with whom he had become intimately involved], who told him that if he loved her, he must leave his family for her.'[7] This he was not prepared to do, so it seemed the best resolution to the affair was to leave New York. At all events, to judge from the lengths Gatti-Casazza and Kahn were prepared to go to try and coax him back, his official excuse does seem threadbare.

The *New York Herald* 'could not help wondering whether it was the outbreak of war in Europe or whether it was *Un Ballo in maschera*, there was comparatively little enthusiasm in the audience, and comparatively little even for an opening night.'[8] The *Press*, however, found space to be expansive about Caruso's contribution: 'The role of Riccardo has always revealed his art to particular advantage, giving him opportunities not only to show his voice and dramatic powers but to disclose the delicacy and charm at his command in music of a distinctly lyric character. . . . He sang the *canzone* in the second act, 'Dì tu se fedele', and the following scene with the quintet, 'E' scherzo od è follia', inimitably.'⁹ Three nights later he appeared as Don José in *Carmen*. It was five years since last he had undertaken it at the Met, and Henderson in the *Sun* wrote that though 'he is not altogether comfortable in uniform, and he is not wholly happy in the opening scenes yet his impersonation last night was generally praiseworthy, and he sang much of the music admirably. The role fitted him well, and he found the music grateful and the action falling to the lot of the luckless brigadier much to his liking.'¹⁰ On November 25 he was Enzo again, but there seemed to have been nothing particularly noteworthy about this performance, save for a new black wig he wore. On December 24 he undertook des Grieux in Massenet's *Manon*. The next day the *Press* was not particularly complimentary, claiming that he had not been vocally 'at ease',¹¹ but Caruso's criticism of that criticism was briefer, and perhaps more telling, for in his press-cutting book he has scrawled under it 'L-I-A-R!' An interesting appraisal of his art appeared in the *New York Tribune*, which compared him with three former des Grieux: Ernst van Dyck, de Reszke and Clément. Van Dyck was

> without question the best actor . . . [but] he was a very poor singer and the dainty elegancies of Massenet's music fared ill in his delivery; [whereas] it was the virility, breadth and fervor of de Reszke's interpretation which was most noteworthy; [while] the exquisite refinement of Clément's des Grieux will be best remembered, [and his] tenderness too was most conspicuous. [Next to theirs] Caruso's can claim special distinction for the directness of its utterance, the positive assertion of its full-blooded passion, voiced in instinct with sensuous quality.¹²

The rest of that season continued with a number of his hardy perennials, including Canio, Radames, the other des Grieux – 'on the theory that two are better than one'¹³ – and he also repeated Raoul in *Gli Ugonotti*. In between performances, on February 11, 1915 at the Aeolian Hall, we catch a glimpse of him in a box at a recital given by the Australian composer/pianist Percy Grainger.

On the 20th he left New York to take part in the Monte Carlo season. Since Conried's day all Caruso's engagements, whether in Europe or America, had been managed by the Met, and inevitably these were not allowed to clash with their needs. But that season Caruso came to undertake his international engagements himself.

Save for four years before, when he was indisposed and obliged to cancel his schedule, he had not quit the Metropolitan so early for more than a decade – in fact, not since his first New York season and his last visit to Monte Carlo in 1904. When Gunsbourg learned of this, he quickly thought out a strategem. After his usual wily fashion he convinced Caruso he should come by arguing that the outbreak of war in France made conditions extremely difficult and the annual cosmopolitan trek to the Casino had been abruptly interrupted. But if Caruso were to come everything would be fine again, and the receipts – or at least part of them – could go for the benefit of the French and Italian Red Cross. Caruso landed at Naples and an offer came immediately for him to appear at a benefit arranged for refugees made homeless by the Avezzano earthquake. He would have been pleased to accept but Gunsbourg insisted on his sticking to the letter of his contract and coming immediately to Monte Carlo; so he never sang in Naples again and had to content himself with making a substantial financial contribution instead.

Camillo Traversi, a sometime Paris critic, engaged that year as secretary to Gunsbourg, recalls some of Caruso's ruminations on the subject of becoming a great box-office draw. 'I feel a role too much,' he laments.

> I always try to give of my best in interpreting a part. I know that I am a singer and an actor but I give an impression of being neither but a real man conceived by the composer. The difficulty does not lie in achieving perfection but in keeping it. As soon as an artist archieves the pinnacle of his success, when he is at the top of the ladder, he is haunted by the terrible question – when will he start to go down? When will he fail? I can never take a step upon the stage without asking myself that.[14]

In the course of the next five years, as his fame grew ever more dramatically, he would utter this plaint increasingly often.

From the first night of his Monte Carlo *rentrée*, which took place on March 11, *Le Petit Monégasque* hailed him: 'His voice has become bigger since last we heard it. [Yet] the highest register is still full of power and authority. The middle range is warmer. It is an organ of incomparable quality; and what art there is in his emission of phrases!'[15] The Aida, the Russian-born soprano Litvinne, wrote admiringly of the 'wonderful Caruso'.[16] On March 21, his Duke was acclaimed by *Le Journal de Monaco*: 'He is altogether remarkable, his voice, his singing and his artistry.'[17] In *Lucia*, on March 28, he was joined by the Spanish 'coloratura' soprano, Graziella Pareto. Years later she told Zirato[18] how after the premiere she had developed a bad cold, lost her voice and been obliged to take to her bed, which had greatly worried Gunsbourg. But Caruso came to her room unexpectedly bearing a throat spray and some other medications. These worked a miraculous cure and so, in fact, she was able to sing her second *Lucia*.

His last appearance at Monte Carlo took place on April 6, as Canio. The outbreak of war having put paid to the rest of his European engagements that spring, it had been his intention to take himself off to Italy for a lengthy vacation. But while he was in Monte Carlo he was approached by Walter Mocchi, the Director of the Costanzi, Rome, husband of Carelli, and a leading South American impresario. He urged him to undertake a tour at the head of a troupe he was organizing to sing in Argentina and Uruguay. Caruso was not particularly keen, so he asked what he fancied was an extortionate fee – about $6,666 a performance. But much to his amazement Mocchi accepted without turning a hair. As Key states in his biography of Caruso, 'How little did the singer, in spite of his steady advancement, suspect his approaching commercial value as an artist.'[19] Yet, however much Caruso was paid, Mocchi was certainly not organizing the company at a loss, as can be judged from the souvenir he gave to Caruso, after the season finished, of a gold cigarette case, which was inscribed: 'To Caruso, the dearest of all friends [and] the least dear of all artists'.[20]

This was Caruso's first appearance in South America in twelve years and it was with typical apprehension that he left Genoa bound for Buenos Aires and his first appearance at the Colón. Mocchi had not been slow sending out advance information of Caruso's imminent arrival. Until then the season's subscriptions had been selling poorly, but no sooner were Caruso posters placarded all over town than a crowd gathered at the box-office that did not disperse until every subscription was taken up. Caruso made his debut opposite the Aida of Rosa Raisa, a celebrated Polish-born dramatic soprano, who had already appeared with him in London in the same opera the previous year. His next role was Canio which he sang on five occasions. It was at a gala concert on June 18 that he was to finish the evening with the first act of *Pagliacci*.

The emotion was at its most intense when Hipolito Lázaro appeared to announce that as the baritone was indisposed,* Caruso, in a fine gesture of camaraderie, was willing to sing Tonio's Prologue. You may well imagine the public's response and the general consternation that swept through the house as the orchestra began the first notes. . . . One cannot describe the excitement as Caruso began to sing 'Si può?' His voice was as dark as a baritone's, but what's more, his was an act so noble, his interpretation so moving, that he received an ovation even before the last chords had sounded. The rest of the first act offered no greater enchantments and only Caruso, even without make-up, dominated the stage, holding the impatient public's attention up to the ineffable final aria at the end of the first act, and when Caruso did at last sing it, there are no words sufficient to describe the effect.[21]

He also sang both des Grieux and he made a couple of appearances as Edgardo in *Lucia*, and these were the last performances of it he was ever to undertake. The Lucia on these occasions was Galli-Curci, a then comparatively unknown Italian 'coloratura' soprano whose big break came nearly a year and a half later at a matinée of *Rigoletto* in Chicago. In 1915 Caruso had written deprecatingly of her to Gatti: she is no more than 'a mediocrity' and Galli-Curci did not come to the Met until 1921, after Caruso's death. So this was the only time they were ever to appear on stage together, though the following year they did both contribute to recordings of the *Lucia* sextet and *Rigoletto* quartet. After visits to three other Argentine cities – Rosario, Córdoba and Tucumán – and some concerts at the Coliseo and the Colón, in one of which he appeared in the first act of *Pagliacci* with Ruffo, his season ended on the other side of the Rio de la Plata, on August 30, with a performance of *Manon Lescaut* at the Urquiza, Montevideo.

Just before he was to re-embark for Italy a request came from Toscanini, then in Milan, for him to sing in two special performances of *Pagliacci*, on September 23 and 26, at the dal Verme; like his Roman appearance the previous year these were in aid of Italian musicians obliged to give up their work in Austro-Hungary and Germany and return home because of the war. Caruso accepted, and these occasions marked his first appearances in Milan since he had created Maurizio in *Adriana Lecouvreur* in 1902. In spite of a vociferously hostile group ensconced in the gallery, Caruso swept all

---

* Mario Sammarco had originally been announced to appear as Tonio but he was unwell and Danise agreed to appear in his stead, although he was already announced to sing in the third act of *Aida* at the beginning of the evening so, not unnaturally, he was relieved to be rid of the Prologue.

before him. The press was unanimous; the *Corriere della sera* praised him: 'He comes again after many years absence with a voice whose high notes are appreciably enhanced, its timbre become fuller and more manly, with a much greater breath span and greater expressive resources. In sum, his singing has a highly dramatic quality which contrasted vividly with Milanese memories of a graceful tenor with an almost feminine delicacy in "Amor ti vieta" from *Fedora* and other celebrated pieces of the same type.'[22]

These were his last European appearances.

After only a month in Italy, on October 12, he left for America with Gatti-Casazza, who joined him on the boat at Naples. No sooner had he arrived in New York than he gave a round of press interviews. In the *New York American* a piece appeared in which he tells how 'the burdens of my life are always greater than the rewards', and then he goes on to complain at length. 'Always life to me is the same. I go from bed to work and from work to bed. On my recent trip to South America, I wanted to give only a dozen performances.'[23] A change was becoming evident in the singer's attitude; his old lightheartedness gradually gave way to a new seriousness of purpose. Perhaps this was in response to the increasingly taxing and dramatically profound repertory he was beginning to undertake. As Key tells: 'How different a man he had become from the Caruso of a decade before! Experience and associations had not been without their influence. The very shape of his head had changed – along with the contour of his features. He was jovial of mood to the many who saw him casually in the streets. . . . But the serious side of the man was having its way. Those who saw him often in his home observed the gradual transformation of the singer.'[24]

The Met season opened again on November 15, 1915, with Saint-Saëns's *Samson et Dalila*, in which Caruso undertook Samson for the first time. Having a biblical subject, the opera had been given there on only one previous occasion, with Tamagno, and it was worlds away from Caruso's typical lyric repertory. Something of the fresh quality of his singing was apparent in 'the second act love duet in which his voice was of melting beauty',[25] and generally the role gave him 'ample opportunities to exhibit . . . the beauty and emotional timbre of his voice . . . [and] it enabled him to practise restraint as well as open the floodgates of impassioned utterance.'[26] Nevertheless, he still had some difficulty with the French language, notwithstanding his eloquent singing of Faust and Don José, both of which roles he sang in the original. 'In the first act, just before the inspired Samson rallies the discouraged Hebrews, he exclaims that he sees a fiery sword in the hands of the angels! But he pronounced it thus, "Je vois dans les mains des anges!" which, with the lyrical elision, sounded like "des singes". There is, of course, a striking difference between "anges" (angels) and "singes" (monkeys)! [He] was horrified when he was told and every time the moment drew near, he grew panicky and could not remember which pronunciation was the right one!'[27]

That season he also appeared in *La Bohème*, *Tosca*, *Pagliacci*, *Manon*, *Un Ballo in maschera*, *Manon Lescaut*, *Rigoletto*, *Carmen* and *Aida*. 'Our public is certainly fortunate in having the opportunity of hearing, on an average of twice a week, the world's most famous singer. Judging from the size of the audiences every time he sings, it is fair to suppose that they do appreciate their good fortune, and they show every sign of continuing to do so.'[28] That he could manage dramatic music was evident from his Samson, but as Lionello in *Marta*, which he undertook again that season after seven years; 'one might have questioned whether the part would sit comfortably on him today. It does. He sang the music gloriously and with lavishness of tone,'[29] (and) 'any doubts that may have existed as to his ability to sing with the lyric fluency which had been his most valuable attribute were convincingly dispelled.'[30] In Puccini's *Manon Lescaut*, Krehbiel, normally a temperate commentator, was moved to describe him as 'the greatest tenor we know and the greatest this generation is likely to know. Last night he overwhelmed his hearers. Caruso's singing had its faults. He oversings his middle voice, as is his custom, and began phrases with an aspirate; but even with these defects his achievement was one of superlative quality. His formation of tone, his legato and his diction were sources of delight appreciated by connoisseur and layman.'[31] On February 11, when he sang the Duke in *Rigoletto** for the first time at the Metropolitan since the 1911/12 season, we can understand after an interval of more than three years that he should have been apprehensive as to the outcome. According to Gatti, Caruso did not think he had sung well and was therefore reluctant to read the notices; nevertheless, the *Times*, the *Tribune* and the *Sun* (i.e. Aldrich, Krehbiel and Henderson) all penned laudatory appreciations. By contrast, the following season, when it was again included in the

---

* In this revival, Giorgio Polacco, the conductor, restored for the first time the duet for Gilda and Rigoletto 'Lassù in cielo', and, as we also noted above, the aria 'Parmi veder le lagrime' was unfamiliar when Caruso sang it in a performance of *Rigoletto* at Bologna in 1901.

repertory and Caruso thought he had sung it well, Gatti tells of the critics writing 'in terms of strong disfavor'.[32] Yet by the time Gatti wrote his autobiography his memory seems to have been playing him false, for the *Sun* extolled '[Caruso's] great beauty of tone',[33] the *Tribune* declared that 'anyone with the love of *bel canto* in his soul should give humble and hearty thanks unto the Almighty',[34] and the *Times* waxed lyric over 'the immense fervor and romance [he put] into the delivery of his airs and recitatives'.[35]

On February 17, 1916 Caruso appeared as Don José opposite Farrar's Carmen, only the second role she had undertaken that season since her return from film-making. She arrived back at the Met sporting extravagant costumes and movie manners that she had acquired, like her swashbuckling film-star husband, Lou Tellegen, in Hollywood. When she tried to import a little new realism into *Carmen*, the impact was more than even she had bargained for: the chorus girls declined to be pushed about, and Alda, who was singing Micaëla, tells how:

[Caruso gripped Farrar] by the wrist to hold her still [and] she turned in his grasp, bent her head swiftly, and bit the hand that held her. Caruso, furious and bleeding, flung her from him [and] she went down smack on her bottom, [but by the time the curtain had fallen she was back] on her feet and she and Caruso were having it out.... The applause ... was tremendous and insistent [and] there was no denying the calls, [so] hand in hand, [they] would come forth to bow, and [then] retire behind the folds where the row was immediately on again.[36]

Farrar told Caruso that if he did not like her new realism then the company could find another Carmen. '"No," the tenor gallantly replied, "we can prevent a repetition of the scene by getting another José."'[37] But by the next performance anyone expecting a renewed outbreak of hostilities was destined to be disappointed.

At the close of the Flower Song, when Don José falls on his knees beside Carmen, who promptly flings her arms about his neck, the two famous singers clung to each other much longer than seemed necessary and as the applause ... threatened to stop, Mrs Lou Tellegen loosened her grip. But her amorous associate showed no sign of wanting to change his posture and, keeping his head comfortably where it was pillowed, held the prima donna firmly in his embrace. Then it was that the crowd burst into hilarious laughter. However irritated Caruso may have been at Farrar a week ago yesterday, he evidently treasured no ill-feeling against [her].[38]

CHAPTER XIV

1916–1918

STRAIGHT AFTER the New York season was done the Metropolitan company paid a visit to Boston. Caruso appeared with it in six of his roles and though each opera was invariably sold out and the house clamorous this seemed to rub up at least one critic the wrong way. After an *Aida* on April 7, 1916 Olin Downes, in the *Boston Globe*, complained at length about his Radames: 'Last night the audience was soon past any dispassionate judgment, [and] as the evening wore on Caruso sang more and more badly.'[1] Downes does not reveal in what way he thought Caruso's singing so bad, but he compared him to Zenatello, whom he claims 'sang this role a hundred times better'. In fact, Downes was in all probability criticising the audience as much as the performance, for when Zenatello had come to sing Radames with the Boston Grand Opera Company the previous December, 'there were seats – a great many seats – empty,'[2] whereas for the Met, 'the house had been sold out some days in advance.'[3] At all events, by the time *Rigoletto* was given on the 12th Downes does not fail to commend Caruso for singing 'a part admirably suited to his voice and his dramatic capabilities. He sang in the majority of scenes with excellent effect, and also with thought for dramatic values and care for dramatic consistency and proportions, more characteristic of the Caruso of later years than in the earlier stages of his remarkable career.'[4]

At the end of April the tour proceeded to Atlanta. Caruso appeared on three evenings and it was here on the morning of the 24th that he sang Samson's lament on his blindness, 'Vois ma misère, hélas', especially for Helen Keller, the blind and deaf woman. So she could 'hear' him, 'she placed her fingers directly to the lips and throat' of Caruso as he sang. Afterwards she exclaimed that though 'I could not see his face . . . I felt the pathos of the song, I felt the soul of Samson in every vibrant touch of my fingertips.'[5] Yet, however Keller may have been affected by their meeting, physiologists denied that it would have been possible for her, in that fashion at least, to have 'heard' anything at all.

While Caruso was in Atlanta he responded to a wire he had received from the Press Club in San Francisco begging him to sing over the telephone on April 30 to three thousand San Franciscans who were all crazy to hear him, and in so doing commemorate the earthquake that had convulsed the town a decade earlier. Caruso had of course been present on that occasion – though there is no evidence to suggest that the San Francisco Press Club remembered this. We can be pretty sure that wild horses would never have dragged the tenor back again; but singing over the phone was another matter, even though transmission would be accomplished in the early hours, and he was happy to agree to be the first artist to telephone his voice over the wires. Three years later, when the Met season was in full swing in New York, a Navy officer representing the San Francisco Press Club came bearing a card of silver plate, giving him life membership.

During the next six months Caruso undertook no further engagements. This summer marked the first extended vacation that he had been able to enjoy in years; he secured a complete rest at the Villa Bellosguardo, surrounded by his stepmother, two sons and other members of his family. He suffered much from an increasingly disturbing indisposition which he had complained of during the previous year while in South America; Dr Holbrook Curtis told him that it was nothing more than a nasal infection but he performed a painful operation. His condition was not immediately alleviated and only gradually did his health recover.

He returned to New York that autumn and the Met opened on November 13, 1916, with Bizet's *Les Pêcheurs de perles*, in which Caruso sang Nadir, De Luca was Zurga and Hempel sang Leïla. The production lasted only three performances – hardly a record for Caruso at this stage of his career. Its inclusion in the repertory was part of the management's increasing tendency to search out earlier and less well-known works by composers of established favorites – Bizet had written *Carmen*. In this way it was hoped to make good the gaps occasioned by the increasingly unsuccessful attempts of living composers such as Puccini's *La Fanciulla del West* and Charpentier's *Julien*. Caruso and De Luca remembered *I Pescatori di perle* from eighteen years before at Genoa. It is surprising, judging from critical enthusiasm, that it did not survive for as many performances as the contemporary works. Although it was a novelty at the Met and had not been heard for nearly a generation, it had been given at San Francisco with Tetrazzini in her salad days, and it had also been heard at the French Opera at New Orleans. In the opinion of Aldrich: 'The performance was one that challenged warm admiration . . . and there was a realization that if the opera was not a masterpiece of the first rank it at least supplied a part admirably fitted for Caruso, in which his voice, his most impassioned style, and his long phrasing [were] heard to advantage.'[6] It seems that Caruso not only lost *Les Pêcheurs de perles* but also his mustache, which had made a reappearance during his Italian sojourn that summer; there was no place for it in the next opera, *Manon Lescaut*, and so off it came again – shades of its initial disappearance at Salerno, twenty years before, for that too was before *Manon Lescaut*.

He made newspaper headlines on two other occasions in November, but not for singing. The first was on the 17th, after he had again received a number of extortion notes from 'The Black Hand' demanding immediate payment of $10,000, which he was told to deliver to an address in New Jersey. The second, on the 26th, was when he was invited to dinner as guest of honor by the Friars' Club, a theatrical group. He was required to raise his voice – but only in a post-prandial speech of thanks to his hosts, among whom were leading song composers, including George M. Cohan, Irving Berlin and Victor Herbert. And this was after they had joined in a carousal – or should it rather be spelled, Carusal – singing, to the tune of 'Pretty baby', 'Everybody loves a tenor, that's why I'm in love with you! Oh, Caruso! Oh, Caruso!'

Meanwhile, on November 24, he appeared as Samson again. The *Morning Telegraph* extolled him: 'Never has he acted with more force and freedom of gesture, never has he sung with a surer command of all resources of an art in which he stands unapproached.'[7] It was from this time that the breadth of his repertory starts to become more apparent. During the next three seasons he would add other dramatic parts, which were offset by two lyric roles that he maintained in his repertory to the last year of his career – he repeated his Lionello in *Marta* on December 25, and later added Nemorino in *L'Elisir d'amore*. The critics were enthusiastic: 'The great tenor's voice has darkened . . . and there are those who doubted whether he would be able to sing the music with his old dexterity. But these doubters were silenced before he had uttered a dozen bars. It was the old Caruso of the graceful, plastic style.'[8] And:

'Una furtiva lagrima' was sung with a perfection of *cantilena*, a finish of phrasing and a musically interpretive art that roused the audience to a pitch of enthusiasm seldom encountered. . . . The Caruso voice had nearly all its former lyric smoothness wherever it was required. Phrases that demanded the light feathery tone were given with a golden quality which this artist alone of all singers we know possesses. And when the contrast of dramatic vocalism was needed the singer did not overdo. It was a masterly achievement like the entire performance.[9]

After he had sung 'Una furtiva lagrima' to a roar of applause, instead of encoring it he stepped out of character and caused a considerable amount of mirth by starting the next recitative: 'It is not allowed' (or words to that effect).[10] But that sort of wile could not be guaranteed to work a second time and at the next performance, on January 10, 1917, 'Caruso pouted and grimaced and wriggled his hands, he curtsied, he caracoled, [but] prettily as he begged, he was forced to do it over, and that huge house had its interlude of heaven twice.'[11]

Throughout the remainder of his Met stint that season he undertook a typical sampling of his regular repertory. As well as Canio and the Duke, he appeared as Cavaradossi opposite the Tosca of Claudia Muzio, who made 'a promising debut [and they had] the honor of facing one of the largest audiences seen at the Metropolitan, which was undoubtedly a tribute to Caruso'.[12] As Don José in *Carmen*, in spite of black marketeers demanding $30 a seat and Farrar whistling the opening measures of the *Séguidille* during the *ritornello*, there were no other untoward events, unlike the previous year. When he sang Radames, according to the *Sun*: 'More than 4,000 people were at the Met, [and another] 5,000 were unable to gain admission.'[13] To celebrate his forty-fourth birthday a special musical evening was held at the West Side apartment of one of his friends, Enrico Scognamillo, also a Neapolitan. On March 4, *The New York Times* had news of some art treasures for which he had paid $30,000 at a 50th Street gallery. Two weeks later, with Alda, De Luca and Amato, he took part in a Met benefit concert, after which it was announced that more than $10,000 had been raised for the relief of Italian reservists; America was yet to enter hostilities but the war fever was escalating precipitately. Caruso sang in *La Bohème* on March 23, and the *Evening Sun* critic was enraptured by 'a high B he took of surpassing beauty [in "Che gelida manina"]'.[14] Something of his vocal progress may be noticed in this. John T. McGovern tells how in his early years, 'Caruso would transpose "Che gelida manina" down a semitone . . . sometimes he would even miss the high B altogether and stay on the G.'[15] By 1917, however, we can see how sure he had become in the delivery of his top notes.

On April 6 that year the United States joined Britain, France and Italy and declared war against Germany and Austro-Hungary. Only eleven days later, at the Metropolitan, Caruso took part in the first of many performances held to benefit one war charity or another. On this occasion not only were Alda, Povla Frijsh and Verlet present, but the proceedings were crowned by the great Sarah Bernhardt who, as Francis Robinson puts it, 'with one leg gone and the foot of the other already in the grave . . . was a symbol of France's heroic resistance.'[16] The Met season came to an end after a performance of *Rigoletto*; there were sixteen curtain calls before the euphoric audience would disband and go home, and Caruso led them in a final three cheers for the United States and for the allies.

The company journeyed down to Atlanta, where he appeared in three operas: *L'Elisir d'amore*, *Tosca* and *Rigoletto*. Amid the hysteria generated by the war and plaudits for the great tenor, one newspaper put it: '"See Naples and die?" Maybe it's better "to hear Caruso first and then die happy!"'[17] And straight afterwards he was off on an American concert tour, to Cincinnati, Toledo and Pittsburgh. At these cities he sang three operatic arias with orchestra: 'O paradiso!' from *L'Africana*, 'Una furtiva lagrima' from *L'Elisir d'amore* and 'Vesti la giubba' from *Pagliacci*. Then, with the piano accompaniment of Barthélemy, he offered the following encores: Widor's 'Mon bras pressait', Duparc's 'Extase', Hüe's 'J'ai pleuré en rêve', Fauré's 'Clair de lune' and Rachmaninoff's 'Primavera'. Here we see how his taste in songs had developed, the result of Barthélemy's influence. But this would be the last time they worked together and henceforth Caruso's song repertory would be made up of more conventional material.

At each city where he stopped, his attentive hosts would escort around the caravan of some thirteen people he brought with him, including the tour manager, his accompanist, press secretary, valet and Scognamillo. Everywhere he was the subject of unfeigned curiosity, although he was always treated respectfully. At his Cincinnati hotel, when he complained to a wedding party assembled on the floor beneath his room that he must have a completely uninterrupted night's sleep if he was to sing well, they immediately moved to the other side of the hotel out of ear-shot. And he was not insensitive to the inconvenience he may have caused, for the next day he sent the young couple a signed photograph of himself with the inscription: 'Thank you for my *not* sleepless night.'[18]

Three days after the last concert he came back to New York, where he was to spend a little more than a week before departing again for South America. On May 8 he found time to sing in front of more than 2,000 members and guests of the Mozart Society, a women's club, at the Astor Hotel in Times Square. The program was similar to the concerts he had undertaken on tour, save for the inclusion of Borodin's 'Dissonance' and 'Come un bel dì di maggio' from *Andrea Chénier*. On May 10 his name headed a company at the Met, including Ignace Paderewski, who, as well as being the world's most celebrated pianist, was soon to become the first Premier of an independent Poland; Jacques Thibaud, the noted French violinist; Lucien Muratore and Homer, all of whom were taking part in a special benefit that helped raised 250,000 French Francs to support Marshall Joffre's charities.

His departure for South America was imminent when he learned with some distress of the damage done to allied shipping by German submarines. He dallied with the idea of trying to re-route himself via the Pacific and Chile, but when he realized the near impossibility of getting over the Andes in the winter, he decided to risk the Atlantic on a neutral Swedish liner. The biggest problem facing Caruso in May 1917 was making a safe journey to South America, and no doubt it was the size of his fee – $200,000 for thirty performances – that helped concentrate his mind. He travelled on board a steamer – photographs show him with a life preserver adroitly placed next to his berth in case of an attack by a German U-boat, so he said. He spent much of his time throughout the voyage studying Mascagni's *Lodoletta*, a new opera in which he was to undertake the role of Flammen in its premieres at Buenos Aires and Rio de Janeiro. The opera season would commence in Buenos Aires but no sooner had he reached Rio than he was met by Mocchi, who was delighted to show him about, as much to satisfy the curiosity of sceptical journalists who never believed he was really coming as to satisfy any curiosity the great tenor may have had in gazing out across the spectacular harbor at the Sugar Loaf. 'Here,' as Caruso tells us himself, 'I was extensively entertained by the

Automobile Club, the Jockey Club and the São Pio Araujo – a society of music editors.'[19] And it was the same story when they reached São Paulo; there he was a lauded guest at the inauguration of the Casade Saude Hospital. After another brief stop at Santos, where he was greeted by representatives from the large Italian colony, he embarked for Buenos Aires.

Caruso made his bow at the Colón as Nemorino on June 17. His fees constituted a large part of the cake, but the scale of the operation was hardly niggardly. Mocchi had got together more than twenty principals, including two successful verismo sopranos, Melis and Dalla Rizza; a noted French lyric soprano, Ninon Vallin; the baritone Giraldoni; a baryton-martin, Armand Crabbé; a first-class bass, Journet; the mezzo-soprano, Fanny Anitua; as well as three other tenors, Charles Hackett, Fernand Francell and Antonio Cortis, then at the very beginning of his career. From the first performance of *L'Elisir d'amore* Caruso himself told how 'the audience was very kind and gave me such a welcome that made me glad I had come back after two years.'[20] His next appearance, as Canio, was deemed 'simply colossal'.[21] He also sang des Grieux in Massenet's *Manon* – 'at which the reception was overwhelming and he was seen to put his hands to his ears so deafening was the applause'[22] – Cavaradossi, Rodolfo and Flammen in *Lodoletta*. But at this some dissenting voices were heard, whether on Caruso's account or Mascagni's it was difficult to tell. Perhaps it was just that Mocchi's prices – an orchestra seat cost $33 – seemed steep. This was not really surprising however, for it was in South America at this stage of his career that Caruso was paid the highest fee since Patti had earned $8,000 a performance at the Politeama Argentino, Buenos Aires, in 1888. His enormous popularity and the interest in him even in remote places in Argentina or Brazil had quickened as a result of the prodigious success of his phonograph records. He had become so well known that 'the various businesses who offered their goods for sale in the daily newspapers, seemed to think that if his name headed the advertisement then it would attract attention. So it was that the sale of special lines in gents' clothing was headed with Caruso's name in bold type'[23] – and perfumes, cigarettes and cough lozenges all took his name, whether they had paid for its use or not.

In Argentina there were German and English speaking immigrants as well as the Spaniards and Italians, and at this time the First World War was beginning to create open friction between the various nationalities. Though the South American countries may have been at peace among themselves, notwithstanding certain border disputes, within their own frontiers they frequently threatened to break into pieces. Mocchi had planned a visit to Rosario (about two hundred miles up the Rio de la Plata from Buenos Aires); he had arranged a performance there for Caruso in 1915. Unfortunately, the theater was owned by a German and this caused so much resentment among the Italians that they hastened to wreck it – but before Caruso had come, instead of waiting until after he had been. The result was that Caruso could not go to Rosario; in such fashion did the Italians cut their own noses off! These peculiar circumstances engendered by the European war went some way to account for the ambiguous attitude to Caruso. He found himself in the middle of a feud. His name had become a byword of contention between the various different-language newspapers of Buenos Aires, although they could not but express the high standard of accomplishment represented in his art.

After leaving Buenos Aires Caruso travelled across to Montevideo and then journeyed north to Rio de Janeiro and São Paulo. The repertory was similar; he did not sing Flammen again until he reached Brazil, but he added Don José. Here, too, the audiences do not appear to have been very sophisticated. Whenever he appeared as Canio he received the typical superlative notices, yet the public regarded itself as cheated at having to pay out full prices when Caruso only sang half an evening. Indeed there would have been many tickets returned but for the fact that the box-office was besieged by would-be purchasers willing to pay practically any price to secure admission to any of the performances. A similar kind of naïvety accounts for the audience reaction during the final performance at São Paulo on October 10 of Massenet's *Manon*. On that evening Vallin was indisposed so Dalla Rizza appeared in the title-role instead, and she sang in Italian. Caruso, of course, still sang in French, but he had only just begun when the audience started chanting, 'Sing in Italian.' At the interval the manager appeared before the curtain and announced that Caruso would comply with their request. '"But," he added, "he tells me that it will take him four months to commit the words to memory, and he fears that you might not have the patience to wait so long."'[24]

Caruso arrived back in New York on November 4, after being away for more than five months – as long as a Metropolitan season. Upon his arrival he bent down and kissed the ground, like a Pope, so expressing his relief at arriving safely back in his 'stepmother country'.

With him – war economics had made it necessary – he was carrying a large part of his fees in gold. And he also brought with him $100,000 from various appearances for the American Red Cross, all of which must have gone some way to console him for the bad news flashed out by telegraph from the war in Europe. After the collapse of Russia, Austro-Hungary had been free to concentrate on her western front and had recently made substantial advances into Italy, securing some 100,000 prisoners of war. Caruso's elder son, Rodolfo, was fighting somewhere at the front and no news from him was bad news. At any rate he had no time for a holiday in 1917 and in only a little over a week the Met season had begun again. On November 12, Caruso was Radames, and this time the company included Muzio, Matzenauer and Amato, but: 'There is, of course, no use blinking the fact that his voice has gradually lost some of its lyric quality. The softly expiring head tone often is replaced by a full-throated utterance, as it was last night in "Celeste Aida", which came to a close with a B flat flung out with tremendous vibrancy and power.'[25] And critical opinion was generally not kind: 'He is so recently up from Buenos Aires that it is no whit surprising he was at first raucous and jerky. Here and there a gold phrase gleamed through the fog, but not until the Nile scene did gold gain easy currency.'[26] In the *World* there was the usual comment on Caruso's 'vocal lustre and beauty', yet 'from an artistic side, however, he did not reach the mark he has set in other seasons. He "scooped" his tone overmuch, and resorted to an explosive delivery which scarcely belongs to *bel canto*.'[27] Sigmund Spaeth was more severe: 'Caruso was about as far from good as he ever permits himself to be. His tones were thick and muffled and in "Celeste Aida" he was shorter of breath than usual, his shouting in the Nile scene did not greatly improve matters, although it won him the enthusiasm of his hearers.'[28] But it was in *Musical America* that the most abrasive criticism appeared:

Candour compels the admission that Caruso was anything but in his best vocal condition. The worshipped tenor did not follow the sensible plan of the previous year and rest during the summer. Instead he worked hard in South America, and on Monday night echoed traces of his fatigue. Except when he forced it to the point of violent, explosive utterance, his voice sounded dark, hollow and unresonant. While beginning with 'Celeste Aida' he exhibited an unfortunate and almost persistent tendency to attack his top notes from beneath and to employ with increasing frequency an unpleasant *coup de glotte*. His vociferous tones at the end of the Nile scene brought him the customary mead of applausive excitement, but their emission cost him obvious effort.[29]

L'Elisir d'amore, three nights later, soon worked an improvement on his form. Henderson observed that

> although it is his fate to impersonate many times chevaliers, knights and even mighty warriors, he is never more satisfying than when playing the unfortunate lovesick countryman chasing the elusive elixir of love. Caruso has a way of impersonating . . . a peasant sometimes when he appears before the curtain in other roles, but his farcical doings are much more at home as Nemorino. He used to sing some of the music better than he does now, especially the beautiful aria 'Una furtiva lagrima', but into whatever manner he elects to wander his public follows him with humble devotion and loyal praises.[30]

At subsequent performances later that season he would introduce fresh bits of business. At one of these, at the end of the first act, he fell to the stage and then rolled towards the footlights, barrel fashion. At another, when the chorus of peasant women were assembled knitting, Caruso helped himself to a pair of needles from one of these ladies, and instantly began to click away. By the time the audience had become aware of it he had finished a row without dropping a stitch. It was later learned that the chorus lady was knitting a sweater for an Italian soldier.

Between performances his name was now often in the news. He conducted an auction of some oranges for the Italian war campaign from which he raised $47,000, and he himself purchased a box for $4,000. He sent off a gift of $10,000 to the Italian Prime Minister for the relief of refugees in the war. Bruno Zirato, a young man in his twenties, was appointed his secretary – after a checkered assortment, at last Caruso secured the services of a full-time professional. He purchased from the Canessa Galleries, for $30,000, four pieces of Limoges enamelled pottery, three of them plaques representing religious subjects and the fourth a cup of classical design. During that autumn, Jascha Heifetz, then a stripling of sixteen, came to New York and created quite a stir with his 'poignant performance of the Bruch [violin] concerto', moving one critic to aver that not 'even the impassioned singing of Caruso as Nemorino could furnish such a musical pleasure'.[31] On November 21 Caruso repeated his Lionello in *Marta*. The *World*[32] thought 'that he might have used less portamento in "Dormi pur" and in "M'appari" but his art was so supreme in nearly every other respect,' and the *Musical Courier* declared: 'If he doesn't furnish an example of *bel canto* then the present reviewer is at a loss to know what *bel canto* is!'[33] At a Washington Square concert he sang the 'Inno di Garibaldi', 'La Marseillaise' and 'The Star Spangled Banner', which he embellished the second time round, interpolating several high notes. After appearing at the Met as Samson he went down to Philadelphia to sing des Grieux in *Manon Lescaut*. The *Record* wrote: 'His rich, expressive voice gave the exquisite music in a way that condoned his failure to look the part, and blinded one to much that was incongrous.'[34] And Huneker modestly observed: 'The art of the greatest tenor must be left to a master of superlatives. Caruso, after his accustomed preliminary vocal mist, sang like the rising sun – one becomes positively lyric in evoking the memory of such art and such a voice.'[35] On December 7 back in New York he sang Canio. On the 10th, although the *Telegram* did not consider Don José to be one of his most effective roles, yet 'he is still the great tenor, and he gives the Flower Song and other melodic moments all the opulence of his golden voice.'[36] Between a Cavaradossi and the Duke on the 27th he appeared at a Musical Morning at the Waldorf Astoria; he sang Godard's 'Chanson de Juin', Buzzi-Peccia's 'Lolita', 'Esprits gardiens' from Reyer's *Sigurd*, Grieg's 'Io t'amo' and Rossini's 'La danza', and the concert ended with Bizet's 'Agnus Dei', in which he was joined by another young violinist, Mischa Elman,* who provided an obbligato.

The last three roles he undertook that season were each of them for the first time in New York. They included Flammen in *Lodoletta*, Jean in Meyerbeer's *Le Prophète* and Avito in Montemezzi's *L'Amore dei tre re*. Of these, a great deal of newspaper space was taken up with his assumption of Flammen. He made his bow in it on January 12, 1918; the opera was by all accounts a failure, but Caruso's singing in it was revealed at its finest and the critics to a man were lost in expatiating on his many virtues. *The New York Times* wrote of 'his virtuosity in difficult intervals and shifting tonality'.[37] Max Smith thought 'the role offers the great tenor opportunities for lyric and dramatic song such as do few roles in his repertory'.[38] Krehbiel was enthusiastic: 'It was Caruso at his best, his golden tone, his feeling and flexibility of utterance.'[39] Even Henderson was unqualified in his praises: 'He has done no more beautiful singing in recent years. It was his finest and

* Forty-five years later, on November 4, 1962, Elman appeared in a televised musical soirée at Covent Garden. The singer on that occasion was Maria Callas.

most lyric style, worthy of his artistic standing and his fame.'[40] In an article in the *World*, Pierre Key, later Caruso's first biographer, gives a full description of his art at this time:

> Coming at a period in his career which many have mistakenly regarded as past his prime, his original achievement and its duplication will set many prognosticators to a reconsideration of their earlier warnings that Caruso has seen his best days and was slipping down hill . . . the fact is that as the years have flown by Caruso has grown steadily in his technical and interpretive skill. The hardest working principal by far in the Metropolitan organization, this superbly gifted singer has never faltered in his constant efforts to improve the resources at his command. To those who have long studied the mechanics of tone production (of emission or formation, as some prefer to designate it), it has been apparent during the past three years that . . . Caruso's actual "making" of his tones has crept steadily nearer perfection. It is true that occasionally he offends by slurring, by using the undesirable aspirate – both unfortunate habits which are the outgrowth of Caruso's fondness for dramatic music, and his insistence upon straying from his metier to gratify his desires to sing it. But these faults are nil when Caruso sings in *Lodoletta*. A unique artist whose like we shall probably never encounter again, he is now at the apex of his career.[41]

Three weeks after Flammen, on February 7, he sang Jean in *Le Prophète*, and after Saint-Saëns's Samson this was his second assumption from a more dramatic repertory. It was altogether sterner stuff than Mascagni's Flammen. 'Sincerity, fervor and repose mark this new impersonation of the famous tenor, and there can be no doubt his favor will grow with it. It is one of his most artistic achievements.'[42] 'He sang superbly . . . with an earnestness and dignity, a beauty of voice and restraint of action.'[43] There was some cavilling ('one could not help feeling that he seemed ill at ease in the dramatic heroics of the role')[44] but, as the *Musical Courier* pointed out: 'It is never fair to judge Caruso in the final estimate when he essays a role for the first time. [He] showed he understands fully its sonorous requirements and he fulfilled them admirably reserving his final vocal graces for the lyrical episodes and saving himself artistically for the resonant climaxes.'[45] 'In short, his Jean is as successful as his Samson vocally and, without reserve, a deeply moving achievement.'[46]

He appeared as Avito in *L'Amore dei tre re* on March 14. *Lodoletta* may have been a poor thing musically but it was composed in a lyrical style to suit the singer, whereas, notwithstanding its musical beauties, *L'Amore dei tre re* was a wholly different kettle of fish, involving the singers in more combative duties with the orchestra. Caruso only undertook Avito on five occasions, and whether he was suffering from a cold, as some journalists surmised, or whether the role induced one, he did not attempt it again. As Max Smith noted, '[He] could hardly be heard through the din of the orchestra';[47] *Plays and Players* thought that 'Caruso labors with the music of Avito [but] it does not suit him';[48] and the *Tribune* felt it was 'a pity that [he] was in far from good voice, with the result that the exquisite love duet became an exceedingly one-sided affair.'[49]

One day that spring he found time to make a journey down town to the Custom House on Lower Broadway to pay his taxes straight across the counter to the commissioner, and not to have an argument with him. He produced his check for almost $60,000, nearly six months before it was due.

On April 5 he played an unfamiliar role, without singing a note, when he became godfather to the son of Fernando Tanara, a well-known accompanist and singing teacher. It was on this occasion at the Tanaras' that Caruso became better acquainted with Dorothy Benjamin, whom he had met only once before.

Perhaps it was not entirely a coincidence, therefore, that, for the first time, that year he did not make his customary summer journey outside the United States but remained working in New York, making sundry concert appearances there and in its purlieus. He received no fee for most of these, since they were charitable occasions, but on July 27, at Ocean Grove, New Jersey, he earned $6,639, a percentage of the takings from an auditorium that accommodated between ten and twelve thousand persons. Here he sang 'Celeste Aida', Rossini's 'La danza', Tosti's 'Addio', 'Vesti la giubba', the duet 'Sento una forza' from Gomes's *Il Guarany* with the American lyric soprano Carolina White, and afterwards he undertook sixteen encores, one of which was the popular war ballad, George M. Cohan's 'Over there', which he was singing for the first time. On August 17, at another out-of-town concert at Saratoga, he was assisted by Nina Morgana, a 'coloratura' soprano, who would later marry his secretary, Zirato.

But that summer Caruso was principally preoccupied making movies. A fee of $100,000 proved irresistible, and between July 15 and September 30, he agreed to make a couple. The first, *My Cousin*, had him playing two roles. But hardly surprisingly – it was *silent!* – the reception was equivocal. It was unfortunate that he did not, as was originally planned, play Canio in a film of Leoncavallo's *Pagliacci*, for had he mimed 'Vesti la giubba' or 'No! Pagliacci non son!' these excerpts might at least have been dubbed with his records. One wonders what Jesse Lasky, the film's director, was thinking of; phonograph records of Pavlova dancing or Picasso painting could hardly have been less revealing. Needless to say, his second film, *A Splendid Romance*, was released only in Europe and South America.

CHAPTER XV

1918–1919

IT WAS on August 20, 1918, that Caruso married Dorothy Park Benjamin.

Her social background was radically different from his. She was the youngest child of a family of old New Yorkers. Her father, a typical 'wasp', sometime editor of *The Scientific American*, was a writer and a successful patent lawyer; her mother was an invalid who had been obliged to live away from New York. After Caruso's death Dorothy wrote two biographies: in an earlier account, *Wings of Song*, published in 1928, she collaborated with her stepsister, Mrs Torrance Goddard, but the second, entitled *Enrico Caruso*, published in 1947, is entirely her own work. There are a number of differences between them – more a comment on her than on him. In both volumes she tells how, after her sisters had married and left home, she had not been inclined to take her domestic duties very seriously, and her father had had to secure the services of an ex-governess who had been employed in the family of his brother. She was a young Italian, Anna Bolchi, who had come to America to study singing, and after some persuasion Mr Benjamin agreed to pay for her lessons in return for her taking charge of his housekeeping. It was shortly after Miss Bolchi began to live with the Benjamins that Dorothy was stricken with a throat complaint, so Miss Bolchi took her to Dr Marafioti, a leading specialist who looked after Caruso and many other opera singers. And it was at his house that Dorothy went to a tea-party given in the tenor's honor. On that occasion they did not exchange more than the usual pleasantries. At the end of the afternoon Caruso offered to drive Miss Bolchi and Dorothy home and, when he discovered that she had left her gloves behind, in a gallant gesture, he insisted that she should take his instead.

It was not for several more years, when Dorothy had grown up, that she went with Miss Bolchi to the christening party at the Tanaras' and there met Caruso again. She tells how 'he raised his eyes and saw me, and stood looking at me [as] he came on upstairs toward me. We both knew from that moment that our lives would be united. . . . Strange as it may seem, from that time until we were engaged to be married we rarely spoke to each other and were never left alone together.'¹ After that, Caruso accepted an invitation from Miss Bolchi and came to dine at the Benjamins' home; but it was not until after several more visits that they were ever alone. Caruso had taken Dorothy, her father and Miss Bolchi out for a drive in his new car – such things were still novelties then – and he was on the point of returning to the Knickerbocker. Dorothy had been invited to a friend's house, so he offered to drop her off there on his way home. No sooner were they in the car together than he proposed marriage. She accepted, but they decided it would be better to keep their engagement secret for a short while until his affairs in Italy had been settled (the war was still on) and the Villa Bellosguardo put in order. Caruso then went to ask for her hand formally from her father. At first, so she relates in both biographies, he raised no objections – perhaps he was too surprised. Then there are some differences. In *Wings of Song* she declares that '[her father] would change completely and would not speak to us or notice us in any way, [for] unknown to himself or any of his family, he was suffering from the beginning of the illness that later caused his death'.² But by the time she wrote *Enrico Caruso*, much later in life after two more marriages – both unsuccessful – she looks back to the far-off halcyon days of her youth, to a world peopled by heroes and villains. Her father she portrays as 'unreasonable, blustering and egotistical'³ and she seems to have grown jealous of Miss Bolchi's ability to divert, pacify and argue with him and to interest him in her own country, as well as to invite her friends to dine. When Miss Bolchi learned of their engagement, according to *Enrico Caruso*, she became highly indignant, claiming she was in love with Caruso herself. She was determined to thwart their marriage. So she went straight to Mr Benjamin and told him it would be unthinkable that she should remain with him unchaperoned under his roof. This, of course, obliged him to find a way of repudiating his initial agreement to the marriage, so he told Dorothy that she must demand of Caruso an immediate cash settlement of half a million dollars. Dorothy was so upset by this that she decided to go at once to the Knickerbocker and ask Caruso what she should do. Although she did not tell her father, she took Miss Bolchi with her, or so she says; but it does seem a little hard to believe that Miss Bolchi should have gone with Dorothy and not told Mr

Benjamin. Perhaps it was that, by the time Dorothy wrote *Enrico Caruso*, she felt that the story would sound more respectable if she took a duenna with her and did not spend a night without escort in New York. At any rate, the next morning Dorothy and Caruso were married at the Marble Collegiate Church, Fifth Avenue. Mr Benjamin never forgave his daughter and a short time later, without notifying any of his family, he adopted Miss Bolchi and, following the death of Dorothy's mother, made her the sole legatee of his estate.

By the autumn of 1918, war fever increasingly preoccupied Caruso: one can understand how relieved he must have felt when the United States came in on the same side as Italy. He was free, when his regular operatic engagements permitted, to participate in a whole catalog of appearances to help raise money for war charities. He journeyed out to Sheepshead Bay speedway track in the New York suburbs on August 31 for a police games benefit in company with Dorothy; this was his first post-marital engagement and an overwhelming reception from an audience of more than 125,000 crowded into the grandstand greeted husband and wife. The company also included McCormack, Amato and Anna Fitziú; and no other event, it was stated, took as much money – more than $300,000 was raised. The weather was hot and sunny and it is from this occasion that the first photographs of Caruso actually singing survive: he was wearing a red tie, white trousers and blue jacket. His program included the 'Inno di Garibaldi' and Cohan's 'Over there'. Three days later he appeared at the Shubert Theater at a San Carlo Company's *Aida* and he received the ovation of the evening, though he was not singing – just sitting in a box. In the course of the next couple of months he headed the bill at a number of war benefits. On Lafayette Day, September 6, he sang 'La Marseillaise' at the Waldorf Astoria before Thomas Masaryk, who was to become first President of the newly-established Czechoslovakia. At the Century Theater for the Tank Corps on September 15 he repeated 'Over there' and led a starry cast of many celebrated names, among them Al Jolson, George M. Cohan and Sophie Tucker, who remembers the occasion in her autobiography. Four nights afterwards in Central Park, at a people's open-air concert at which he gave his services, more than 50,000 heard him sing. At the end, the band played an orchestral composition of Caruso's, the march 'Liberty forever'. On September 30, at Carnegie Hall, for the Allied Music Division of the Liberty

Loan, a glittering quartet – Caruso, Galli-Curci, Heifetz and McCormack – helped raise the colossal sum of $4 million. He contributed five solos, including an English version of the 'Inno di Garibaldi' entitled 'Victory! Victory!', with words translated by Dorothy. On October 5 at Madison Square Gardens, he opened the National Motion Picture Exposition, having stipulated that half the contributions should go to the Italian Red Cross.

In the midst of this welter of charity appearances he was to give only three performances for his own benefit. The first time, at Buffalo, however, had to be postponed at the last minute, as a result of an epidemic of Spanish 'flu – not because he caught it, but because nearly everyone else did. So, instead, he gave an impromptu concert at his hotel to help raise money for the Liberty Loan. After another charity gala at the Metropolitan, he sang the next time for his own benefit, at the Arcadia Theater, Detroit, on October 15. On that occasion he went alone to undertake Canio, for Dorothy had been stricken by the 'flu. The local impresario had originally wanted him for a concert, but Caruso had not been keen; it was too far away, he said, so he asked $7,000, thinking this would shy him off. But it proved perfectly acceptable. He then demanded that his fee be put in escrow, but to this too no objections were raised. So he insisted it could not be a concert, it must be a performance of *Pagliacci*. The impresario was delighted as Canio was Caruso's *chef d'œuvre* and he assented with alacrity. At the event, which 5,000 attended, the cast was completed with Muzio and Amato, and Giorgio Polacco conducted a local orchestra and semi-professional chorus. Back in New York on November 3, he sang in a couple of concerts on the same day: in the morning at Madison Square Garden in aid of the U.S. Naval Relief Society and in the evening at the Hippodrome in aid of the United War Work Campaign. His last appearance before the Met resumed once again was for his own benefit at the Biltmore on the 8th, in a company that included Galli-Curci, Alda, Martinelli and John O'Sullivan.

The season opened on Armistice Day, November 11, 1918. Caruso's Samson brought the house down and the evening was a clamorous occasion culminating in handfuls of confetti being added to the tumbling pillars. After the final curtain he re-emerged and led the company in 'The Star Spangled Banner', the 'Inno di Garibaldi', 'La Marseillaise' and 'God Save the King', and 'what boots it if the veracious chronicler declared that Caruso betrayed a patriot-fatigued larynx'.⁴ His next appearance, on the 15th, was a new role for him –

Alvaro in Verdi's *La Forza del destino*. Like *Le Prophète* this marked another stage in his dramatic evolution. 'Caruso's interpretation can be summarised in the word 'wonderful'.[5] 'He interpreted the role as it should be interpreted, robustly. He was the impetuous soldier, the ardent lover. [It] was a stirring impersonation.'[6] 'All of his singing was good, some of it, especially in the scene where he is wounded, was exquisite.'[7] The role of Leonora, originally to have been sung by Muzio, was undertaken by Rosa Ponselle, a new young American dramatic soprano. Thereafter came *L'Elisir d'amore* and *Le Prophète*, affording quite a contrast in styles. 'It is a far cry from Italian opera to John of Leyden, but not too far for this master of them all, who was dramatic in effect and splendid of voice. Impressive in appearance and acting finely, he roused his audience frequently to a typical frenzy.'[8] 'He sang with a perfection of art, of beauty, of taste that makes praise a vain thing. Such legato, such phrasing and such purity and richness of tone as marked his delivery of the scene in the inn must be the goal of singing.'[9] On December 1 he appeared at a Sunday Afternoon Vaudeville Show given at the Manhattan Opera House for 4,500 soldiers, sailors and marines. On the 6th at a Biltmore Friday Morning Musicale in company with Marguerite Namara his program included Cesti's 'Intorno all'idol mio', Sgambati's arrangement of the Italian folk song 'Separazione', Carissimi's 'Vittoria, vittoria', the air 'Echo lointain de ma jeunesse' from *Eugène Onéguine*, Uterhart's 'Romance', Seismit-Doda's 'Dream' and Silesu's 'Star of my life', and to these he added Buzzi-Peccia's 'Povero Pulcinella', Alvarez's 'A Granada', Rossini's 'La danza', Sibella's 'Désir', Tosti's 'Pour un baiser' and Leoncavallo's 'Serenata', with Salvatore Fucito his accompanist. That Caruso was never completely at his ease at this kind of recital and always liked to have the music handy was confirmed by an incident that took place; apparently the stage was not lit sufficiently for him, and at one point he had a standard lamp brought on to shed a stronger light on his copy of the songs.

At the Metropolitan during that autumn he also sang Lionello, Flammen in *Lodoletta* and Canio – 'when he was in splendid voice and high spirits . . . Never has the-greatest-tenor-of-them-all held an audience so completely in the palm of his hand. When he grinned, it grinned as well, when he frolicked, it guffawed and applauded; and when he sobbed – oh! when he sobbed, it held its breath and thrilled to the tones of that golden voice of his. It fairly shrieked itself hoarse over "Vesti la giubba" – in joyous surprise, one might think, that it could sound the same as it has sounded so interminably on the Victrola.'[10] On December 23, he took part in another of Mr Bagby's Musical Matinées at the Waldorf Astoria and on Christmas Day, as usual, he went down to the Met to distribute $2,000 in ten and twenty dollar gold pieces to members of the chorus, stage assistants and others, as well as scarf pins of differing designs to every member of the staff.

During a performance of *Samson* no fewer than eleven newspapers were quick to report an accident he suffered: while the stage was in darkness, as he rushed down the steps of Dalila's residence, his foot caught on a step and he fell heavily; the house physician was summoned for Caruso had cut his knee badly. But he did not miss the next performance; as the *Evening Journal* recorded: 'He cut his knee [and] not his golden throat . . . and he declined to permit an injury to his "pedal" to interfere with his *vox humana*.'[11]

On New Year's Day, 1919, the Carusos were 'at home' at the Knickerbocker. More than a thousand friends and acquaintances in society, in musical, social and dramatic circles, responded to their invitation. The entire second floor with its ballrooms, foyers and series of salons, extending along the Forty-second Street and Broadway fronts, was decorated with palms grouped in the corners of rooms, while tall vases with flowers added touches of contrasting color. Two orchestras played melodies from the classics and ragtime, for those who wished to dance the latest foxtrots and one-steps. Dorothy remembers how 'Enrico and I stood under a bower of roses, shaking hands with everyone and receiving their wishes for happiness. I thought all the strangers were his friends and he thought they were mine: later we discovered that neither of us knew any of them!'[12] On January 3 the police were round at the Knickerbocker – but only on a friendly visit. They were there to make him an honorary captain in the New York force, a thank-you present for his songs at their games benefit at Sheepshead Bay the previous August. 'As the gold medal was pinned on his coat he asked the commissioner, "Can I arrest people now?" He was told he could. "Then I must go to the Metropolitan right away. I will play a funny on Mr Gatti."'[13] By this time, as Key assures us, 'he [spoke] English with a trace of a foreign accent to be sure, yet with none of that exaggeration which is sometimes inexactly put into his mouth. One should remember that Caruso has been living [in New York] for fifteen years.'[14]

On the 7th, in the *Telegraph* there appeared a comparative

appraisal of Caruso's art in an article entitled 'Leave Caruso Alone' by Nicola Gigliotto, a sometime critic of the Neapolitan *l'Occhialetto*:

> Caruso is a unique artist and he stands absolutely by himself. De Lucia, in spite of very limited vocal powers, succeeded in becoming one of the great tenors of the last generation. Bonci would have been, too, if he had not been as cold as an icicle and I have heard Gayarré, Marconi, Stagno and de Reszke, who made up a glorious constellation, but the voice of Caruso has all the good traits of theirs. True, Lázaro's upper register is wonderful and he may develop into a great singer, but so far he is quite far from being one. His voice is not even and his lower register can stand some improvement. To herald him as the greatest tenor since Rubini is ridiculous. Caruso, in spite of his forty-five years, is unique as a tenor. The quality of his voice is even, warm, perfect, round and rich from the lowest to the highest register. He is in a place by himself that admits of no comparison.[15]

That Caruso was indeed someone special may be noted by just how much his income tax bill had soared: in 1918 he paid out $154,000, nearly three times as much as he had the previous year. In those last years of his career, as his income began to escalate, so his investments became increasingly manifold and he acquired a prodigious collection of works of art. This had begun modestly enough in 1904 with stamps, then rare gold coins, finally *objets d'art*. As his wife described it: 'To walk through his collection was to move through an atmosphere of romance that opened the heart and stirred the imagination with its remembrance of the great ages of the world.'[16] At the sale of the Pierpont Morgan collection he had managed to acquire some choice bronzes and enamels. Afterwards he bought a few fine bas-reliefs, including one by a fifteenth century master; after his death this was for a time hung in the Caruso chapel at the Cimitero del pianto in Naples. He also made a choice selection of antique snuff boxes which were worth more than $60,000. There were delicately wrought silver and gold ones, studded with precious stones, or graced with some exquisite miniature of a lady of the court of the period of Louis XIV or XV. Among the more curious were two quaint Japanese snuff boxes with glass stoppers and one with an unusual uncut amethyst. Magnificent, too, was a Marie Antoinette medallion, once thought to have adorned the neck of the Queen herself. In the center was a painting after the style of Gainsborough encircled with diamonds and turquoises.

On March 2 he took part in a concert at Ann Arbor, Michigan, but it was hardly over when he received a summons from Kahn which sent him racing back to New York to sing 'The Star Spangled Banner' on the evening President Wilson came to the Metropolitan to deliver his League of Nations address. The tenor's train, however, did not arrive until 7.45 p.m. and he only just got to the theater in time. Less than three weeks later, on the 22nd, he celebrated the twenty-fifth anniversary of his operatic debut at a Met gala. (Actually, Caruso's debut had taken place on March 15, 1895, and so on March 22, 1919 he was really celebrating the twenty-fourth anniversary of his operatic debut.) The program included an act each out of *L'Elisir d'amore*, *Pagliacci* and *Le Prophète*. It was Kahn who addressed Caruso afterwards:

> When offering you the tribute of our admiration, it is not the glory of your voice which I have in mind primarily, though it is the most perfect and glorious voice of a generation, for having heard you posterity will envy us. But in your case we admire the voice, the art and the man. I have in mind your boundless generosity, your modesty, kindliness and simplicity, your unfailing consideration for others. Bearing a name which has become a household word throughout the world, you have retained the plain human qualities of a man and a gentleman, which have won you the affection of those whose privilege it is to know you personally.[17]

During the remainder of that season he undertook Radames and a solitary Don José, as well as singing Rodolfo for the last time in his career in Philadelphia with Muzio: 'He was in voice and sang beautifully, barring a slight tendency to 'scoop' some of his higher notes, but he carried off the music both vocally and dramatically so well that this slip can hardly be noticed.'[18]

It would be wrong to assume that this so-called 'scooping' or 'slurring', for which Caruso was increasingly criticised in the later years of his career, represented some marked deterioration in his singing technique. Doubtless there were occasions, such as the opening night of the Met season in 1917, when he was obviously fatigued after a strenuous South American tour and was obliged to reach for high notes, but that is another matter. By the end of the second decade of the twentieth century the romantic style of perform-ance was fast going out of fashion, and the liberal use of portamento had been one of its basic ingredients; it is not surprising, therefore, to find it referred to slightingly. The introduction of the phonograph and the ready availability of Caruso's records made it easy for the next generation to copy much of his vocal style and yet at the same time ignore this salient feature of his art: the perfection of the relationship between his legato and portamento. It was crucial to his technique; it enabled his singing, one might say, to speak eloquently. It was the logical extension of Maria Celloni's axiom – 'Chi sa respirare, sa cantare'[19] (He who knows how to breathe, knows how to sing). This fundamental concept was what writers from Giustiniani to Burney had meant by portamento, not, as the term is too often used today, simply to indicate an ornament in just a narrow sense, nor to imply a slipshod attack. 'By portamento', Pier Francesco Tosi writes, 'I mean the passing and blending of the voice from one tone to another with perfect proportion in descending as well as ascending phrases.'[20] It continues by implication through passages where the singer does not join notes obviously, yet he could do so if he wished, for the voice is so limpid and perfectly placed. As with so many other vocal devices it came to be copied by violinists from Paganini, or simulated by pianists such as Liszt, so as to give to their art its maximum eloquence. Today it can still be heard on any number of recordings made by instrumentalists as well as singers at the beginning of this century – perhaps most potently from the violinist Fritz Kreisler, whose fiddling is so telling we almost expect it to break into words. Nor was it merely confined to soloists; in the later nineteenth century it was the modish basis of music making – as a glance at the scores of Mahler symphonies or Strauss tone poems reveals. It survives too on recordings, most expressively on those made by Willem Mengelberg and the Concertgebouw Orchestra, in music of Brahms and Tchaikovsky as well as Mahler and Strauss. (Both Mahler and Strauss dedicated works to Mengelberg, and they were also conductors of consequence.) He preserved the portamento style – if we can so dignify it – even on recordings he made into the 1940s.

Caruso's records provide us with many perfect examples. In the duet 'Solo, profugo' from *Marta* he begins the phrases with portamento underlying them, and yet only occasionally does he link tones, though this is implicit throughout all his singing, and the tension in the phrasing does not slacken even if he draws a breath. His voice is so free and easily produced he can introduce portamento with varying shades of intensity, singing it lightly or very markedly, according to the width of the interval and the speed of the music. It is interesting to compare him with the other singer, Journet, for they echo similar musical phrases. By today's standards, doubtless, Journet seems a revelation of a smooth and expressive *bel canto* bass; yet, heard in duet with Caruso, certain limitations become apparent. Journet's singing may be limpid but it is not poised on the breath, so it does not flow freely in the way Caruso's does, which is what the portamento style is all about.

Four more titles from *Marta* were recorded consecutively on January 7, 1912, and each of these has the same perfect legato and portamento. One of them, the *notturno* 'Dormi pur', is an ineffable creation. Towards the end his restatement of the melody, its line limpidly drawn and eloquently shaped, shows how to convey to the fullest sentiment and yet not sentimentality. On the same day he also recorded Fauré's 'Crucifix', notable for a high B natural, tremendously attacked – yet 'attacked' is not the right word, for he seems merely to open his mouth and the note is there, without glottal betrayal. Then comes one of his finest records, the trio 'Qual voluttà' from *I Lombardi*. He takes it at a leisurely pace – andantino, the score says – shaping the phrasing expressively and creating an impression of grandeur. Journet and Alda both make a fine effect too, but they have little of Caruso's dynamic range and he sings rings round them, even on an acoustic record. Towards the end he embellishes his music and on the repeated phrase 'tu lo schiudesti a me!' he joins Alda in a full-voiced climax and, as if by some *léger de voix* on the repeated high Bs, it seems to be his voice that rises an octave above hers; then, by contrast, in the next phrase, he produces a *piano* note, much softer than anything Alda attempts, yet still projecting with consummate ease. Those who know this trio from this recording alone will probably be surprised to hear it performed these days without Caruso's *oppure* and shorn of ritards and portamento, and they are unlikely to recognize it until it is half way through. It is an interesting comment on the standards of that day that Caruso, Alda and Journet should sing this piece so freely and so musically yet show such complete unanimity in their mastery of the style – and only on this occasion, for there is no record of any of them ever having sung it before.

That Caruso's art was ever dynamic and in a constant state of change becomes plainly evident if we compare this group of recordings made in 1912 with those of another session that he essayed seven and a half years later. By this time his voice has grown darker and the instrument more resplendent, much of which had to do with his being caught up in the rapidly accelerating development of opera in those last years of verismo. The phonograph had established Caruso's art as a precursor of the changes then implicit in the style. In the last years of his life, before the introduction of the microphone, the pressure to live up to the enormous acclaim generated by his records caused him to undertake an increasing number of tours through the United States, singing before vast popular audiences not only in the restricted circumstances of concert halls but at improvised routs held at all sorts of places, including speedway tracks and cow palaces.

At the session on September 11, 1919, he sang a number of songs which he seems never to have sung publicly, including Fucito's 'Scordame', de Curtis's 'Senza nisciuno' and Bracco's 'Serenata' (to words he wrote himself), as well as the aria 'Mia piccirella' from Gomes's *Salvator Rosa*. This is written for a soprano and he transposes it down a ninth. It is remarkable for its fine finish and polished rubato. The formidable run at the end to a climactic high B flat displays that complete sense of security discernible in every detail of his art by this stage of his career. In Bracco's 'Serenata' we get some clue as to what the Philadelphia critic was alluding when he noted Caruso's tendency to scoop. This song is notable for a rising phrase – E, E sharp, F sharp, G sharp and A – which may not be exactly effortless, yet his singing is supremely accomplished and the effect overwhelming. As his voice ascends he covers the tone, contriving a great arch of sound, and, when he reaches the top, the climax, he lets out an exultant snarl; this is an increasingly more common device on his later recordings. To describe it as scooping, however, betrays not so much Caruso's fallibility as the changing critical standards of the day.

Caruso as a young man. He often related the story of how he was photographed, at his hotel at Trapani in Sicily in 1896, draped toga-like in a bedspread. He claimed his shirt was drying on the line.

Caruso's birthplace, now above a sweet shop, much the same today as it was in 1 in the crowded back streets of Naples.

Caruso (*left*) with friends in Luigi Denza's garden in Hampstead, London, in 1 Also in the picture are Scotti and Tirindelli.

As Nemorino in Donizetti's
L'Elisir d'amore.

As Don José in Bizet's *Carmen*.

As the Duke in Verdi's *Rigoletto*.

As Enzo in Ponchielli's *La Gioconda*.

Caruso as Radames in Verdi's *Aida*, in a photograph by Mishkin and as he saw himse:
in his own sketch.

Caricatures by Caruso of himself: as Julien in Charpentier's *Julien*, in Toronto in 190
and in London in 1913.

uso as Dick Johnson, the role he created in Puccini's *La Fanciulla del West*, in 1912 at the Metropolitan.

Titta Ruffo, Enrico Caruso and Feodor Chaliapin. The only time the three artists were por
together, painted by Tadè Styka, Paris, 1912.

On the S.S. *Canopic*, from Naples to Boston, 1914. Caruso is in the centre, near the fron
group. Among a large contingent of artists from the Met are Arturo Toscanini, Ge
Farrar, Elisabeth Schumann, Amelita Galli-Curci and Lucrezia Bori with the Director,
Gatti-Casazza.

so with his wife, Dorothy, and daughter, Gloria, on S.S. *Presidente Wilson*, in May, 1921.

On the balcony of the Hotel Vittoria, Sorrento. July, 1921, one of the last photographs taken of Caruso.

CHAPTER XVI

1919–1920

THAT SPRING Dorothy went to St Patrick's Cathedral to be baptised a Roman Catholic, and then she and Caruso could be married again according to the Roman rite.

On April 2, with Garden, Elman and Rubinstein, Caruso took part in a musical evening held to commemorate the opening of the Commodore Hotel. On the 7th, six months after his first visit to Buffalo when the 'flu epidemic had prevented his singing, he made an appearance at the Auditorium. He was driven out to see Niagara Falls, 'where he bought a china shop out of business – took the entire shop – and his comment was, "if I come to this city and ask people to pay me $7,000, I have to leave something for the merchants."'[1] He declined an invitation to return to Boston that year – after the critical reception he had determined not to go again – but he made his customary trip to Atlanta for three operas. There, at the instigation of Mrs Caruso, on April 25, he went out to the Morris Brown University. He was described by the President of the Theological Seminary 'as a man whose body is strung together from head to toe with silver chords which, when played on by the wings of friendship, give forth music that make the angels stoop to listen'.[2] The student choir saluted the king of song, singing number after number of haunting Negro melodies, including 'Every time I feel the spirit', 'My Lord, what a morning!', 'Deep river', 'Soldiers of the cross' and 'Swing low, sweet chariot'. So great was the effect they created that Caruso at once despatched Zirato in a hurry to procure him some music, and he was able to reply, singing for them Tosti's ''A vucchella', Duparc's 'Extase' and Fatuo's 'Sento che t'amo'.

At this time an offer came from Cleofonte Campanini, Director of the Chicago Opera, to sing Canio with them that autumn, and he was offered $5,000 a performance – twice his Met fee. He took the proposal at once to Gatti-Casazza who, not surprisingly, intimated that he should not accept; Caruso thereupon wrote a note to Campanini declining the offer. From Atlanta he proceeded to Nashville, where he commenced a concert tour taking in eight other cities as well, including Saint Louis, Kansas City, Saint Paul, Chicago, Milwaukee, Canton, Newark and Springfield. The *Kansas City Times* had not heard him for twelve years and

> since that time his art has become almost entirely remodelled. His style today is very much more refined. There is not the prodigality of tone that used to thrill audiences and cause some critics to predict an early end to [his] career . . . but, unlike most adventures in penuriousness, Caruso has the effect of enriching those with whom he deals. The audiences are gainers rather than losers through his restraint. The baritone quality which has always been a striking characteristic of his voice was more in evidence than in the past. There has never been a robust tenor with more resonance and power in his deepest notes. But there has been no sacrifice of beauty. Rather has the effect of musical beauty been increased by the singer's new habit of restraint. His *mezza voce* is intensively lovely in quality, and in his high notes, whether sung softly or forte, there is the old magic quality that many know as 'the golden tone'.[3]

Straight after the concert tour was finished, Caruso set sail for Italy and for the first time he took Dorothy with him. She has left us an account of life that summer at the Villa Bellosguardo.[4] There she came to meet for the first time his Italian family: his stepmother, brother, sons, nephew and niece, a total *dramatis personae* of more than twenty people. His stepmother was an intensely religious old lady of seventy-five with beautiful white hair who spoke Neapolitan with such a thick accent that even Caruso had difficulty understanding her. She worshipped him but distrusted everyone else and hated his brother Giovanni – Dorothy has nothing nice to say of him either. In character she could find no resemblance between them, for Enrico was open and good but Giovanni closed and false. Fofo, Caruso's elder son, was twenty-one. He had been a private in the army and was still in uniform, and he too left an unfortunate impression on her; she can only recall his sitting at table weeping bitterly. Caruso's younger son, Mimmi, was a large lad of nearly fourteen, dressed in a sailor suit and always accompanied by his governess, Miss Saer. He succeeded in ingratiating himself with Dorothy – he spoke English; though he had not been allowed to mix with other children, he had spent most of his childhood in London. By that time his voice was breaking and he had a slight mustache. Dorothy decided he had been in the governess's care quite long enough and she persuaded his father to let him come back to America with them.

During the stay at his villa Caruso studied Eléazar in Halévy's *La Juive*, which he was to sing for the first time next season at the Metropolitan. In the mornings he would work in the music room with his accompanist, Bruno Bruni, and then in the afternoons amuse himself building the scenery for an enormous *crèche* for which he had bought some five or six hundred figurines some years before in Paris. They were more than two hundred years old and were dressed in costumes made by the ladies-in-waiting of the Queen of Naples. The stage for this had been built in a room next to the chapel and Dorothy tells how she 'couldn't stay [there] long without feeling ill [from the] hot fish glue, [for] even with the doors and windows open the fumes were overpowering'. Outside, beyond the villa and park with its pools, statues, formal gardens and long vistas of cypress trees, Italy was in a state of turmoil. The country was on the verge of financial collapse, and there was widespread failure of social discipline, which would culminate in 1922 in the march on Rome and the seizure of power by Mussolini. Before the war the men had always worked late in the vineyards, cultivating grapes, and the women and girls were never seen without a package of straws under one arm and a strip of braid running through their fingers, busily weaving the fine Leghorn hats that were famous throughout the world. But by 1919 all this had changed dramatically, as Caruso himself was made aware when a hundred and fifty neighbours came to the villa gates.

I went and spoke with them and they told me with tears in their eyes that they had been without wine and cheese throughout the war. So I opened the gates and bade them enter. They covered the lawn and I had wine and cheese brought out to them and they feasted and we were all very happy. And then they went away. But on the next day they were back, twice as many of them, and they showed me papers with ribbons and seals on them and they told me to read. The papers showed that the leaders were representatives of what we now call in Italy the public commissary, with power to confiscate all surplus food and wine. I protested. I temporised, I said I would sing to them. And I did. I sang as well as I could and they applauded tremendously. Then they broke down the gates. They swarmed through my house. They carried away twenty-seven demi-johns of wine, a hogshead of olive oil and four Virginia hams. They were very happy and very rough, but very polite. My wife averted one tragedy. They were about to take all my chickens also, and wring their necks and cook them. The chickens were my wife's pets. Many of them she had named; she pleaded with the crowd and her Italian became quite eloquent. The people were moved. They relented and the chickens were saved.[5]

And they did at least leave Caruso his car so that he and his wife were eventually able to reach Genoa, where they took a boat to New York.

Nearly two weeks after his return to America, he departed to undertake a season of opera in Mexico City. On this occasion, for the first time since they were married, Dorothy did not accompany him, for she was pregnant. Mexico was another country going through political crisis. Its generally bad reputation for bandits had encouraged the government to take no chances, and from his arrival at Santillo, almost five hundred miles north of Mexico City, Caruso's train was accompanied by a posse of fifty soldiers. Every effort was made to secure his comfort and a house was booked for him for the season. Four days after his arrival, on September 26, a special performance was organized at the Teatro Arbeu, where Mexican members of the opera company were assembled to sing and be reviewed by Caruso, 'to prove to him,' so says José Mojica, 'that he would not be appearing with inferior, provincial talent.'[6] The producers had been unselective, however, and many of the artists were forced to retire from the stage amidst a barrage of jeers, ribald comments and whistles. But Caruso thought that at least some of the singers did have 'nice, beautiful voices'.[7] Three nights later he made his Mexican debut at the Esperanza Iris as Nemorino in L'Elisir d'amore and a variety of newspaper reviews square well with his own opinion of the performance.

> The success last night was plain. At the beginning I was nervous, and the public was excited; and you could hear a fly moving in the theater. I sang my first little aria ['Quanto è bella!'] with great emotion. What explosion! Everybody was crazy and we stop awhile. My heart nearly stop to beat. When we went on we had the public with us. I never heard such a big noise after my big aria ['Una furtiva lagrima'] even at the Metropolitan. Hats, handkerchiefs, coats waved like banners. For nearly ten minutes they applauded – five calls for encores – but I could not, as my nerves were so excited. I am glad because they like me. I feel so happy.[8]

The impresario, José del Rivera, had a doubtful financial reputation.[9] Earlier that year a company he had brought to Mexico City led by Ruffo had failed to draw the public – Ruffo had wanted too much money and he bankrupted del Rivera. Nevertheless del Rivera had no difficulty finding a consortium of guarantors for his Caruso season, but apart from Gabriella Besanzoni, who was in the grand tradition of Italian contraltos, the other singers were all deplorable. At the next opera, *Un Ballo in maschera*, Gennaro Papi, who was the only conductor, refused to direct, so it was put into the hands of a repetiteur. Caruso was understandably nervous, for he had not undertaken Riccardo for more than three years, but in the event he enjoyed a considerable success, and he hauled out the rest of the cast at the end of the acts, so that they might enjoy a little of the applause. The third opera, *Carmen*, with Besanzoni, took place in the bull ring in front of 22,000 spectators. The weather in Mexico City is peculiarly changeable and during the performance clouds rolled up and the heavens opened, but the people stayed put. As Caruso recalls: 'Thousands of umbrellas opened up and cover all the area of the plaza. We don't see any heads or hear the orchestra,'[10] yet the opera continued without interruption to the end. But, at the next open-air performance, *Un Ballo in maschera*, 'the clouds open and wather come down as storm. . . . We stay . . . for half an hour and the public was there with umbrellas and overcoats on the head. When I saw [this] I went out . . . and ask . . . the public . . . "Watte we go to do?" They answer me, "Go home". . . . I think it is the first time in my artistic career that I bring home some money without work!'[11]

There were also two performances of *Samson et Dalila* (one at the Esperanza and the other in the bull ring) and these revealed to his Mexican audiences yet another aspect of his art, for 'Caruso sang in French, though it is better to say that he sang in the French style, with all the virtuosity of that school. It is a new proof of the adaptability of his talent.'[12] For *Marta*, his next opera at the Esperanza, the frenetic audience was in its place nearly an hour before the curtain rose. 'Caruso earned the most emotional ovation yet heard in Mexico and he received six curtain calls after "M'apparì".'[13] It was during this performance that his presence of mind saved the day: he noticed that the soprano, who was to sing 'The last rose of summer', had forgotten to bring one with her. He whispered, 'Take a rose from your hat and give it to me.' But she paid no heed. So instead of the words in the score he sang 'Gi-i-ve m-e-ee the r-o-ose, t-a-ake o-o-ne fr-o-om y-our h-a-at.'[14] Still she did not understand. Whereupon Caruso plucked a flower from her hat, placed it in her hand, then smilingly received it back from her. The reception was equally overwhelming after his Canio, Radames and des Grieux in *Manon Lescaut*. He made his last appearance on November 2 in the bull ring in an act each out of *L'Elisir*, *Marta* and *Pagliacci*.

Throughout his entire stay in Mexico he was constantly troubled by the altitude: Mexico City is 9,000 feet above sea-level, and this often has a deleterious effect on a visitor. He seems to realize something of this when he complains, in a letter to Dorothy: 'During the night I had the idea to cut my nek and let go out the blood! I don't know if this pain, so strong, is the effect of the weather.'[15]

Although at that time he was still robust, photographs show him beginning to look middle-aged.[16] Any personal criticism levelled against him as a young man had long been obliterated under the softening influences of an inner growth and quietude. His own assiduous love of hard work made him a severe taskmaster, demanding the utmost of every member of his staff – it was enough, in his view, that an employee should be permitted to stay with him. Even in those years Caruso still made it his practice to keep his own books of accounts and to attend to many other seemingly minor matters himself. He insisted on cutting the coupons from his bonds and, indeed, one of his many diversions was to go round with a pair of scissors to his safety deposit box where he kept his securities. His cash credits and debits he would enter himself in his own hand and he would be able to account for every entry made. He bought only government stocks, for he did not care to play the market.

Caruso had been back in New York little more than a week, on November 17, 1919, when he opened the Metropolitan season as Cavaradossi opposite Farrar's Tosca. Apart from the first act of *Pagliacci*, which he sang in a gala to honor the Prince of Wales on his first visit to New York the following evening, Caruso's next appearance was as Eléazar in *La Juive*. This new and final addition to his repertory followed in the heavier and more heroic style of his later undertakings, like Samson and Jean in *Le Prophète*, but unlike these, Eléazar has none of the typically amorous preoccupations of an operatic tenor. Henderson in the *Sun* complimented him on his interpretation: 'He conceived the part in earnest study and he sang and acted it with an art as far removed as possible from that of his more familiar Italian roles. There were dignity and beauty in his cantilena. His chanting in the second act was a lyric utterance of exquisite character, while his delivery of the pealing air of the fourth act

["Rachel, quand du Seigneur"] might have excited the envy of Nourrit himself.'[17] Krehbiel, too, in the *Tribune*, wrote equally enthusiastically. 'A new part must be found for him each year, and Eléazar is a character which gives him an opportunity for the display of his voice and vocal resources. . . . [His] performance was, on the whole, admirable. In Eléazar [he] has found a part both dramatically and vocally extraordinarily suited to him. In face, figure and bearing he makes of this operatic Shylock an interpretation which will remain long in the memory of those who saw it. Indeed, it is perhaps the first time in his career when the greatest tenor has succeeded in giving perfect verisimilitude to a tragic impersonation. And he sang the music with a passion, yet restraint, which revealed only the more exquisitely the golden voice.'[18] It was his culminating achievement at the Metropolitan. He spent some time in the New York Public Library investigating the subject and studying the Shylock-like character of Eléazar, paying particular attention to his costuming. He approached a friend, Mrs Selma Shubart, and asked her to help him obtain a shawl that a rabbi uses when saying his prayers. She obtained for him a white and black silk scarf. He used this in the scene where Eléazar presents the unleavened bread at the ceremony immediately before Princess Eudoxie arrives. And he devoted the same scrupulous attention to every detail throughout the opera.

The rest of that season was made up of a parade of his more familiar undertakings: Canio, Alvaro in *La Forza del destino*, Samson, Lionello, Nemorino, des Grieux in *Manon Lescaut* and Jean in *Le Prophète*. On December 18 his daughter Gloria was born, and when the news reached the Met next evening, at a performance of *L'Elisir d'amore*, appropriately enough, the public greeted him with shouts of 'Long live Papa'. He made his customary appearance for Mr Bagby at the Waldorf on January 19, 1920. The press tried to celebrate his birthday as usual on February 25, but he told the *Sun* that in fact he had not been born until the 27th. During that season at the Metropolitan he went out of town to appear in recitals in Pittsburgh and Waterbury, and on March 28 he took part in an 'Italian loan concert' at the Lexington. Here he sang Tosti's 'A' vucchella' for a man who had purchased $50,000 in bonds. On this occasion he appeared with Riccardo Stracciari and Tetrazzini, and before it she came round to see Caruso. She was suffering from a cold and very apprehensive as to her ability to sing. Caruso took her into the bathroom and sprayed her throat with a mixture of ether and iodoform. Dorothy recalls the occasion: 'I can still see Tetrazzini balancing on the rim of the tub, in full evening dress, while Enrico, wearing his gold-rimmed spectacles, hung over like an anxious owl. As he sprayed she had to pant quickly and not stop for a moment or the ether would have gone down into her lungs and anaesthetised her.'[19] Caruso undertook two further concert engagements at Scranton and Detroit, before making the customary Met postscript of three performances in Atlanta.

That May he accepted an engagement from Adolfo Bracale in Cuba, where he was to earn his highest fee. It was a quarter of a century since last he had sung for Bracale in a season in Cairo. The Cuba company was superior to that of his Mexican adventure and included Maria Barrientos, who was that season at the Met and had been vying with Hempel as the company's leading 'coloratura' soprano, Melis, a verismo soprano, Stracciari, a noted baritone whose career was mostly in Italy, Mardones, the Spanish bass, and Besanzoni.

Caruso was on his way to Havana when a piece of bad news broke. The Knickerbocker was sold. He was very upset and wrote to Dorothy, who was still in New York with Gloria, their five month old daughter, that 'if such things were in [Regan, the manager's] mind before I left for Atlanta he was not kind with me because I [never] had time to pack everything [for] myself.'[20] But there was nothing he could do, for the first night at Havana took place on May 12 with a performance of *Marta*. Although the reception was warm it was at first a little reserved and it was not until he began the duet ('Il suo sguardo è dolce tanto') that 'I went crazy and took my public. I forgot that there [was] a lady singing with me and . . . transport . . . everybody, maestro, orchestra . . . [and] the public. I was obliged to come out . . . five time[s].'[21] It was the same thing, too, with 'Dormi pur', when his singing created no less of an effect. On May 19, directly after *L'Elisir d'amore*, he wrote to Dorothy again:

> My voice was fine, I begin the performance very nicely and at the middle of the duet . . . I took the public . . . the callings were [innumerable]. The second act I amuse [everyone and again there were] many [recalls] at the end. . . . Then came ['Una furtiva lagrima']. I never see such things! It was a storm of clappings . . . at the end of the opera there was a big dimostration. . . . From now on I will make this people go crazy with all the opera which I go to sing next.[22]

But the following performance three nights later of *Un Ballo in maschera*, when he sang as well as ever, the evening was unexpectedly ruined by the Amelia, and Caruso could only lament, 'What work for me!'[23] Thereafter he sang through a typical repertory: he was Canio, and 'everybody is crazy about [me]',[24] Cavaradossi, in which 'Cubans who [have] heard me in New York says that I never sang better',[25] and Don José in *Carmen*, but it was probably as Alvaro in *La Forza del destino* that he enjoyed his most spontaneous success. 'At the moment [when I threw] down the pistol at the end of the first act, the people [backstage] dont shoot, [so] I make a big noise with my mouth like this, BUUUM!!!! and I kill the father of Leonora. You can immagine [how the public laughed. And] six time[s] I was obliged to go out.'[26]

Almost from the time of his arrival in Havana, Bracale had been trying to persuade Caruso to extend his stay and get him to come on down to Puerto Rico, Venezuela and Peru. If he had already made prior engagements at New Orleans and Atlantic City, there was no reason why he should not go there first and come back again; and if Mrs Caruso and baby Gloria needed him, then why not take the opportunity of stopping in New York and bringing them along too? Bracale was persuasive and persistent: '[He] is [an] old impresario and he knows how to [treat an] artist like me – with kindness and sommission, and I cannot treat him in a bad way. . . . With this money of Lima, I will be covered for two years for the income tax in Italy and in the U.S.A.'[27] By this time Caruso was nearly half way there, and it was only when Dorothy dug her heels in and insisted that the doctor had told her the South American climate and food might be harmful to Gloria that he finally abandoned the idea.

Caruso may have been unaware of the prodigious growth in his reputation during those last years of his career; although at the Metropolitan his fee remained $2,500, in Buenos Aires in 1915 it had risen to $6,666, in Mexico City in 1919 to $7,000 and by 1920 in Havana it reached $10,000 a night. There also seems little doubt that, had he gone off to other venues in the West Indies or South America, it would have been for even more money. Bracale's way of whetting the public's appetite, by blatantly advertising Caruso's fee, inevitably caused deep resentment. There was a strong reaction to the wave of publicity he set off. At that time the standard of living in Cuba was wretched and the ticket prices represented more than a year's work for the average inhabitant – orchestra seats cost $35. That this created a potentially explosive situation, literally, became increasingly apparent and made itself felt palpably on the last night in Havana when, during a performance of *Aida*, a bomb blast rent the air 'with a tremendous noise and the most dreadful odor. Caruso, alias Radames, picked up the skirts of his gorgeous white robe, hopped out of the theater and into the street, and galloped across the square to the hotel, pursued by a crowd of reporters. . . . Of course, Bracale and the stage manager ran to the hotel, where they calmed the hero of the Ethiopian wars, and brought him back to his triumph.'[28]

CHAPTER XVII

1920–1921

MEANWHILE IN New York Dorothy had been looking round for a new home and, after considering several, she finally reserved an apartment at the Vanderbilt; this included the entire top floor of a block at Thirty-fourth Street and Park Avenue. 'Despite the fact that a thousand others will be under the same roof, [Caruso] will have absolute privacy . . . his wife will have her garden and her daughter a playground, yet they will be removed from the throbbing world which passes their door as though they were at a Long Island estate.'¹ That summer the Carusos did in fact rent an estate on Long Island – that of Alfred Herter at East Hampton. Memories of the unfortunate events in Italy the previous summer had persuaded them that with baby Gloria it would be more judicious to take their vacation in the United States, so it was to East Hampton that Dorothy went to await the return of Caruso from Cuba. It was there on the night of June 8, when she and her stepsister Mrs Goddard were relaxing after dinner, that the burglar alarm suddenly went off in her bedroom. They rushed upstairs and found the safe gone. The butler 'wanted to pursue the burglars, but I forbade anyone to leave the house, reminding them that we were unarmed and that men who could steal such valuable jewels would kill to keep them.'² '[I] started for the room of the chauffeur [Fitzgerald, an Irish-American], but [a] maid [told me] he was not in. Then I tried to telephone the lodge house, where he might be, when he came running in. [I] did not see he had a revolver, [and] when he dashed out . . . a moment later [I] heard two shots fired.'³ The only evidence of burglars seemed to have been a slit in the wire wide enough for a hand to have reached through and raised the bolt. Some minutes later the chauffeur returned. He was out of breath and appeared to have been running, and he was carrying with him the safe which he had opened and which, he claimed, he had found in the garden. There were no jewels in it, but he had picked up a diamond comb and

earrings from the grass. It was not until the police arrived and
everyone else in the house had by that time touched the safe that
Dorothy thought of finger-prints. One of the detectives recognized the
chauffeur as having been involved some years previously in a case
connected with the theft of an automobile, but 'it was recalled that he
was exonerated'.[4] At first the butler (Ferraro, an Italo-American) had
started out with one story but, cross-examined by the police, he later
admitted that he had not been telling the truth when he claimed to
have seen the chauffeur standing in front of the studio at the time the
jewels had been stolen. 'I did not see him fire a shot in the air [nor] did I
see him pick up the jewel box and start the bell ringing. I did not like
him . . . [for] when I first came here he hit me and I wanted to get back
at him.'[5] The whole affair began to look like a replay of various earlier
events in Caruso's career: the cast included Irish-Americans and
Italo-Americans feuding with one another, and Caruso seemed to be
ever unlucky with his chauffeurs. At all events, and in spite of the
intense search conducted by the police and his insurance company,
save for the diamond comb and earrings, and a pearl headband valued
between $15,000 and $20,000, the missing jewels, worth at least
$370,000, were never recovered. At length, when Caruso was in
Naples in 1921, the brokers eventually paid up.

The season in Cuba came to an end with performances in Santa
Clara and Cienfuegos, after which Caruso left Havana for New
Orleans. On June 26 he appeared there in a concert at the Atheneum.
Noel Straus praised his 'delicacy of tone . . . in "Che gelida manina".
The suavity and breadth of the main theme . . . after the introduction
was one of the unforgettable moments in a superlative performance,
and the great climax with its superb high C [sic], dwelt upon subtly
and without over emphasis, was accomplished with consummate
art.'[6] His last appearance that season took place at a special benefit
given by Victor artists for the National Association of Talking
Machine Jobbers at the Ambassador Hotel, Atlantic City. He shared
this occasion with the great Russian composer Sergei Rachmaninoff,
who was almost his exact contemporary. Yet, whereas Caruso's career
was almost done, Rachmaninoff's, as a concert pianist, had only just
begun, for he had yet to make his first Victor recordings, and he would
continue to occupy himself with these for more than twenty years.

On July 1 Caruso rejoined Dorothy and Gloria in East Hampton,
and, save for another concert in the middle of his holiday on August
14, he spent the rest of the summer there. By this time photography

was sufficiently sensitive to record him in a variety of impromptu shots: in one group he is dressed in plus fours attempting to lob a tennis ball over the net, another shows him daubing a paint brush against the side of a boat, but these were cosmetic exercises for he did not play tennis and though he used pencils to sketch with, it was years since he had tried painting. Although his singing remained unimpaired, and he continued to show off his voice to its best advantage, the strain was beginning to show, and he complained of a cold he could not shake off. On September 3 he despatched an irate letter to a Cuban daily, the *Nacion*, for he had had time to look over his Havana notices and great was his wrath when he read that, by their account, the season had been his Waterloo. If they wanted 'historical' allusions, he countered, accusing them of a 'treachery equal to Judas'.

On September 12 the Carusos returned to New York and moved in to the Vanderbilt. It was surprising, as Stanley Jackson observed, 'that he saw nothing ominous in the fate of Alfred Gwynne Vanderbilt, for whom the luxurious suite was originally designed. [For] he had drowned when the *Lusitania* had been torpedoed.'[7] A couple of days later he went down to Camden, New Jersey, and there in the course of three sessions he made his last recordings, among them 'Rachel, quand du Seigneur' from *La Juive*. Manuel Garcia II, brother of Malibran and Viardot and the most famous singing teacher of the nineteenth century, singles this aria out as an example of the *canto declamato* style. In his treatise *L'Art du chant*, he writes: 'In order to excel in this dramatic style, it is necessary to have a soul of fire and gigantic power: the actor must constantly dominate the singer. But one should be careful to approach this style with moderation and reserve, for it quickly exhausts the resources of the voice. Only the singer whose constitution is strong, but who, through long practice of his art, has lost the freshness, youth and flexibility of voice should take it up.'[8] Judging from all the more reliable accounts, as well as his incomparable recording, when Caruso undertook Eléazar he had certainly not 'lost the freshness, youth and flexibility of [his] voice', yet it was just as well that he sang the part when he did, for his constitution, as subsequent events were all too soon to prove, was not strong and this was, in fact, the last role he would add to his repertory. It was at the end of September, at the beginning of his final concert tour, that his fatal illness was foreshadowed in his allusion to starting it with a little cold. '"I feel it is in my chest and he will take a long time to go on." As though a presentiment of his death cast a shadow over him, he began to long for Italy . . . [and] again he cried out like a man who is fast exhausting his strength: "I must stop to work and go back to my country, otherwise I will go down like a fruit goes down from the tree." [9]

His first performance in the new season was at Montreal on September 27. Here he earned $10,000; 8,000 people were present and the takings amounted to $30,000. One newspaper noted that 'it was a mistake to poster Jack Dempsey as the best-known man in the world [for] Caruso is known personally on four continents. He has sung in Europe, Africa, North and South America.' [10] After stopping in Toronto he went on to Chicago, 'and to listen to Caruso's equipment is to marvel at the plenitude of tone, the ring and resonance, the surety of attack and sustaining power still present in a voice that has been generously given to the world for the last twenty five years. Notes of glowing color are there, glorious high B naturals are his to evoke enthusiasm. Nobody seems to care what he sings, nor how he interprets, it is his voice that they have come to hear.' [11]

The aria from *Marta* was an intensely emotional expression almost of the robust type, and not the perfect expression of the old Italian *bel canto*, with its tones of exquisite purity sustained in a line of curving grace. The tones have grown deeper and more baritonal, even since last we heard him [in another concert in May 1919]. . . . At times there was his old buoyancy in the songs which lay in the lower part of his range. He evidently liked to feel the depth of the lower tones, and many a baritone would give his old boots, or even some brand new ones, to have the same richness of quality down below. But he has paid for it up above, and he no longer cares to toy with the long sustained high note. He can do it still, yet not with the old nonchalance. The upper phrases are now things that must be attended to and with no nonsense permitted. In other days there was a very different impression. You felt that he was singing for the joy of it, and the tones flowed forth from a super abundant store, whereas yesterday afternoon he had to add quite a bit of propulsion. As the oil man would say, he used to be a gusher, but now he is settled down into a pumper. When he calls on it the voice is there. He squares his shoulders and sends out a high B flat which sails up to the roof just the way Babe Ruth can pound the ball over the fence, and you realize that there had to be about as much muscle back of one as of the other. [12]

Caruso then continued his magnificent progress through Saint Paul, Denver, Omaha, Tulsa, Fort Worth, Houston, Charlotte and Norfolk. At these he would sing normally three operatic arias: among them

'Che gelida manina' from *La Bohème*, 'Una furtiva lagrima' from *L'Elisir d'amore*, 'O paradiso!' from *L'Africana*, 'M'apparì' from *Marta* and 'Vesti la giubba' from *Pagliacci* – all with orchestral accompaniment – and between these he would intersperse a number of encores, all piano accompanied, including Tosti's ''A vucchella' and 'Pour un baiser', Duparc's 'Extase', Rossini's 'La danza', Bartlett's 'A dream', Geehl's 'For you alone', Fatuo's 'Sento che t'amo', Pasadas's 'Noche feliz', Massenet's 'Elégie' and Donaudy's 'Spirate'.

By the time he commenced his ultimate season at the Metropolitan, on November 15, 1920, 'few of the vast number [present] . . . realized the responsibility Caruso's artistic position had wrought.'[13] The man was already in failing health on the opening night, yet his performance in *La Juive* brought forth encomiums. Aldrich spent a considerable amount of space on him:

> Although his voice may not have been in its best condition, [yet it was] the finest representation of his art in certain ways that can be recalled in recent years. His Eléazar is one of the creations of his maturity, of his middle age. In his singing it shows the Caruso whose voice has become so very considerably changed from that lyric tenor which he first disclosed on the Met stage . . . the deeper burnished gold of a dramatic voice heavier in quality but still profoundly beautiful. . . . A notable passage of which he gives his best is in the Passover scene . . . [where] he reveals the fullest beauty of his voice, the sustained tones, the expressive color, the long phrases are of his best. Another capital point is in the fourth act of the opera. . . . Here Caruso is a tragic actor [who] discloses resources of tragic power that he never disclosed before. It is a scene that he has evidently studied seriously; as his composition of it, pose, gesture and facial expression are matched by the poignant intensity of his declamation in the baleful color he imparts to the musical phrase.[14]

And the consensus of opinion was equally enthusiastic. Finck in the *Evening Post* acclaimed him: 'Caruso completely merges his individuality in the character he impersonates. . . . [He] sang the soft measures with exquisite *mezza voce*. His singing of "Rachel, quand du Seigneur" was the best thing he has ever done.'[15] For Krehbiel in the *Tribune*, too, 'his performance of the part of the vengeful Jew was as notable a thing as he has ever put to his credit. He was not only electrifying in his moments of passion, his suave and beautiful singing in the scene of the Pesach meal was transporting.'[16] But perhaps it was the *Evening Telegram* which best expressed the critical affection for the great artist: 'He has had a long career and lovers of beautiful singing follow his voice year by year, watching fearfully for decay that never comes.'[17]

Three nights later, however, the reception for his Nemorino was hardly as warm: Aldrich thought that in this 'all thoughts of suitability and appropriateness of singing, all feeling for artistic propriety seemed to be simply cast aside. Caruso's treatment of Donizetti's music, fragile enough in its substance, but expressive of the spirit of the comedy, is exaggerated; an attempt to make pretentious and orotund in expression what is really very simple and straightforward.'[18] In effect custom, not to mention the demands of a score so dramatic as *La Juive*, had staled his interpretation. Whereas his new-found manners might have suited roles like Eléazar, Alvaro, Samson and Jean in *Le Prophète*, as Nemorino 'he let [his] voice [free] in all its power, [and turned on] the emotional stop . . . in full voice.'[19] When Caruso came to read criticism like this his self-doubts, exacerbated by his generally run-down condition, caused him to write to Gatti-Casazza protesting: 'If I sing as [they] say I sing it is time I appeared no more before the New York public.'[20] But Gatti was over at the Vanderbilt in a trice and persuaded him to disregard such notices. At any rate, on November 24, when he undertook Samson, Aldrich was reassuring: 'He takes the music seriously and sings it artistically, [and] not for the benefit of the groundlings. Samson is to be placed alongside of Eléazar as one of his finest parts, one that he has found congenial and the music of which he treats with respect.'[21] There was the usual unanimity of opinion in the press reviews as to the high quality of both his singing and his acting in the Saint-Saëns opera, and he used his voice so as to convince those who had criticised him that he was in no such vocal condition as might have been assumed by readers of the reviews he had earned for *L'Elisir*. On November 27 when he sang Alvaro, Huneker wrote: 'There is but one word to characterise his singing – Superb!'[22]

It was on December 3, as Samson again, that at end of the evening he was struck by a falling pillar from the temple, and perhaps this may have accounted for his suddenly feeling unwell the next day when he was out for a drive with Dorothy. They immediately made a diversion to call on his physician, Dr Horowitz, who ordered him straight home to bed. At this time he was beginning to suffer from a pain in his side, but instead of taking a rest he insisted on fulfilling his engagements. On December 8 he was back at the Met as Canio. Everything passed off as usual until he reached the end of the first act and 'Vesti la giubba', when a top A failed and he was suddenly stricken by an excruciating pain in his left flank. As he later told, 'I felt sick all over . . . [and] saw black.'[23] In order to create a diversion he affected to stumble up the steps of the set. In the interval in his dressing room he was determined to continue with the performance; Dr Horowitz dismissed it as 'nothing serious'. During the following three days, notwithstanding the indisposition he was suffering from, he continued to lead a normal life. One day he gave an audition to a young singer and on another he invited Mrs Shubart to dine.

The next part he was due to sing, on December 11 at the Brooklyn Academy, was Nemorino, but directly before this performance he started to cough up blood. Dorothy was with him at the time in his dressing room, and he immediately ordered her to take her seat out front and behave absolutely normally. She was terrified. She did as she was bid but she could not help recalling that once he had told her how tenors sometimes died on stage after a high note, from a haemorrhage. From the moment he appeared in the first scene people situated in the boxes could see that he was in distress. From time to time he turned round partly as if to cough, then he resorted to a handkerchief, as though clearing his throat. After finishing the aria 'Quanto è bella' he stepped to the well built into the set, and dropped a handkerchief over the side. Members of the cast came to his assistance, passing out more handkerchiefs, and when the curtain came down it was announced that the performance could not continue. Backstage a prodigious flurry of activity had been going on. Gatti had been informed and as he later tells: 'At that very moment I had a fleeting premonition that Caruso was lost. It was the only time, during my entire career as an opera director, that I was obliged to end a performance in the middle. I could have sent [for] another tenor, but after the excitement it was impossible.'[24]

According to Dr Horowitz it was still only a case of 'intercostal neuralgia'; a vein had burst at the bottom of Caruso's tongue and all he needed was to be swathed in tight bandages. The bleeding stopped and two days later something of the old Caruso was on show when he undertook Alvaro in La Forza del destino, 'beaming all over his countenance with happiness over his complete recovery'[25] – or so Aldrich thought, for the pain in his side had only abated temporarily and it returned on the 21st. His condition became so agonising that he had little sleep that night and was obliged to cancel an appearance in L'Elisir d'amore. On Christmas Eve he was scheduled to undertake Eléazar again. He determined to be well enough to face the music; on December 23 he began rehearsing with his accompanist and swept aside suggestions that he first have a thorough medical investigation. At the performance Toscanini was in the audience. He was touring America with the orchestra from La Scala, Milan and afterwards he went round to see Gatti. 'What is wrong with Caruso? The man must be sick. He looks very bad, I am anxious about him.'[26] Yet Caruso had managed to conceal his indisposition and only someone who knew the singer well, like Toscanini, was aware that something was profoundly wrong. For Henderson was also present and he wrote in the *Sun*: 'Caruso, Well Again; Sings *La Juive* to Large Audience'. Lumbago faded into obscurity before the approaching joys of Christmas, and therefore Caruso was himself once more. Accordingly the perform-ance of *La Juive* scheduled for last night was sung . . . The opera was heard with loudly proclaimed delight by a large audience.'[27] But 'when he got home that night,' Dorothy remembers, 'I was horrified at his color, which was a curious greyish green.'[28]

Caruso himself has left an account of the progress of his illness during the next weeks, in a letter he wrote on February 1, 1921 to his brother Giovanni in Naples:

From Xmas day until today there are but tortures that I am suffering. I will tell you what happened to me. Since some time I was not feeling well. Pains on my side, blood from my throat made me very much worried and although I used to be visited by a doctor every day, they told me it was nothing and [I] should not be alarmed. On Xmas Day – which I thought I would spend happily because beside a big Xmas tree full of presents for my friends, Doro, under the mantel piece, mounted up a *presepe* with big figures of the Saints etc and thus everything promised [to be] a splendid holiday if you add that on the Eve I sang a splendid performance of *La Juive* and after it we had many friends [to] supper. On about 12.30 [p.m.] of that Xmas day while I was giving away some tips . . . to the waiters and maids [at] the hotel I felt a general weakness which [I had never] experience[d] before. I thought it was something [to do] with my stomach. I went to the bath room, but as soon as I started to [bru]sh my teeth, some kind of fainting spell possessed me. I thought a hot bath would help me and . . . immediately turned on the water and tried to descend in the tub. I hadn't time to sit down I fell [and] my body ben[t] like a willow and I started to scream like a madman. Mario and Zirato ran to me and tried to get me out of the tub. I lost every bit of strength . . . and with my hand . . . pressed [against] my left side which ached terribly. I remember the yells I emitted like a wounded dog. They tell me that people outside heard me, and we [a]re on the eighteenth floor! Doro and the others helped me to a chair. They called the doctor and the house physician who arrived immediately but not knowing me well was a little embarrassed [at] what to do at first but [at length] he gave me something until my doctor arrived. They [told] me that if my wife and friend[s] had not insisted [o]n getting some other doctors, by this time I would be cold in Brooklyn.* . . . When my doctor [arrived] he said it was the usual ailment and that with some morphine everything would be all right. Five days [and] I passed between life and death for the stubborness of that good doctor. Finally my wife and . . . friends and a consultation of [new] doctors [confirmed] that I was a very sick man with . . . painful pleurisy. 'If this man is not operated [on with] in twenty-four hours there is no hope.' This was the result of [their immediate] consultation. They decided to call a surgeon; [he] came and on the same evening operated on me for empyema. I do not remember anything but [the] awful noise of surgical instruments, then I felt . . a point of a knife in my side and immediately screams of 'Hurra'. What happened? On cutting . . . my side the surgeon found an enormous quantity of pus, which came out like an explosion. [But] he did not cut my ribs as he thought [he might have had to] on account of a large intercostal space I have. Have you any idea what a pleurisy is? It is what we call a stitch in the side 'na puntura', as we say in dialect. Mine, however, is of the worst class because it is purulent. I think I had this for years and [it] was the cause of all my headaches . . . Now I feel well. I eat like a wolf because I have to gain the many kilos I have lost. I started to walk round the rooms and stay up for four or five hours daily in the salon where I enjoy myself playing with Gloria. I think I have to stay with caution for another month at least. The wound is still open. I hope in March to go somewhere near the sea and at the end of that month [I shall] come to Naples. Now you can be satisfied without worr[ying] about me. I am all right. I still have that superstition, you know, that until the time . . . I lose a tooth nothing will happen to me. Thank you for your cables and please let [all] of our friends know that I am well [again]. Embraces to you and yours. Affectionately, Enrico.[29]†

But in less than two weeks, on February 12, it was necessary to operate again, and Dr Erdman, Professor of Surgery at Columbia University, was called back. He reopened the incision in Caruso's side.[30] The poison found in the deepest part of the cavity had become so viscid that now only the most drastic drainage could save his life and 'when his chest was opened, out poured the foulest pus I think I have ever seen and smelled'.[31] To facilitate this operation it was necessary to remove four inches of the rib, although Caruso was not told of this. During the next few days his condition was front-page

* By this time there were no longer any cemeteries in Manhattan.
†This is an English translation contained in Zirato's draft biography.

news. Fears were expressed that he would not recover and his family were summoned to his bedside. 'He never stirred, he scarcely seemed to breathe,' Dorothy remembered. 'I looked into a face I did not recognize, drained of all expression, shrunken and empty.'[32]

Nearly another two weeks passed before there was any noticeable improvement in his condition. Then one morning the Italian ambassador came to call. He bent over the bed and said: 'Caruso. You must live for your country and your king.' At first the tenor did not respond, but then he spoke softly, just begging to be allowed to return home to Italy and die. 'Caruso,' the ambassador repeated in a louder voice: 'Listen to me! Here is an emblem from your king, who wants you to get well,' and he took a carnation from his button hole and then reminded Caruso of when he had heard him sing for the first time in 1898 at Genoa in *Il Cid*. This gingered Caruso into life: 'No,' he murmured. 'It was in *I Pescatori*.'[33]

During the next month the poisonous seepage from the pleura obliged the doctors to undertake a total of five more operations and these were carried out without general anaesthetics. After the fifth it was decided that his weakness and prodigious loss of weight necessitated a blood transfusion, and eventually he had two. He talked incessantly of wanting to return to Italy, to the sunshine of Tuscany. 'I heard in that appeal,' writes Dorothy, 'far off, like the echo of a bad dream – "Let me die in my own country. I want to die in Italy."'[34] Years later she speculates over whether Caruso might have survived had he stayed in America. Though medical skills were more advanced there, she believes that 'he would have died of a broken heart. [And] if that sounds romantic, he would have died, I will say, of frustrated hopes.'[35] From this time there was a slow but gradual improvement in his condition. By the beginning of April he was well enough to get up a short while each day, and on the 21st be began to take car rides out in Central Park again. One day he went down to the Metropolitan, but whether this was to say 'hullo' or bid 'good bye', it was hard to know, for by then he looked like an old man – he stooped and had lost more than fifty pounds in weight. X-rays of his chest revealed that his left lung had contracted and he had a circulatory problem in the fingers of his right hand, for the flesh had begun to shrink away from the bones and he was obliged to wear gloves. 'It would seem likely that [he] was injured in some way perhaps while under anaesthetic.'[36]

It was when the Carusos were packing preparing for their imminent departure for Italy that a new doctor let the cat out of the bag, congratulating him on the way the incision in his ribs was growing. 'Caruso was horrified. The prevailing opinion was that to remove a piece of rib was to remove the voice.'[37] He at once instructed Fucito, his accompanist, to unpack all his music, for he would not need it now.

On May 28, Enrico, Dorothy and Gloria, together with their entourage, left New York for Naples on the *Presidente Wilson*. By this time photographs show him looking older and thinner but recognizably the same man. After arriving in Naples the party proceeded by boat across the bay to Sorrento and took a floor of the Hotel Vittoria. During most of June he followed a strict regime. A tub of mud was brought over each morning by boat from Agnano Terme and he would hold his right hand and arm in it while he took his breakfast coffee. Then he would swim or play with Gloria on the beach, teaching her her first Italian words. His face gradually became bronzed and he began to look much fitter; he put on twenty-five pounds and a photograph of him on the hotel balcony at the beginning of July shows him without gloves, beginning to look like the Caruso of old. As the days passed in the summer sun he began to make strolls about Sorrento stopping to buy some linen and antiques. Everywhere he went he was greeted with respect – even awe.

Early in July a party of his New York cronies, including Scognamillo, came down to Naples and it was not long before they caught Caruso up in various schemes. They invited him out to Capri; Dorothy did her best to dissuade him, but to no avail. He was determined to prove that he was as well as anyone. When they got back that night he collapsed but, before Dorothy could get him to bed, he insisted on watching a firework display from the balcony. And it was that night, as she tells us, 'that I noticed his face was flushed, but thinking it was only a reflection of the lights outside . . . I did not treat the symptom seriously. When I felt his hand, it was hot, and then I soon discovered, to my consternation, that he already had a high temperature.'[38]

The next morning, however, he seemed well again, and a few days later he determined to go to Pompei – he would go to church to thank its patron saint, the Madonna, for making him well again, and then he would visit the ruins. Although it was a fiercely hot day, he refused to take a sedan chair. By chance they met Crown Prince Hirohito of Japan and the officials who welcomed him insisted on introducing him to the Emperor's heir. They walked on through the sweltering streets, narrow alleys, passed temples and courtyards, all roofless, the sun glaring down upon them. At length Caruso could go no further: ' "I think now we send for chairs," he panted.'[39] Before leaving Pompei a young man came up and begged him to give him an audition, and it was arranged that he would come the next day. A night's rest seemed to have refreshed Caruso and when the youth arrived Dorothy was sitting out on the balcony. She heard him trying to sing, then 'suddenly there was a flood of golden tone. It was the aria from *Marta* poured into the room as it could be by only one. I rushed into the room. And Enrico was calling "Doro! Doro! I can sing, I haven't lost my voice as they said I would. I have all my strength and am not even tired!" I hurried to him and found that singing had not wearied him.'[40] And all they could think of was that, notwithstanding all his operations, it was still there, the same incomparable voice. They sat down at once and began to make elaborate plans for the future. What happened to the young man Dorothy could never recall.

But that evening Caruso's temperature returned and, despite the happiness of the day, Dorothy decided that she must find a doctor at once. She knew that De Luca was also staying in Sorrento so that night she managed to slip out and ask him what she should do. He suggested calling in two famous Roman surgeons, the Signori Bastianelli. They came down in response to her request and after carrying out an examination of Caruso they urged him to come up to Rome as soon as possible so that they might remove another abscess which was close to his kidneys. For some reason he did not depart at once – according to Dottore Raffaele Bastianelli, he did not know why Caruso delayed coming.[41] Perhaps the long chapter of operations in New York made it difficult for him to face up to another again. In an interview given by Dorothy, after her return to New York, she claimed: 'He did not realize how weak he was after so many months of illness.'[42] It was not for another couple of days that the Carusos finally left Sorrento by boat for Naples, where they would take a train for Rome. But when they reached Naples, Caruso's temperature had risen to 104°, and he was again suffering from the agonising pain in his side so they were forced to stop at the Hotel Vesuvio. During the next two days Dorothy did her best to secure him some relief but it was the height of summer and the whole city was on vacation. Finally she did manage to find a doctor who brought some morphine and at length Caruso was able to get some sleep. Then six other doctors arrived and Dorothy did her best to urge them to operate at once, but after consideration they told her his heart was too weak to withstand surgery.

There are three versions of his last moments, in the small hours of the morning of August 2, 1921, all by Dorothy. There is that from her 1945 *Enrico Caruso, His Life and Death*:

> In spite of what [the doctors] said I could not believe he was near death. . . . Hours passed. . . . He opened his eyes and looked at me.
> 'Doro-I-am-thirsty–' he gave a little cough. 'Doro-they-hurt-me-again.' He began to gasp for air.
> 'Don't be afraid. Rico darling – everything is all right.'
> 'Doro-I-can't-get-my-breath–'
> I saw his eyes close and his hand drop. I hid my face and thought, 'at last Enrico is well . . .'[43]

The second version is from *Wings of Song*, which Dorothy wrote in 1928:

> 'Doro, I can't seem to get my breath.'
> 'You're all right, Rico. Everything is all right, dear.'
> 'Doro, don't let me die!' His eyes looked at me full of appeal.
> 'He is not dying?' I cried to the doctor, who, in answer, laid the limp hand he held gently on the sheet and turned away.
> Suddenly a piercing cry broke the stillness of the room – the wail of one lost in the darkness. 'Doro-Doro, Doro!' and he died.'[44]

But the account she gave to the newspapers less than three months after he died, immediately upon her return to New York, is a lot less novelettish and has the ring of truth about it. 'It was a miserable hot day, and Enrico got so tired. And then after we got [to the hotel], he went to sleep and never woke up.'[45]

Thirty-eight years after his death, Dr Robert Prichard published an article entitled 'The Death of Enrico Caruso' in *Surgery, Gynecology and Obstetrics*.[46] Famous public personalities, like Caruso, he writes, often do not get the best medical treatment; perhaps because of an inclination to secure the services of a fashionable rather than a reputable doctor. Caruso's infection was serious and resistant; it proved difficult, and eventually impossible, to effect an adequate drainage. This resulted in the end in his inevitable death. 'It seems likely that he had pneumonia, empyema, satellite abscesses in the fascia and muscles of the left side of the chest, a subphrenic abscess, possibly a perirenal abscess, and terminally, general peritonitis.'[47] It is curious, Dr Prichard goes on, why, in the face of this ineluctable evidence, public opinion should prefer that he died from cancer.

Possibly 'the association of singing and respiratory difficulties, taken with the episode of hemoptysis during *L'Elisir d'amore*, was too hard to resist and to replace such a romantic flourish with a protracted and complex infection would seem to be too much to ask of the public.'[48]

Today, now that more than sixty-five years have passed since Caruso's death, it is possible to say, however cavalier it may seem, that he died at exactly the right time for his reputation. It was not until several years later that the introduction of the microphone was to bring in its wake a whole bevy of popular singers, or crooners, whose voices did not any longer need the breath support necessary to project across the spaces of a theater or concert auditorium. So it was that the classical and popular idioms began to grow rapidly apart. At the same time opera composers largely abandoned traditional lyricism – or perhaps it was that the prodigious growth of popular music, occasioned after the invention of the microphone, led to its inevitably abandoning them – and instead they began to embark upon all manner of abstruse and rarefied experiments. In the generation following Caruso's there were a number of fine tenors whose art was still, like his, in varying degrees dynamic. Gigli, for example, remained all his lengthy career a renowned popular musician. Unfortunately, however, when he sang ballads and songs on the radio, records or in recital, this led to a general coarsening of his delivery, a plethora of aspirates and sobs, which inevitably corrupted his style in opera – although not his singing. Tauber, on the other hand, was widely acclaimed by composers as various as Richard Strauss and Franz Lehár, and his later records include not only Strauss Lieder and arias of Weber, but also popular songs by Irving Berlin and Richard Rodgers. In its heyday, of course, the opera house had not been a temple of enlightenment, but a place of entertainment. By the forties, however, even an artist of Tauber's remarkable virtuosity could not disguise a gap between popular and classical music grown too wide for any one singer to bridge stylishly. Tito Schipa at the end of his career had recourse to a microphone at his concerts; we are not surprised that his singing on records becomes reminiscent of Tino Rossi or Rudy Vallee, or even the light baritone Bing Crosby. In our own day this tradition may be said to have been followed by Placido Domingo, who has recorded a recital with John Denver. This, however, is more a comment on Domingo's prodigious musicianship and his ability to adopt almost any kind of disguise, while Tauber and Schipa attempted to convert the popular music of their day to their own style – Tauber even tried to do so with Cole Porter's 'Night and Day'. Most opera singers have been content to succeed with just the operatic repertory and to keep themselves aloof from the world of popular music. Their art has thus remained immutable through the years. We may think of Martinelli, Pertile or Melchior (notwithstanding Melchior's Hollywood postscript to his career, for Romberg and Herbert remained, for him at least, always Wagner).

The invention of the microphone did not at once affect opera singers in blatant fashion, as it did popular singers. Nevertheless, over the last half century and more, it has worked, albeit subtly, a profound influence. Profound, because reputations, though not contrived, are certainly confirmed by electric means: recordings, films, television and video. The impact that singers used once to create only in the opera house or concert hall, in the days before electric amplification, has come to be less significant in their careers than their impact on record or tape. Who today would think it telling to write of a singer's art, as Shaw did of Patti's: 'Her voice is so perfectly produced and controlled that its most delicate pianissimo reaches the remotest listener in [London's Royal] Albert Hall'?[49] The fact is that this 'third dimension' to the opera singer's art has been lost by the listener as surely as by the singer.

In the nineteenth century tenors from Rubini to de Reszke were greatly admired, but their reputations had not spread far beyond the society that patronised opera. Undoubtedly the phonograph, even in its acoustic period, was the principal factor in translating Caruso into an international figure; it took his voice into the homes of thousands who never heard him in person, and even today it continues to keep his legend alive. As a singer of songs he replaced the genteel accents of the salon singers with something more expansive and better suited to the larger popular audiences to whom he sang in America and, via the phonograph, throughout the world. In the last years of his life the phonograph was so whetting the public's appetite that it succeeded in making Caruso as great a singer of songs as he was an operatic tenor. The tremendous pressure this generated piled up cumulatively until his untimely death, as we can see from press interviews he gave. He told readers of the *Brooklyn Eagle* on December 31, 1916: 'I strain myself to keep my voice from sounding strained. It is only after the hardest training that a man can regulate his voice so that it always sounds easy and natural. The audience should not think I am straining my voice but they should realize that I am straining every nerve to make my notes smooth and natural.'[50] Something had to yield, and if it was not the voice then it had to be the man himself. The effect of this rapidly accelerating popularity in those last years of his career can be seen all too obviously if we examine photographs of him; he aged rapidly and by 1920 he looked as if he were nearer sixty than forty-seven. It is a measure of his artistic greatness that no vocal strain shows on his later recordings; and we should be careful not to confuse the greater tension in his singing style with physical effort, for this was a development of the verismo style, and we can hear it too in recordings made by Martinelli and Pertile.

The toll the repertory took was of his health rather than his voice. Caruso may have been a greater master of comedy than tragedy, yet there was no levity in his approach to his art, for as each year passed and he became an ever more celebrated singer, his fame – ably demonstrated by frequent new issues of ever improving records – made increasing demands of him. In those last years he rode a tiger.

PART TWO

The Works

A CHRONOLOGY OF CARUSO'S APPEARANCES

Thomas G. Kaufman

This chronology owes a debt to the pioneering work of Bruno Zirato, contained in Pierre V. R. Key's biography, on which it is based. Nevertheless, Zirato omitted several important engagements in Caruso's early career; the spring 1898 seasons in Fiume and Milan, as well as the month he spent in Warsaw in autumn 1901. He is generally weak on the later German tours, omitting the entire 1911 tour and leaving those of 1912 and 1913 incomplete. He also included several seasons that are unlikely to have taken place. In many of the seasons otherwise correctly listed there is a quantity of errors relating to the operas Caruso actually sang. Finally, he left out a number of concerts and special appearances.

A list of songs, operatic arias and ensembles sung by Caruso in concert is included with the Notes, and is referred to in the Chronology by a letter coding. This has been included by Michael Scott and, regrettably, his information is by no means complete.

Since Caruso created a number of roles and took part in the local premieres of an even larger number of works, these are indicated as follows:

    **   world premiere
    *   local premiere

However, no attempt has been made to indicate all local premieres; this would have been impossible to do with any degree of accuracy.

ACKNOWLEDGMENTS

This chronology would not have been possible without the assistance of many persons. Of these, Michael Scott deserves special thanks for sharing information that he had himself accumulated over the years;

Lim Lai for looking up dates and casts in his fabulous collection of books and programs; Charles Mintzer who is a walking encyclopaedia of information pertaining to opera singers and opera houses; and Bob Tuggle, Director of the Metropolitan Opera Archives, for providing me with information pertaining to Caruso's appearances with the Metropolitan Opera. Dr Mario Moreau of Lisbon, Drs Eduardo Arnosi, and Horacio Sanguinetti of Buenos Aires, as well as Mr Juan Dzazopulos of Santiago, Chile, were also particularly helpful. I am just as indebted to Andrew Farkas for his constant encouragement and many suggestions.

Equally important are the invaluable contributions made by several librarians. Ms Janet Bone, Mrs Ruth Schultz, and Mrs Susan Rowe of the Morris County Free Library, Mrs Josepha Cooke of the Drew University Library, and Ms Linda Naru of the Centre for Research Libraries, helped me locate and borrow many of the books, newspapers and periodicals which were essential to compiling this list.

I also want to express my sincere thanks to the following individuals and institutions and, at the same time, apologize to anyone who has been inadvertently omitted: Mr Larry Lustig, Mr Michael Henstock, Mr Lewis Hall, Professor Guglielmo Berutto, Dr Antonino Defraia, Mr Donald Wisdom of the Newspapers and Periodicals Division of the Library of Congress and his staff, Ms Jean Lee of the Holmes Library in Boonton, the staffs of the Princeton University Library, the University of Illinois Library, the University of North Carolina Library, the Music Division of the Library of Performing Arts, and the Music Division of the Library of Congress and to countless other Research Libraries all over the United States.

And finally, I am indebted to my wife, Marion, without whose patience and encouragement this listing would have been equally impossible.

Chronology

1895

	CASERTA – CATTEDRALE	
Jan 2	Vespers (2 perf.)	

	NAPLES – TEATRO NUOVO	
Mar 15	**L'Amico Francesco* (Morelli) (2 perf.)	Belvetti s. U. Ciabò b.

	CASERTA – TEATRO CIMAROSA	
Mar 28	*Faust* (Gounod)	Ferrara-Moscati s. E. Molinari ms. E. Pignataro b. A. Sternaiolo bs.

Apr 23	*Cavalleria rusticana* (Mascagni)	Ferrara-Moscati s. E. Pignataro b.
	Camoëns (Musone)	Ferrara-Moscati s. E. Pignataro b. A. Sternaiolo bs.

	COTRONE – CATTEDRALE	
June	Mass	

	NAPLES – TEATRO BELLINI	
June 9	*Faust*	E. Pignataro b. E. Foggi bs.
July 21	*Rigoletto* (Verdi)	A. Pane s. C. Molinari ms. G. Ferrari b. Fari bs.
Aug 25	*La Traviata* (Verdi)	A. Antinori s. G. Ferrari b.

	CAIRO – EZBEKIEH GARDENS	
Oct. ?	*Cavalleria rusticana*	E. Bianchini-Cappelli s. V. Ferraguti b.
Oct. ?	*Rigoletto*	
Oct. ?	*La Gioconda* (Ponchielli)	E. Bianchini-Cappelli s. V. Ferraguti b.
Oct. ?	*Manon Lescaut* (Puccini)	E. Bianchini-Cappelli s. V. Ferraguti b; A. Sarmiento cond.

1895–96

	NAPLES – TEATRO MERCADANTE	
Nov. 29	*La Traviata* (15 perf.)	K. Bensberg s. (later A. Franco s., then Castelriva s.) L. Magni b. (later F. M. Bonini b.); C. Sebastiani cond.
Dec 7	*I Capuleti ed i Montecchi* (Bellini) (15 perf.)	A. Franco s. E. Carelli s. R. De Falco bs.; C. Sebastiani cond.
Dec 25	*Rigoletto* (10 perf.)	A. Franco s. V. Ferraguti b. (later F. M. Bonini b.); V. Galassi cond.
Jan 11	*Faust* (10 perf.)	A. Franco s. E. Riso ms. F. M. Bonini b. L. Rossato bs.; V. Galassi cond.

THE WORKS

1896

Feb   CASERTA – TEATRO CIMAROSA
Faust

TRAPANI – TEATRO GARIBALDI
Feb 15   *Lucia di Lammermoor* (Donizetti)   A. Franco s. G. La Puma b. Franchetti bs.; O. Anselmi cond.

Mar 10   *Cavalleria rusticana*   E. Cavalieri s. E. Pignataro b.; O. Anselmi cond.

Mar 21   *Malia* (Frontini)

Mar 24   *La Sonnambula* (Bellini)   A. Franco s. G. La Puma b.; O. Anselmi cond.

MARSALA
Rigoletto
May 2?   *Cavalleria rusticana*   A. Franco s. E. Pignataro b.; O. Anselmi cond.

NAPLES – TEATRO BELLINI
May 20?   *Rigoletto*   Ariberti s. E. Riso ms. V. Ferraguti b.; G. Scognamiglio cond.

La Traviata
Faust

June 23   *Mariedda* (Bucceri)   A. Scalera s. E. Riso ms. V. Morghen b.

SALERNO – TEATRO MUNICIPALE
Sep 10   *I Puritani* (Bellini)   A. Franco s. V. Ferraguti b. R. Di Falco bs.

Sep 17   *Cavalleria rusticana*   A. Franco s. V. Ferraguti b.

SALERNO – CATTEDRALE SAN MATEO
Sep 27   Concert   E. Pignataro b. V. Ferraguti b.; V. Lombardi cond.

SALERNO – TEATRO MUNICIPALE
Oct   *La Traviata*   A. Franco s. E. Pignataro b.; Bossi cond.

Nov 22   *La Favorita* (Donizetti)   M. Masula ms. E. Pignataro b. C. Gagliardi bs.; V. Lombardi cond.

Nov 23   { *A San Francisco* (Sebastiani)   M. Masula ms. E. Pignataro b.; V. Lombardi cond.

    Pagliacci (Leoncavallo)   A. Franco s. E. Pignatoro b.; Bossi cond.

Dec 6   *Carmen* (Bizet)   A. Scalera ms. M. Masula ms. E. Pignataro b.

1896–97

NAPLES – TEATRO MERCADANTE
Dec 16   *La Traviata*   N. Barbareschi s. F. Guarini b.; A. Siragusa cond.

Dec 30   *La Favorita*

Jan 19   *La Gioconda*   A. Penchi s. A. Dombrowska ms. A. Nava ms. F. Guarini b. E. Brancaleoni bs.; Scalisi cond.

Feb 1	*Un Dramma in vendemmia* (Fornari)	Ducci s. A. Dombrowska ms. Salvi ms. F. Guarini b.; V. Fornari cond.
Mar 6	**Celeste* (D. Lamonica and G. Biondi)	N. Barbareschi s. F. Guarini b.; Scalisi cond.

1897

SALERNO – TEATRO MUNICIPALE

Mar 11	*La Traviata*	C. Zucchi-Ferrigno s. (later A. Franco s.) E. Pignataro b.
Mar	*La Favorita*	M. Masula ms. E. Pignataro b. R. Di Falco bs.
Mar 24	**Manon Lescaut*	A. Franco s. E. Pignataro b.; V. Lombardi cond.
Apr 8	**Il Profeta velato* (Napolitano)	A. Franco s. M. Masula ms. E. Pignataro b.; Bossa cond.
Apr 18?	*La Gioconda*	C. Zucchi-Ferrigno s. M. Masula ms. E. Pignataro b. R. Di Falco bs.; Bossa cond.

PALERMO – TEATRO MASSIMO

May 29	*La Gioconda* (13 perf.)	M. Borelli s. E. Borlinetto ms. M. Paolicchi-Mugnone ms. T. Terzi b. P. Wulmann bs.; L. Mugnone cond.

LEGHORN – TEATRO GOLDONI

July 7?	*La Traviata*	A. Giachetti s. (later F. Rapisardi s.) A. Pini-Corsi b.; V. Podesti cond.
Aug 14	*La Bohème* (Puccini)	A. Giachetti s. A. Campagnoli s. G. Pini-Corsi t. R. Galli b. A. Silvestri bs.; V. Podesti cond.

1897–98

MILAN – TEATRO LIRICO

Nov 3	*La Navarrese* (Massenet)	Z. De Nuovina s. E. Dufriche b. L. Aristi b. M. Wigley b.; R. Ferrari cond.
Nov 10	**Il Voto* (Giordano)	R. Storchio s. O. Synnerberg ms. L. Aristi b.; G. Barone cond.
Nov 23	*Cavalleria rusticana*	Passeri s. L. Aristi b.
Nov 27	**L'Arlesiana* (Cilea)	M. Tracey s. L. Casini b. L. Aristi b.; G. Zuccani cond.
Dec 31?	*Pagliacci*	L. Cassandro s. L. Casini b. L. Aristi b.

1898

GENOA – TEATRO CARLO FELICE

Jan 20	*La Bohème* (Leoncavallo) (13 perf.)	E. Corsi s. R. Storchio s. R. Angelini-Fornari b. A. Pini-Corsi b.; A. Pomé cond.
Feb 3	*I Pescatori di perle* (Bizet) (8 perf.)	R. Pinkert s. G. De Luca b. O. Carozzi bs.; A. Pomé cond.

THE WORKS

1898 cont.

GENOA – TEATRO PAGANINI

Feb 14   Concert

MILAN – TEATRO LIRICO

Mar 8   *La Bohème* (Leoncavallo) — A. Sedelmayer s. A. Santarelli s. R. Angelini-Fornari b.; G. Zuccani cond.

Mar 16   *Carmen* — F. Strakosch s. I. Monti-Baldini ms. F. Le Borne cond.

Apr 2   **Hedda* (Le Borne) — Garnier s. E. Lorini ms. L. Casini b.

FIUME – TEATRO COMUNALE

Apr 10?   *La Bohème* — A. Giachetti s. V. Novelli s. P. Giacomello b. L. Contini bs.; G. Cimini cond.

Apr 19?   *La Traviata* — A. Giachetti s. A. Nava b.; G. Cimini cond.

May 4   *Mefistofele* (Boito) — A. Giachetti s. L. Contini bs.; G. Cimini cond.

TRENTO – TEATRO SOCIALE

June 4   **Saffo* (Massenet) — A. Pandolfini s. S. Aifos s. A. Borda ms. L. Aristi b.; G. Zuccani cond.

June 13?   *Pagliacci* — S. Aifos s. R. Angelini-Fornari b.; G. Zuccani cond.

LEGHORN – POLITEAMA LIVORNESE

July 27?   *Pagliacci* — M. Ticci s. E. Barbieri b. S. Arrighetti b.; E. Martini cond.

Aug 4   *Cavalleria rusticana* — A. Antinori s. S. Arrighetti b.; E. Martini cond.

MILAN – TEATRO LIRICO

Oct 22   *L'Arlesiana* — A. Santarelli s. I. Timroth s. E. Pignataro b.; G. Zuccani cond.

Nov 8   *La Bohème* (Leoncavallo) — A. Santarelli s. B. Sorel s. Menotti b.

Nov 17   **Fedora* (Giordano) — G. Bellincioni s. D. Menotti b.; U. Giordano cond.

Dec   *Saffo* — G. Bellincioni s. (later F. Strakosch s.) I. Timruth s. Manfredi b. L. Aristi b.

1899

ST PETERSBURG – GRAND THEATRE DU CONSERVATOIRE

Jan 27   *La Traviata* (2 perf.) — S. Arnoldson s. M. Battistini b.; V. Podesti cond.

Jan 30   **La Bohème* (Puccini) (4 perf.) — S. Arnoldson s. L. Tetrazzini s. M. Battistini b. V. Brombara b. V. Arimondi bs. A. Silvestri bs.; V. Podesti cond.

206

A CHRONOLOGY OF CARUSO'S APPEARANCES

Feb 22	*Lucia di Lammermoor* (2 perf.)	L. Tetrazzini s. V. Brombara b. A. Silvestri bs.; V. Podesti cond.
	Cavalleria rusticana (2 perf.)	A. Giachetti s. T. Carotini ms. V. Brombara b.

MILAN – TEATRO LIRICO

Mar 1	*Fedora* (8 perf.)	G. Bellincioni s.

BUENOS AIRES – TEATRO DE LA OPERA

May 14	**Fedora* (4 perf.)	G. Bellincioni s. D. Menotti b.; O. Anselmi cond.
May 24	*La Traviata* (2 perf.)	G. Bellincioni s. I. Tabuyo b.; E. Mascheroni cond.
June 4	**Saffo* (2 perf.)	G. Bellincioni s. R. Angelini-Fornari b.; O. Anselmi cond.
June 8	*La Gioconda* (1 perf.)	E. Petri s. E. Lorini ms. I. Tabuyo b.; E. Mascheroni cond.
June 22	**Iris*(Mascagni) (7 perf.)	M. De Lerma s. R. Angelini-Fornari b. R. Ercolani bs.; E. Mascheroni cond.
July 4	**La Regina di Saba* (Goldmark) (6 perf.)	M. De Lerma s. E. Lorini ms. I. Tabuyo b. A. Didur bs.; E. Mascheroni cond.
July 25	***Yupanky* (Berutti) (3 perf.)	E. Petri s. I. Tabuyo b. R. Ercolani bs.; E. Mascheroni cond.
Aug 8	*Cavalleria rusticana* (1 perf.)	E. Petri s. I. Tabuyo b.; E. Mascheroni cond.

ROME – TEATRO COSTANZI

Nov 4	*Iris* (9 perf.)	E. Carelli s. E. Moreo b. R. Galli bs.; L. Mugnone cond.
Nov 11	*La Gioconda* (5 perf.)	M. D'Arneyro s. I. Monti-Baldini ms. S. Carobbi b. G. Balisardi bs.; L. Mugnone cond.
Nov 22	*Mefistofele* (8 perf.)	E. Carelli s. I. Monti-Baldini ms. E. Borucchia bs.; L. Mugnone cond.

1899–1900

ST PETERSBURG – GRAND THEATRE DU CONSERVATOIRE

Dec 28	*La Traviata* (2 perf.)	S. Arnoldson s. M. Battistini b.; V. Podesti cond.
Jan 3	*Aida* (Verdi) (3 perf.)	S. Kruszelnicka s. A. Cucini ms. M. Battistini b. V. Arimondi bs.
Jan 11	*Un Ballo in maschera* (Verdi) (4 perf.)	S. Kruszelnicka s. L. Tetrazzini s. T. Carotini ms. M. Battistini b.; V. Podesti cond.

1899–1900 cont.

Jan 17	*La Bohème* (3 perf.)	S. Arnoldson s. L. Tetrazzini s. V. Brombara b. V. Arimondi bs.; V. Podesti cond.
Jan 22	*Mefistofele* (3 perf.)	S. Kruszelnicka s. T. Carotini ms. V. Arimondi bs.
Feb 13	*La Resurrezione di Lazaro* (Perosi) (2 perf.)	S. Kruszelnicka s. T. Carotini ms. M. Battistini b. A. Silvestri bs.; V. Podesti cond.
	Stabat Mater (Rossini)	S. Kruszelnicka s. A. Cucini ms. T. Carotini ms. A. Silvestri bs.; V. Podesti cond.
Feb 28	*Lucia di Lammermoor* (1 perf.)	L. Tetrazzini s. V. Brombara b.
Mar 2	*Maria di Rohan* (Donizetti) (1 perf.)	S. Kruszelnicka s. T. Carotini ms. M. Battistini b.

1899–1900

ST PETERSBURG – THEATRE IMPERIAL
(Concurrent with season at the Grand Théâtre du Conservatoire)

Dec 30	*Aida* (1 perf.)	S. Kruszelnicka s. A. Cucini ms. M. Battistini b. V. Arimondi bs.
Feb 10	*La Traviata* (1 perf.)	S. Arnoldson s. M. Battistini b.

1900

MOSCOW – TEATR BOLSHOI

Mar 11	*Aida* (2 perf.)	M. De Lerma s. A. Cucini ms. G. Pacini b. V. Arimondi bs.
Mar 17	*La Traviata* (1 perf.)	S. Arnoldson s. G. Pacini b.
Mar 20	*Un Ballo in maschera* (2 perf.)	M. De Lerma s. L. Tetrazzini s. T. Carotini ms. M. Battistini b. V. Arimondi bs. A. Silvestri bs.; V. Podesti cond.
Mar 24	*Faust* (1 perf.)	S. Arnoldson s. T. Carotini ms. M. Battistini b. V. Arimondi bs.
Mar 27	*La Resurrezione di Lazaro* (2 perf.)	M. De Lerma s. G. Pacini b. A. Silvestri bs.; V. Podesti cond.
	Stabat Mater	M. De Lerma s. A. Cucini ms. A. Silvestri bs.; V. Podesti cond.
Mar 28	*Lucia di Lammermoor*	L. Tetrazzini s. V. Brombara b. A. Silvestri bs.
Mar 6	Concert	Song by Cosentino

BUENOS AIRES – TEATRO DE LA OPERA

May 10	*Mefistofele* (3 perf.)	E. Carelli s. R. Ercolani bs.; V. Vanzo cond.
May 17	*Iris* (5 perf.)	E. Carelli s. R. Angelini-Fornari b. R. Ercolani bs.; V. Mingardi cond.
June 9	*La regina di Saba* (6 perf.)	O. Carrera s. Mendioroz s. E. Giraldoni b. R. Ercolani bs.; V. Vanzo cond.
June 23	*La Bohème* (6 perf.)	E. Carelli s. R. Angelini-Fornari b. R. Ercolani bs. O. Luppi bs.; V. Mingardi cond.
July 12	*Cavalleria rusticana* (1 perf.)	E. Carelli s. G. Pacini b.; V. Vanzo cond.
July 28	*Manon* (1 perf.)	O. Carrera s. E. Giraldoni b.; V. Mingardi cond.

BUENOS AIRES – CATEDRAL

Aug 9	Concert	(A) w. E. Carelli s. E. Giraldoni b.

BUENOS AIRES – PROGRESS CLUB

Aug 12	Concert	(CL)

TREVISO – TEATRO SOCIALE

Oct 23	*Tosca* (Puccini) (12 perf.)	A. Giachetti s. A. Magini-Coletti b.; E. Tango cond.

BOLOGNA – TEATRO COMUNALE

Nov 17	*Tosca* (12 perf.)	A. Giachetti s. E. Giraldoni b.; L. Mugnone cond.
	Iris	M. Farneti s. R. Angelini-Fornari b. C. Nicolai bs.; L. Mugnone cond.

1900–01

MILAN – TEATRO ALLA SCALA

Dec 26	*La Bohème* (10 perf.)	E. Carelli s. L. Pasini-Vitale s. A. Arcangeli b.; A. Toscanini cond.
Jan 17	**Le Maschere* (Mascagni) (3 perf.)	L. Brambilla s. E. Carelli s. A. Arcangeli b. O. Luppi bs.; A. Toscanini cond.
Feb 1	Concert	(B) w. L. Brambilla s. E. Ghibaudo ms. A. Arcangeli b.
Feb 17	*L'Elisir d'amore* (Donizetti) (12 perf.)	R. Pinkert s. (later Brambilla s.) A. Magini-Coletti b. Carbonetti bs.; A. Toscanini cond.
Mar 16	*Mefistofele* (9 perf.)	E. Carelli s. A. Pinto s. F. Chaliapin bs.; A. Toscanini cond.

THE WORKS

1901

BUENOS AIRES – TEATRO DE LA OPERA

May 18	*Tosca* (8 perf.)	H. Darclée s. E. Giraldoni b.; A. Toscanini cond.
June 1	*La Regina di Saba* (3 perf.)	M. Pinto s. M. D'Arneyro s. E. Giraldoni b.; A. Toscanini cond.
June 9	*Rigoletto* (4 perf.)	H. Darcleé s. M. Sammarco b. R. Ercolani bs.; A. Toscanini cond.
June 23	*L'Elisir d'amore* (4 perf.)	H. Darclée s. M. Sammarco b. R. Ercolani bs.; A. Toscanini cond.
July 7	*Lohengrin* (in It.) (Wagner) (3 perf.)	M. D'Arneyro s. A. Degli Abate ms. E. Giraldoni b.; A. Toscanini cond.
July 8	*Iris* (3 perf.)	H. Darclée s. M. Sammarco b. R. Ercolani bs.; A. Toscanini cond.
July 27	*La Traviata* (2 perf.)	H. Darclée s. E. Giraldoni b.; A. Toscanini cond.
July 29	Concert	(A)

WARSAW – TEATR WIELKI

Oct 10	*Rigoletto* (1 perf.)	J. Korolewicz-Wayda s. T. Carotini ms. V. Grombczewski b. ?A. Sillich bs.; V. Podesti cond.
Oct 12	*Carmen* (1 perf.)	J. Korolewicz-Wayda s. ? B. Sorel s.
Oct 14	*Aida* (2 perf.)	S. Kruszelnicka s. V. Grombczewski b. A. Sillich bs.; V. Podesti cond.
Oct 16	*Un Ballo in maschera* (2 perf.)	S. Kruszelnicka s. T. Carotini ms. V. Grombczewski b. A. Sillich bs.; V. Podesti cond.
Oct 18	*La Traviata* (1 perf.)	B. Sorel s. V. Grombczewski b.; V. Podesti cond.
Oct 21	*La Bohème* (1 perf.)	B. Sorel s.; J. Korolewicz-Wayda s. ? V. Grombczewski b. ? A. Sillich bs. ?; V. Podesti cond.
Oct 28	*Mefistofele* (1 perf.)	S. Kruszelnicka s. A. Sillich bs.; V. Podesti cond.

BOLOGNA – TEATRO COMUNALE

Nov 30	*Rigoletto* (5 perf.)	A. Padovani s. A. Giacomini ms. E. Nani b. E. Borucchia bs.; L. Mugnone cond.

TRIESTE – POLIETEAMA ROSSETTI

Dec 14	*L'Elisir d'amore* (2 perf.)	A. Padovani s. G. Caruson b. E. Borelli bs.; G. Gialdini cond.

A CHRONOLOGY OF CARUSO'S APPEARANCES

1901–02

NAPLES – TEATRO SAN CARLO

Dec 30   *L'Elisir d'amore*   R. Pinkert s. E. Bucalo b. E. Borelli bs.; E.
          (5 perf.)   Mascheroni cond.

Jan 16   *Manon*   R. Giachetti s. E. Bucalo b. C. Thos bs.;
          (5 perf.)   E. Mascheroni cond.

1902

MONTE CARLO – SALLE GARNIER

Feb 1   *La Bohème*   N. Melba s. M. Boyer s. G. Soulacroix b.
         (3 perf.)   M. Boudouresque bs.; A. Vigna cond.

Feb 16   *Rigoletto*   N. Melba s. M. Renaud b. M. Boudour-
         (1 perf.)   esque bs. A. Vigna cond.

NICE – THEATRE DE L'OPERA
(Concurrent with Monte Carlo season)

Feb 13?   *Rigoletto*   N. Melba s. M. Renaud b. M. Boudour-
         (1 perf.)   esque bs.; A. Vigna cond.

MILAN – TEATRO ALLA SCALA

Mar 11   **Germania** (Franchetti)   A. Pinto s. M. Sammarco b.; A.
         (14 perf.)   Toscanini cond.

LONDON – COVENT GARDEN

May 14   *Rigoletto*   N. Melba s. L. Kirkby-Lunn ms. M.
         (5 perf.)   Renaud b. (later Seveilhac b.) M. Journet
                                 bs.; L. Mancinelli cond.

May 24   *La Bohème*   N. Melba s. F. Scheff s. A. Scotti b. C.
         (4 perf.)   Gilibert b. (later A. Pini-Corsi b.) M.
                                 Journet bs.; L. Mancinelli cond.

June 4   *Lucia di Lammermoor*   R. Pacini s. A. Scotti b. M. Journet bs.; L.
         (3 perf.)   Mancinelli cond.

June 6   *Aida*   L. Nordica s. (later S. Strong s.; then F.
         (4 perf.)   Litvinne s.) L. Kirkby-Lunn ms. A. Scotti
                                 b. P. Plançon bs.; L. Mancinelli cond.

June 14   *L'Elisir d'amore*   R. Pacini s. A. Scotti b. A. Pini-Corsi b.;
         (2 perf.)   L. Mancinelli cond.

June 28   *Cavalleria rusticana*   E. Calvé s. E. Dufriche b.; L. Mancinelli
         (2 perf.)   cond.

July 4   *La Traviata*   N. Melba s. Seveilhac b. (later A. Scotti
         (2 perf.)   b.); L. Mancinelli cond.

July 19   *Don Giovanni* (Mozart)   F. Litvinne s. S. Adams s. F. Scheff s. M.
         (2 perf.)   Renaud b. (later A. Scotti b.) C. Gilbert
                                 b. A. Pini-Corsi b. M. Journet bs.; L.
                                 Mancinelli cond.

MILAN – TEATRO LIRICO

Nov 6   **Adriana Lecouvreur** (Cilea)   A. Pandolfini s. E. Ghibaudo ms. G. De
         (13 perf.)   Luca b.; C. Campanini cond.

THE WORKS

1902 cont.

TRIESTE – POLITEAMA ROSSETTI

Dec 10   *Rigoletto* (2 perf.)   F. Torresella s. A. Arcangeli b.; G. Gialdini cond.

1902–03   ROME – TEATRO COSTANZI

Dec 26   *Rigoletto* (5 perf.)   F. Torresella s. E. Bruno ms. G. Pacini b. E. Borucchia bs.; E. Vitale cond.

Jan 10   *Mefistofele* (5 perf.)   F. Labia s. E. Borucchia bs.; E. Vitale cond.

Jan 20   *Manon Lescaut* (6 perf.)   L. Pasini-Vitale s. E. D'Albore b.; E. Vitale cond.

Jan 31   *Aida* (4 perf.)   F. Labia s. E. Bruno ms. G. Pacini b. M. Spoto bs.; E. Vitale cond.

1903   LISBON – TEATRO SAO CARLOS

Feb 14   *Fedora* (2 perf.)   A. Pandolfini s. A. Cerratelli b.; C. Campanini cond.

Feb 20   *Aida* (2 perf.)   A. Pandolfini s. V. Guerrini ms. M. Bensaude b. G. Rossi bs.; C. Campanini cond.

Feb 27   *Tosca* (3 perf.)   H. Darclée s. R. Blanchart b.; C. Campanini cond.

Mar 4   **Adriana Lecouvreur* (5 perf.)   A. Pandolfini s. A. Torretta ms. R. Stracciari b. (later M. Bensaude b.); C. Campanini cond.

Mar 10   *Lucrezia Borgia* (Donizetti) a(2 perf.)   H. Darclée s. A. Torretta ms. G. Mansueto bs.; J. Goula cond.

Mar 19   *Rigoletto* (3 perf.)   R. Pacini s. V. Guerrini ms. R. Stracciari b. G. Rossi bs.; C. Campanini cond.

MONTE CARLO – SALLE GARNIER

Mar 28   **Tosca* (3 perf.)   H. Darclée s. M. Renaud b.; A. Vigna cond.

BUENOS AIRES – TEATRO DE LA OPERA

May 19   *Tosca* (2 perf.)   M. Mei-Figner s. E. Giraldoni b.; A. Toscanini cond.

May 21   *Germania* (3 perf.)   M. Farneti s. G. De Luca b.; A. Toscanini cond.

June 4   *L'Elisir d'amore* (3 perf.)   E. Clasenti s. G. De Luca b. R. Ercolani bs.; A. Toscanini cond.

June 18   *Iris* (3 perf.)   M. Farneti s. P. Giacomello b. R. Ercolani bs.; A. Toscanini cond.

June 26   *Mefistofele* (1 perf.)   M. Farneti s. V. Arimondi bs.; A. Toscanini cond.

A CHRONOLOGY OF CARUSO'S APPEARANCES

July 7	*Adriana Lecouvreur* (4 perf.)	M. Mei-Figner s. V. Guerrini ms. G. De Luca b.; A. Toscanini cond.
July 25	*Manon Lescaut* (4 perf.)	M. Farneti s. P. Giacomello b. R. Ercolani bs. ; A. Toscanini cond.

MONTEVIDEO – TEATRO SOLIS
(71)

Aug 16	*Manon Lescaut* (1 perf.)	M. Farneti s. P. Giacomello b. R. Ercolani bs.; A. Toscanini cond.
Aug 20	*Adriana Lecouvreur* (2 perf.)	M. Mei-Figner s. V. Guerrini ms. G. De Luca b.; A. Toscanini cond.
Aug 23	*Iris* (1 perf.)	M. Farneti s. P. Giacomello b. R. Ercolani bs.; A. Toscanini cond.
Aug 24	*L'Elisir d'amore* (1 perf.)	E. Clasenti s. G. De Luca b. R. Ercolani bs.; A. Toscanini cond.
Aug 30	*Tosca* (1 perf.)	H. Darclée s. E. Giraldoni b.; A. Toscanini cond.

RIO DE JANEIRO – TEATRO LYRICO

Sep 8	*Rigoletto* (2 perf.)	L. Brambilla s. E. De Cisneros ms. F. Cigada b.; A. Bovi cond.
Sep 12	*Tosca* (3 perf.)	E. Carelli s. T. Parvis b.; A. Bovi cond.
Sep 17	*Manon Lescaut* (2 perf.)	B. Adami s. T. Parvis b.; A. Bovi cond.
Sep 22	*Iris* (2 perf.)	E. Carelli s. T. Parvis b. L. Lucenti bs.; A. Bovi cond.
Sep 26	Concert	The last two acts of both *Rigoletto* and *Tosca* with the casts as above.

1903–4

NEW YORK – METROPOLITAN OPERA

Nov 23	*Rigoletto* (4 perf.)	M. Sembrich s. (later J. Norelli s.) L. Homer ms. (later J. Jacoby ms.) A. Scotti b. M. Journet bs.; A. Vigna cond.
Nov 30	*Aida* (4 perf.)	J. Gadski s. E. Walker ms. (later L. Homer ms.) A. Scotti b. (later G. Campanari b.) P. Plançon bs.; A. Vigna cond.
Dec 2	*Tosca* (3 perf.)	M. Ternína s. A. Scotti b.; A. Vigna cond.
Dec 5	*La Bohème* (2 perf.)	M. Sembrich s. E. Liebling s. (later C. Seygard s.) G. Campanari b. A. Rossi bs. M. Journet bs.; A. Vigna cond.
Dec 9	*Pagliacci* (4 perf.)	M. Sembrich s. (later C. Seygard s.) A. Reiss t. A. Scotti b. M. Guardabassi b.; A. Vigna cond.

1903–4 cont.

Dec 23   *La Traviata*   M. Sembrich s. A. Scotti b.; A. Vigna cond.
           (1 perf.)

Jan 8   *Lucia di Lammermoor*   M. Sembrich s. G. Campanari b. M. Journet
           (3 perf.)   bs.; A. Vigna cond.

Jan 23   *L'Elisir d'amore*   M. Sembrich s. A. Scotti b. A. Rossi bs.;
           (4 perf.)   A. Vigna cond.

1903–4

PHILADELPHIA – ACADEMY OF MUSIC
(With New York season)

Dec 29   *Rigoletto*   M. Sembrich s. L. Homer ms. A. Scotti b. M.
           (1 perf.)   Journet bs.; A. Vigna cond.

Jan 12   *Pagliacci*   C. Seygard s. A. Reiss t. A. Scotti b. M.
           (1 perf.)   Guardabassi b.; A. Vigna cond.

Jan 19   *Tosca*   M. Ternina s. A. Scotti b.; A. Vigna cond.
           (1 perf.)

Feb 2   *Aida*   J. Gadski s. E. Walker ms. A. Scotti b. P.
           (1 perf.)   Plançon bs.; A. Vigna cond.

1904

NEW YORK – HOME OF MRS W. PAYNE WHITNEY

Jan 14   Concert

NEW YORK – HOME OF MRS ORME WILSON

Jan 21   Concert

MONTE CARLO – SALLE GARNIER

Mar 3   *Rigoletto*   A. Zeppilli s. L. Arbell ms. M. Renaud b. M.
           (3 perf.)   Baer bs.; A. Vigna cond.

Mar 10   *La Bohème*   G. Farrar s. I. Timroth s. M. Renaud b. G.
           (3 perf.)   Gravina bs.; A. Vigna cond.

Mar 19   Concert   Act III of *La Bohème* and Act IV of
                                     Rigoletto, casts as above

Mar 22   *L'Elisir d'amore*   R. Pacini s. G. Soulacroix b. F. Carbonetti
           (2 perf.)   bs.; A. Vigna cond.

Mar 26   *Aida*   G. Russ s. V. Guerrini ms. M. Renaud b. V.
           (2 perf.)   Arimondi bs.; A. Vigna cond.

PARIS – THEATRE SARAH BERNHARDT

Apr 14   *Rigoletto*   L. Cavalieri s. C. Thevenet ms. M. Renaud
           (1 perf.)   b. V. Arimondi bs.; A. Vigna cond.

BARCELONA – TEATRO DEL LICEO

Apr 20   *Rigoletto*   E. Clasenti s. M. Claessens ms. M. Berriel b.
           (2 perf.)   M. Munoz bs.; G. Barone cond.

PRAGUE – DEUTSCHES LANDES THEATER

May 4   *Rigoletto*   R. Pinkert s. J. Schaffer ms. E. Pignataro b.
           (1 perf.)   V. Arimondi bs.; A. Vigna cond.

| May 6 | *L'Elisir d'amore*
(1 perf.) | R. Pinkert s. E. Pignataro b., V. Arimondi bs.; A. Vigna cond. |

DRESDEN – HOFTHEATER

| May 8 | *Rigoletto*
(1 perf.) | R. Pinkert s. E. Pignataro b. V. Arimondi bs.; A. Vigna cond. |

LONDON – COVENT GARDEN

May 17	*Rigoletto* (4 perf.)	N. Melba s. (later M. Sylva s.; then S. Kurz s.) L. Kirkby-Lunn ms. (later M. Hertzer-Deppe ms.) M. Renaud b. M. Journet bs; L. Mancinelli cond.
May 19	*Pagliacci* (5 perf.)	E. Destinn s. (later A. Revy s.) A. Reiss t. A. Scotti b. P. Seveilhac b.; L. Mancinelli cond.
May 28	*La Bohème* (6 perf.)	N. Melba s. E. Parkina s. A. Scotti b. C. Gilibert b. M. Journet bs.; L. Mancinelli cond.
June 13	*Aida* (4 perf.)	G. Russ s. L. Kirkby-Lunn ms. A. Scotti b. P. Plançon bs. M. Journet bs.; L. Mancinelli cond.
June 15	*La Traviata* (3 perf.)	N. Melba s. A. Scotti b.; L. Mancinelli cond.
June 29	*Un Ballo in maschera* (4 perf.)	G. Russ s. S. Kurz s. N. Frascani ms. A. Scotti b.; L. Mancinelli cond.

BERLIN – THEATER DES WESTENS

| Oct 5 | *Rigoletto*
(1 perf.) | Stoller s. von Martinowska ms. E. Nawiasky b. Stammer bs.; Roth cond. |
| Oct 7 | *La Traviata*
(1 perf.) | Stoller s. R. Leonhardt b.; Roth cond. |

LONDON – COVENT GARDEN

Oct 17	*Manon Lescaut* (3 perf.)	R. Giachetti s. R. Angelini-Fornari b. V. Arimondi bs.; C. Campanini cond.
Oct 21	*Carmen* (3 perf.)	A. Nielsen s. Gianoli ms. P. Amato b.; C. Campanini cond.
Oct 27	*La Bohème* (2 perf.)	A. Nielsen s. E. Trentini s. P. Amato b. V. Arimondi bs.; C. Campanini cond.
Nov 2	*Pagliacci* (1 perf.)	J. Korolewicz-Wayda s. M. Sammarco b. R. Angelini-Fornari b.; C. Campanini cond.

1904–5

NEW YORK – METROPOLITAN OPERA

| Nov 21 | *Aida*
(4 perf.) | E. Eames s. (later L. Nordica s.) E. Walker ms. A. Scotti b. P. Plançon bs. (later M. Journet bs.); A. Vigna cond. |
| Nov 23 | *Lucia di Lammermoor*
(2 perf.) | M. Sembrich s. T. Parvis b. M. Journet bs.; A. Vigna cond. |

1904–5 cont.

Nov 26	*La Traviata* (3 perf.)	M. Sembrich s. A. Scotti b.; A. Vigna cond.
Nov 28	*La Gioconda* (4 perf.)	L. Nordica s. L. Homer ms. E. Walker ms. E. Giraldoni b. P. Plançon bs.; A. Vigna cond.
Dec 5	*Lucrezia Borgia* (1 perf.)	M. De Macchi s. E. Walker ms. A. Scotti b.; A. Vigna cond.
Dec 16	*La Bohème* (2 perf.)	N. Melba s. (later M. Sembrich s.) B. Alten s. A. Scotti b. T. Parvis b. M. Journet bs.; A. Vigna cond.
Dec 21	*Rigoletto* (2 perf.)	M. Sembrich s. L. Homer ms. E. Giraldoni b. M. Journet bs.; A. Vigna cond.
Dec 24	*L'Elisir d'amore* (1 perf.)	M. Sembrich s. A. Scotti b. A. Rossi bs.; A. Vigna cond.
Dec 26	*Pagliacci* (3 perf.)	B. Alten s. (later C. Talma s.) A. Reiss t. A. Scotti b. T. Parvis b.; A. Vigna cond.
Jan 16	*Tosca* (2 perf.)	E. Eames s. A. Scotti b.; A. Vigna cond.
Feb 3	*Gli Ugonotti* (Meyerbeer) (4 perf.)	L. Nordica s. (later M. De Macchi s.) M. Sembrich s. E. Walker ms. A. Scotti b. M. Journet bs. P. Plançon bs.; A. Vigna cond.
Feb 6	*Un Ballo in maschera* (2 perf.)	E. Eames s. B. Alten s. L. Homer ms. A. Scotti b. M. Journet bs. P. Plançon bs.; A. Vigna cond.
Feb 16	Ballroom scene of *Die Fledermaus* (Strauss)	(B) w. L. Nordica s. L. Homer ms. E. Giraldoni b.
Mar 3	Concert	Act IV of *La Gioconda* and Act I of *Pagliacci*

PHILADELPHIA – ACADEMY OF MUSIC
(Concurrent with New York season)

Dec 13	*Aida* (1 perf.)	E. Eames s. E. Walker ms. A. Scotti b. P. Plançon bs.; A. Vigna cond.
Dec 27	*Pagliacci* (1 perf.)	B. Alten s. A. Reiss t. A. Scotti b. T. Parvis b.; A. Vigna cond.
Jan 10	*Lucia di Lammermoor* (1 perf.)	M. Sembrich s. T. Parvis b. M. Journet bs.; A. Vigna cond.
Jan 24	*La Bohème* (1 perf.)	M. Sembrich s. B. Alten s. A. Scotti b. T. Parvis b. M. Journet bs.; A. Vigna cond.
Feb 28	*La Gioconda* (1 perf.)	L. Nordica s. L. Homer ms. E. Walker ms. E. Giraldoni b. P. Plançon bs.; A. Vigna cond.

A CHRONOLOGY OF CARUSO'S APPEARANCES

1905

NEW YORK – HOME OF MR J. M. SMITH
Jan 12   Concert   (C), (D), (E) and (F).

NEW YORK – HOTEL WALDORF ASTORIA
Jan 23   Concert

Tour of the Metropolitan Opera Company from Boston to Los Angeles
BOSTON – BOSTON THEATRE

Mar 6	*Lucia di Lammermoor* (1 perf.)	M. Sembrich s. T. Parvis b. M. Journet bs.; A. Vigna cond.
Mar 8	*Pagliacci* (1 perf.)	B. Alten s. A. Reiss t. A. Scotti b. T. Parvis b.; A. Vigna cond.
Mar 10	*La Gioconda* (1 perf.)	L. Nordica s. L. Homer ms. E. Walker ms. E. Giraldoni b. P. Plançon bs.; A. Vigna cond.

PITTSBURGH – NIXON THEATRE

Mar 13	*Lucia di Lammermoor* (1 perf.)	M. Sembrich s. T. Parvis b. M. Journet bs.; A. Vigna cond.
Mar 16.	*La Gioconda* (1 perf.)	M. De Macchi s. L. Homer ms. E. Walker ms. E. Giraldoni b. P. Plançon bs.; A. Vigna cond.

CINCINNATI – MUSIC HALL

Mar 18	*La Gioconda* (1 perf.)	M. De Macchi s. L. Homer ms. E. Walker ms. E. Giraldoni b. P. Plançon bs.; A. Vigna cond.

CHICAGO – AUDITORIUM

Mar 20	*Lucia di Lammermoor* (1 perf.)	M. Sembrich s. T. Parvis b. M. Journet bs.; A. Vigna cond.
Mar 22	*Pagliacci* (1 perf.)	B. Alten s. A. Reiss t. A. Scotti b. T. Parvis b.; A. Vigna cond.
Mar 24	*La Gioconda* (1 perf.)	L. Nordica s. L. Homer ms. E. Walker ms. E. Giraldoni b. P. Plançon bs.; A. Vigna cond.

MINNEAPOLIS – AUDITORIUM

Mar 28	*Pagliacci* (1 perf.)	B. Alten s. A. Reiss t. O. Goritz b. T. Parvis b.; A. Vigna cond.

OMAHA – AUDITORIUM

Mar 30	*Lucia di Lammermoor* (1 perf.)	M. Sembrich s. T. Parvis b. M. Journet bs.; A. Vigna cond.

KANSAS CITY – CONVENTION HALL

Apr 1	*Pagliacci* (1 perf.)	B. Alten s. A. Reiss t. O. Goritz b. T. Parvis b.; A. Vigna cond.

217

1905 cont.

SAN FRANCISCO – GRAND OPERA

Apr 6	*Rigoletto* (1 perf.)	M. Sembrich s. L. Homer ms. A. Scotti b. (T. Parvis b. in Act III) M. Journet bs.; A. Vigna cond.
Apr 8	*Pagliacci* (2 perf.)	M. Lemon s. (later B. Alten s.) A. Reiss t. A. Scotti b. (later O. Goritz b.) T. Parvis b.; A. Vigna cond.
Apr 10	*Lucia di Lammermoor* (1 perf.)	M. Sembrich s. T. Parvis b. M. Journet bs.; A. Vigna cond.
Apr 12	*La Gioconda* (2 perf.)	L. Nordica s. L. Homer ms. J. Jacoby ms. A. Scotti b. M. Journet bs.; A. Vigna cond.

LOS ANGELES – AUDITORIUM

Apr 18	*Lucia di Lammermoor* (1 perf.)	M. Sembrich. s. T. Parvis b. M. Journet bs.; A. Vigna cond.

NEW YORK – HOTEL WALDORF ASTORIA

Apr 26	Concert	L. Nordica s.; Victor Herbert and his orchestra

PARIS – THEATRE SARAH BERNHARDT

May 13	*Fedora* (6 perf.)	L. Cavalieri s. T. Ruffo b.; C. Campanini cond.

LONDON – COVENT GARDEN

May 22	*La Bohème* (6 perf.)	N. Melba s. (later P. Donalda s.) A. Scotti b. C. Gilibert b. M. Journet bs. (later Vanni-Marcoux bs.); C. Campanini cond.
May 26	*Rigoletto* (3 perf.)	S. Kurz s. E. Thornton ms. A. Scotti b. (later M. Sammarco b.) M. Journet bs.; C. Campanini cond.
June 3	*Gli Ugonotti* (3 perf.)	E. Destinn s. S. Kurz s. B. Alten s. A. Scotti b. M. Journet bs. C. Whitehill bs.; C. Campanini cond.
June 8	Concert	Act III of *La Bohème* and Act IV of *Gli Ugonotti*
June 10	*Aida* (2 perf.)	E. Destinn s. L. Kirkby-Lunn ms. (later R. Olitzka ms.) A. Scotti b. (later M. Sammarco b.) M. Journet bs.; C. Campanini cond.
June 19	*Un Ballo in maschera* (4 perf.)	J. Raunay s. (later M. Thecla s.) S. Kurz s. E. Thornton ms. (later R. Olitzka ms.) A. Scotti b. (later M. Sammarco b.) M. Journet bs. E. Cotreuil bs.; L. Mancinelli cond. (later C. Campanini cond.)
July 1	*Don Giovanni* (2 perf.)	E. Destinn s. P. Donalda s. A. Nicholls s. A. Scotti b. C. Gilibert b. M. Journet bs. Vanni-Marcoux bs.; A. Messager cond.

July 10	*Madama Butterfly* (Puccini) (4 perf.)	E. Destinn s. G. Lejeune ms. A. Scotti b.; C. Campanini cond.
	LONDON – SAVOY HOTEL	
July 26	Concert	
	OSTEND – THEATRE ROYAL	
Aug 3	*Rigoletto* (1 perf.)	L. Miranda s. Beronne b.
	OSTEND – KURSAAL	
Aug 6	Concert	(H), (I), (J) and (G)

1905–6

	NEW YORK – METROPOLITAN OPERA	
Nov 20	*La Gioconda* (3 perf.)	L. Nordica s. L. Homer ms. J. Jacoby ms. A. Scotti b. P. Plançon bs.; A. Vigna cond.
Nov 24	*Rigoletto* (4 perf.)	M. Sembrich s. J. Jacoby ms. A. Scotti b.; M. Journet bs.; A. Vigna cond.
Nov 29	*La Favorita* (4 perf.)	E. Walker ms. A. Scotti b. P. Plançon bs.; A. Vigna cond.
Dec 9	*L'Elisir d'amore* (2 perf.)	M. Sembrich s. A. Scotti b. A. Rossi bs.; A. Vigna cond.
Dec 15	*La Sonnambula* (Bellini) (2 perf.)	M. Sembrich s. P. Plançon bs.; A. Vigna cond.
Dec 18	*La Bohème* (4 perf.)	M. Sembrich s. B. Alten s. A. Scotti b. T. Parvis, b. M. Journet bs.; A. Vigna cond.
Jan 3	*Faust* (4 perf.)	E. Eames s. J. Jacoby ms. A. Scotti b. P. Plançon bs.; N. Franke cond.
Jan 8	*Tosca* (1 perf.)	E. Eames s. A. Scotti b.; A. Vigna cond.
Jan 15	*Aida* (3 perf.)	L. Nordica s. E. Walker ms. G. Campanari b. P. Plançon bs.; A. Vigna cond.
Jan 20	*Lucia di Lammermoor* (3 perf.)	M. Sembrich s. T. Parvis b. M. Journet bs.; A. Vigna cond.
Jan 31	*Pagliacci* (2 perf.)	B. Alten s. A. Reiss t. G. Campanari b. T. Parvis b. (later A. Mühlmann bs.); A. Vigna cond.
Feb 9	*Marta* (Flotow) (4 perf.)	M. Sembrich s. E. Walker ms. P. Plançon bs.; A. Vigna cond.
Feb 12	*La Traviata* (1 perf.)	M. Sembrich s. A. Scotti b.; A. Vigna cond.
Feb 15	Concert	(K) w. A. Scotti b.
Mar 5	*Carmen* (2 perf.)	B. Abott s. O. Fremstad s. M. Journet bs.; A. Vigna cond.

THE WORKS

PHILADELPHIA – ACADEMY OF MUSIC
(Concurrent with New York season)

Dec 5   *La Favorita*   E. Walker ms. A. Scotti b. P. Plançon bs.;
(1 perf.)   A. Vigna cond.

Dec 26   *Rigoletto*   M. Sembrich s. J. Jacoby ms. A. Scotti b.;
(1 perf.)   A. Vigna cond.

Jan 23   *La Bohème*   M. Sembrich s. B. Alten s. G. Campanari
(1 perf.)   b. T. Parvis b. M. Journet bs.; A. Vigna
cond.

Feb 6   *Aida*   E. Eames s. E. Walker ms. G. Campanari
(1 perf.)   b. P. Plançon bs.; A. Vigna cond.

Feb 29   *Carmen*   B. Abott s. O. Fremstad s. A. Scotti b.; A.
(1 perf.)   Vigna cond.

Mar 1   *Faust*   B. Abott s. J. Jacoby ms. G. Campanari b.
(1 perf.)   P. Plançon bs.; A. Vigna cond.

1906

NEW YORK – HOME OF MR J. H. SMITH

Jan 18   Concert   (L) and some Tosti songs; M. Rappold s.
L. Abarbanell s.; N. Franke cond.

NEW YORK – HOTEL WALDORF ASTORIA

Jan 22   Concert   Victor Herbert and his orchestra

WASHINGTON – HOME OF MR P. BELMONT

Jan 24   Concert   (M) (N) w. B. Abott and a Buzzi-Peccia
song.

NEW YORK – HOME OF MRS ORME WILSON

Feb 27   Concert

NEW YORK – HOTEL WALDORF ASTORIA

Mar 17   Concert   A. Scotti b.

Tour of the Metropolitan Opera Company from Baltimore to San Francisco
BALTIMORE – LYRIC THEATRE

Mar 19   *Marta*   M. Sembrich s. E. Walker ms. P. Plançon
(1 perf.)   bs.; A. Vigna cond.

Mar 21   *Faust*   E. Eames s. J. Jacoby ms. G. Campanari b.
(1 perf.)   P. Plançon bs.; A. Vigna cond.

WASHINGTON – NATIONAL THEATRE

Mar 23   *Lucia di Lammermoor*   M. Sembrich s. T. Parvis b. M. Journet
(1 perf.)   bs.; A. Vigna cond.

Mar 24   *Pagliacci*   B. Alten s. A. Reiss t. G. Campanari b. T.
(1 perf.)   Parvis b.; A. Vigna cond.

PITTSBURGH – NIXON THEATRE

Mar 27	*Carmen* (1 perf.)	B. Abott s. O. Fremstad s. M. Journet bs. A. Vigna cond.
Mar 29	*La Bohème* (1 perf.)	B. Abott s. B. Alten s. G. Campanari b. T. Parvis b. M. Journet bs.; A. Vigna cond.
Mar 31	*Faust* (1 perf.)	E. Eames s. J. Jacoby ms. G. Campanari b. P. Plançon bs.; A. Vigna cond.

CHICAGO – AUDITORIUM

Apr 3	*Faust* (1 perf.)	E. Eames s. J. Jacoby ms. A. Scotti b. P. Plançon bs.; A. Vigna cond.
Apr 5	*Carmen* (1 perf.)	B. Abott s. O. Fremstad s. M. Journet bs.; A. Vigna cond.
Apr 7	*Marta* (1 perf.)	M. Sembrich s. L. Homer ms. P. Plançon bs.; A. Vigna cond.

ST. LOUIS – OLYMPIC THEATRE

Apr 9	*Marta* (1 perf.)	M. Sembrich s. E. Walker ms. P. Plançon bs.; A. Vigna cond.
Apr 11	*Faust* (1 perf.)	E. Eames s. J. Jacoby ms. G. Campanari b. P. Plançon bs.; A. Vigna cond.

KANSAS CITY – CONVENTION HALL

Apr 12	*Marta* (1 perf.)	M. Sembrich s. E. Walker ms. P. Plançon bs.; A. Vigna cond.

SAN FRANCISCO – GRAND OPERA

Apr 17	*Carmen* (1 perf.)	B. Abott s. O. Fremstad s. M. Journet bs.; A. Vigna cond.

LONDON – COVENT GARDEN

May 15	*Rigoletto* (4 perf.)	P. Donalda s. (later N. Melba s., then F. Alda s.) L. Kirkby-Lunn ms. A. Scotti b. (later M. Battistini b.) M. Journet bs.; C. Campanini cond.
May 17	*La Bohème* (9 perf.)	N. Melba s. F. Parkina s. M. Sammarco b. (later A. Scotti b.) M. Journet bs.; C. Campanini cond.
May 24	*Pagliacci* (3 perf.)	E. Destinn s. A. Scotti b. (later M. Sammarco b.) P. Seveilhac b.; C. Campanini cond.
May 26	*Madama Butterfly* (5 perf.)	E. Destinn s. A. Scotti b.; C. Campanini cond.
June 9	*Tosca* (2 perf.)	R. Giachetti s. A. Scotti b.; C. Campanini cond.
June 25	*Aida* (2 perf.)	R. Giachetti s. L. Kirkby-Lunn ms. A. Scotti b. M. Journet bs.; C. Campanini cond.

1906 cont.

July 7   *La Traviata*   N. Melba s. M. Battistini b.; C.
         (2 perf.)   Campanini cond.

July 17   *Don Giovanni*   E. Destinn s. P. Donalda s. A. Nicholls s.
         (2 perf.)   M. Battistini b. (later A. Scotti b.) C.
                                Gilibert b. M. Journet bs. Vanni-
                                Marcoux bs.; A. Messager cond.

LONDON – FRENCH EMBASSY
May 28   Concert

LONDON – THEATRE ROYAL, DRURY LANE
June 12   Concert   Songs by and acc. by Tosti

OSTEND – KURSAAL
Aug 5   Concert   (D), (E) and arias of Mascagni and Puccini
Aug 9   Concert   (*Manon Lescaut* and *Tosca*). Also sang at
Aug 12   Concert   these concerts, though not in duet with
Aug 15   Concert   Caruso: Marthe Chenal s. Zina Brozia s.
Aug 19   Concert   Louise Kirkby-Lunn ms. Lina Cavalieri s.
Aug 23   Concert   Selma Kurz s. Jean Noté b. Marguerite
Aug 26   Concert   Carré s. Fany Carthant ? Alice Verlet s.
Aug 29   Concert   Elsa Szamosy m.s. Marie Louise
                                Hubert ms. Marthe de Saint-Loup ? Edith
                                Buyens ? Rachel Jean ? Mlle Delhaye ?

VIENNA – HOFOPER
Oct 6   *Rigoletto*   S. Kurz s. H. Kittel ms. T. Ruffo b.; F.
         (1 perf.)   Spetrino cond.

BERLIN – KONIGLICHES OPERNHAUS
Oct 9   *Rigoletto*   G. Farrar s. B. Hoffmann b.; E. von
         (1 perf.)   Strauss cond.

Oct 11   *Carmen*   T. Rothauser ms. R. Berger b.; L. Blech
         (1 perf.)   cond.

Oct 13   *Aida*   E. Destinn s. M. Goetze ms. B. Hoffmann
         (1 perf.)   b. J. Moedlinger bs.; L. Blech cond.

HAMBURG – STADTTHEATER
Oct 16   *Rigoletto*   A. Hindermann s. O. Metzger ms. M.
         (1 perf.)   Dawison b. M. Hohfing bs.; J. Stransky
                                cond.

Oct 18   *Carmen*   H. Offenberg s. O. Metzger ms. M.
         (1 perf.)   Dawison b.; J. Stransky cond.

PARIS – TROCADÉRO
Oct 25   Concert   (CJ), (CK), (G) and (B) w. E. Calvé s. M.
                                Flathaut ms. J. Noté b.

1906–7

NEW YORK – METROPOLITAN OPERA
Nov 28   *La Bohème*   M. Sembrich s. (later L. Cavalieri s.; then
         (5 perf.)   G. Farrar s.) B. Alten s. A. Scotti b. (later
                                R. Stracciari b.) M. Simard b. M. Journet
                                bs.; A. Vigna cond.

Dec 1	*La Traviata* (2 perf.)	M. Sembrich s. R. Stracciari b. (later A. Scotti b.); A. Vigna cond.
Dec 3	*Marta* (2 perf.)	M. Sembrich s. L. Homer ms. M. Journet bs.; A. Vigna cond.
Dec 5	**Fedora* (4 perf.)	L. Cavalieri s. B. Alten s. A. Scotti b.; A. Vigna cond.
Dec 12	*Lucia di Lammermoor* (1 perf.)	M. Sembrich s. R. Stracciari b. M. Journet bs.; A. Vigna cond.
Dec 21	*Aida* (5 perf.)	C. Boninsegna s. (later E. Eames s.) L. Kirkby-Lunn ms. (later L. Homer ms.) R. Stracciari b. (later A. Scotti b.) P. Plançon bs.; A. Vigna cond.
Jan 2	*Tosca* (4 perf.)	E. Eames s. (later L. Cavalieri s.) A. Scotti b.; A. Vigna cond.
Jan 11	*L'Africana* (Meyerbeer) (2 perf.)	O. Fremstad s. M. Rappold s. R. Stracciari b. P. Plançon bs. M. Journet bs.; A. Vigna cond.
Jan 16	*Pagliacci* (2 perf.)	B. Alten s. A. Reiss. t. A. Scotti b. M. Simard b.; A. Vigna cond.
Jan 18	*Manon Lescaut* (3 perf.)	L. Cavalieri s. A. Scotti b. A. Rossi bs.; A. Vigna cond.
Jan 22	Concert	(O)
Feb 11	*Madama Butterfly* (4 perf.)	G. Farrar s. L. Homer ms. A. Scotti b. (later R. Stracciari b.); A. Vigna cond.
Feb 27	*Rigoletto* (2 perf.)	M. Sembrich s. L. Homer ms. R. Stracciari b. M. Journet bs.; A. Vigna cond.

PHILADELPHIA – ACADEMY OF MUSIC
(Concurrent with New York season)

Dec 27	*Fedora* (1 perf.)	L. Cavalieri s. B. Alten s. A. Scotti b.; A. Vigna cond.
Jan 15	*Marta* (1 perf.)	M. Sembrich s. L. Homer ms. M. Journet bs.; A. Vigna cond.
Feb 7	*Aida* (1 perf.)	E. Eames s. L. Homer ms. R. Stracciari b. P. Plançon bs.; A. Vigna cond.
Feb 14	*Madama Butterfly* (1 perf.)	G. Farrar s. L. Homer ms. R. Stracciari b.; A. Vigna cond.
Feb 21	*Manon Lescaut* (1 perf.)	L. Cavalieri s. A. Scotti b. A. Rossi bs.; A. Vigna cond.
Mar 5	*Pagliacci* (1 perf.)	G. Farrar s. A. Reiss t. R. Stracciari b. M. Simard b.; A. Vigna cond.

1906–7 cont.

Mar 7	*La Bohème* (1 perf.)	M. Sembrich s. B. Alten s. A. Scotti b. M. Simard b. M. Journet bs.; A. Vigna cond.

1907

Tour of the Metropolitan Opera Company from Baltimore to Milwaukee
BALTIMORE – LYRIC THEATRE

Mar 25	*La Bohème* (1 perf.)	M. Sembrich s. B. Alten s. A. Scotti b. M. Simard b. M. Journet bs.; A. Vigna cond.
Mar 26	*Pagliacci* (1 perf.)	B. Alten s. J. Bars t. R. Stracciari b. M. Simard b.; A. Vigna cond.

WASHINGTON – BELASCO THEATRE

Mar 28	*Madama Butterfly* (1 perf.)	G. Farrar s. L. Homer ms. R. Stracciari b.; A. Vigna cond.
Mar 30	*Aida* (1 perf.)	M. Rappold s. L. Homer ms. R. Stracciari b. M. Journet bs.; A. Vigna cond.

BOSTON – BOSTON THEATRE

Apr 2	*Tosca* (1 perf.)	E. Eames s. A. Scotti b.; A. Vigna cond.
Apr 4	*Marta* (4 perf.)	M. Mattfeld. s. J. Jacoby ms. M. Journet bs.; A. Vigna cond.
Apr 6	*Aida* (1 perf.)	E. Eames s. J. Jacoby ms. R. Stracciari b. P. Plançon bs.; A. Vigna cond.

CHICAGO – AUDITORIUM

Apr 8	*L'Africana* (1 perf.)	O. Fremstad s. M. Rappold s. R. Stracciari b. P. Plançon bs. M. Journet bs.; A. Vigna cond.
Apr 10	*Aida* (1 perf.)	E. Eames s. J. Jacoby ms. R. Stracciari b. P. Plançon bs.; A. Vigna cond.
Apr 12	*La Bohème* (1 perf.)	G. Ciaparelli s. B. Alten s. A. Scotti b. M. Simard b. M. Journet bs.; A. Vigna cond.
Apr 13	*Pagliacci* (1 perf.)	B. Alten s. A. Reiss t. R. Stracciari b. M. Simard b.; A. Vigna cond.

CINCINNATI – MUSIC HALL

Apr 15	*Aida* (1 perf.)	M. Rappold s. J. Jacoby ms. R. Stracciari b. M. Journet bs.; A. Vigna cond.

ST. LOUIS – ODEON THEATRE

Apr 17	*Aida* (1 perf.)	E. Eames s. J. Jacoby ms. R. Stracciari b. M. Journet bs.; A. Vigna cond.
Apr 19	*La Bohème* (1 perf.)	G. Ciaparelli s. B. Alten s. R. Stracciari b. M. Simard b. M. Journet bs.; A. Vigna cond.

KANSAS CITY – CONVENTION HALL

Apr 20	*La Bohème* (1 perf.)	G. Farrar s. B. Alten s. R. Stracciari b. M. Simard b. M. Journet bs.; A. Vigna cond.

A CHRONOLOGY OF CARUSO'S APPEARANCES

Apr 22
OMAHA – AUDITORIUM
La Bohème
(1 perf.)

G. Ciaparelli s. B. Alten s. R. Stracciari b. M. Simard b. M. Journet bs.; A. Vigna cond.

Apr 24
ST. PAUL – AUDITORIUM
La Bohème
(1 perf.)

G. Ciaparelli s. M. Mattfeld s. R. Stracciari b. M. Simard b. M. Journet bs.; A. Vigna cond.

Apr 26
MINNEAPOLIS – AUDITORIUM
Aida
(1 perf.)

M. Rappold s. J. Jacoby ms. R. Stracciari b. M. Journet bs.; A. Vigna cond.

Apr 27
MILWAUKEE – ALHAMBRA THEATRE
Pagliacci
(1 perf.)

B. Alten s. A. Reiss t. R. Stracciari b. M. Simard b.; A. Vigna cond.

May 15
LONDON – COVENT GARDEN
La Bohème
(8 perf.)

P. Donalda s. (later N. Melba s.) A. Zeppilli s. (later E. Parkina s.) A. Scotti b. C. Gilibert b. M. Journet bs.; L. Mancinelli cond.

May 17
Madama Butterfly
(4 perf.)

E. Destinn s. A. Scotti b.; L. Mancinelli cond.

May 25
La Traviata
(5 perf.)

P. Donalda s. (later N. Melba s.) A. Scotti b.; C. Campanini cond.

May 29
Aida
(3 perf.)

E. Destinn s. L. Kirkby-Lunn ms. A. Scotti b. M. Journet bs. Vanni-Marcoux bs.; C. Campanini cond.

June 6
Carmen
(2 perf.)

P. Donalda s. L. Kirkby-Lunn ms. A. Scandiani b.; C. Campanini cond.

June 11
Concert

Act I of *Butterfly* and Act I of *La Bohème*

June 13
Tosca
(3 perf.)

R. Giachetti s. A. Scotti b.; C. Campanini cond.

June 28
Un Ballo in maschera
(1 perf.)

M. Scalar s. S. Kurz s. E. De Cisneros ms. M. Sammarco b. Vanni-Marcoux bs. M. Journet bs.; E. Panizza cond.

July 3
Fedora
(2 perf.)

R. Giachetti s. A. Zeppilli s. A. Scotti b. E. Panizza cond.

July 20
Andrea Chénier (Giordano)
(2 perf.)

E. Destinn s. M. Sammarco b.; E. Panizza cond.

July 26
Pagliacci
(1 perf.)

E. Destinn s. M. Sammarco b.; C. Campanini cond.

THE WORKS

1907 cont.

PARIS – TROCADÉRO
May 18 Concert

LONDON
July 18 Concert

BUDAPEST – KIRALYI OPERAHAZ
Oct 2 *Aida* H. Ney s. G. Flatt ms. M. Takáts b. R.
(1 perf.) Erdös bs.; H. Benkö cond.

VIENNA – HOFOPER
Oct 4 *Aida* L. Weidt s. (later E. Bland s.) C. Cahier
(2 perf.) ms. F. Weidemann b. W. Hesch bs.;
G. Mahler cond.

Oct 6 *La Bohème* S. Kurz s. G. Forst s. G. Stehmann b. R.
(1 perf.) Mayr bs.; F. Spetrino cond.

Oct 11 *Rigoletto* S. Kurz s. H. Kittel ms. L. Demuth b. W.
(1 perf.) Hesch bs.; F. Spetrino cond.

LEIPZIG – STADTTHEATER
Oct 13 *Aida* Osborne-Hannach s. Wrbaczek ms.
(1 perf.) W. Soomer b.; Porst cond.

HAMBURG – STADTTHEATER
Oct 15 *Rigoletto* A. Hindermann s. O. Metzger ms. M.
(1 perf.) Dawison b. M. Lohfing bs.; J. Stransky
cond.

Oct 17 *Pagliacci* H. Offenburg s. R. vom Scheidt b.; J.
(1 perf.) Stransky cond.

Oct 19 *Aida* M. Kuhnel s. O. Metzger ms. M. Dawison
(1 perf.) b. A. Hinkley bs.; G. Brechner cond.

BERLIN – KONIGLICHES OPERNHAUS
Oct 23 *Rigoletto* F. Hempel s. B. Hoffmann b. E. von
(1 perf.) Strauss cond.

Oct 25 *Aida* E. Destinn s. M. Goetze ms. B. Hoffmann
(2 perf.) b. P. Knupfer bs.; L. Blech cond.

Oct 27 *Lucia di Lammermoor* F. Hempel s.; E. von Strauss cond.
(1 perf.)

FRANKFURT – OPERNHAUS
Oct 31 *Aida* E. Hensel-Schweitzer s. E. Schroeder ms.
(1 perf.) R. Breitenfeld b. E. Lankow bs.; L. Rottenberg cond.

Nov 2 *Rigoletto* R. Breitenfeld b.; H. Reichenberger cond.
(1 perf.)

A CHRONOLOGY OF CARUSO'S APPEARANCES

1907–8

NEW YORK – METROPOLITAN OPERA

Nov 18	*Adriana Lecouvreur* (2 perf.)	L. Cavalieri s. J. Jacoby ms. A. Scotti b.; R. Ferrari cond.
Nov 21	Aida (6 perf.)	J. Gadski s. (later M. Rappold s.) L. Kirkby-Lunn ms. A. Scotti b. M. Journet bs. (later R. Blass bs., then P. Plançon bs.); R. Ferrari cond.
Nov 23	La Bohème (1 perf.)	G. Farrar s. F. Dereyne s. A. Scotti b. B. Bégué b. M. Journet bs.; R. Ferrari cond.
Dec 6	Iris (5 perf.)	E. Eames s. A. Scotti b. M. Journet bs.; R. Ferrari cond.
Dec 14	Madama Butterfly (5 perf.)	G. Farrar s. J. Jacoby ms. A. Scotti b. (later R. Stracciari b.); R. Ferrari cond.
Dec 19	Fedora (3 perf.)	L. Cavalieri s. B. Alten s. A. Scotti b.; R. Ferrari cond.
Dec 21	Tosca (5 perf.)	E. Eames s. A. Scotti b.; R. Ferrari cond.
Jan 6	Faust (5 perf.)	G. Farrar s. (later E. Eames s.) J. Jacoby ms. A. Scotti b. (later R. Stracciari b.) F. Chaliapin bs. (later P. Plançon bs.); R. Ferrari cond.
Jan 25	Manon Lescaut (4 perf.)	L. Cavalieri s. A. Scotti b. A. Baracchi b. R. Ferrari cond.
Feb 6	Pagliacci (3 perf.)	F. Dereyne s. (later L. Cavalieri s.; then G. Farrar s.) A. Reiss t. A. Scotti b. A. Sarto b.; R. Ferrari cond.
Feb 26	Il Trovatore (Verdi) (6 perf.)	E. Eames s. (later R. Fornia s.) L. Homer ms. R. Stracciari b. A. Mühlmann bs.; R. Ferrari cond.
Mar 24	Concert	Act IV, Scene 1, Il Trovatore, Act II, Faust and Act I, Pagliacci.

PHILADELPHIA – ACADEMY OF MUSIC
(Concurrent with New York season)

Dec 17	Madama Butterfly (1 perf.)	G. Farrar s. J. Jacoby ms. A. Scotti b.; R. Ferrari cond.
Jan 14	Adriana Lecouvreur (1 perf.)	L. Cavalieri s. J. Jacoby ms. A. Scotti b.; R. Ferrari cond.
Feb 4	Iris (1 perf.)	E. Eames s. A. Scotti b. M. Journet bs.; R. Ferrari cond.
Mar 3	Il Trovatore (1 perf.)	E. Eames s. L. Homer ms. R. Stracciari b. A. Mühlmann bs.; R. Ferrari cond.

1907–8 cont.

Mar 17   *Aida*   E. Eames s. L. Kirkby-Lunn ms. A. Scotti
           (1 perf.)   b. P. Plançon bs.; R. Ferrari cond.

Mar 31   *Tosca*   E. Eames s. A. Scotti b.; R. Ferrari cond.
           (1 perf.)

1908

NEW YORK – HOTEL WALDORF ASTORIA

Jan 13   Concert

Apr 3   Concert   (P) w. G. Farrar s.

Tour of the Metropolitan Opera Company from Boston to Pittsburgh
BOSTON – BOSTON THEATRE

Apr 6   *Iris*   E. Eames s. A. Scotti b. A. Mühlmann bs.;
           (1 perf.)   R. Ferrari cond.

Apr 8   *Il Trovatore*   R. Fornia s. L. Homer ms. R. Stracciari b.
           (1 perf.)   A. Mühlmann bs.; R. Ferrari cond.

Apr 10   *Manon Lescaut*   L. Cavalieri s. A. Scotti b.; R. Ferrari
           (1 perf.)   cond.

BALTIMORE – LYRIC THEATER

Apr 13   *Manon Lescaut*   L. Cavalieri s. R. Stracciari b.; R. Ferrari
           (1 perf.)   cond.

Apr 15   *Il Trovatore*   E. Eames s. L. Homer ms. R. Stracciari b.
           (1 perf.)   B. Bégué bs.; R. Ferrari cond.

WASHINGTON – NEW NATIONAL THEATER

Apr 18   *Pagliacci*   F. Dereyne s. A. Reiss t. A. Scotti b.; A.
           (1 perf.)   Sarto b.; R. Ferrari cond.

CHICAGO – AUDITORIUM

Apr 21   *Il Trovatore*   E. Eames s. L. Homer ms. R. Stracciari b.
           (1 perf.)   A. Mühlmann bs.; R. Ferrari cond.

Apr 23   *Pagliacci*   B. Alten s. A. Reiss t. A. Scotti b. A.
           (1 perf.)   Mühlmann bs.; R. Ferrari cond.

Apr 25   *Iris*   E. Eames s. A. Scotti b. A. Mühlmann bs.;
           (5 perf.)   R. Ferrari cond.

PITTSBURGH – NIXON THEATER

Apr 27   *Faust*   E. Eames s. J. Jacoby ms. G. Campanari b.
           (1 perf.)   P. Plançon bs.; R. Ferrari cond.

Apr 29   *Il Trovatore*   E. Eames s. L. Homer ms. G. Campanari
           (1 perf.)   b. A. Mühlmann bs.; R. Ferrari cond.

COLUMBUS – MEMORIAL HALL

May 1   Concert

TORONTO – MASSEY HALL

May 4   Concert   (I), (L), (Q) and (B) w. G. Allen s. M.
                                   Keyes ms. H. Scott b.

A CHRONOLOGY OF CARUSO'S APPEARANCES

DETROIT – LIGHT GUARD ARMORY
May 6   Concert

BUFFALO – CONVENTION HALL
May 8   Concert   (as Toronto) w. G. Allen s. M. Keyes ms. H. Scott b.

CLEVELAND – HIPPODROME
May 11   Concert   (as above) w. G. Allen s. M. Keyes ms. H. Scott b.

ROCHESTER – CONVENTION HALL
May 13   Concert

MONTREAL – ARENA
May 18   Concert   (I), (L), (Q) and (B) w. G. Allen s. M. Keyes ms. H. Scott b.

LONDON – ROYAL ALBERT HALL
May 30   Concert   (D), (I) and (B) w. N. Melba s. E. Thornton ms. M. Sammarco b.

PARIS – OPERA
June 11   *Rigoletto*   N. Melba s. E. Petrenko ms. M. Renaud b. A. Gresse bs.; T. Serafin cond.

WIESBADEN
Oct 1   *Rigoletto* (1 perf.)   B. Engel s. Geisse-Winkell b.; Mannstaedt cond.

FRANKFURT – OPERNHAUS
Oct 3   *La Bohème* (1 perf.)   L. Sellin s. B. Kernic s. R. Breitenfeld b. Lankow bs.; L. Rottenberg cond.

Oct 7   *Pagliacci* (1 perf.)   B. Kernic s. R. Breitenfeld b. R. Brinkmann b.; F. Neumann cond.

BREMEN – STADTTHEATER
Oct 11   *Pagliacci* (1 perf.)

HAMBURG – STADTTHEATER
Oct 13   *La Bohème* (1 perf.)   K. Fleischer s. A. Hindermann s. M. Dawison b. R. vom Scheidt b. M. Lohfing bs.; J. Stransky cond.

Oct 15   *Pagliacci* (1 perf.)   B. Alten s. F. Weidmann t. R. vom Scheidt b.; J. Stransky cond.

LEIPZIG – STADTTHEATER
Oct 17   *Rigoletto* (1 perf.)   Eichholz s. W. Soomer b.

BERLIN – KONIGLICHES OPERNHAUS
Oct 20   *Pagliacci* (1 perf.)   G. Farrar s. W. Kirchhoff t. A. Scotti b. C. Bronsgeest b. E. von Strauss cond.

THE WORKS

1908 cont.

Oct 22   *Aida*   M. Salvatini s. M. Goetze ms. A. Scotti b.
          (1 perf.)   P. Knuepfer bs.; L. Blech cond.

Oct 24   *La Bohème*   G. Farrar s. A. Scotti b. C. Bronsgeest b.
          (1 perf.)   H. Bachmann b.; L. Blech cond.

1908–09

BROOKLYN – ACADEMY OF MUSIC
(Concurrent with New York season)

Nov 14   *Faust*   G. Farrar s. R. Fornia s. J. Noté b. A.
          (1 perf.)   Didur bs.; F. Spetrino cond.

Jan 4   *Il Trovatore*   E. Eames s. M. Gay ms. P. Amato b. G.
         (1 perf.)   Rossi bs.; F. Spetrino cond.

Jan 14   *Carmen*   M. Rappold s. M. Gay ms. J. Noté b.; A.
         (1 perf.)   Toscanini cond.

NEW YORK – METROPOLITAN OPERA

Nov 16   *Aida*   E. Destinn s. (later E. Eames s. then M.
         (6 perf.)   Rappold s.) L. Homer ms. (later M.
                                Flahaut ms. then M. Gay ms.) A. Scotti b.
                                (later P. Amato b.; then G. Campanari b.)
                                A. Didur bs.; A. Toscanini cond.

Nov 19   *Madama Butterfly*   G. Farrar s. R. Fornia ms. A. Scotti b.; A.
         (1 perf.)   Toscanini cond.

Nov 20   *La Traviata*   M. Sembrich s. P. Amato b. (later G.
         (3 perf.)   Campanari b.); F. Spetrino cond.

Nov 21   *Tosca*   E. Eames s. A. Scotti b.; F. Spetrino cond.
         (2 perf.)   (later A. Toscanini cond.)

Dec 3   *Carmen*   G. Farrar s. M. Gay ms. J. Noté b.; A.
        (3 perf.)   Toscanini cond.

Dec 5   *Faust*   G. Farrar s. (later F. Alda s.) I. L'Huillier
        (3 perf.)   ms. J. Noté b. A. Didur bs.; F. Spetrino
                                cond.

Dec 7   *Rigoletto*   F. Alda s. L. Homer ms. P. Amato b. A.
        (1 perf.)   Didur bs.; F. Spetrino cond.

Dec 17   *Cavalleria rusticana*   E. Destinn s. M. Gay ms. P. Amato b.; A.
        (3 perf.)   Toscanini cond.

Dec 26   *Pagliacci*   G. Farrar s. (later E. Destinn s.) A. Bada t.
        (2 perf.)   G. Campanari b. (later A. Lecomte b.); F.
                                Spetrino cond.

Feb 3   *Manon* (Massenet)   G. Farrar s. (later F. Alda s.) A. Scotti b. J.
        (3 perf.)   Noté b. (later G. Rossi bs.); F. Spetrino
                                cond.

PHILADELPHIA – ACADEMY OF MUSIC
(Concurrent with New York season)

Nov 17   *La Bohème*   M. Sembrich s. I. L'Huillier s. A. Scotti b.
        (1 perf.)   A. Rossi bs.; F. Spetrino cond.

A CHRONOLOGY OF CARUSO'S APPEARANCES

Nov 24	*Faust* (1 perf.)	G. Farrar s. R. Fornia s. J. Noté b. A. Didur bs.; Hagemann cond.
Dec 1	*Aida* (1 perf.)	E. Destinn s. L. Homer ms. A. Scotti b. A. Didur bs.; A. Toscanini cond.
Dec 29	*Madama Butterfly* (1 perf.)	E. Destinn s. R. Fornia ms. P. Amato b.; A. Toscanini cond.
Jan 12	*Carmen* (1 perf.)	M. Rappold s. M. Gay ms. J. Noté b.; A. Toscanini cond.
Jan 28	*Il Trovatore* (1 perf.)	M. Rappold s. M. Flahaut ms. G. Campanari b. Bazzano bs.; F. Spetrino cond.
Mar 2	*Pagliacci* (1 perf.)	B. de Pasquali s. A. Bada t. P. Amato b. E. Cibelli b.; F. Spetrino cond.

1909

NEW YORK – HOTEL WALDORF ASTORIA

Jan 18	Concert	(I), (O), (D), (R) and (S)

BALTIMORE – LYRIC THEATRE
(Concurrent with New York season)

Jan 20	*Madama Butterfly* (1 perf.)	E. Destinn s. R. Fornia ms. A. Scotti b.; A. Toscanini cond.
Mar 8	*Pagliacci* (1 perf.)	B. De Pasquali s. A. Bada t. P. Amato b. A. Lecomte b.; F. Spetrino cond.

NEW YORK – HOME OF MRS G. GOULD

Feb 5	Concert

OSTEND – KURSAAL

Aug 1	Concert	(O), (H) and (I)

DUBLIN – THEATRE ROYAL

Aug 20	Concert	(I), (O), (Q) and (U), (AO), (C), (CC), and (K) w. A. Lecomte b.

PLYMOUTH – GUILDHALL

Aug 25	Concert

BLACKPOOL – WINTER GARDEN

Aug 29	Concert

GLASGOW – ST ANDREW'S HALL

Sep 3	Concert	(Q), (O), (I), (T), (U), (R), (H), (V), (W)

EDINBURGH – McEWAN HALL

Sep 7	Concert	(X), (O), (C) and (K) w. A. Lecomte b.

NEWCASTLE – TOWN HALL

Sep 10	Concert

THE WORKS

	MANCHESTER – FREE TRADE HALL	
Sep 13	Concert	(Q), (O), (I) and (K) w. A. Lecomte b.

	BELFAST – ULSTER HALL	
Sep 15	Concert	

	LONDON – ROYAL ALBERT HALL	
Sep 18	Concert	(Q), (O), (I) and (K) w. A. Lecomte b., T. Beecham cond.

	LIVERPOOL – PHILHARMONIC HALL	
Sep 20	Concert	

	FRANKFURT – OPERNHAUS	
Sep 29	*Tosca* (1 perf.)	E. Hensel-Schweitzer s. R. Breitenfeld b.; L. Rottenberg cond.
Oct 1	*Carmen* (1 perf.)	E. Gentner-Fischer s. E. Schroeder ms. R. Breitenfeld b.; L. Rottenberg cond.
Oct 3	*Pagliacci* (1 perf.)	L. Sellin s. R. Breitenfeld b.; F. Neumann cond.

	NUREMBERG – STADTTHEATER	
Oct 7	*Rigoletto* (1 perf.)	

	HAMBURG – STADTTHEATER	
Oct 11	*Lucia di Lammermoor* (1 perf.)	A. Hindermann s. M. Dawison b. T. Lattermann bs.; J. Stransky cond.
Oct 13	*Carmen* (1 perf.)	B. Alten s. O. Metzger ms. H. Wiedemann b.; J. Stransky cond.
Oct 15	*Tosca* (1 perf.)	E. Walker s. M. Dawison b.; G. Brecher cond.

	BERLIN – KONIGLICHES OPERNHAUS	
Oct 19	*Carmen* (1 perf.)	L. Artôt de Padilla s. F. Rose ms.; L. Blech cond.
Oct 21	*La Bohème* (1 perf.)	F. Hempel s. M. Dietrich s. B. Hoffmann b. C. Bronsgeest b. H. Bachmann b.
Oct 23	*Pagliacci* (1 perf.)	E. Destinn s. W. Kirchhoff t. van Hulst b. C. Bronsgeest b.

	BREMEN – STADTTHEATER	
Oct 25	*Carmen* (1 perf.)	Rudiger s. O. Metzger ms. Bodenklebe b.; E. Pollak cond.

1909–10

	PHILADELPHIA – ACADEMY OF MUSIC (Concurrent with New York season)	
Nov 9	*Aida* (2 perf.)	J. Gadski s. L. Homer ms. P. Amato b. A. Hinkley bs.; A. Toscanini cond.

Nov 30	*La Gioconda* (1 perf.)	E. Destinn s. G. Fabbri ms. P. Amato b. A. De Segurola bs.; A. Toscanini cond.
Dec 28	*Pagliacci* (1 perf.)	J. Noria s. A. Bada t. P. Amato b. V. Reschiglian b.; E. Tango cond.
Feb 10	*Rigoletto* (1 perf.)	B. De Pasquali s. M. von Niessen-Stone ms. P. Amato b. A. De Segurola bs.; V. Podesti cond.
Feb 15	**Germania* (1 perf.)	E. Destinn s. P. Amato b.; A. Toscanini cond.

NEW YORK – METROPOLITAN OPERA

Nov 15	*La Gioconda* (6 perf.)	E. Destinn s. L. Homer ms. A. Meitschik ms. P. Amato b. A. De Segurola bs.; A. Toscanini cond.
Nov 18	*La Traviata* (2 perf.)	L. Lipkowska s. (later B. De Pasquali s.) P. Amato b. (later G. Campanari b.); V. Podesti cond.
Nov 24	*Pagliacci* (5 perf.)	J. Noria s. (later B. Alten s.) A. Bada t. A. Scotti b. (later P. Amato b.) D. Gilly b.; E. Tango cond.
Dec 3	*Aida* (4 perf.)	J. Gadski s. (later E. Destinn s.) L. Homer ms. P. Amato b. A. Didur bs.; A. Toscanini cond.
Dec 11	*Tosca* (1 perf.)	O. A. Didur bs.; V. Podesti cond.
Jan 4	*La Bohème* (3 perf.)	G. Ciaparelli s. (later F. Alda s.; then G. Farrar s.) J. Noria s. A. Scotti b. A. Didur bs. A. De Segurola bs.; V. Podesti cond.
Jan 22	*Germania* (5 perf.)	E. Destinn s. P. Amato b.; A. Toscanini cond.
Feb 18	*Rigoletto* (1 perf.)	L. Lipowska s. A. Meitschik ms. P. Amato b. A. Didur bs.; V. Podesti cond.
Mar 1	Concert	Act I, *Pagliacci* and Act III, *La Gioconda*

BROOKLYN – ACADEMY OF MUSIC
(Concurrent with New York season)

Nov 22	*Madama Butterfly* (1 perf.)	E. Destinn s. R. Fornia ms. A. De Segurola bs.; V. Podesti cond.
Jan 17	*Aida* (1 perf.)	E. Destinn s. M. Flahaut ms. P. Amato b. A. Didur bs.; A. Toscanini cond.
Mar 7	*La Gioconda* (1 perf.)	E. Destinn s. L. Homer ms. P. Amato b. A. De Segurola bs.; A. Toscanini cond.

1909–10 cont.

Mar 21	*Rigoletto* (1 perf.)	E. De Hidalgo s. J. Mauburg ms. G. Campanari b. A. De Segurola bs.; E. Tango cond.

BALTIMORE – LYRIC THEATRE

Dec 17	*Pagliacci* (1 perf.)	J. Noria s. A. Bada t. P. Amato b. D. Gilly b.; M. Bendix cond.

1910

BOSTON – BOSTON THEATRE

Jan 15	*Pagliacci* (1 perf.)	J. Noria s. A. Bada t. P. Amato b. V. Reschiglian b.; E. Tango cond.
Feb 2	*La Gioconda* (1 perf.)	E. Destinn s. G. Fabbri ms. P. Amato b. A. De Segurola bs.; A. Toscanini cond.
Mar 28	*Aida* (1 perf.)	E. Destinn s. L. Homer ms. P. Amato b. A. De Segurola bs.; A. Toscanini cond.
Mar 30	*La Bohème* (1 perf.)	A. Gluck s. L. Sparkes s. D. Gilly b. A. Pini-Corsi b.; V. Podesti cond.

NEW YORK – HOTEL WALDORF ASTORIA

Jan 24	Concert	

Tour of the Metropolitan Opera Company from Chicago to Atlanta

CHICAGO – AUDITORIUM

Apr 4	*La Gioconda* (1 perf.)	E. Destinn s. L. Homer ms. P. Amato b. A. De Segurola bs.l; A. Toscanini cond.
Apr 6	*La Bohème* (2 perf.)	A. Nielsen s. (later G. Ciaparelli s.) L. Sparkes s. G. Campanari b. A. Didur bs. (later A. Pini-Corsi b.) G. Rossi bs. (later A. De Segurola bs.); V. Podesti cond.
Apr 9	**Germania* (1 perf.)	E. Destinn s. P. Amato b.; A. Toscanini cond.
Apr 13	*Aida* (1 perf.)	E. Destinn s. L. Homer ms. D. Gilly b. A. De Segurola bs.; A. Toscanini cond.
Apr 16	*Pagliacci* (2 perf.)	B. Alten s. A. Bada t. P. Amato b. V. Reschiglian b.; E. Tango cond.
Apr 20	*Faust* (1 perf.)	A. Gluck s. R. Fornia ms. D. Gilly b. A. De Segurola bs.; V. Podesti cond.

CLEVELAND – KEITH'S HIPPODROME

Apr 11	*Marta* (1 perf.)	B. De Pasquali s. L. Homer ms. A. Didur bs.; T. Voghera cond.

MILWAUKEE – AUDITORIUM

Apr 18	*Aida* (1 perf.)	E. Destinn s. L. Homer ms. G. Campanari b. A. Didur bs.; V. Podesti cond.

ST PAUL – AUDITORIUM

Apr 22	*Pagliacci* (1 perf.)	J. Noria s. A. Bada t. J. Forsell b. V. Reschiglian b.; E. Tango cond.

A CHRONOLOGY OF CARUSO'S APPEARANCES

ST LOUIS – COLISEUM

Apr 25   *La Bohème*   A. Gluck s. V. Courtenay s. P. Amato b. V.
(1 perf.)   Reschiglian b. A. De Segurola bs.; V. Podesti cond.

ATLANTA – AUDITORIUM

May 4   *Aida*   J. Gadski s. L. Homer ms. P. Amato b. R.
(1 perf.)   Blass bs.; F. Tanara cond.

May 7   *Pagliacci*   J. Noria s. A. Bada t. P. Amato b. V.
(1 perf.)   Reschiglian b.; E. Tango cond.

PARIS – TROCADÉRO

May 18   Concert

PARIS – THÉÂTRE DU CHATELET
Visit of Metropolitan Opera, New York

May 21   *Aida*   E. Destinn s. L. Homer ms. P. Amato b. A.
(3 perf.)   De Segurola bs.; A. Toscanini cond.

May 23   *Pagliacci*   B. Alten s. A. Bada t. P. Amato b. A. Costa
(3 perf.)   b.; V. Podesti cond.

June 9   **Manon Lescaut*   L. Bori s. P. Amato b.; A. Toscanini cond.
(5 perf.)

PARIS – OPERA

June 19   Concert   Act III, *La Bohème* w. G. Farrar s.
B. Alten s. A. Scotti b.
Act V, *Faust* w. G. Farrar s. A. De Segurola bs.

BRUSSELS – THEATRE DE LA MONNAIE

Sep 24   *La Bohème*   F. Alda s. B. Alten s. P. Amato b.; S.
(2 perf.)   Dupuis cond.

FRANKFURT – OPERNHAUS

Oct 2   *Aida*   E. Hensel-Schweitzer s. B. Halbaerth ms.
R. Breitenfeld b. Hagedorn bs.; L. Rottenberg cond.

Oct 4   *Carmen*   E. Gentner-Fischer s. I. Tervani ms. R.
Breitenfeld b.; L. Rottenberg cond.

MUNICH – HOF-UND NATIONALTHEATER

Oct 8   *Carmen*   E. Burg-Zimmermann s. M. Matzenauer
(1 perf.)   ms. F. Brodersen b.; O. Rohr cond.

Oct 11   *La Bohème*   M. Craft s. von Vadung s. F. Brodersen
(1 perf.)   b. P. Bender bs. M. Gillmann bs.; O. Rohr cond.

HAMBURG – STADTTHEATER

Oct 15   *Rigoletto*   A. Hindermann s. M. Dawison b.; O.
(1 perf.)   Klemperer cond.

Oct 18   *Marta*   A. Hindermann s. M. Mosel-Tomschik
(1 perf.)   ms. M. Lohfing bs.; O. Klemperer cond.

1910 cont.

Oct 20   *Carmen*   K. Fleischer s. O. Metzger ms. H. Wied-
                (1 perf.)   emann b.; O. Klemperer cond.

POTSDAM – IMPERIAL PALACE
Oct 22   Concert

BERLIN – NEUES OPERNTHEATER
Oct 24   *Aida*   F. Easton s. M. Goetze ms. C. Bronsgeest
                (1 perf.)   b. P. Knuepfer bs.; L. Blech cond.

Oct 27   *Carmen*   L. Artôt de Padilla s. F. Rose ms.
                (1 perf.)

Oct 30   *L'Elisir d'amore*   F. Hempel s. Rafe b. L. Mantlers bs.; L.
                (1 perf.)   Blech cond.

1910–11

NEW YORK – METROPOLITAN OPERA
Nov 14   **Armide* (Gluck)   O. Fremstad s. L. Homer ms. A. Gluck s.
                (3 perf.)   P. Amato b. D. Gilly b.; A. Toscanini
                                             cond.

Nov 17   *Aida*   E. Destinn s. (later M. Rappold s.) L.
                (4 perf.)   Homer ms. (later M. Claessens ms.) P.
                                             Amato b. (later A. Scotti b.) A. Didur bs.
                                             (later A. De Segurola bs.); A. Toscanini
                                             cond.

Nov 23   *La Gioconda*   E. Destinn s. L. Homer ms. (later F.
                (4 perf.)   Wickham ms.) M. Claessens ms. P.
                                             Amato b. A. De Segurola bs.; A.
                                             Toscanini cond.

Nov 25   *Pagliacci*   B. Alten s. A. Bada t. P. Amato b. D. Gilly
                (3 perf.)   b.; V. Podesti cond.

Dec 10   ***La Fanciulla del West* (Puccini)   E. Destinn s. P. Amato b. A. Didur bs. A.
                (7 perf.)   De Segurola bs.; A. Toscanini cond.

Feb 1   *Germania*   E. Destinn s. P. Amato b.; A. Toscanini
                (2 perf.)   cond.

PHILADELPHIA – ACADEMY OF MUSIC
(Concurrent with New York season)
Dec 20   **La Fanciulla del West*   E. Destinn s. P. Amato b. A. Didur bs. A.
                (1 perf.)   De Segurola bs.; A. Toscanini cond.

1911

BROOKLYN – ACADEMY OF MUSIC
Jan 3   *Pagliacci*   A. Gluck s. P. Amato b. V. Reschiglian b.;
                (1 perf.)   V. Podesti cond.

CHICAGO – AUDITORIUM
(With the Chicago Opera)
Jan 14   *Pagliacci*   M. Sylva s. M. Sammarco b.; C.
                (1 perf.)   Campanini cond.

Jan 18   *La Fanciulla del West*   C. White s. M. Sammarco b.; C.
                (1 perf.)   Campanini cond.

A CHRONOLOGY OF CARUSO'S APPEARANCES

CLEVELAND – KEITH'S HIPPODROME
(With the Chicago Opera)

Jan 19   *Pagliacci*   A. Zeppilli s. E. Venturini t. A. Costa b. A.
(1 perf.)   Crabbé b.; C. Campanini cond.

NEW YORK – HOME OF MRS CORNELIUS VANDERBILT

Jan 24   Concert

NEW YORK – HOTEL WALDORF ASTORIA

Jan 30   Concert

VIENNA – HOFOPER

Sep 20   *Pagliacci*   B. Kiurina s. A. Preuss t. J. Schwarz b. C.
(1 perf.)   Rittmann b.; F. Schalks cond.

Sep 23   *Rigoletto*   H. Francillo-Kaufmann s. H. Kittel ms. J.
(1 perf.)   Schwarz b. J. Betetto b.; B. Walter cond.

Sep 25   *Carmen*   B. Kiurina s. M. Gutheil-Schroder ms. R.
(1 perf.)   Hofbauer b.; B. Walter cond.

MUNICH – HOF-UND NATIONALTHEATER

Sep 28   *Pagliacci*   H. Bosetti s.
(1 perf.)

Oct 1   *Aida*   M. Fay s. Clairmont ms. F. Feinhals b.
(1 perf.)   Gieglitz bs.; O. Rohr cond.

FRANKFURT – OPERNHAUS

Oct 4   *La Bohème*   L. Sellin s. B. Kernic s. R. Breitenfeld b. R.
(1 perf.)   Brinkmann b. R. Erdös bs.; L. Rottenberg
cond.

Oct 6   *Carmen*   E. Gentner-Fischer s. I. Tervani ms. R.
(1 perf.)   Brinkmann b.; L. Rottenberg cond.

HANOVER – HOFTHEATER

Oct 9   *Carmen*   Cassel s. Schmid-Hammerstein ms. R.
(1 perf.)   Moest bs.; Weigman cond.

Oct 12   *Rigoletto*   Stein s. Aigner b.; C. Gille cond.
(1 perf.)

HAMBURG – STADTTHEATER

Oct 15   *Pagliacci*   M. Winternitz s. R. vom Scheidt b.; A.
(1 perf.)   Winternitz cond.

Oct 18   *Carmen*   M. Winternitz s. O. Metzger ms. H.
(1 perf.)   Wiedemann b.; O. Selberg cond.

Oct 20   *Un Ballo in maschera*   H. Pfeil-Schneider s. M. Winternitz s. O.
(1 perf.)   Metzger ms. M. Dawison b.; O. Selberg
cond.

BERLIN – KÖNIGLICHES OPERNHAUS

Oct 24   *L'Elisir d'amore*   F. Hempel s. C. Bronsgeest b. E. Habich
(1 perf.)   b.; L. Blech cond.

THE WORKS

1911 cont.

Oct 27	*Rigoletto* (1 perf.)	F. Hempel s. B. Hoffmann b.; E. von Strauss cond.
Oct 29	*Pagliacci* (1 perf.)	C. Dux s. J. Bischoff b. B. Hoffmann b.; L. Blech cond.

1911–12

NEW YORK – METROPOLITAN OPERA

Nov 13	*Aida* (5 perf.)	E. Destinn s. (later M. Rappold s.; then J. Gadski s.) M. Matzenauer ms. (later T. Orridge ms.; then M. Claessens ms.) P. Amato b. (later D. Gilly b.; then A. Scotti b.) A. Didur bs.; A. Toscanini cond.
Nov 16	*La Fanciulla del West* (5 perf.)	E. Destinn s. P. Amato b. D. Gilly b. A. Didur bs. A. De Segurola bs.; A. Toscanini cond.
Nov 24	*Pagliacci* (9 perf.)	B. Alten s. (later A. Gluck s.; still later E. Destinn s.; then B. De Pasquali s.) A. Bada t. A. Scotti b. (later P. Amato b.) D. Gilly b. (later V. Reschiglian b.); G. Sturani cond.
Nov 29	*La Gioconda* (5 perf.)	E. Destinn s. F. Wickham ms. T. Orridge ms. P. Amato b. A. De Segurola bs.; A. Toscanini cond.
Dec 16	*Armide* (4 perf.)	O. Fremstad s. A. Gluck s. M. Matzenauer ms. P. Amato b. D. Gilly b. A. De Segurola bs.; A. Toscanini cond.
Dec 21	*Tosca* (2 perf.)	E. Destinn s. (later O. Fremstad s.) P. Amato b.; A. Toscanini cond.
Jan 17	*Cavalleria rusticana* (1 perf.)	E. Destinn s. D. Gilly b.; G. Sturani cond.
Jan 25	Concert	Act I, *Pagliacci*
Feb 6	*Rigoletto* (3 perf.)	L. Tetrazzini s. (later B. De Pasquali s.) L. Homer ms. (later M. Duchène ms.) M. Renaud b. (later P. Amato b.) L. Rothier bs.; G. Sturani cond.
Feb 19	*La Bohème* (1 perf.)	G. Farrar s. B. Alten s. D. Gilly b. A. Didur bs. A. De Segurola bs.; G. Sturani cond.
Mar 30	*Manon* (3 perf.)	G. Farrar s. D. Gilly b. L. Rothier bs.; A. Toscanini cond.
Apr 29	Concert	(Y)

PHILADELPHIA – ACADEMY OF MUSIC
(Concurrent with New York season)

Nov 21	*La Gioconda* (1 perf.)	E. Destinn s. F. Wickham ms. T. Orridge ms. P. Amato b. A. De Segurola bs.; A. Toscanini cond.

Jan 9	*La Bohème* (1 perf.)	A. Gluck s. L. Sparkes s. D. Gilly b. A. Didur bs. A. De Segurola bs.; G. Sturani cond.
Jan 30	*Pagliacci* (1 perf.)	R. Fornia s. A. Bada t. D. Gilly b. V. Reschiglian b.; G. Sturani cond.

1912

BROOKLYN – ACADEMY OF MUSIC

Jan 2	*La Bohème* (1 perf.)	A. Gluck s. L. Sparkes s. D. Gilly b. A. Didur bs. G. Rossi bs.; G. Sturani cond.
Jan 27	*Pagliacci* (1 perf.)	A. Gluck s. A. Bada t. P. Amato b. V. Reschiglian b.; G. Sturani cond.
Mar 12	*Aida* (1 perf.)	J. Gadski s. M. Matzenauer ms. D. Gilly b. A. De Segurola bs.; G. Sturani cond.

BOSTON – BOSTON OPERA HOUSE
(With the Boston Opera)

Mar 5	*La Fanciulla del West* (1 perf.)	C. Melis s. G. Polese b. R. Blanchart b. J. Mardones bs.; R. Moranzoni cond.

Tour of the Metropolitan Opera Company from Boston to Atlanta
BOSTON – BOSTON OPERA HOUSE

Apr 17	*Pagliacci* (1 perf.)	A. Nielsen s. A. Reiss t. P. Amato b. D. Gilly b.; G. Sturani cond.

PHILADELPHIA – ACADEMY OF MUSIC

Apr 19	*Aida* (1 perf.)	J. Gadski s. L. Homer ms. P. Amato b. A. De Segurola bs.; G. Sturani cond.

ATLANTA – AUDITORIUM

Apr 22	*Aida* (1 perf.)	J. Gadski s. L. Homer ms. D. Gilly b. A. De Segurola bs.; G. Sturani cond.
Apr 25	*Pagliacci* (1 perf.)	B. Alten s. A. Bada t. A. Scotti b. V. Reschiglian b.; G. Sturani cond.
Apr 27	*Rigoletto* (1 perf.)	A. Gluck s. F. Wickham s. D. Gilly b. A. De Segurola bs.; G. Sturani cond.

PARIS – OPÉRA
Visit of the Monte Carlo Opera to Paris

May 12	*Rigoletto* (3 perf.)	A. Nezhdanova s. N. Lollini ms. T. Ruffo b.; L. Jehin cond. (later A. Pomé cond.)
May 16	**La Fanciulla del West* (3 perf.)	C. Melis s. (later T. Poli-Randaccio s.) T. Ruffo b.; T. Serafin cond.

PARIS – SALLE RUE NITOT

May 31	Concert	C. Melis s. T. Ruffo b.

VIENNA – HOFOPER

Sep 14	*Carmen* (1 perf.)	B. Kiurina s. M. Gutheil-Schoder ms. J. Schwarz b.; H. Reichenberger cond.

THE WORKS

1912 cont.

Sep 17	*Un Ballo in maschera* (1 perf.)	E. Elizza s. S. Kurz s. H. Kittel ms. J. Schwarz b.; H. Reichenberger cond.
Sep 20	*Tosca* (1 perf.)	E. Elizza s. R. Hochbauer b.; H. Reichenberger cond.

MUNICH – HOF UND NATIONAL THEATER

Sep 23	*Carmen* (1 perf.)	Tordek s. Mme C. Cahier ms. F. Brodersen b.; O. Rohr cond.
Sep 26	*Tosca* (1 perf.)	M. Fay s. F. Feinhals b.; S. Meyrowitz cond.
Sep 28	*Rigoletto* (1 perf.)	H. Bosetti s. Lippe ms. F. Feinhals b.; O. Rohr cond.

STUTTGART – HOFTHEATER

Oct 1	*Pagliacci* (1 perf.)	I. Hangers s. H. Weil b.; P. Drach cond.
Oct 3	*La Bohème* (1 perf.)	M. Burchardt s. H. Weil b.; P. Drach cond.

BERLIN – KÖNIGLICHES OPERNHAUS

Oct 7	*Carmen* (1 perf.)	L. Artôt de Padilla s. M. Sylva ms. B. Hoffmann b.; L. Blech cond.
Oct 10	*La Bohème* (1 perf.)	C. Dux s. A. von Andrejewa Skilondz s. C. Bronsgeest b. E. Babich b. H. Bachmann bs.; L. Blech cond.
Oct 12	*Un Ballo in maschera* (1 perf.)	M. Kurt s. L. Artôt de Padilla s. M. Ober ms. C. Bronsgeest b.; L. Blech cond.

POTSDAM – IMPERIAL PALACE

Oct 22	Concert	

HAMBURG – STADTTHEATER

Oct 15	*Carmen* (1 perf.)	V. Pawlovska s. O. Metzger ms. C. Armster b.; Szendrei cond.
Oct 18	*Aida* (1 perf.)	L. Marcel s. O. Metzger ms. C. Armster b. M. Lohfing bs.; Szendrei cond.
Oct 20	*La Traviata* (1 perf.)	H. Francillo-Kaufmann s. M. Dawison b.; L. Schottlaender cond.

1912–13

NEW YORK – METROPOLITAN OPERA

Nov 11	*Manon Lescaut* (5 perf.)	L. Bori s. A. Scotti b. A. De Segurola bs.; G. Polacco cond. bs.
Nov 14	*La Gioconda* (3 perf.)	E. Destinn s. L. Homer ms. (later M. Matzenauer ms.) M. Duchène ms. P. Amato b. A. De Segurola bs.; G. Polacco cond.

Nov 20	*Pagliacci* (6 perf.)	L. Bori s. (later B. Alten s., then E. Destinn s.) A. Bada t. P. Amato b. (later A. Scotti b., then D. Gilly b.) D. Gilly b. (later V. Reschiglian b.); G. Polacco cond.
Nov 25	*La Fanciulla del West* (4 perf.)	E. Destinn s. P. Amato b. A. Didur bs. A. De Segurola bs.; G. Polacco cond. (later A. Toscanini cond.)
Nov 28	*La Bohème* (3 perf.)	L. Bori s. (later F. Alda s.) D. Gilly b. (later P. Amato b.) A. Didur bs. A. De Segurola bs.; G. Polacco cond.
Dec 9	*Aida* (4 perf.)	E. Destinn s. (later J. Gadski s.) L. Homer ms. D. Gilly b. (later P. Amato b.) L. Rothier bs. (later A. Didur bs., then A. De Segurola bs.); G. Polacco cond. (later A. Toscanini cond.)
Dec 24	*Gli Ugonotti* (5 perf.)	E. Destinn s. F. Hempel s. B. Alten s. A. Scotti b. (later D. Gilly b.) A. Didur bs. (later C. Braun bs.) L. Rothier bs.; G. Polacco cond.
Jan 4	*Tosca* (4 perf.)	G. Farrar s. (later O. Fremstad s.) A. Scotti b.; A. Toscanini cond. (later G. Sturani cond.)
Jan 22	*Manon* (5 perf.)	G. Farrar s. D. Gilly b. L. Rothier bs.; A. Toscanini cond.
Feb 17	*Cavalleria rusticana* (1 perf.)	J. Gadski s. D. Gilly b.; G. Polacco cond.
Feb 18	Concert	Act I, *Pagliacci*

PHILADELPHIA – ACADEMY OF MUSIC
(Concurrent with New York season)

Dec 3	*La Bohème* (1 perf.)	G. Farrar s. L. Sparkes s. P. Amato b. A. Didur bs. A. De Segurola bs.; G. Polacco cond.
Jan 7	*La Gioconda* (1 perf.)	E. Destinn s. L. Homer ms. M. Duchène ms. D. Gilly b. A. De Segurola bs.; G. Polacco cond.
Jan 28	*Manon* (1 perf.)	G. Farrar s. D. Gilly b. L. Rothier bs.; A. Toscanini cond.
Mar 25	*Gli Ugonotti* (1 perf.)	E. Destinn s. F. Hempel s. B. Alten s. D. Gilly b. C. Braun bs. L. Rothier bs.; G. Polacco cond.

BROOKLYN – ACADEMY OF MUSIC

Dec 24	*Pagliacci* (1 perf.)	L. Bori s. A. Bada t. P. Amato b. V. Reschiglian b.; G. Polacco cond.

THE WORKS

1912–13 cont.

Mar 4   *Tosca*   O. Fremstad s. A. Scotti b.; A. Toscanini
         (1 perf.)   cond.

1913

NEW YORK – HOTEL WALDORF ASTORIA
Jan 27   Concert

BOSTON – BOSTON OPERA HOUSE
(With The Boston Opera)
Mar 18   *Pagliacci*   C. Melis s. E. Giaccone t. A. Rossi b. G.
         (1 perf.)   Everett b.; R. Moranzoni cond.

ATLANTA – AUDITORIUM
Tour of the Metropolitan Opera Company
Apr 21   *Manon Lescaut*   L. Bori s. A. Scotti b. A. De Segurola bs.;
         (1 perf.)   G. Sturani cond.

Apr 24   *La Gioconda*   E. Destinn s. L. Homer ms. M. Duchène
         (1 perf.)   ms. D. Gilly b. A. De Segurola bs.; G.
                                       Polacco cond.

Apr 26   *Tosca*   E. Destinn s. A. Scotti b.; A. Toscanini
         (1 perf.)   cond.

ATLANTA – PENITENTIARY
Apr 23   Concert   (O), (C) and (I); L. Bori s.

LONDON – COVENT GARDEN
May 20   *Pagliacci*   C. Melis s. M. Sammarco b. A. Crabbé b.;
         (2 perf.)   E. Panizza cond.

May 24   *Aida*   E. Destinn s. L. Kirkby-Lunn ms. A. Scotti
         (5 perf.)   b. J. Goddard bs.; G. Polacco cond.

June 5   *Tosca*   E. Destinn s. A. Scotti b.; G. Polacco cond.
         (3 perf.)

June 18   *La Bohème*   C. Melis s. (later N. Melba s.) L. Sparkes s.
         (3 perf.)   M. Sammarco b. P. Malatesta b. J.
                                       Aquistipace bs.; E. Panizza cond.

VIENNA – HOFOPER
Sep 15   *Carmen*   B. Kiurina s. M. Gutheil-Schoder ms. J.
         (1 perf.)   Schwarz b.; H. Reichenberger cond.

Sep 18   *La Bohème*   S. Kurz s. B. Kiurina s. J. Schwarz b.; H.
         (1 perf.)   Reichenberger cond.

Sep 21   *Rigoletto*   S. Kurz s. H. Kittel ms. J. Schwarz b.; H.
         (1 perf.)   Reichenberger cond.

MUNICH – HOF-UND NATIONALTHEATER
Sep 25   *Pagliacci*   H. Bosetti s. F. Brodersen b.; O. Rohr
         (1 perf.)   cond.

Sep 28   *Carmen*   C. Kuhn-Brunner s. C. Dahmen s. F.
         (1 perf.)   Brodersen b.; O. Hess cond.

Sep 30	*La Bohème* (1 perf.)	L. Perard-Petzl s. Von Fladung s. F. Brodersen b. M. Gillmann bs.

STUTTGART – HOFTHEATER

Oct 3	*Tosca* (1 perf.)	H. Brugelmann s. B. Ziegler b.; Band cond.
Oct 6	*Carmen* (1 perf.)	M. Burchardt s. S. Onegin ms. H. Weil b.; Band cond.
Oct 10	*Rigoletto* (1 perf.)	

BERLIN – KÖNIGLICHES OPERNHAUS

Oct 16	*Aida* (1 perf.)	B. Kemp s. M. Ober ms. B. Hoffmann b. P. Knupfer bs.; L. Blech cond.
Oct 19	*La Bohème* (1 perf.)	C. Dux s. Alferman s. C. Bronsgest b. E Habich b. H. Bachmann bs.; L. Blech cond.
Oct 22	*Carmen* (1 perf.)	L. Artôt de Padilla s. M. Salvatini s. H. Wiedemann b.; L. Blech cond.
Oct 24	*Pagliacci* (1 perf.)	C. Dux s. Funck t. H. Wiedemann b. R. Philipp b.; E. von Strauss cond.

HAMBURG – STADTTHEATER

Oct 27	*La Bohème* (1 perf.)	M. Cavan s. T. Jansen s. C. Armster b. T. Lattermann bs. M. Lohfing bs.; Kaiser cond.
Oct 30	*Pagliacci* (1 perf.)	H. Francillo-Kaufmann s. W. Buers b.; C. Gotthardt cond.
Nov 2	*La Fanciulla del West* (1 perf.)	F. Easton s. Buers b. T. Lattermann bs.; C. Gotthardt cond.

1913–14

NEW YORK – METROPOLITAN OPERA

Nov 17	*La Gioconda* (4 perf.)	E. Destinn s. M. Matzenauer ms. (later M. Ober ms.; then L. Homer ms.) M. Duchène ms. P. Amato b. (later D. Gilly b.) A. De Segurola bs.; A. Toscanini cond.
Nov 22	*Un Ballo in maschera* (5 perf.)	E. Destinn s. F. Hempel s. (later B. Alten s.) M. Matzenauer ms. (later M. Duchène ms.) P. Amato b. A. De Segurola bs. L. Rothier bs.; A. Toscanini cond.
Nov 27	*Manon Lescaut* (4 perf.)	L. Bori s. A. Scotti b. A. De Segurola bs.; G. Polacco cond.
Dec 5	*Pagliacci* (7 perf.)	L. Bori s. (later E. Destinn s.; then R. Fornia s.) A. Bada t. P. Amato b. (later A. Scotti b.; then D. Gilly b.) V. Reschiglian b. (later D. Gilly b.); G. Polacco cond. (later R. Hageman cond.)

1913–14

Dec 8   *Aida* (3 perf.)   E. Destinn s. M. Matzenauer ms. (later L. Homer ms.; then M. Ober ms.) P. Amato b. (later D. Gilly b.) A. Didur bs. (later L. Rothier bs.); A. Toscanini cond.

Dec 19   *Tosca* (4 perf.)   E. Destinn s. (later G. Farrar s.) A. Scotti b; A. Toscanini cond. (later G. Polacco cond.)

Dec 31   *Manon* (4 perf.)   G. Farrar s. (later F. Alda s.) D. Gilly b. L. Rothier bs.; A. Toscanini cond.

Jan 30   *La Bohème* (2 perf.)   F. Alda s. (later G. Farrar s.) B. Alten s. D. Gilly b. A. Didur bs. L. Rothier bs. cond. Polacco.

Feb 4   *La Fanciulla del West* (3 perf.)   E. Destinn s. P. Amato b. V. Reschiglian b. A. Didur bs. A. De Segurola bs.; G. Polacco cond.

Feb 26   **Julien* (Charpentier) (5 perf.)   G. Farrar s. M. Duchène ms. D. Gilly b.; G. Polacco cond.

Mar 5   Concert   Act I, *Pagliacci* w. L. Bori s. P. Amato b.

Apr 14   Concert   Act I, *La Bohème* w. F. Alda s. D. Gilly b.

PHILADELPHIA ACADEMY OF MUSIC
(Concurrent with New York season)

Nov 25   *Aida* (1 perf.)   E. Destinn s. M. Matzenauer ms. D. Gilly b. L. Rothier bs.; G. Polacco cond.

Dec 23   *La Bohème* (1 perf.)   F. Alda s. B. Alten s. A. Scotti b. A. Pini-Corsi b. A. De Segurola bs.; G. Polacco cond.

Feb 10   *Tosca* (1 perf.)   O. Fremstad s. A. Scotti b.; A. Toscanini cond.

Mar 3   *Pagliacci* (1 perf.)   B. Alten s. P. Amato b. V. Reschiglian b.; G. Polacco cond.

1914

BROOKLYN – ACADEMY OF MUSIC
(With New York season)

Jan 27   *Pagliacci* (1 perf.)   B. Alten s. P. Amato b. V. Reschiglian b.; G. Polacco cond.

Mar 24   *La Gioconda* (1 perf.)   E. Destinn s. L. Homer ms. M. Duchène ms. P. Amato b. A. De Segurola bs.; G. Polacco cond.

ATLANTA – AUDITORIUM
Tour of the Metropolitan Opera Company

Apr 27   *Manon* (1 perf.)   G. Farrar s. D. Gilly b. L. Rothier bs.; A. Toscanini cond.

May 30	*Un Ballo in maschera* (1 perf.)	J. Gadski, s, F. Hempel s, M. Duchène ms, P. Amato b. A. De Segurola bs. L. Rothier bs.; G. Polacco cond.
May 2	*Pagliacci* (1 perf.)	R. Fornia s. A. Scotti b. V. Reschiglian b.; G. Polacco cond.
	LONDON – COVENT GARDEN	
May 14	*Aida* (3 perf.)	E. Destinn s. (later R. Raisa s.) L. Kirkby- Lunn ms. D. Gilly b. (later C. Van Hulst b.; then A. Scotti b.) A. Didur bs.; G. Polacco cond.
May 16	*Tosca* (1 perf.)	C. Muzio s. A. Scotti b.; G. Polacco cond.
May 25	*Madama Butterfly* (1 perf.)	E. Destinn s. E. Leveroni ms. A. Scotti b.; G. Polacco cond.
May 28	*Un Ballo in maschera* (2 perf.)	E. Destinn s. A. Zeppilli s. L. Berat ms. C. Van Hulst b. G. Huberdeau bs.; G. Polacco cond.
June 6	*La Bohème* (2 perf.)	N. Melba s. (later C. Muzio s.) R. Buckman s. A. Scotti b. (later F. Cigada b.) P. Malatesta b. J. Aquistipace bs.; G. Polacco cond. (later E. Panizza cond.)
	ROME – TEATRO COSTANZI	
Oct 19	*Pagliacci* (1 perf.) Act I	L. Bori s. A. Bada t. G. De Luca b. R. Tegani b.; A. Toscanini cond.

1914–15

	NEW YORK – METROPOLITAN OPERA	
Nov 16	*Un Ballo in maschera* (2 perf.)	E. Destinn s. F. Hempel s. M. Matzenauer ms. (later M. Duchène ms.) P. Amato b. A. De Segurola bs. L. Rothier bs.; A. Toscanini cond.
Nov 19	*Carmen* (7 perf.)	F. Alda s. (later L. Bori s.) G. Farrar s. P. Amato b. (later C. Whitehill b.); A. Toscanini cond.
Nov 25	*La Gioconda* (2 perf.)	E. Destinn s. M. Ober ms. (later M. Matzenauer ms.) M. Duchène ms. P. Amato b. A. De Segurola bs. (later L. Rothier bs.); G. Polacco cond.
Dec 5	*Pagliacci* (4 perf.)	L. Bori s. (later E. Destinn s.) P. Audisio t. (later A. Bada t.) P. Amato b. (later A. Didur bs.) R. Tegani b.
Dec 12	*Aida* (2 perf.)	E. Destinn s. M. Ober ms. (later M. Matzenauer ms.) P. Amato b. A. Didur bs.; G. Polacco cond.
Dec 24	*Manon* (3 perf.)	G. Farrar s. (later F. Alda s.) A. Scotti b. L. Rothier bs.; A. Toscanini cond.

1914–15 cont.

Dec 30	*Gli Ugonotti* (3 perf.)	E. Destinn s. F. Hempel s. M. Garrison s. A. Scotti b. C. Braun bs. L. Rothier bs.; G. Polacco cond.
Jan 1	*Manon Lescaut* (1 perf.)	L. Bori s. P. Amato b. A. De Segurola bs.; G. Polacco cond.
Jan 19	Concert	Act I, *Pagliacci*

PHILADELPHIA – ACADEMY OF MUSIC
(Concurrent with New York season)

Dec 1	*La Gioconda* (1 perf.)	E. Destinn s. M. Matzenauer ms. M. Duchène ms. P. Amato b. A. De Segurola bs.; G. Polacco cond.
Dec 15	*Aida* (1 perf.)	M. Rappold s. M. Duchène ms. P. Amato b. A. Didur bs.; G. Polacco cond.
Jan 12	*Pagliacci* (1 perf.)	L. Bori s. P. Amato b. R. Tegani b.; G. Polacco cond.

1915

BROOKLYN – ACADEMY OF MUSIC
(Concurrent with New York season)

Feb 2	*Carmen* (1 perf.)	F. Alda s. G. Farrar s. P. Amato b.; A. Toscanini cond.

MONTE CARLO – SALLE GARNIER

Mar 11	*Aida* (3 perf.)	F. Litvinne s. G. Bailac ms. A. Maguenat b. M. Journet bs.; G. Lauweryns cond.
Mar 21	*Rigoletto* (2 perf.)	A. Zeppilli s. V. Carton ms. Skouffi b. M. Journet bs.; A. Pomé cond.
Mar 28	*Lucia di Lammermoor* (3 perf.)	G. Pareto s. A. Maguenat b. M. Journet bs.; A. Pomé cond.
Apr 6	*Pagliacci* (1 perf.)	A. Zeppilli s. Skouffi b. A. Maguenat b. G. Lauweryns cond.

BUENOS AIRES – TEATRO COLÓN

May 20	*Aida* (2 perf.)	R. Raisa s. N. Frascani ms. G. Danise b. G. Cirino bs.; G. Marinuzzi cond.
May 26	*Pagliacci* (5 perf.)	M. Roggero s. (later H. Spani s.) L. Nardi t. G. Danise b. (later M. Sammarco b.) D. Lusardi b. (later E. Caronna b.); G. Sturani cond.
June 10	*Manon Lescaut* (3 perf.)	G. Dalla Rizza s. M. Sammarco b.; G. Marinuzzi cond.
June 18	Concert	Act I, *Pagliacci* w. M. Roggero s. G. Danise b.
June 20	*Manon* (7 perf.)	G. Vix s. M. Sammarco b. B. Berardi bs.; G.. Sturani cond.

June 27	*Lucia di Lammermoor* (2 perf.)	A. Galli-Curci s. G. Danise b. B. Berardi bs.; G. Sturani cond.
Aug 4	Concert	Act I, *Pagliacci* w. H. Spani s. T. Ruffo b.
Aug. 10	Concert	Act I & II, *Manon*, Act I, *Pagliacci* w. H. Spani s. G. Danise b.
Aug 11	Concert	(I)

BUENOS AIRES – TEATRO COLISEO
(With the season at Teatro Colón)

June 7	Concert	
July 5	Concert	

ROSARIO – TEATRO DE LA OPERA

July 9	*Manon Lescaut* (1 perf.)	G. Dalla Rizza s. M. Sammarco b. G. Cirino bs.; G. Armani cond.

CORDOBA – TEATRO RIVERA INDARTE

July 11	*Manon Lescaut* (1 perf.)	G. Dalla Rizza s. E. Caronna b.; G. Armani cond.
July 13	*Pagliacci* (1 perf.)	H. Spani s. N. Olivero t. G. Danise b. Vail b.; G. Armani cond.

TUCUMAN – TEATRO ODEON

July 14?	*Pagliacci* (1 perf.)	H. Spani s. G. Danise b. E. Caronna b.; G. Armani cond.
	Manon Lescaut?	

ROSARIO – TEATRO DE LA OPERA

July 22	*Pagliacci* (1 perf.)	H. Spani s. G. Danise b. E. Caronna b.; G. Armani cond.

MONTEVIDEO – TEATRO SOLIS

Aug 14	*Manon* (1 perf.)	G. Vix s. M. Sammarco b.; G. Sturani cond.

MONTEVIDEO – TEATRO URQUIZA

Aug 16	*Pagliacci* (1 perf.)	H. Spani s. T. Ruffo b.; G. Marinuzzi cond.

MILAN – TEATRO DAL VERME

Sep 23	*Pagliacci* (2 perf.)	C. Muzio s. A. Bada t. L. Montesanto b. L. Paci b. (later A. Crabbé b.); A. Toscanini cond.

1915–16

NEW YORK – METROPOLITAN OPERA

Nov 15	*Samson et Dalila* (Saint-Saëns) (5 perf.)	M. Matzenauer ms. P. Amato b. L. Rothier bs. C. Schlegel bs.; G. Polacco cond.

THE WORKS

1915–16 cont.

Nov 19	*La Bohème* (4 perf.)	F. Alda s. I. Cajatti s. A. Scotti b. (later G. De Luca b.; then P. Amato b.) R. Tegani b. A. De Segurola bs. (later A. Didur bs.; then L. Rothier bs.); G. Bavagnoli cond.
Nov 27	*Tosca* (1 perf.)	L. Edvina s. A. Scotti b.; G. Polacco cond.
Dec 2	*Pagliacci* (4 perf.)	I. Cajatti s. A. Bada t. (later P. Audisio t.) P. Amato b. (later A. Scotti b.; then G. De Luca b. R. Tegani b.); G. Bavagnoli cond.
Dec 11	*Marta* (4 perf.)	F. Hempel s. M. Ober ms. G. De Luca b.; G. Bavagnoli cond.
Dec 15	*Manon* (1 perf.)	F. Alda s. A. Scotti b. L. Rothier bs.; G. Polacco cond.
Jan 1	*Un Ballo in maschera* (1 perf.)	M. Kurt s. E. Mason s. M. Duchène ms. P. Amato b. A. De Segurola bs. L. Rothier bs.; G. Polacco cond.
Jan 6	*Manon Lescaut* (3 perf.)	F. Alda s. G. De Luca b. (later A. Scotti b.; then P. Amato b.) A. De Segurola bs.; G. Bavagnoli cond.
Feb 11	*Rigoletto* (5 perf.)	M. Barrientos s. F. Perini ms. (later L. Homer ms.) G. De Luca b. (later P. Amato b.) G. Polacco cond.
Feb 17	*Carmen* (5 perf.)	F. Alda s. (later E. Mason s.) G. Farrar s. P. Amato b.; G. Polacco cond.
Mar 16	Concert	Act I, *Pagliacci*
Mar 24	*Aida* (1 perf.)	M. Rappold s. L. Homer ms. G. De Luca b. H. Scott bs.; G. Bavagnoli cond.

PHILADELPHIA – ACADEMY OF MUSIC
(Concurrent with New York season)

Nov 30	*Manon* (1 perf.)	F. Alda s. A. Scotti b. L. Rothier bs.; G. Polacco cond.
Dec 21	*Un Ballo in maschera* (1 perf.)	M. Kurt s. E. Mason s. M. Duchène ms. P. Amato b. A. De Segurola bs. L. Rothier bs.
Jan 25	*La Bohème* (1 perf.)	F. Alda s. I. Cajatti s. A. Scotti b. R. Tegani b. A. De Segurola bs.; G. Bavagnoli cond.
Mar 14	*Pagliacci* (1 perf.)	I. Cajatti s. P. Audisio t. G. De Luca b. R. Tegani b.; G. Bavagnoli cond.

1916

BROOKLYN – ACADEMY OF MUSIC
(Concurrent with New York season)

Jan 4	*Aida* (1 perf.)	M. Rappold s. M. Ober ms. R. Tegani b. H. Scott bs.; G. Bavagnoli cond.

Feb 1	*Manon* (1 perf.)	F. Alda s. G. De Luca b. L. Rothier bs.; G. Polacco cond.

NEW YORK – HOTEL WALDORF ASTORIA

Jan 10	Concert	(Z), (AA), (AB), (AC) and (AD) w. M. Elman violin

NEW YORK – BILTMORE HOTEL

Jan 21	Concert	

Tour of the Metropolitan Opera Company to Boston and Atlanta
BOSTON – BOSTON OPERA HOUSE

Apr 4	*La Bohème* (1 perf.)	F. Alda s. I. Cajatti s. G. De Luca b. R. Tegani b. A. De Segurola bs.; G. Bavagnoli cond.
Apr 7	*Aida* (1 perf.)	M. Rappold s. L. Homer ms. P. Amato b. H. Scott bs.; G. Bavagnoli cond.
Apr 12	*Rigoletto* (1 perf.)	M. Barrientos s. F. Perini ms. G. De Luca b. A. Didur bs.; G. Polacco cond.
Apr 15	*Pagliacci* (1 perf.)	I. Cajatti s. A. Bada t. P. Amato b. R. Tegani b.; G. Bavagnoli cond.
Apr 18	*Un Ballo in maschera* (1 perf.)	J. Gadski s. M. Garrison s. M. Duchène ms. P. Amato b. A. De Segurola bs. L. Rothier bs.; G. Bavagnoli cond.
Apr 21	*Marta* (1 perf.)	M. Barrientos s. F. Perini ms. G. De Luca b.; G. Bavagnoli cond.

ATLANTA – AUDITORIUM

Apr 24	*Samson et Dalila* (1 perf.)	M. Ober ms. P. Amato b. C. Schlegel bs.; G. Polacco cond.
Apr 28	*Marta* (1 perf.)	M. Barrientos s. F. Perini ms. G. De Luca b.; G. Bavagnoli cond.
Apr 29	*La Bohème* (1 perf.)	I. Cajatti s. L. Sparkes s. P. Amato b. A. Didur bs. L. Rothier bs.; G. Polacco cond.

1916–17

NEW YORK – METROPOLITAN OPERA

Nov 13	*Les Pêcheurs de perles* (3 perf.)	F. Hempel s. G. De Luca b. L. Rothier bs.; G. Polacco cond.
Nov 16	*Manon Lescaut* (3 perf.)	F. Alda s. (later C. Muzio s.) A. Scotti b. (later G. De Luca b.) A. De Segurola bs.; G. Papi cond.
Nov. 24	*Samson et Dalila* (5 perf.)	L. Homer ms. (later M. Matzenauer ms.) P. Amato b. (later G. De Luca b.) C. Schlegel bs. L. Rothier bs.; G. Polacco cond.
Dec. 4	*Tosca* (1 perf.)	C. Muzio s. A. Scotti b.; G. Polacco cond.

THE WORKS

1916–17 cont.

Dec 15	*Pagliacci* (4 perf.)	C. Muzio s. A. Bada t. (later P. Audisio t.) P. Amato b. (later A. Scotti b.; then G. De Luca b.) R. Tegani b.; G. Papi cond.
Dec 25	*Marta* (3 perf.)	F. Hempel s. (later M. Barrientos s.) M. Ober ms. (later F. Perini ms.) G. De Luca b.; G. Papi cond.
Dec 30	*L'Elisir d'amore* (5 perf.)	F. Hempel s. (later M. Barrientos s.) A. Scotti b. A. Didur bs.; G. Papi cond.
Jan 5	*Carmen* (5 perf.)	E. Mason s. (later A. Case s.) G. Farrar s. P. Amato b. (later G. De Luca b.); G. Polacco cond.
Feb 7	*Rigoletto* (5 perf.)	M. Barrientos s. P. Perini ms. G. De Luca b. A. De Segurola bs.; G. Polacco cond.
Feb 12	*Aida* (4 perf.)	C. Muzio s. M. Ober ms. (later M. Matzenauer ms.) P. Amato b. L. Rothier bs. (later A. Didur bs.; then H. Scott bs.); G. Polacco cond. (later G. Papi cond.)
Mar 18	Concert	(M) and (AE) w. P. Amato b.; (B) w. F. Alda s. Perini ms. G. de Luca b.
Mar 23	*La Bohème* (1 perf.)	F. Alda s. L. Sparkes s. P. Amato b. A. Didur bs.; A. De Segurola bs.; G. Papi cond.
Mar 29	Concert	Act IV, *Rigoletto*
Apr 17	Concert	3 French songs
May 10	Concert	L. Homer ms. L. Muratore t.

PHILADELPHIA – ACADEMY OF MUSIC
(Concurrent with New York season)

Nov 28	*Samson et Dalila* (1 perf.)	L. Homer ms. G. De Luca b. C. Schlegel bs. L. Rothier bs.; G. Polacco cond.
Dec 19	*Marta* (1 perf.)	F. Hempel s. M. Ober ms. G. De Luca b.; G. Papi cond.
Jan 23	*La Bohème* (1 perf.)	F. Alda s. E. Mason s. P. Amato b. R. Tegani b. E. De Segurola bs.; G. Papi cond.
Mar 6	*Rigoletto* (1 perf.)	M. Barrientos s. F. Perini ms. G. De Luca b. A. De Segurola bs.; G. Polacco cond.
Apr 10	*Pagliacci* (1 perf.)	C. Muzio s. A. Bada t. P. Amato b. R. Tegani b.; G. Papi cond.

1917

BROOKLYN – ACADEMY OF MUSIC
(Concurrent with New York season)

Jan 2	*Aida* (1 perf.)	M. Rappold s. L. Homer ms. G. De Luca b. L. Rothier bs.; G. Papi cond.

| Feb 27 | *Marta*
(1 perf.) | M. Barrientos s. F. Perini ms. G. De Luca
b.; G. Papi cond. |

NEW YORK – HOTEL WALDORF ASTORIA

| Jan 8 | Concert | (M) and (AF) w. J. Thibaud violin |

ATLANTA – AUDITORIUM
Tour of the Metropolitan Opera Company

Apr 23	*L'Elisir d'amore* (1 perf.)	M. Barrientos s. A. Scotti b. A. Didur bs.; G. Papi cond.
Apr 26	*Tosca* (1 perf.)	C. Muzio s. A. Scotti b.; G. Polacco cond.
Apr 28	*Rigoletto* (1 perf.)	M. Barrientos s. F. Perini ms. G. De Luca b. L. Rothier bs.; G. Polacco cond.

CINCINATTI – MUSIC HALL

| May 1 | Concert | (O), (M) and (I) w. orch. acc. and (AG),
(AF), (AI), (AJ), (AK), (AL) w. piano acc. |

TOLEDO – TERMINAL AUDITORIUM

| May 3 | Concert | As above |

PITTSBURGH – SYRIA MOSQUE

| May 5 | Concert | As above |

NEW YORK – HOTEL ASTOR

| May 8 | Concert | (O), (AH), (AJ), (AM), (AL), (AI), (AG),
(AK) and (AN) |

BUENOS AIRES – TEATRO COLÓN

June 17	*L'Elisir d'amore* (3 perf.)	N. Marmora s. (later M. Barrientos s.) T. Parvis b. G. Azzolini bs.; G. Marinuzzi cond.
June 20	*Pagliacci* (4 perf.)	N. Marmora s. A. Cortis t. A. Crabbé b. (later M. Urizar b.) E. De Franceschi b.; V. Bellezza cond.
June 26	*Manon* (3 perf.)	N. Vallin s. (later C. Melis s.) A. Crabbé b. M. Journet bs.; G. Marinuzzi cond.
July 2	Concert	
July 4	Concert	
July 6	Concert	
July 11	*Tosca* (1 perf.)	G. Dalla Rizza s. E. Giraldoni b.; G. Marinuzzi cond.
July 15	*La Bohème* (2 perf.)	G. Dalla Rizza s. N. Marmora s. A. Crabbé b. E. De Franceschi b. M. Journet bs.; V. Bellezza cond.

THE WORKS

1917 cont.

July 29	*Lodoletta* (Mascagni) (2 perf.)	G. Dalla Rizza s. M. Urizar b. E. De Franceschi b. T. Dentale bs.; G. Marinuzzi cond.
July 30	Concert	
Aug. 13	Concert	(AO), (AP), (AQ), (AR)

BUENOS AIRES – TEATRO SAN MARTÍN
(Concurrent with season at Teatro Colón)

Aug 6	Concert	(C), (W), (AR), (AO), (AN)

BUENOS AIRES – TEATRO COLISEO

Aug 12	*Pagliacci* (1 perf.)	N. Marmora s. A. Cortis t. J. Segura-Tallien b. E. De Franceschi b.; A. Padovani cond.

MONTEVIDEO – TEATRO SOLIS

Aug 16	*L'Elisir d'amore* (1 perf.)	N. Vallin s. E. De Franceschi b. G. Azzolini bs.; G. Marinuzzi cond.
Aug 18	*Pagliacci* (2 perf.)	N. Vallin s. A. Cortis t. M. Urizar b. E. De Franceschi b.; V. Bellezza cond.
Aug 21	*Tosca* (1 perf.)	G. Dalla Rizza s. E. Giraldoni b.; G. Marinuzzi cond.
Aug 26	*Carmen* (1 perf.)	N. Vallin s. F. Anitua ms. M. Journet bs.; G. Marinuzzi cond.

MONTEVIDEO – TEATRO URQUIZA
(Concurrent with the season at Teatro Solis)

Aug 23	*Carmen* (1 perf.)	N. Vallin s. F. Anitua ms. M. Journet bs.; G. Marinuzzi cond.

RIO DE JANEIRO – TEATRO MUNICIPAL

Sep 3	*Pagliacci* (2 perf.)	N. Vallin s. A. Cortis t. M. Urizar b. (later A. Crabbé b.) E. De Franceschi b.
Sep 6	*Carmen* (1 perf.)	N. Vallin s. F. Anitua ms. M. Journet bs.; G. Marinuzzi cond.
Sep 12	*Tosca* (1 perf.)	G. Dalla Rizza s. E. Giraldoni b.; G. Marinuzzi cond.
Sep 15	*L'Elisir d'amore* (1 perf.)	A. Giacomucci s. E. De Franceschi b. G. Azzolini bs.; G. Marinuzzi cond.
Sep 17	**Lodoletta* (1 perf.)	G. Dalla Rizza s. M. Urizar b. E. De Franceschi b. T. Dentale bs.; G. Marinuzzi cond.
Sep 19	Concert	
Sep 20	*La Bohème* (1 perf.)	G. Dalla Rizza s. A. Giacomucci s. A. Crabbé b. E. De Franceschi b. M. Journet bs.; V. Bellezza cond.

Sep 22	*Manon* (1 perf.)	N. Vallin s. A. Crabbé b. M. Journet bs.; G. Marinuzzi cond.

SÃO PAULO – TEATRO MUNICIPAL

Sep 25	*L'Elisir d'amore* (1 perf.)	A. Giacomucci s. E. De Franceschi b. G. Azzolini bs.; G. Marinuzzi cond.
Sep 27	*Carmen* (1 perf.)	A. Giacomucci s. F. Anitua ms. M. Journet bs.; G. Marinuzzi cond.
Sep 30	*Tosca* (1 perf.)	G. Dalla Rizza s. E. Giraldoni b.; G. Marinuzzi cond.
Oct 2	*La Bohème* (1 perf.)	G. Dalla Rizza s. A. Giacomucci s. A. Crabbé b. E. De Franceschi b. T. Dentale bs.; V. Bellezza cond.
Oct 5	*Pagliacci* (1 perf.)	A. Giacomucci s. A. Cortis t. A. Crabbé b. E. De Franceschi b.; V. Bellezza cond.
Oct 7	*Lodoletta* (1 perf.)	G. Dalla Rizza s. M. Urizar b. E. De Franceschi b. T. Dentale bs.; G. Mar- inuzzi cond.
Oct 8	Concert	(M) and Act I, *Pagliacci*
Oct 10	*Manon* (1 perf.)	G. Dalla Rizza s. A. Crabbé b. M. Journet bs.; G. Marinuzzi cond.

RIO DE JANEIRO – TEATRO MUNICIPAL

Oct 13	*Carmen* (1 perf.)	A. Giacomucci s. F. Anitua ms. M. Journet bs.; G. Marinuzzi cond.
Oct 16	*Manon Lescaut* (1 perf.)	G. Dalla Rizza s. A. Crabbé b. G. Azzolini bs.; V. Bellezza cond.

1917–18

NEW YORK – METROPOLITAN OPERA

Nov 12	*Aida* (3 perf.)	C. Muzio s. M. Matzenauer ms. (later L. Homer ms.) P. Amato b. J. Mardones bs. (later A. De Segurola bs.); R. Moranzoni cond. (later G. Papi cond.)
Nov 15	*L'Elisir d'amore* (5 perf.)	F. Hempel s. (later M. Barrientos s.) A. Scotti b. A. Didur bs.; G. Papi cond.
Nov 21	*Marta* (5 perf.)	F. Hempel s. (later M. Barrientos s.) F. Perini ms. G. De Luca b. (later A. Didur bs.); A. Bodansky cond.
Nov 23	*Samson et Dalila* (4 perf.)	J. Claussen ms. (later L. Homer ms.; then M. Matzenauer ms.) C. Whitehill b. (later P. Amato b.) C. Schlegel b. L. Rothier bs.; P. Monteux cond.
Dec 5	*Manon Lescaut* (3 perf.)	F. Alda s. (later C. Muzio s.) P. Amato b. A. De Segurola bs.; G. Papi cond.

1917–18 cont.

Dec 7	*Pagliacci* (3 perf.)	C. Muzio s. A. Bada t. P. Amato b. M. Laurenti b.; R. Moranzoni cond.
Dec 10	*Carmen* (2 perf.)	M. Peterson s. G. Farrar s. C. Whitehill b.; P. Monteux cond.
Dec 15	*Tosca* (1 perf.)	C. Muzio s. A. Scotti b.; R. Moranzoni cond.
Dec 29	*Rigoletto* (1 perf.)	F. Hempel s. S. Braslau ms. G. De Luca b. J. Mardones bs.; R. Moranzoni cond.
Jan 12	*Lodoletta* (5 perf.)	G. Farrar s. (later F. Easton s.) P. Amato b. (later G. De Luca b.) A. Didur bs.; R. Moranzoni cond.
Feb 7	*Le Prophète* (Meyerbeer) (5 perf.)	C. Muzio s. M. Matzenauer ms. J. Mardones bs. A. Didur bs. (later L. Rothier bs.); A. Bodanzky cond.
Mar 14	*L'Amore dei tre re* (Montemezzi) (4 perf.)	C. Muzio s. P. Amato b. A. Didur bs. (later J. Mardones bs.); R. Moranzoni cond.
Mar 21	Concert	Act I, *Pagliacci*; F. Easton s. G. De Luca b.
Apr 14	Concert	(I), (K) w. A. Scotti b.; (AS) w. F. Alda s. L. Sparkes ms. A. Scotti b.

NEW YORK – WASHINGTON SQUARE

Nov 22	Concert	(AT), (AU), (AV)

PHILADELPHIA – ACADEMY OF MUSIC
(Concurrent with New York season)

Nov 27	*Manon Lescaut* (1 perf.)	F. Alda s. P. Amato b. A. De Segurola bs.; G. Papi cond.
Dec 18	*Pagliacci* (1 perf.)	C. Muzio s. P. Audisio t. P. Amato b. M. Laurenti b.; R. Moranzoni cond.
Feb 19	*Lodoletta* (1 perf.)	F. Easton s. P. Amato b. A. Didur bs.; R. Moranzoni cond.
Mar 19	*L'Amore dei tre re* (1 perf.)	C. Muzio s. P. Amato b. J. Mardones bs.; R. Moranzoni cond.
Apr 9	*Samson et Dalila* (1 perf.)	M. Matzenauer ms. C. Whitehill b. C. Schlegel bs. L. Rothier bs.; P. Monteux cond.

NEW YORK – HOTEL WALDORF ASTORIA

Dec 27	Concert	
Jan 7	Concert	(AW), (AX), (AY), (AZ), (BA) and (BB) w. M. Elman violin

1918

BROOKLYN – ACADEMY OF MUSIC
(Concurrent with New York season)

Jan 15   *Rigoletto*
(1 perf.)
     M. Conde s. F. Perini ms. G. De Luca b. J.
Mardones bs.; R. Moranzoni cond.

NEW YORK – BILTMORE HOTEL

Feb 18   Concert   (BA), (I), (BD) and (BE) w. G. Walska s.

NEW YORK – 48TH ST. THEATRE

Mar 10   Concert

BOSTON – BOSTON OPERA HOUSE
Tour of the Metropolitan Opera Company

Apr 22   *Le Prophète*
(1 perf.)
     C. Muzio s. M. Matzenauer ms. J.
Mardones bs. L. Rothier bs.; A.
Bodanzky cond.

Apr 25   *Pagliacci*
(1 perf.)
     C. Muzio s. A. Bada t. P. Amato b. M.
Laurenti b.; R. Moranzoni cond.

Apr 27   *Samson et Dalila*
(1 perf.)
     J. Claussen ms. C. Whitehill b. L. D'An-
gelo bs. L. Rother bs.; P. Monteux cond.

NEW YORK – CARNEGIE HALL

May 1   Concert

WASHINGTON – POLI'S THEATRE

May 20   Concert   (I), (BA), (BF), (BG), (BI), (BJ), (BK),
and (AT) w. G. De Luca b.; F. Alda s.

NEW YORK – METROPOLITAN OPERA

May 24   Concert   F. Alda s. A. Case s. C. Muzio s. S.
Braslau ms. G. Martinelli t. P. Amato b.
G. De Luca b. A. Scotti b.

May 27   Concert   F. Alda s. A. Fitziu s. C. Muzio s. S.
Braslau ms. P. Amato b. R. Stracciari b.
A. Scotti b. A. Didur bs. J. Mardones bs.
L. Rothier bs. A. De Segurola bs.

June 10   Concert   (I); F. Alda s. C. Muzio s. S. Braslau ms. H.
Lazaro t. G. Martinelli t. J. McCormack
t. L. Muratore t. A. Scotti b. P. Amato b.
G. De Luca b. L. Rothier bs.

BOONTON N. J. – MOUNT CARMEL SCHOOL

July 3?   Concert

OCEAN GROVE N.J. – AUDITORIUM

July 27   Concert   (BA), (Q), (BM), (R), (I) and (BL) w.
C. White s.

SARATOGA SPRINGS – CONVENTION HALL

Aug 17   Concert   (H), (M), (BM), (AV), (I)

NEW YORK – SHEEPSHEAD BAY

Aug 31   Concert   (BM), (AT)

1918 cont.

NEW YORK – HOTEL WALDORF ASTORIA
Sep 6   Concert   (AU)

NEW YORK – CENTURY THEATRE
Sep 15   Concert   (BM)

NEW YORK – CENTRAL PARK MALL
Sep 19   Concert   (AT), (BM)

NEW YORK – CARNEGIE HALL
Sep 30   Concert   (AT) (Eng.) w. A. Galli-Gurci s. J. McCormack t.

NEW YORK – MADISON SQUARE GARDEN
Oct 5   Concert   (AV), (AT) (Eng.), (BM)

BUFFALO – HOTEL IROQUOIS
Oct 9   Concert   (BM)

NEW YORK – METROPOLITAN OPERA
Oct 12   Concert   (BM) w. M. Garrison s.

DETROIT – ARCADIA AUDITORIUM
Oct 15   *Pagliacci*   C. Muzio s. F. Daddi t. P. Amato b. M. Picco b.; G. Polacco cond.

NEW YORK – MADISON SQUARE GARDEN
Nov 3   Concert – morning   (AV), (BM)

HIPPODROME
Concert – evening   (BM); w. C. Muzio s.

NEW YORK – BILTMORE HOTEL
Nov 8   Concert   F. Alda s. A. Galli Curci s. G. Martinelli t. J. O'Sullivan t.

1918–19

NEW YORK – METROPOLITAN OPERA
Nov 11   *Samson et Dalila*   L. Homer ms. (later M. Matzenauer ms. (5 perf.)   R. Couzinou b. (later G. De Luca b.) L. Rothier bs.; P. Monteux cond.

Nov 15   *La Forza del destino* (Verdi)   R. Ponselle s. A. Gentle ms. (later S. (6 perf.)   Braslau ms.) G. De Luca b. T. Chalmers b. J. Mardones bs.; G. Papi cond.

Nov 20   *L'Elisir d'amore*   F. Hempel, s. (later M. Barrientos s.) A. (5 perf.)   Scotti b. (later G. De Luca b.) A. Didur bs. (later P. Malatesta bs.); G. Papi cond.

Nov 23   *Le Prophète*   C. Muzio s. (later F. Easton s.) L. Homer ms. (6 perf.)   (later M. Matzenauer ms.) J. Mardones bs. L. Rothier bs.; A. Bodanzky cond.

Dec 7   *Marta*   F. Hempel s. (later M. Barrientos s.) L. (5 perf.)   Homer ms. (later F. Perini ms.) A. Didur b.; A. Bodanzky cond.

Dec 18	*Lodoletta* (3 perf.)	F. Easton s. T. Chalmers b. A. Didur bs.; R. Moranzoni cond.
Dec 25	*Pagliacci* (3 perf.)	C. Muzio s. (later F. Easton s.) G. Patrinieri t. L. Montesanto b. (later T. Chalmers b.) M. Laurenti b. (later R. Werrenrath b.); R. Moranzoni cond.
Jan 8	*La Bohème* (2 perf.)	F. Alda s. L. Sparkes s. L. Montesanto b. A. Didur bs. (later L. D'Angelo bs.) A. De Segurola bs.; G. Papi cond.
Feb 12	*Aida* (2 perf.)	C. Muzio s. J. Claussen ms. (later M. Matzenauer ms.) C. Whitehill b. (later P. Amato b. J. Mardones bs. (later H. Scott bs.); R. Moranzoni cond.
Mar 4	League of Nations Rally	(AV)
Mar 22	Concert	Act III, *L'Elisir d'amore*, Act I, *Pagliacci*, and Act IV, *Le Prophète*
Apr 3	Concert	Act III, *Aida*
Apr 14	*Carmen* (1 perf.)	M. Sundelius s. G. Farrar s. C. Whitehill b.; P. Monteux cond.

PHILADELPHIA – METROPOLITAN OPERA
(Concurrent with New York season)

Nov 26	*L'Elisir d'amore* (1 perf.)	F. Hempel s. G. De Luca b. A. Didur bs.; G. Papi cond.
Dec 10	*Pagliacci* (1 perf.)	F. Easton s. A. Reiss t. L. Montesanto b. M. Laurenti b.; G. Papi cond.
Jan 21	*Samson et Dalila* (1 perf.)	M. Matzenauer ms. R. Couzinou b. P. Ananian bs. J. Mardones bs.; G. Setti cond.
Mar 11	*La Bohème* (1 perf.)	C. Muzio s. L. Sparkes s. L. Montesanto b. L. D'Angelo bs. A. De Segurola bs.; G. Papi cond.

NEW YORK – MANHATTAN OPERA

Dec 1	Concert	

NEW YORK – BILTMORE HOTEL

Dec 6	Concert	(BO), (BP, (BQ), (BR), (BS), (BT), (BU) and (AC), (BV), (BA), (Z), (U), (BW) w. M. Namara s.

NEW YORK – HOTEL WALDORF ASTORIA

Dec 23	Concert	(H), (BX), (BY), (M)

1919

ANN ARBOR – HILL AUDITORIUM

Mar 2	Concert	(Q), (M), (I) and (AV) w. N. Morgana s.

NEW YORK – COMMODORE HOTEL

Apr 2	Concert	(X) and (BN) w. M. Garden s.

BUFFALO–BROADWAY AUDITORIUM

Apr. 7	Concert	(as at Ann Arbor, see above.)

1919 cont.

ATLANTA – AUDITORIUM
Tour of the Metropolitan Opera Company

Apr 21	*La Forza del destino* (1 perf.)	R. Ponselle s. R. Delaunois ms. G. De Luca b. P. Malatesta b. J. Mardones bs.; G. Papi cond.
Apr 24	*Marta* (1 perf.)	M. Barrientos s. K. Howard ms. A. Didur bs.; G. Papi cond.
Apr 26	*Pagliacci* (1 perf.)	F. Easton s. G. Paltrinieri t. A. Scotti b. M. Laurenti b; R. Moranzoni cond.

NASHVILLE – RYMAN AUDITORIUM

Apr 29	Concert	Each concert (Apr 29 – May 22) included: (Q), (M) and (I) orchestrally acc. plus many of the following, piano acc.: (BZ), (CA), (U), (CB), (AR), (C), (AH), (BA), (W), (CC), (AC) and (AV) w. N. Morgana s.

ST. LOUIS – COLISEUM

May 2	Concert	See above

KANSAS CITY – CONVENTION HALL

May 5	Concert	See above

ST. PAUL – AUDITORIUM

May 8	Concert	See above

CHICAGO – MEDINAH TEMPLE

May 11	Concert	See above

MILWAUKEE – AUDITORIUM

May 13	Concert	See above

CANTON – AUDITORIUM

May 16	Concert	See above

NEWARK – FIRST REGIMENT ARMORY

May 19	Concert	See above

SPRINGFIELD, MASS. – AUDITORIUM

May 22	Concert	See above, but w. E. Bianchini-Cappelli s.

MEXICO CITY – TEATRO ESPERANZA IRIS

Sep 29	*L'Elisir d'amore* (1 perf.)	A. Navarrete s. R. Blanchart b.; G. Papi cond.
Oct 2	*Un Ballo in maschera* (1 perf.)	C. Sanchez s. M. Santillan s. G. Besanzoni ms. A. Ordonez b.
Oct 9	*Samson et Dalila* (1 perf.)	G. Besanzoni ms. A. Ordonez b.; G. Papi cond.
Oct 17	*Marta* (1 perf.)	A. Navarrete s. G. Besanzoni ms. R. Blanchart b.; G. Papi cond.

Oct 23	*Pagliacci* (1 perf.)	M. Santillan s. A. Ordonez b.; G. Papi cond.
Oct 28	Concert	C. Mayer s. G. Besanzoni ms. A. Ordonez b.
Oct 30	*Manon Lescaut* (1 perf.)	M. Santillan s. R.. Blanchart b.; G. Papi cond.

MEXICO CITY – PLAZA EL TOREO
(Concurrent with the season at the Esperanza Iris)

Oct 5	*Carmen* (1 perf.)	A. Navarrete s. G. Besanzoni ms. A. Ordonez b.; G. Papi cond.
Oct 12	*Un Ballo in maschera* (1 perf.)	C. Sanchez s. M. Santillan s. G. Besanzoni ms. A. Ordonez b.; G. Papi cond.
Oct 19	*Samson et Dalila* (1 perf.)	G. Besanzoni ms. A. Ordonez b.; G. Papi cond.
Oct. 25	*Aida* (1 perf.)	M. L. Escobar s. G. Besanzoni ms. A. Ordonez b.; G. Papi cond.
Nov 2	Concert	Act III, *L'Elisir d'amore*, Act III, *Marta*, Act I, *Pagliacci*

1919–20

NEW YORK – METROPOLITAN OPERA

Nov 17	*Tosca* (1 perf.)	G. Farrar s. A. Scotti b.; R. Moranzoni cond.
Nov 18	Concert	Act I, *Pagliacci*
Nov 22	*La Juive* (Halévy) (7 perf.)	R. Ponselle s. E. Scotney s. O. Harrold t. L. Rothier bs. (later J. Mardones bs.); A. Bodanzky cond.
Nov 26	*Pagliacci* (5 perf.)	C. Muzio s. A. Bada t. P. Amato b. M. Laurenti b.; R. Moranzoni cond.
Nov 28	*La Forza del destino* (5 perf.)	R. Ponselle s. R. Delaunois ms. (later J. Gordon ms.; then G. Besanzoni ms.) P. Amato b. (later R. Zanelli b.) T. Chalmers b. J. Mardones bs.; G. Papi cond.
Dec 10	*Samson et Dalila* (5 perf.)	G. Besanzoni ms. (later M. Matzenauer ms.) R. Couzinou b. (later P. Amato b.; then C. Whitehill b.) P. Ananian bs. L. Rothier bs. (Later J. Mardones bs.); A. Wolff cond.
Dec 13	*Marta* (4 perf.)	M. Garrison s. (later M. Barrientos s.) F. Perini ms. G. De Luca b.; A. Bodanzky cond.
Dec 19	*L'Elisir d'amore* (5 perf.)	M. Garrison s. (later M. Barrientos s.) A. Scotti b. (later G. De Luca b.) A. Didur bs. (later P. Malatesta bs.); G. Papi cond.
Jan 15	*Manon Lescaut* (1 perf.)	F. Alda s. A. Scotti b. A. De Segurola bs. G. Papi cond.

1919–20 cont.

Feb 4   *Le Prophète*   C. Muzio s. (later F. Easton s.) M. Matzen-
       (5 perf.)   auer ms. J. Mardones bs. L. Rothier bs.; A.
             Bodanzky cond.

Mar 15   Concert   Act I, *Pagliacci* w. C. Muzio s. R. Zanelli b.

BROOKLYN – ACADEMY OF MUSIC
(Concurrent with New York season)

Dec 23   *Marta*   M. Garrison s. F. Perini ms. G. De Luca b.;
       (1 perf.)   A. Bodanzky cond.

Feb 24   *La Juive*   R. Ponselle s. E. Scotney s. R. Diaz t. L.
       (1 perf.)   Rothier bs.; A. Bodanzky cond.

1920

PHILADELPHIA – ACADEMY OF MUSIC

Jan 6   *La Juive*   R. Ponselle s. E. Scotney s. O. Harrold t. J.
       (1 perf.)   Mardones bs.; A. Bodanzky cond.

Mar 2   *Marta*   M. Barrientos s. F. Perini ms. G. De Luca b.;
       (1 perf.)   A. Bodanzky cond.

Mar 30   *La Forza del destino*   R. Ponselle s. J. Gordon ms. P. Amato b. T.
       (1 perf.)   Chalmers b. J. Mardones bs.; G. Papi cond.

NEW YORK – HOTEL WALDORF ASTORIA

Jan 19   Concert

PITTSBURGH – SYRIA MOSQUE

Feb 28   Concert   (Q), (I), (BZ), (BA), (CB) and some other
             Tosti songs w. N. Morgana s.

WATERBURY CONN. – AUDITORIUM

Mar 14   Concert

NEW YORK – LEXINGTON OPERA HOUSE

Mar 28   Concert   (CB) w. L. Tetrazzini s. R. Stracciari b.

SCRANTON – ARMORY

Apr 5   Concert

DETROIT – ARCADIA THEATRE

Apr 18   Concert   (Q), (M), (H), (AH), (CC), (CB), (BZ),
             (BA) M. Kent ms.

ATLANTA – AUDITORIUM
Tour of the Metropolitan Opera Company

Apr 26   *Samson et Dalila*   M. Matzenauer ms. P. Amato b. P. Ananian
       (1 perf.)   bs. J. Mardones bs.; A. Wolff cond.

Apr 29   *La Juive*   R. Ponselle s. E. Scotney s. O. Harrold t. J.
       (1 perf.)   Mardones bs.; A. Bodanzky cond.

May 1   *L'Elisir d'amore*   M. Barrientos s. A. Scotti b. P. Malatesta
       (1 perf.)   bs.; G. Papi cond.

HAVANA – TEATRO NACIONAL

May 12   *Marta*   M. Barrientos s. F. Perini ms. T. Parvis b.; A.
       (2 perf.)   Padovani cond.

A CHRONOLOGY OF CARUSO'S APPEARANCES

May 18	*L'Elisir d'amore* (1 perf.)	M. Barrientos s. T. Parvis b. G. La Puma bs.; A. Padovani cond.
May 21	*Un Ballo in maschera* (1 perf.)	M. L. Escobar s. G. Besanzoni ms. R. Stracciari b.; A. Padovani cond.
May 25	*Pagliacci* (2 perf.)	C. Melis s. R. Stracciari b.; A. Padovani cond.
May 28	*Tosca* (1 perf.)	C. Melis s. R. Stracciari b.; A. Padovani cond.
June 2	*Carmen* (2 perf.)	M. L. Escobar s. G. Besanzoni ms. R. Stracciari b.; A. Padovani cond.
June 6	*La Forza del destino* (1 perf.)	M. L. Escobar s. G. Besanzoni ms. R. Stracciari b. J. Mardones bs.; A. Padovani cond.
June 8	*Aida* (1+ perf.)	M. L. Escobar s. G. Besanzoni ms. R. Stracciari b. J. Mardones bs.; A. Padovani cond.
June 11	Concert	Act III, *L'Elisir d'amore*, Act I, *Pagliacci*

SANTA CLARA – TEATRO LA CARIDAD

June 17	*Pagliacci* (1 unfinished perf.)	C. Melis s. R. Stracciari b.; A. Padovani cond.

CIENFUEGOS – TEATRO TERRY

June 19	*Aida* (1 perf.)	M. L. Escobar s. G. Besanzoni ms. R. Stracciari b. J. Mardones bs.; A. Padovani cond.

NEW ORLEANS – ATHENAEUM

June 26	Concert	N. Morgana s.

ATLANTIC CITY – AMBASSADOR HOTEL

June 30	Concert	

OCEAN GROVE – AUDITORUM

Aug 14	Concert	N. Morgana s.

MONTREAL – MOUNT ROYAL ARENA

Sep 27	Concert	Each concert (Sep 27 – Oct 28) included three of the following operatic arias with piano acc.: (H), (M), (I), (O) and (CD); with a substantial collection of encores, including (CB), (U), (BZ), (CC), (AH), (BA), (CE), (CF), (CH) and (CI) w. A. Miriam s.

TORONTO – MASSEY HALL

Sep 30	Concert	See above

CHICAGO – MEDINAH TEMPLE

Oct 3	Concert	See above

ST. PAUL – AUDITORIUM

Oct 6	Concert	See above

1920 cont.

| | DENVER – AUDITORIUM | |
| Oct 9 | Concert | See over |

| | OMAHA – AUDITORIUM | |
| Oct 12 | Concert | See over |

| | TULSA – CONVENTION HALL | |
| Oct 16 | Concert | See over |

| | FORT WORTH – COLISEUM | |
| Oct 19 | Concert | See over |

| | HOUSTON – CITY AUDITORIUM | |
| Oct 22 | Concert | See over |

| | CHARLOTTE – CITY AUDITORIUM | |
| Oct 25 | Concert | See over |

| | NORFOLK – TABERNACLE | |
| Oct 28 | Concert | See over |

	NEW YORK – METROPOLITAN OPERA	
Nov 15	*La Juive* (2 perf.)	R. Ponselle s. (later F. Easton s.) E. Scotney s. O. Harrold t. L. Rothier bs.; A. Bodanzky cond.
Nov 18	*L'Elisir d'amore* (2 perf.)	M. Garrison s. A. Scotti b. A. Didur bs.; G. Papi cond.
Nov 24	*Samson et Dalila* (3 perf.)	M. Matzenauer ms. G. De Luca b. (later C. Whitehill b.) P. Ananian bs. L. Rothier bs.; A. Wolff cond.
Nov 27	*La Forza del destino* (2 perf.)	R. Ponselle s. R. Delaunois ms. (later J. Gordon ms.) G. Danise b. T. Chalmers b. G. Martino bs. (later J. Mardones bs.); G. Papi cond.
Dec 8	*Pagliacci* (1 perf.)	E. Destinn s. A. Bada t. G. De Luca b. M. Laurenti b.; R. Moranzoni cond.

| | PHILADELPHIA – METROPOLITAN OPERA
(Concurrent with New York season) | |
| Nov 30 | *La Juive*
(1 perf.) | R. Ponselle s. E. Scotney s. R. Diaz t. L. Rothier bs.; A. Bodanzky cond. |

| | BROOKLYN – ACADEMY OF MUSIC
(Concurrent with New York season) | |
| Dec 11 | *L'Elisir d'amore* | E. Scotney s. G. De Luca b. P. Malatesta bs.; G. Papi cond. |

Songs, Operatic Arias and Ensembles sung by Caruso in concert.

(A)	Rossini, *Stabat Mater*, 'Cujus animam.'
(B)	Verdi, *Rigoletto*, 'Bella figlia dell'amore.'
(C)	Tosti, 'Ideale.'
(D)	*Ibid*, 'La mia canzone.'

(E)	Tirindelli, 'Di te'.
(F)	Denza, 'Non t'amo più'.
(G)	Verdi, *Rigoletto*, 'La donna è mobile'.
(H)	Puccini, *La Bohème*, 'Che gelida manina'.
(I)	Leoncavallo, *Pagliacci*, 'Vesti la giubba'.
(J)	Ponchielli, *La Gioconda*, 'Cielo e mar!'
(K)	Verdi, *La forza del destino*, 'Solenne in quest' ora'.
(L)	Gounod, *Faust*, 'Salut demeure!'
(M)	Donizetti, *L'Elisir d'amore*, 'Una furtiva lagrima'.
(N)	Puccini, *La Bohème*, 'O soave fanciulla'.
(O)	Meyerbeer, *L'Africana*, 'O paradiso!'
(P)	Puccini, *Madama Butterfly*, 'O quanti occhi fisi'.
(Q)	Verdi, *Aida*, 'Celeste Aida'.
(R)	Tosti, 'Addio'.
(S)	Schubert, 'Serenade'.
(T)	Tosti, 'Triste ritorno'.
(U)	*Ibid*, 'Pour un baiser'.
(V)	Puccini, *Tosca*, 'E lucevan le stelle'.
(W)	Gastaldon, 'Musica proibita'.
(X)	Verdi, *La forza del destino*, 'O tu che in seno'.
(Y)	Sullivan, 'The lost chord'.
(Z)	Sibella, 'Desir'.
(AA)	Gounod, *La Reine de Saba*, 'Inspirez-moi'.
(AB)	Buzzi-Peccia, 'Mal d'amore'.
(AC)	*Ibid.*, 'Povero pulcinella'.
(AD)	Franck, 'La Procession'.
(AE)	Ponchielli, *La Gioconda*, 'Enzo Grimaldo'.
(AF)	Faure, 'Santa Maria'.
(AG)	Widor, 'Mon bras pressait'.
(AH)	Duparc, 'Extase'.
(AI)	Barthélemy, 'Triste ritorno'.
(AJ)	Hüe, 'J'ai pleuré en rêve'.
(AK)	Fauré, 'Claire de la lune'.
(AL)	Rachmaninoff, 'Primavera' (Spring Waters).
(AM)	Borodin, 'Dissonance'.
(AN)	Giordano, *Andrea Chénier*, 'Come un bel dì di maggio'.
(AO)	Tosti, 'L'alba separa dalla luce l'ombra'.
(AP)	*Ibid.*, 'Carmela'.
(AQ)	Nutile, 'Mamma mia'.
(AR)	Leoncavallo, 'Mattinata'.
(AS)	Puccini, *La Bohème*, 'Addio dolce svegliare'.
(AT)	'Inno di Garibaldi.'
(AU)	'La Marseillaise'.
(AV)	'The Star Spangled Banner'.
(AW)	Godard, 'Chanson de Juin'.
(AX)	Buzzi-Peccia, 'Lolita'.
(AY)	Grieg, 'Io t'amo'.
(AZ)	Reyer, *Sigurd*, 'Esprits gardiens'.
(BA)	Rossini, 'La danza'.
(BB)	Bizet, 'Agnus Dei'.
(BD)	Auber, *Fra Diavolo*, aria.
(BE)	Bizet, *Les Pêcheurs de perles*, duet.
(BF)	Costa, 'Sei morta nella vita mia'.
(BG)	Tosti, 'Luna d'estate'.
(BI)	Mrs Lawrence Townsend, Chanson.
(BJ)	*Ibid.*, 'La vie est brève'.
(BK)	*Ibid.*, 'Vous-toi'.
(BL)	Gomes, *Il guarany*, 'Sento una forza'.

(BM)	Cohan, 'Over There'.
(BN)	Massenet, *Manon*, 'Ah! fuyez, douce image'.
(BO)	Cesti, 'Intorno all'idol mio'.
(BP)	Sgambati, 'Separazione'.
(BQ)	Carissimi, 'Vittoria, vittoria'.
(BR)	Tchaikovsky, *Eugène Oneguine*, 'Echo lointain'.
(BS)	Uterhart, 'Romance'.
(BT)	Seismit-Doda, 'Dream'.
(BU)	Silesu, 'Star of My Life'.
(BV)	Alvarez, 'A Granada'.
(BW)	Leoncavallo, 'Serenade'.
(BX)	Niedermeyer, 'Pietà, Signore'.
(BY)	Adam, 'Cantique de Noël'.
(BZ)	Geehl, 'For You Alone'.
(CA)	Arona, 'La Campana di San Giusto'.
(CB)	Tosti, ''A vucchella'.
(CC)	Fatuo, 'Sento che t'amo'.
(CD)	Flotow, *Marta*, 'M'apparì'.
(CE)	Bartlett, 'A Dream.'
(CF)	Pasadas, 'Noche felíz'.
(CG)	Massenet, 'Elégie'.
(CH)	Lully, 'Bois Epais'.
(CI)	Donaudy, 'Spirate'.
(CJ)	Barthélemy, 'Serenata Napolitana'.
(CK)	Pons, *Laura*, air.
(CL)	Massenet, *Il Re di Lahore*, aria.

A CARUSO DISCOGRAPHY

By Dr. John R. Bolig

Researchers have been able to document 498 Caruso recordings, of which 245 are known still to exist. It should be noted that almost all of the records which were not published probably do not exist today because they were not approved by Caruso or his fellow artists. The masters were destroyed by the recording companies. Fortunately, all but 20 of these were alternate takes of published material. There may be a few unpublished Caruso records in private collections.

The discography on the following pages is in chronological order, demonstrating the development of Caruso as a recording artist. Each entry is identified by title, matrix number, and take number. If the title was re-recorded, subsequent matrix and take numbers are reported. The titles are not always the same as those shown on record labels because record companies made errors on many such labels.

The matrix and take numbers are very important in identifying records. A matrix number was assigned to each title an artist was to record. Each time that title was recorded, a new take number was assigned. These numbers usually appear on the surface of the published record. In Europe, the matrix and take number were etched or embossed in the area surrounding the label of a record. In the United States, the matrix number was rarely shown, but the take number was usually etched or embossed in the space to the left of the label.

Collectors of '78 RPM' records have become quite skilled at identifying different versions of Caruso recordings by visual inspection of the surface surrounding labels. Collectors of long-playing records are forced to rely on the liner or album notes, and it should be noted that the number of errors or omissions on these are countless.

Caruso records were reissued which were made from transcribed or pantographed stampers, as well as some with the addition of symphony orchestra or organ accompaniment. Again, markings next to the label can be used to determine which version was published. Pantographed versions have the fraction S/8 embossed on them, and most of the re-recordings have a new matrix number or the symbol VE in the area next to the grooves.

Since there are so many errors on long-playing reissues, not to mention the editing done by recording engineers, the only long-playing records of any merit are those published by RCA Victor and its affiliates after the year 1975.

The index, below, is keyed to recordings in the text. Numbers in italics refer to recordings which have been published or which are known to exist.

Marta (Flotow):
Act 1: Solo, profugo, reietto! *132*
Act 2: Siam giunti, o giovinette 179, *180*
Act 2: Questo camero è per voi; Che vuol dir ciò? *181*
Act 2: Presto, presto andiam *182*, 183
Act 2: T'ho raggiunta, sciagurata; Dormi pur *184*
Act 3: M'apparì tutt'amor 49, *359*, 360
Mattinata (Leoncavallo; written for the phonograph) 42
Mefistofele (Boito):
Act 1: Dai campi, dai prati 8, *11*
Epilog: Giunto sul passo estremo 6
Messa da Requiem (Verdi):
Ingemisco 295, 296, 297
Mia canzone, La (Tosti) *18*, 285, 286, 292
Mia sposa sarà la mia bandiera (Rotoli) 318, *319*
Milagro de la Virgen, El (Gomes):
Flores purisimas 270, 271
Musica proibita (Gastaldon) 283, 284, 290, 291, *361*
Néron (Rubinstein):
Act 2: Oh! lumière du jour 366, 367
Noche felíz (Pasadas) 467, 468, 469, 470, 475, 476
Non t'amo più (Denza) *17*
O sole mio (di Capua) *315*
Otello (Verdi):
Act 2: Ora e per sempre addio sante memorie 147, *148*
Act 2: Oh! mostruosa colpa!; Si, pel ciel 167, 247, *248*
Over There/Par là-bas (Cohan) 382, 383, 384, *385*
Pagliacci (Leoncavallo):
Act 1: Recitar, mentre preso; Vesti la giubba *15*, 40, *64*, 65
Act 2: No, Pagliaccio non son 145, *146*
Parce que (d'Hardelot) 210, 211
Parted (Tosti) 263
Partida, La (Alvarez) 268, 269, *376*, 377, 378
Pecchè? (Pennino) *293*
Pescatori di Perle, I (Bizet):
Act 1: Del tempio al limitar 68
Act 1: Je crois entendre encore 347, 348, *349*
Act 1: Mi Par d'udir ancora 43, 74, 86, 87
Act 2: De mon amie, fleur endormie 350, *351*
Petite Messe Solennelle (Rossini):
Crucifixus 497, 498
Domine Deus 495, 496
Pietà, Signore (Niedermeyer) 372, 373, 374, 375, *392*, *393*, 394
Pimpinella ('Florentine Air') (Tchaikovsky) 221, 222
Pour un baiser (Tosti) *104*
Pourquoi? (Tchaikovsky) 338, 339, *340*
Povero Pulcinella (Buzzi-Peccia) 414, 415, 416
Première caresse (de Crescenzo) 444, 445, 446, 447
Procession, La (Franck) 307, 308, *309*
Rameaux, Les (Fauré) 242, 243, *257*
Régiment de Sambre et Meuse, Le (Planquette) 409, 410, *411*
Regina di Saba, La (Goldmark):
Act 2: Magiche note 95, *112*
Reine de Saba, La (Gounod):
Act 2: Faiblesse de la race humaine; Inspirez-moi 316, *317*
Rigoletto (Verdi):
Act 1: Questa o quella 2, *31*, 91
Act 3: Ella mi fu rapita; Parmi veder le lagrime 176, 223

Gramophone & Typewriter. *Milan*, Friday, April 11, 1902.   71.29 RPM.
1 *Germania*: Studenti! Udite
   Matrix 1782 Accompanied by Cottone, piano
2 *Rigoletto*: Questa o quella
   Matrix 1783 Accompanied by Cottone, piano
3 *Aïda*: Celeste Aïda
   Matrix 1784 Accompanied by Cottone, piano
4 *Manon*: Chiudo gli occhi ('Il sogno')
   Matrix 1785 Accompanied by Cottone, piano
5 *L'Elisir d'amore*: Una furtiva lagrima
   Matrix 1786 Accompanied by Cottone, piano
6 *Mefistofele*: Giunto sul passo estremo
   Matrix 1787 Accompanied by Cottone, piano
7 *Germania*: No, non chiuder gli occhi vaghi
   Matrix 1788 Accompanied by Cottone, piano
8 *Mefistofele*: Dai campi, dai prati
   Matrix 1789 Accompanied by Cottone, piano
9 *Tosca*: E lucevan le stelle
   Matrix 1790 Accompanied by Cottone, piano
10 *Iris*: Apri la tua finestra ('Serenata')
   Matrix 1791 Accompanied by Cottone, piano

Gramophone & Typewriter. *Milan*, Sunday, November 30, 1902.   67.92 RPM.
11 *Mefistofele*: Dai campi, dai prati
   Matrix 2871 Accompanied by Cottone, piano
12 *Fedora*: Amor ti vieta
   Matrix 2872 Accompanied by Cottone, piano
13 *Aïda*: Celeste Aïda
   Matrix 2873 Accompanied by Cottone, piano
14 *La Gioconda*: Cielo e mar
   Matrix 2874 Accompanied by Cottone, piano
15 *Pagliacci*: Recitar, mentre preso dal delirio; Vesti la giubba
   Matrix 2875 Accompanied by Cottone, piano
16 *Cavalleria rusticana*: O Lola ch'ai di latti ('Siciliana')
   Matrix 2876 Accompanied by Cottone, piano
17 Non t'amo più
   Matrix 2877 Accompanied by Cottone, piano

Gramophone & Typewriter. *Milan*, December 1 or 2, 1902.   67.92 RPM.
18 La mia canzone
   Matrix 2879 Accompanied by Cottone, piano
19 *Adriana Lecouvreur*: No, più nobile
   Matrix 2880 Accompanied by the composer, Cilea, piano
20 Luna fedel
   Matrix 2882 Accompanied by Cottone, piano

Anglo-Italian Commerce Co. *Milan*, Sunday, April 19, 1903.   75.00 RPM.
Announced, probably by Caruso; accompanied by an unknown pianist.
21 Un bacio ancora
   Matrix X–1550
22 Luna fedel
   Matrix X–1551
23 *L'Elisir d'amore*: Una furtiva lagrima
   Matrix X–1552
24 *Tosca*: E lucevan le stelle
   Matrix X–1553
25 *Germania*: No, non chiuder gli occhi vaghi
   Matrix X–1554

26 *Rigoletto*: La donna è mobile
Matrix X–1555
27 *Cavalleria rusticana*: O Lola ch'ai di latti ('Siciliana')
Matrix X–1556

Anglo-Italian Commerce Co. *Milan*. Vertical cut, speeds vary. Announced, probably by Caruso; accompanied by an unknown pianist. Probably recorded between October 7 and December 20, 1903.
28 Tu non mi vuoi più ben
Matrix 84003 (Master cylinder)
29 *Tosca*: E lucevan le stelle
Matrix 84004 (Master cylinder)
30 *Gli Ugonotti*: Qui sotto il ciel
Matrix 84006 (Master cylinder)

Victor. *New York*, Monday, February 1, 1904. Piano.   78.26 RPM.
31 *Rigoletto*: Questa o quella
Matrix B 994
32 *Rigoletto*: La donna è mobile
Matrix B 995
33 *L'Elisir d'amore*: Una furtiva lagrima
Matrix B 996
34 *L'Elisir d'amore*: Un solo istante i palpiti
Matrix C 996–1
35 *Aïda:* Celeste Aïda
Matrix C 997
36 *Tosca*: E lucevan le stelle
Matrix B 998
37 *Tosca*: Recondita armonia
Matrix B 999
38 *Cavalleria rusticana*: O Lola ch'ai di latti ('Siciliana')
Matrix B 1000
39 *Manon*: Chiudo gli occhi ('Il sogno')
Matrix B 1001–1 *Held*
40 *I Pagliacci*: Recitar, mentre preso dal delirio; Vesti la giubba
Matrix B 1002

Victor. *New York*, Tuesday, February 9, 1904. Piano.   78.26 RPM.
41 *Manon*: Chiudo gli occhi ('Il sogno')
Matrix B 1001–2

Gramophone & Typewriter. *Milan*, Friday, April 8, 1904.   73.47 RPM.
42 Mattinata
Matrix 2181–h Accompanied by the composer, Leoncavallo, piano
43 *I Pescatori di Perle*: Mi par d'udir ancora
Matrix 268–i Accompanied by Cottone, piano

Victor. *New York*, Monday, February 27, 1905. Piano.   76.60 RPM.
44 *Don Pasquale*: Com'è gentil ('Serenata')
Matrix C2340
45 *Carmen*: Il fior che avevi a me tu dato
Matrix C2341
46 *Gli Ugonotti*: Bianca al par di neve alpina
Matrix C2342
47 *La Gioconda*: Cielo e mar
Matrix C 2343
48 *Cavalleria rusticana*: Viva il vino spumeggiante ('Brindisi')
Matrix B 2344

Victor. *New York*, Sunday, February 11, 1906. Orchestra. 76.60 RPM.
  49 *Marta*: M'apparì tutt'amor
     Matrix C 3100–1
  50 *La Bohème*: Che gelida manina
     Matrix C 3101
  51 *Faust*: Salut, demeure chaste et pure
     Matrix C 3102
  52 *Il Trovatore*: Di quella pira
     Matrix B 3103
  53 *La Favorita*: Spirto gentil, ne' sogni miei
     Matrix C 3104

Victor. *New York*, Tuesday, March 13, 1906. Orchestra. 76.60 RPM.
  54 *La Forza del destino*: Solenne in quest'ora
     Matrix C 3179 Accompanied by Scotti
     Matrix CS 74802 Rerecorded with symphony orchestra; Shilkret, conductor,
         December 3, 1932. (3 takes, unpublished)
  55 *Aïda*: Celeste Aïda
     Matrix C 3180–1

Victor. *New York*, Sunday, December 30, 1906. Orchestra. 76.60 RPM.
  56 Triste ritorno
     Matrix C 4159
  57 *L'Africana*: Mi batte il cor; O paradiso
     Matrix C 4160–1 *Held*
  58 *Andrea Chénier*: Un dì all'azzurro spazio
     Matrix C 4161 *Held*
  59 Ideale
     Matrix C 4162

Victor. *New York*, Wednesday, February 20, 1907. Orchestra. 76.60 RPM.
  60 *L'Africana*: Mi batte il cor; O paradiso
     Matrix C 4160–2
     Matrix 2EA 4012–1 Rerecorded with symphony orchestra.
  61 *Rigoletto*: Bella figlia dell'amore 80.00 RPM.
     Matrix C 4259 Accompanied by Abott, Homer, Scotti
     Matrix 2EA 272–7 Remastered fragment of C 4259.

Victor. *New York*, Sunday, March 17, 1907. Orchestra. 76.60 RPM.
  62 *La Bohème*: O Mimì, tu più non torni
     Matrix C 4315 Accompanied by Scotti
  63 *Andrea Chénier*: Un dì all'azzurro spazio
     Matrix C 4316
  64 *Pagliacci*: Recitar, mentre preso dal delirio; Vesti la giubba
     Matrix C 4317–1
     Matrix CS 58966–1A Rerecorded with symphony orchestra; Shilkret, conductor,
         August 15, 1932. (Alternate take)
     Matrix 2EA 272–7 Remastered fragment of CS 58966–1A.

Victor. *New York*, Sunday, March 24, 1907. Orchestra. 76.60 RPM.
  65 *Pagliacci*: Recitar, mentre preso dal delirio; Vesti la giubba
     Matrix C 4317–2 *Held*
  66 *La Bohème*: O soave fanciulla
     Matrix C 4326–1 Accompanied by Melba
  67 *La Bohème*: O soave fanciulla
     Matrix C 4326–2 Accompanied by Melba *Destroyed*
  68 *I Pescatori di perle*: Del tempio al limitar
     Matrix C 4327 Accompanied by Ancona

Victor. *New York*, Monday, April 1, 1907. Orchestra.
69 *La Bohème*: O soave fanciulla
Matrix C 4326–3 Accompanied by Melba *Destroyed*
70 *La Bohème*: O soave fanciulla
Matrix C 4326–4 Accompanied by Melba *Destroyed*

Victor. *New York*, Friday, January 10, 1908. Orchestra.   80.00 RPM.
71 *Don Sebastiano*: Deserto in terra
Matrix C 5008–1
72 *Don Sebastiano*: Deserto in terra
Matrix C 5008–2
73 Adorables tourments
Matrix C 5009
74 *I Pescatori di Perle*: Mi par d'udir ancora
Matrix C 5010–1 *Held*

Victor. *New York*, Monday, February 3, 1908. Orchestra.
75 *Lucia di Lammermoor*: Chi mi frena in tal momento? *Destroyed*
Matrix C 5052–1 Accompanied by Daddi, Journet, Scotti, Sembrich, Severina
76 *Lucia di Lammermoor*: Chi mi frena in tal momento? *Destroyed*
Matrix C 5052–2 Accompanied by Daddi, Journet, Scotti, Sembrich, Severina
77 *Lucia di Lammermoor*: Chi mi frena in tal momento? *Destroyed*
Matrix C 5052–3 Accompanied by Daddi, Journet, Scotti, Sembrich, Severina
78 *Rigoletto*: Bella figlia dell'amore
Matrix C 5053–1 Accompanied by Jacoby, Scotti, Sembrich *Destroyed*
79 *Rigoletto*: Bella figlia dell'amore
Matrix C 5053–2 Accompanied by Jacoby, Scotti, Sembrich *Destroyed*
Note: RCA Victor allegedly included this recording in LP album ARM4–0302,
but they probably used 82.

Victor. *New York*, Friday, February 7, 1908. Rogers, conductor.   78.26 RPM.
80 *Lucia di Lammermoor*: Chi mi frena in tal momento?
Matrix C 5052–4 Accompanied by Daddi, Journet, Scotti, Sembrich, Severina
81 *Lucia di Lammermoor*: Chi mi frena in tal momento? *Destroyed*
Matrix C 5025–5 Accompanied by Daddi, Journet, Scotti, Sembrich, Severina
82 *Rigoletto*: Bella figlia dell'amore
Matrix C 5053–3 Accompanied by Scotti, Sembrich, Severina
83 *Rigoletto*: Bella figlia dell'amore
Matrix C 5053–4 Accompanied by Scotti, Sembrich, Severina *Destroyed*

Victor. *New York*, Tuesday, March 10, 1908. Rogers, conductor.   76.60 RPM.
84 *La Bohème*: Addio, dolce svegliare alla mattina
Matrix C 6025 Accompanied by Farrar, Scotti, Viafora
85 *Madama Butterfly*: Un po' di vero c'e; O quanti occhi fisi
Matrix C 6026 Accompanied by Farrar

Victor. *Camden*, Monday, March 16, 1908. Orchestra.   76.60 RPM.
86 *I Pescatori di perle*: Mi par d'udir ancora
Matrix C 5010–2 *Destroyed*
87 *I Pescatori di perle*: Mi par d'udir ancora
Matrix C 5010–3 *Destroyed*
88 Lolita
Matrix C 6032
89 *Rigoletto*: La donna è mobile
Matrix B 6033
Matrix BS 71800–1 Re-recorded with symphony orchestra; Shilkret, conductor,
December 3, 1932. (4 takes)

90 *Il Trovatore*: Ah sì, ben mio
   Matrix C 6034
91 *Rigoletto*: Questa o quella
   Matrix B 6035

Victor. *Camden*, Tuesday, March 17, 1908. Orchestra.   75.00 RPM.
92 *Il Trovatore*: Se m'ami ancor; Ai nostri monti
   Matrix C 6036–1 Accompanied by Homer

Victor. *Camden*, Sunday, March 29, 1908. Orchestra.   76.60 RPM.
93 *Aïda*: Celeste Aïda
   Matrix C 3180–2 *Destroyed*
94 *Aïda*: Celeste Aïda
   Matrix C 3180–3
95 *La Regina di Saba*: Magiche note
   Matrix C 6062 *Destroyed*

Gramophone Company Ltd. *London*, circa August 10, 1908. Pitt, conductor.
96 Auld Lang Syne
   Matrix number unknown
97 *Rigoletto*: La donna è mobile
   Matrix 8972e
   Note: October 8 has been suggested as the date, but Caruso was in Germany at that
   time, so August seems more plausible.

Victor. *New York*, Saturday, December 19, 1908. Orchestra.
98 *Faust*: Alerte! ou vous êtes perdus!
   Matrix C 6679–1 Accompanied by Farrar, Vieulle *Destroyed*
99 *Faust*: Alerte! ou vous êtes perdus!
   Matrix C 6679–2 Accompanied by Farrar, Vieulle *Destroyed*
100 *Il Trovatore*: Perigliarti ancor languente
   Matrix C 6680 Accompanied by Homer *Destroyed*
101 *Faust*: Que voulez-vous, messieurs?
   Matrix C 6681–1 Accompanied by De Gogorza, Vieulle *Destroyed*
102 *Faust*: Que voulez-vous, messieurs?
   Matrix C 6681–2 Accompanied by De Gogorza, Vieulle *Destroyed*
103 *Il Trovatore*: Mal reggendo all'aspro assalto
   Matrix C 6682–1 Accompanied by Homer *Destroyed*

Victor. *Camden*, Saturday, November 6, 1909. Orchestra.   75.00 RPM.
104 Pour un baiser
   Matrix B 8343
105 Mamma mia, che vo' sapè
   Matrix C 8344–1 *Held*
106 Mamma mia, che vo' sapè
   Matrix C 8344–2
107 *La Forza del destino*: O tu che in seno agli angeli
   Matrix C 8345
108 *Tosca*: E lucevan le stelle
   Matrix B 8346
109 *Tosca*: Recondita armonia
   Matrix B 8347
   Matrix 2EA 1570–2A Re-recorded with symphony orchestra.
110 *Aïda*: O terra addio
   Matrix C 8348–1 Accompanied by Gadski *Held*
111 *Aïda*: O terra addio
   Matrix C 8348–2 Accompanied by Gadski

THE WORKS

Victor. *Camden*, Sunday, November 7, 1909. Orchestra.   75.00 RPM.
  112 *La Regina di Saba*: Magiche note
      Matrix B 6062
  113 *Carmen*: Il fior che avevi a me tu dato
      Matrix C 8349
      Matrix 2EA 4093–2A Re-recorded with symphony orchestra.
  114 *Carmen*: La fleur que tu m'avais jetée
      Matrix C 8350
  115 *Gli Ugonotti*: Bianca al par di neve alpina
      Matrix C 8351
  116 *Il Trovatore*: Miserere; Ah! che la morte ognora
      Matrix C 8352–1 Accompanied by Gadski *Destroyed*
  117 *Il Trovatore*: Miserere; Ah! che la morte ognora
      Matrix C 8352–2 Accompanied by Gadski *Held*
  118 *Aïda*: La fatal pietra
      Matrix C 8353 Accompanied by Gadski

Victor. *Camden*, Monday, December 27, 1909. Orchestra.   75.00 RPM.
  119 *Il Trovatore*: Ah! che la morte ognora ('Miserere')
      Matrix C 8506–1 Accompanied by Alda

Victor. *New York*, Thursday, January 6, 1910. Rogers, conductor.   76.60 RPM.
  120 *Il Trovatore*: Ah! che la morte ognora ('Miserere')
      Matrix C 8506–2 Accompanied by Alda, Met. Opera Chorus *Held*
  121 *Il Trovatore*: Ah! che la morte ognora ('Miserere')
      Matrix C 8506–3 Accompanied by Alda, Metropolitan Opera Chorus
  122 *Faust*: Il se fait tard; Laisse-moi
      Matrix C 8533 Accompanied by Farrar
  123 *Faust*: Éternelle! O nuit d'amour
      Matrix C 8534–1 Accompanied by Farrar *Destroyed*
  124 *Faust*: Éternelle! O nuit d'amour
      Matrix C 8534–2 Accompanied by Farrar

Victor. *New York*, Wednesday, January 12, 1910. Rogers, conductor.   76.60 RPM.
  125 *Faust*: Mon coeur est pénétré d'épouvante
      Matrix C 8542–1 Accompanied by Farrar *Destroyed*
  126 *Faust*: Mon coeur est pénétré d'épouvante
      Matrix C 8542–2 Accompanied by Farrar
  127 *Faust*: Attends! voici la rue
      Matrix C 8543–1 Accompanied by Farrar *Destroyed*
  128 *Faust*: Attends! voici la rue
      Matrix C 8543–2 Accompanied by Farrar
  129 *Faust*: Seigneur dieu, que vois-je!
      Matrix C 8544 Accompanied by Farrar, Gilibert, Journet
  130 *Faust*: Alerte! ou vous êtes perdus!
      Matrix C 8545–1 Accompanied by Farrar, Journet *Destroyed*
  131 *Faust*: Alerte! ou vous êtes perdus!
      Matrix C 8545–2 Accompanied by Farrar, Journet *Held*
  132 *Marta*: Solo, profugo, reietto!
      Matrix C 8546 Accompanied by Journet
  133 *Faust*: Eh! quoi! toujours seule?
      Matrix C 8547 Accompanied by Farrar, Gilibert, Journet

Victor. *New York*, Sunday, January 16, 1910. Rogers, conductor.   76.60 RPM.
  134 *Faust*: Alerte! ou vous êtes perdus!
      Matrix C 8545–3 Accompanied by Farrar, Journet *Held*
  135 *Faust*: Alerte! ou vous êtes perdus!
      Matrix C 8545–4 Accompanied by Farrar, Journet

136 *Faust*: Ô merveille!
 Matrix C 8555–1 Accompanied by Journet *Held*
137 *Faust*: Ô merveille!
 Matrix C 8555–2 Accompanied by Journet
138 *Faust*: Que voulez-vous, messieurs?
 Matrix C 8556 Accompanied by Journet, Scotti

Victor. *New York*, Monday, March 14, 1910. Orchestra.   76.60 RPM.
 139 *Germania*: Studenti! Udite
  Matrix B 8710
 140 *Madama Butterfly*: Amore o grillo
  Matrix C 8711 Accompanied by Scotti
 141 *Madama Butterfly*: Non ve l'avevo detto?
  Matrix C 8712 Accompanied by Scotti
 142 *Germania*: No, non chiuder gli occhi vaghi
  Matrix B 8713
 143 *La Gioconda*: Cielo e mar!
  Matrix C 8718

Victor. *New York*, Thursday, March 17, 1910. Orchestra.
 144 *Luisa Miller*: Quando le sere al placido
  Matrix C 8725 *Destroyed*

Victor. *Camden*, Wednesday, December 28, 1910. Orchestra.   75.00 RPM.
 145 *Pagliacci*: No, Pagliaccio non son
  Matrix C 9742–1 *Held*
 146 *Pagliacci*: No, Pagliaccio non son
  Matrix C 9742–2
 147 *Otello*: Ora e per sempre addio sante memorie
  Matrix B 9743–1 *Held*
 148 *Otello*: Ora e per sempre addio sante memorie
  Matrix B 9743–2
 149 For You Alone
  Matrix B 9744–1
  Matrix OB 5102–3 Re-recorded with symphony orchestra.
 150 For You Alone
  Matrix B 9744–2 *Held*
 151 *Cavalleria rusticana*: O Lola ch'ai di latti ('Siciliana')
  Matrix B 9745 Accompanied by Lapitino, harp

Victor. *Camden*, Thursday, December 29, 1910. Orchestra.   75.00 RPM.
 152 *Il Trovatore*: Se m'ami ancor; Ai nostri monti
  Matrix C 6036–2 Accompanied by Homer
 153 *Il Trovatore*: Mal reggendo all'aspro assalto
  Matrix C 6682–2 Accompanied by Homer
 154 Canta pe' me
  Matrix B 9746 *Held*
 155 Addio ('Good-bye')
  Matrix C 9747
  Matrix 2EA 5828–1 Re-recorded with symphony orchestra.
 156 *Aïda*: Già i sacerdoti adunansi
  Matrix C 9748 Accompanied by Homer
 157 *Aïda*: Misero appien mi festi; Aïda, a me togliesti
  Matrix C 9749 Accompanied by Homer

Victor. *Camden*, Sunday, November 19, 1911. Orchestra.   75.00 RPM.
 158 *Un Ballo in maschera*: Di' tu se fedele
  Matrix B 11270–1 Acc. by Metropolitan Opera Chorus *Held*

THE WORKS

159 *Un Ballo in maschera*: Di' tu se fedele
    Matrix B 11270–2 Accompanied by Metropolitan Opera Chorus
160 Eternamente
    Matrix C 11271
161 *La Bohème*: Musetta! O gioia della mia dimora; Testa adorata
    Matrix C 11272
162 *Lo Schiavo*: L'importuna insistenza; Quando nascesti tu
    Matrix C 11273–1 *Destroyed*
163 *Lo Schiavo*: L'importuna insistenza; Quando nascesti tu
    Matrix C 11273–2
164 Core 'ngrato
    Matrix C 11274

Victor. *Camden*, Sunday, November 26, 1911. Orchestra.   75.00 RPM.
165 *L'Elisir d'amore*: Una furtiva lagrima
    Matrix C 996–2
    Matrix CS 74801 Re-recorded with symphony orchestra; Shilkret, conductor, December 3, 1932. (2 takes, unpublished)
    Matrix 2EA–8402–1 Re-recorded with symphony orchestra.
166 *La Bohème*: Io non ho che una povera stanzetta
    Matrix C 11276
167 *Otello*: Oh! mostruosa colpa; Si, pel ciel
    Matrix C 11285 Accompanied by Amato *Destroyed*
168 *La Forza del destino*: Invano, Alvaro
    Matrix C 11286–1 Accompanied by Amato *Held*
169 *La Forza del destino*: Invano, Alvaro
    Matrix C 11286–2 Accompanied by Amato
170 *La Forza del destino*: Le minnaccie
    Matrix C 11286–1 (Mx. number used twice) Accompanied by Amato
171 Canta pe' me
    Matrix B 11306–1 *Held*
172 Canta pe' me
    Matrix B 11306–2

Victor. *Camden*, Wednesday, December 27, 1911. Orchestra.   76.60 RPM.
173 Love Is Mine
    Matrix B 11419–1 *Held*
174 Love Is Mine
    Matrix B 11419–2
175 *Un Ballo in maschera*: Forse la soglia; Ma se m'e forza
    Matrix C 11420
176 *Rigoletto*: Ella mi fu rapita; Parmi veder le lagrime
    Matrix C 11421–1 *Destroyed*
177 *Manon*: Je suis seul; Ah! fuyez, douce image
    Matrix C 11422
178 *Aïda*: Se quel guerrier io fossi; Celeste Aïda
    Matrix C 11423
    Matrix CS 74803–1 Re-recorded with symphony orchestra; Shilkret, conductor, December 3, 1932. (3 takes)

Victor. *New York*, Sunday, January 7, 1912. Rogers, conductor   76.60 RPM.
179 *Marta*: Siam giunti, o giovinette
    Matrix C 11437–1 Accompanied by Alda, Jacoby, Journet *Destroyed*
180 *Marta*: Siam giunti, o giovinette
    Matrix C 11437–2 Accompanied by Alda, Jacoby, Journet
181 *Marta*: Questo camero e per voi; Che vuol dir ciò?
    Matrix C 11438 Accompanied by Alda, Jacoby, Journet
182 *Marta*: Presto, presto andiam
    Matrix C 11439–1 Accompanied by Alda, Jacoby, Journet

183 *Marta*: Presto, presto andiam
    Matrix C 11439–2 Accompanied by Alda, Jacoby, Journet *Destroyed*
184 *Marta*: T'ho raggiunta, sciagurata! Dormi pur
    Matrix C 11440 Accompanied by Alda, Jacoby, Journet
185 *I Lombardi*: Qual voluttà trascorrere
    Matrix C 11441 Accompanied by Alda, Journet
186 Crucifix
    Matrix C 11442 Accompanied by Journet

Victor. *New York*, Wednesday, January 10, 1912. Orchestra.
187 *Lucia di Lammermoor*: Chi mi frena in tal momento? *Destroyed*
    Matrix C 11446–1 Accompanied by Amato, Bada, Jacoby, Journet, Tetrazzini
188 *Lucia di Lammermoor*: Chi mi frena in tal momento? *Destroyed*
    Matrix C 11446–2 Accompanied by Amato, Bada, Jacoby, Journet, Tetrazzini
189 *Rigoletto*: Bella figlia dell'amore
    Matrix C 11447–1 Acc. by Amato, Jacoby, Tetrazzini *Held*

Victor. *New York*, Friday, January 19, 1912. Rogers, conductor   76.60 RPM.
190 *Lucia di Lammermoor*: Chi mi frena in tal momento?
    Matrix C 11446–3 Accompanied by Amato, Bada, Jacoby, Journet, Tetrazzini
191 *Lucia di Lammermoor*: Chi mi frena in tal momento? *Held*
    Matrix C 11446–4 Accompanied by Amato, Bada, Jacoby, Journet, Tetrazzini
192 *Rigoletto*: Bella figlia dell'amore
    Matrix C 11447–2 Accompanied by Amato, Jacoby, Tetrazzini *Held*
193 Tarantella sincera
    Matrix C 11472

Victor. *New York*, Tuesday, February 13, 1912. Orchestra.   76.60 RPM.
194 *Rigoletto*: Bella figlia dell'amore
    Matrix C 11447–3 Accompanied by Amato, Jacoby, Tetrazzini *Held*
195 *Rigoletto*: Bella figlia dell'amore
    Matrix C 11447–4 Accompanied by Amato, Jacoby, Tetrazzini
196 Tarantella Napolitana 'La danza'
    Matrix C 11590

Victor. *New York*, Tuesday, February 27, 1912. Orchestra.
197 Dreams of Long Ago
    Matrix C 11616–1 *Held*
198 *La Bohème*: O soave fanciulla
    Matrix C 11617–1 Accompanied by Farrar *Destroyed*
199 *La Bohème*: O soave fanciulla
    Matrix C 11617–2 Accompanied by Farrar *Destroyed*
200 *Tosca*: Perché chiuso?
    Matrix C 11618–1 Accompanied by Farrar *Destroyed*
201 *Tosca*: Perché chiuso?
    Matrix C 11618–2 Accompanied by Farrar *Destroyed*
202 *Tosca*: Or lasciami al lavoro
    Matrix C 11619 Accompanied by Farrar *Destroyed*
203 *Tosca*: Ah, franchigia a Floria Tosca
    Matrix C 11620 Accompanied by Farrar *Destroyed*
204 *Tosca*: O dolci mani mansuerte e pure
    Matrix C 11621 Accompanied by Farrar *Destroyed*
205 *Tosca*: Amaro sol per te m'era il morine
    Matrix C 11622 Accompanied by Farrar *Destroyed*

Victor. *Camden*, Thursday, April 18, 1912. Orchestra.   76.60 RPM.
206 Dreams of Long Ago
    Matrix C 11616–2 *Destroyed*

207 Dreams of Long Ago
    Matrix C 11616–3

Victor. *Camden*, Monday, April 29, 1912. Orchestra.   76.60 RPM.
208 The Lost Chord
    Matrix C 11942–1
    Matrix 2B 3570–2A Re-recorded with organ.
209 The Lost Chord
    Matrix C 11942–2 *Held*

Victor. *New York*, Saturday, December 7, 1912. Orchestra.   76.60 RPM.
210 Parce que 'Because'
    Matrix B 12680–1 *Destroyed*
211 Parce que 'Because'
    Matrix B 12680–2
    Matrix OB 5151–1 Re-recorded with symphony orchestra.
212 Hosanna
    Matrix C 12681–1 *Destroyed*
213 Hosanna
    Matrix C 12681–2
    Matrix 2EA 4188–1 Re-recorded with symphony orchestra.

Victor. *New York*, Monday, December 30, 1912. Orchestra.   76.60 RPM.
214 *Manon*: On l'appelle Manon
    Matrix C 12750–1 Accompanied by Farrar *Destroyed*
215 *Manon*: On l'appelle Manon
    Matrix C 12750–2 Accompanied by Farrar
216 *La Bohème*: O soave fanciulla
    Matrix C 12751–1 Accompanied by Farrar
217 *La Bohème*: O soave fanciulla
    Matrix C 12751–2 Accompanied by Farrar *Destroyed*

Victor. *New York*, Friday, January 17, 1913. Orchestra.   76.60 RPM.
218 *Don Carlo*: Domanda al ciel; Dio, che nell'alma infondere
    Matrix C 12752 Accompanied by Scotti
219 *Il Trovatore*: Se m'ami ancor; Ai nostri monti
    Matrix C 12804–1 Accompanied by Schumann-Heink? *Destroyed*
220 *Il Trovatore*: Se m'ami ancor; Ai nostri monti
    Matrix C 12804–2 Accompanied by Schumann-Heink?
221 Pimpinella ('Florentine Air')
    Matrix B 12805–1 Accompanied by Scognamiglio, piano *Held*
222 Pimpinella ('Florentine Air')
    Matrix B 12805–2 Accompanied by Scognamiglio, piano

Victor. *New York*, Monday, February 24, 1913. Orchestra.   76.60 RPM.
223 *Rigoletto*: Ella mi fu rapita; Parmi veder le lagrime
    Matrix C 11421–2
    Matrix 2EA 8403–1 Re-recorded with symphony orchestra.
224 Agnus Dei
    Matrix C 12942 Accompanied by Scognamiglio, piano
    Matrix 2EA 1571–2A Re-recorded with symphony orchestra.
225 *Manon Lescaut*: Donna non vidi mai
    Matrix B 12945 Accompanied by Madame A. Regis Rossini, harp

Victor. *New York*, Thursday, March 20, 1913   76.60 RPM.
226 Ave Maria
    Matrix C 13004–1 Accompanied by Elman, violin; Kahn, piano
227 Ave Maria
    Matrix C 13004–2 Accompanied by Elman, violin; Kahn, piano *Destroyed*

228 Ave Maria
   Matrix C 13004–3 Accompanied by Elman, violin; Kahn, piano *Destroyed*
229 Elégie
   Matrix C 13005–1 Accompanied by Elman, violin; Kahn, piano
230 Elégie
   Matrix C 13005–2 Accompanied by Elman, violin; Kahn, piano *Destroyed*
231 Elégie
   Matrix C 13005–3 Accompanied by Elman, violin; Kahn, piano *Destroyed*

Victor. *New York*, Thursday, April 10, 1913. Orchestra.   76.60 RPM.
   232 Lasciati amar
      Matrix B 13104–1 *Destroyed*
   233 Lasciati amar
      Matrix B 13104–2
   234 Guardann' 'a luna
      Matrix B 13105–1 Accompanied by Lapitino, harp *Destroyed*
   235 Guardann' 'a luna
      Matrix B 13105–2 Accompanied by Lapitino, harp
   236 Your Eyes Have Told Me What I Did Not Know
      Matrix B 13106–1 *Destroyed*
   237 Your Eyes Have Told Me What I Did Not Know
      Matrix B 13106–2
      Matrix OEA 6753–2 Re-recorded with symphony orchestra.
   238 Fenesta che lucive
      Matrix C 13107–1 *Destroyed*
   239 Fenesta che lucive
      Matrix C 13107–2

Victor. *New York*, Monday, December 15, 1913. Orchestra.   76.60 RPM.
   240 *Stabat Mater*: Cujus animam
      Matrix C 14200–1
   241 *Stabat Mater*: Cujus animam
      Matrix C 14200–2 *Destroyed*
   242 Les rameaux
      Matrix C 14201–1 *Held*
   243 Les rameaux
      Matrix C 14201–2
      Matrix 2EA 4187–1 Re-recorded with symphony orchestra.
   244 *Cavalleria rusticana*: Addio alla madre
      Matrix C 14202–1 *Destroyed*
   245 *Cavalleria rusticana*: Addio alla madre
      Matrix C 14202–2
      Matrix 2EA 4125–1 Rerecorded with symphony orchestra.
   246 Trusting Eyes
      Matrix B 14203–1 *Destroyed*

Victor. *New York*, Thursday, January 8, 1914. Orchestra.   76.60 RPM.
   247 *Otello*: Oh! mostruosa colpa; Si, pel ciel
      Matrix C 14272–1 Accompanied by Ruffo
   248 *Otello*: Oh! mostruosa colpa; Si, pel ciel
      Matrix C 14272–2 Accompanied by Ruffo *Destroyed*
   249 *La Gioconda*: Enzo Grimaldo
      Matrix C 14723 Accompanied by Ruffo *Destroyed*

Victor. *New York*, Wednesday, January 21, 1914. Orchestra.   76.60 RPM.
   250 Trusting Eyes
      Matrix C 14203 *Destroyed* (There is no take 2)
   251 Trusting Eyes
      Matrix B 14203–3 *Destroyed*

252 Sérénade de Don Juan
 Matrix B 14355
253 Amor mio
 Matrix B 14356
254 Hantise d'amour
 Matrix C 14357–1 *Destroyed*
255 Manella mia
 Matrix C 14358
256 Sérénade Espagnole
 Matrix B 14359–1 *Destroyed*

Victor. *New York*, Monday, March 9, 1914. Scognamiglio, conductor   76.60 RPM.
257 Les Rameaux
 Matrix C 14203–3
258 Trusting Eyes
 Matrix B 14203–4
 Matrix OEA 5832–1 Re-recorded with symphony orchestra.
259 Hantise d'amour
 Matrix C 14357–2 *Destroyed*
260 Hantise d'amour
 Matrix B 14357–1 *Destroyed*
261 Sérénade Espagnole
 Matrix B 14359–2 *Destroyed*
262 Sérénade Espagnole
 Matrix B 14359–3
263 Parted
 Matrix B 14550
 Matrix 2EA 5829–1 Re-recorded with symphony orchestra.

Victor. *New York*, Friday, April 3, 1914. Scognamiglio, conductor   76.60 RPM.
264 *Un Ballo in maschera*: La rivedrà nell'estasi
 Matrix C 14659–1 Accompanied by De Segurola, Hempel, Rothier, Metropolitan
 Opera Chorus; Setti, director *Held*
265 *Un Ballo in maschera*: La rivedrà nell'estasi
 Matrix C 14659–2 Accompanied by De Segurola, Hempel, Rothier, Metropolitan
 Opera Chorus; Setti, director
266 *Un Ballo in maschera*: E scherzo od è follia
 Matrix C 14660–1 Accompanied by De Segurola, Duchene, Hempel, Rothier,
 Metropolitan Opera Chorus; Setti, director
267 *Un Ballo in maschera*: E scherzo od è follia
 Matrix C 14660–2 Accompanied by De Segurola, Duchene, Hempel, Rothier, Met.
 Opera Chorus; Setti, director *Destroyed*
268 La partida
 Matrix C 14661–1 Accompanied by Scognamiglio, piano *Destroyed*
269 La partida
 Matrix C 14661–2 Accompanied by Scognamiglio, piano
270 *El Milagro de la Virgen*: Flores purisimas
 Matrix B 14662 Accompanied by Scognamiglio, piano *Destroyed*
271 *El Milagro de la Virgen*: Flores purisimas
 Matrix C 14662 Accompanied by Scognamiglio, piano
272 Tu-Habanera
 Matrix B 14663–1 Accompanied by Scognamiglio, piano *Destroyed*
273 Tu-Habanera
 Matrix B 14663–2 Acompanied by Scognamiglio, piano *Destroyed*
274 Ave Maria
 Matrix C 14664 Accompanied by Kreisler, violin; Scognamiglio, piano *Destroyed*

A CARUSO DISCOGRAPHY

Victor. *New York*, Monday, April 20, 1914. Setti, conductor   76.60 RPM.
   275 *La Traviata*: Libiamo, libiamo ne' liete calici 'Brindisi'
        Matrix B 14729–1 Accompanied by Gluck, Met. Opera Chorus *Destroyed*
   276 *La Traviata*: Libiamo, libiamo ne' liete calici 'Brindisi'
        Matrix B 14729–2 Accompanied by Gluck, Metropolitan Opera Chorus
   277 *La Traviata*: Libiamo, libiamo ne' liete calici 'Brindisi'
        Matrix B 14729–3 Accompanied by Gluck, Met. Opera Chorus *Destroyed*
   278 *Il Guarany*: Sento una forza indomita
        Matrix C 14730–1 Accompanied by Destinn
   279 *Il Guarany*: Sento una forza indomita
        Matrix C 14730–2 Accompanied by Destinn *Held*
   280 *Lucrezia Borgia*: Della duchesa ai prieghi
        Matrix C 14731 Accompanied by Destinn, Scotti *Destroyed*

Victor. *New York*, Thursday, December 10, 1914. Rogers, conductor   75.00 RPM.
   281 Hantise d'amour
        Matrix B 14357–2
   282 Hantise d'amour
        Matrix B 14357–3 *Destroyed*
   283 Musica proibita
        Matrix C 15480–1 *Destroyed*
   284 Musica proibita
        Matrix C 15480–2 *Held*
   285 La mia canzone
        Matrix B 15481–1 *Destroyed*
   286 La mia canzone
        Matrix B 15481–2 *Destroyed*
   287 *Carmen*: Parle-moi de ma mère
        Matrix C 15483–1 Accompanied by Alda *Destroyed*
   288 *Carmen*: Parle-moi de ma mère
        Matrix C 15483–2 Accompanied by Alda *Destroyed*
   289 *Carmen*: Parle-moi de ma mère
        Matrix C 15483–3 Accompanied by Alda

Victor. *New York*, Thursday, January 7, 1915. Rogers, conductor   75.00 RPM.
   290 Musica proibita
        Matrix B 15480–3 *Destroyed*
   291 Musica proibita
        Matrix B 15480–4 *Destroyed*
   292 La mia canzone
        Matrix B 15481–3
        Matrix OB 5990–2 Rerecorded with symphony orchestra.
   293 Pecchè?
        Matrix C 15568 Accompanied by Bianculli, mandolin
   294 Cielo turchino
        Matrix B 15569
   295 *Messa da Requiem*: Ingemisco
        Matrix C 15570–1 *Destroyed*
   296 *Messa da Requiem*: Ingemisco
        Matrix C 15570–2 *Held*
   297 *Messa da Requiem*: Ingemisco
        Matrix C 15570–3
   298 'A luna
        Matrix B 15571–1 Accompanied by Bianculli, mandolin *Destroyed*
   299 'A luna
        Matrix C 15571–2 (no mandolin) *Held*
   300 *Il Duca d'Alba*: Angelo casto e bel
        Matrix C 15572–1 *Destroyed*

301 *Il Duca d'Alba*: Angelo casto e bel
    Matrix C 15572–2

Victor. *New York*, Saturday, February 6, 1915   75.00 RPM.
  302 Si vous l'aviez compris
    Matrix C 15682–1 Accompanied by Elman, violin; Scognamiglio, piano *Destroyed*
  303 Si vous l'aviez compris
    Matrix C 15682–2 Accompanied by Elman, violin; Scognamiglio, piano *Destroyed*
  304 Si vous l'aviez compris
    Matrix C 15682–3 Accompanied by Elman, violin; Scognamiglio, piano
  305 Les deux sérénades 'Sérénade Française'
    Matrix C 15683–1 Accompanied by Elman, violin; Scognamiglio, piano *Destroyed*
  306 Les deux sérénades 'Sérénade Francaise'
    Matrix C 15683–2 Accompanied by Elman, violin; Scognamiglio, piano

Victor. *Camden*, Saturday, February 5, 1916. Rogers, conductor   75.00 RPM.
  307 La procession
    Matrix C 17121–1 *Destroyed*
  308 La procession
    Matrix C 17121–2 *Held*
  309 La procession
    Matrix C 17121–3
    Matrix 2EA 4186–1 Re-recorded with symphony orchestra.
  310 *Le Cid*: Ah, tout est bien fini; Ô Souverain, ô Juge, o Père
    Matrix C 17122–1 *Held*
  311 *Le Cid*: Ah, tout est bien fini; Ô Souverain, ô Juge, o Père
    Matrix C 17122–2
  312 Luna d'estate
    Matrix B 17123–1 *Destroyed*
  313 Luna d'estate
    Matrix B 17123–2 *Destroyed*
  314 Luna d'estate
    Matrix B 17123–3
    Matrix BVE 17123 Re-recorded with symphony orchestra; Shilkret, conductor,
      April 26, 1928. (8 takes, unpublished)
  315 O sole mio
    Matrix B 17124
    Matrix BS 58967–1A Re-recorded with symphony orchestra; Shilkret, conductor,
      August 15, 1932. (Alternate take)
  316 *La Reine de Saba*: Faiblesse de la race humaine; Inspirez-moi
    Matrix C 17125–1 *Destroyed*
  317 *La Reine de Saba*: Faiblesse de la race humaine; Inspirez-moi
    Matrix C 17125–2
    Matrix 2EA 4126–1 Re-recorded with symphony orchestra.

Victor. *Camden*, Wednesday, February 23, 1916. Rogers, conductor.   75.00 RPM.
  318 Mia sposa sarà la mia bandiera
    Matrix C 17195–1 *Destroyed*
  319 Mia sposa sarà la mia bandiera
    Matrix C 17195–2
  320 The rosary
    Matrix B 17196–1 *Destroyed*
  321 The rosary
    Matrix B 17196–2 *Destroyed*
  322 The rosary
    Matrix B 17196–3 *Destroyed*
  323 The rosary
    Matrix B 17196–4 *Destroyed*

324 *Macbeth*: Ah, la paterna mano
    Matrix C 17197
325 *La Bohème*: Vecchia zimarra
    Matrix B 17198 *Destroyed, copies exist*
    Matrix D9 QB 7758–1A Remastered.
    Matrix D9 QB 7758–1A–R Remastered.
326 Cantique de Noël
    Matrix C 17218–1 *Destroyed*
327 Cantique de Noël
    Matrix C 17128–2 *Destroyed*
328 Cantique de Noël
    Matrix C 17128–3

Victor. *New York*, Monday, March 20, 1916. Rogers, conductor.   76.60 RPM.
329 The rosary
    Matrix B 17196–5 *Destroyed*
330 The rosary
    Matrix B 17196–6 *Destroyed*
331 *La Gioconda*: O sommo Dio
    Matrix C 17341–1 *Destroyed*
332 *La Gioconda*: O sommo Dio
    Matrix C 17341–2 *Destroyed*
333 Sancta Maria
    Matrix C 17342–1 Accompanied by Bourdon, cello *Held*
334 Sancta Maria
    Matrix C 17342–2 Accompanied by Bourdon, cello
335 Tiempo antico
    Matrix C 17343–1 *Held*
336 Tiempo antico
    Matrix C 17343–2
337 Santa Lucia
    Matrix C 17344 Accompanied by Bianculli, mandolin
    Matrix 2EA 652–2 Rerecorded with symphony orchestra.

Victor. *New York*, Friday, November 3, 1916. Pasternack, conductor.   78.26 RPM.
338 Pourquoi?
    Matrix B 18656–1 *Destroyed*
339 Pourquoi?
    Matrix B 18656–2 *Destroyed*
340 Pourquoi?
    Matrix B 18656–3
341 *Eugène Onéguine*: Pour moi ce jour est tout mystère
    Matrix C 18657–1
342 *Eugenio Oneghin*: Aria di Lenski (In Italian)
    Matrix C 18657–2 *Held*
343 Chanson de Juin
    Matrix C 18658
344 *Andrea Chénier*: Come un bel dì di maggio
    Matrix B 18659

Victor. *Camden*, Thursday, December 7, 1916. Pasternack, conductor.   76.60 RPM.
345 *Samson et Dalila*: Vois ma misère, hélas
    Matrix C 18821–1 Accompanied by Metropolitan Opera Chorus
346 *Samson et Dalila*: Vois ma misère, hélas
    Matrix C 18821–2 Accompanied by Metropolitan Opera Chorus *Destroyed*
347 *Les Pêcheurs de perles*: Je crois entendre encore
    Matrix C 18822–1 *Destroyed*
348 *Les Pêcheurs de perles*: Je crois entendre encore
    Matrix C 18822–2 *Destroyed*

349 *Les Pêcheurs de perles*: Je crois entendre encore
   Matrix C 18822–3
   Matrix CS 74804–1 Re-recorded with symphony orchestra; Shilkret, conductor, December 3, 1932. (3 takes)
350 *Les Pêcheurs de perles*: De mon amie, fleur endormie
   Matrix B 18823–1 Accompanied by Adams, oboe; Lapitino, harp *Held*
351 *Les Pêcheurs de perles*: De mon amie, fleur endormie
   Matrix B 18823–2 Accompanied by Adams, oboe; Lapitino, harp

Victor. Camden, Thursday, January 25, 1917. Pasternack, conductor.   75.00 RPM.
352 *Rigoletto*: Bella figlia dell'amore (Fragment)
   Matrix number unknown
      Note: Only the tenor's opening phrases are sung.
353 *Rigoletto*: Bella figlia dell'amore
   Matrix C 19132–1 Accompanied by De Luca, Galli-Curci, Perini *Held*
354 *Rigoletto*: Bella figlia dell'amore
   Matrix C 19132–2 Accompanied by De Luca, Galli-Curci, Perini
355 *Rigoletto*: Bella figlia dell'amore
   Matrix C 19132–3 Accompanied by De Luca, Galli-Curci, Perini *Destroyed*

Victor. Camden, Thursday, January 25, 1917. Pasternack, conductor.   75.00 RPM.
356 *Lucia di Lammermoor*: Chi mi frena in tal momento?
   Matrix C 19133–1 Accompanied by Bada, De Luca, Egener, Galli-Curci, Perini *Held*
      Note: RCA Victor allegedly included this recording in LP album ARM4-0302; they may have used take 2.
357 *Lucia di Lammermoor*: Chi mi frena in tal momento?
   Matrix C 19133–2 Acompanied by Bada, De Luca, Egener, Galli-Curci, Perini
358 *Lucia di Lammermoor*: Chi mi frena in tal momento?
   Matrix C 19133–3 Acc. by Bada, De Luca, Egener, Galli-Curci, Perini *Destroyed*

Victor. New York, Sunday, April 15, 1917. Pasternack, conductor.   75.00 RPM.
359 *Marta*: M'apparì tutt' amor
   Matrix C 3100–2
   Matrix CS 58965–1A Re-recorded with symphony orchestra; Shilkret, conductor, August 15, 1932. (3 takes)
360 *Marta*: M'apparì tutt' amor
   Matrix C 3100–3 *Held*
361 Musica proibita
   Matrix C 15480–5
   Matrix OEA 6752–2 Re-recorded with symphony orchestra.
362 Uocchie celeste
   Matrix C 19483–1 Accompanied by Lapitino, harp *Held*
363 Uocchie celeste
   Matrix C 19483–2 Accompanied by Lapitino, harp
364 L'alba separa dalla luce l'ombra
   Matrix B 19484–1 *Held*
      Note: A copy of this recording exists, and RCA Victor allegedly included it in LP album ARM4-0302; but they may have used 365.
365 L'alba separa dalla luce l'ombra
   Matrix B 19484–2
366 *Néron*: Oh! lumière du jour
   Matrix C 19485–1 Accompanied by Lapitino, harp *Held*
      Note: A copy of this recording exists, and RCA Victor allegedly included it in LP album ARM4-0302; but they may have used 367.
367 *Néron*: Oh! lumière du jour
   Matrix C 19485–2 Accompanied by Lapitino, harp

Victor. Camden, Tuesday, April 16, 1918. Pasternack, conductor.   76.60 RPM.
368 A la luz de la luna
   Matrix C 21773–1 Accompanied by De Gogorza *Destroyed*

369 A la luz de la luna
    Matrix C 21773–2 Accompanied by De Gogorza
370 Sei morta ne la vita mia
    Matrix B 21774–1 Accompanied by Bellezza, piano *Destroyed*
371 Sei morta ne la vita mia
    Matrix B 21774–2 Accompanied by Bellezza, piano

Victor. *Camden*, Wednesday, July 10, 1918. Pasternack, conductor.   75.00 RPM.
372 Pietà, Signore
    Matrix C 22121–1 *Destroyed*
373 Pietà, Signore
    Matrix C 22121–2 *Destroyed*
374 Pietà, Signore
    Matrix C 22121–3 *Destroyed*
375 Pietà, Signore
    Matrix C 22121–4 *Held*
376 La partida
    Matrix C 22122–1
        Matrix BS 76052 Re-recorded with symphony orchestra; Cibelli, director,
        April 24, 1933. (3 takes, unpublished)
        Matrix CS 76053 Re-recorded with symphony orchestra; Cibelli, director, April 24,
        1933. (3 takes, unpublished)
377 La partida
    Matrix C 22122–2 *Destroyed*
378 La partida
    Matrix C 22122–3 *Destroyed*
379 *La Forza del destino*: Ne gustare m'e dato; Sleale, il segreto
    Matrix C 22123–1 Accompanied by De Luca *Destroyed*
380 *La Forza del destino*: Ne gustare m'e dato; Sleale, il segreto
    Matrix C 22123–2 Accompanied by De Luca
381 A Granada
    Matrix C 22124–1 *Held*
382 Over there/Par là-bas
    Matrix B 22125–1 *Held*

Victor. *Camden*, Thursday, July 11, 1918. Pasternack, conductor.   75.00 RPM.
383 Over there/Par là-bas
    Matrix B 22125–2 *Destroyed*
384 Over there/Par là-bas
    Matrix B 22125–3 *Held*
385 Over there/Par là-bas
    Matrix B 22125–4
386 Dopo
    Matrix C 22126–1 *Destroyed*
387 Dopo
    Matrix C 22126–2 *Held*
388 Dopo
    Matrix C 22126–3 *Destroyed*
389 Maria, Mari'
    Matrix C 22127–1 Accompanied by Bianculli, mandolin *Destroyed*
390 Maria, Mari'
    Matrix C 22127–2 Accompanied by Bianculli, mandolin *Destroyed*
391 Maria, Mari'
    Matrix C 22127–3 Accompanied by Bianculli, mandolin *Destroyed*

Victor. *Camden*, Thursday, September 26, 1918. Pasternack, conductor.   75.00 RPM.
392 Pietà, Signore
    Matrix C 22121–5 *Destroyed*

393 Pietà, Signore
    Matrix C 22121–6
394 Pietà, Signore
    Matrix C 22121–7 *Destroyed*
395 A Granada
    Matrix C 22124–2 *Held*
396 A Granada
    Matrix C 22124–3
    Matrix BS 76050–1 Re-recorded with symphony orchestra; Cibelli, director, April 24, 1933. (3 takes)
    Matrix CS 76051 Re-recorded with symphony orchestra; Cibelli, director, April 24, 1933. (1 take, unpublished)
397 Campane a sera
    Matrix C 22259–1 *Held*
398 Campane a sera
    Matrix C 22259–2 *Destroyed*
399 Campane a sera
    Matrix C 22259–3
400 Inno di Garibaldi ('Garibaldi's Hymn')
    Matrix B 22260–1 *Destroyed*
401 Inno di Garibaldi ('Garibaldi's Hymn')
    Matrix B 22260–2
402 Inno di Garibaldi ('Garibaldi's Hymn')
    Matrix B 22260–3 *Destroyed*

Victor. *Camden*, Monday, January 6, 1919. Pasternack, conductor.   75.00 RPM.
403 La campana di San Giusto
    Matrix C 22514–1
404 La campana di San Giusto
    Matrix C 22514–2 *Destroyed*
405 Sultanto a te
    Matrix B 22515–1 *Held*
406 Sultanto a te
    Matrix B 22515–2 *Destroyed*
407 Sultanto a te
    Matrix B 22515–3 *Destroyed*
408 Sultanto a te
    Matrix B 22515–4 *Destroyed*
409 Le Régiment de Sambre et Meuse
    Matrix C 22516–1 *Destroyed*
410 Le Régiment de Sambre et Meuse
    Matrix C 22516–2 *Destroyed*
411 Le Régiment de Sambre et Meuse
    Matrix C 22516–3
412 A Rose, a Kiss, and You
    Matrix B 22517–1 *Destroyed*
413 A Rose, a Kiss, and You
    Matrix B 22517–2 *Held*

Victor. *Camden*, Monday, January 6, 1919. Pasternack, conductor.   75.00 RPM.
414 Povero Pulcinella
    Matrix B 22518–1 *Destroyed*
415 Povero Pulcinella
    Matrix B 22518–2 *Destroyed*
416 Povero Pulcinella
    Matrix B 22518–3 *Held*

A CARUSO DISCOGRAPHY

Victor. *Camden*, Monday, February 10, 1919. Pasternack, conductor.   76.60 RPM.
417 Sultanto a te
   Matrix B 22515–5
   Matrix OB 6071–2 Re-recorded with symphony orchestra.
418 A Rose, a Kiss, and You
   Matrix B 22517–3 *Destroyed*
419 A Rose, a Kiss, and You
   Matrix B 22517–4 *Destroyed*
420 *Samson et Dalila*: Je viens célébrer la victoire
   Matrix C 22575–1 Accompanied by Homer, Journet *Destroyed*
421 *Samson et Dalila*: Je viens célébrer la victoire
   Matrix C 22575–2 Accompanied by Homer, Journet
422 *Samson et Dalila*: Je viens célébrer la victoire
   Matrix C 22575–3 Accompanied by Homer, Journet *Held*
423 *L'Elisir d'Amore*: Venti scudi
   Matrix C 22576–1 Accompanied by De Luca *Held*
424 *L'Elisir d'Amore*: Venti scudi
   Matrix C 22576–2 Accompanied by De Luca

Victor. *Camden*, Monday, September 8, 1919. Pasternack, conductor.   75.00 RPM.
425 'A vucchella
   Matrix B 23138–1 *Destroyed*
426 'A vucchella
   Matrix B 23138–2 *Destroyed*
427 'A vucchella
   Matrix B 23138–3
   Matrix BVE 23138 Re-recorded with symphony orchestra; Shilkret, conductor,
       April 26, 1928. (7 takes, unpublished)
428 'A vucchella
   Matrix B 23138–4 *Held*
429 Vieni sul mar
   Matrix B 23139–1 *Held*
430 Vieni sul mar
   Matrix B 23139–2
431 L'Addio a Napoli
   Matrix B 23140–1 *Destroyed*
432 L'Addio a Napoli
   Matrix B 23140–2 *Destroyed*
433 L'Addio a Napoli
   Matrix B 23140–3 *Held*
434 Tu, ca nun chiagne
   Matrix B 23141

Victor. *Camden*, Tuesday, September 9, 1919. Pasternack, conductor.   75.00 RPM.
435 L'Addio a Napoli
   Matrix B 23140–4 *Destroyed*
436 L'Addio a Napoli
   Matrix B 23140–5 *Destroyed*
437 L'Addio a Napoli
   Matrix B 23140–6
   Matrix OEA 6751–1 Re-recorded with symphony orchestra.
438 *I Lombardi*: La mia letizia infondere
   Matrix C 23142–1 *Destroyed*
439 *I Lombardi*: La mia letizia infondere
   Matrix C 23142–2 *Destroyed*
440 Tre giorni son che nina
   Matrix B 23143–1 *Destroyed*

441 Tre giorni son che nina
   Matrix B 23143–2 *Destroyed*
442 Tre giorni son che nina
   Matrix B 23143–3 *Destroyed*
443 Tre giorni son che nina
   Matrix B 23143–4
444 Première caresse
   Matrix B 23144–1 *Destroyed*
445 Première caresse
   Matrix B 23144–2 *Destroyed*
446 Première caresse
   Matrix B 23144–3 *Destroyed*
447 Première caresse
   Matrix B 23144–4

Victor. *Camden*, Thursday, September 11, 1919. Pasternack, conductor. 75.00 RPM.
448 Senza nisciuno
   Matrix B 23149–1 *Destroyed*
449 Senza nisciuno
   Matrix B 23149–2 *Destroyed*
450 Senza nisciuno
   Matrix B 23149–3 *Held*
451 Senza nisciuno
   Matrix B 23149–4
452 *Salvator Rosa*: Mia piccirella
   Matrix B 23150–1 *Destroyed*
453 *Salvator Rosa*: Mia piccirella
   Matrix C 23150–1
454 Serenata
   Matrix B 23151–1 *Destroyed*
455 Serenata
   Matrix C 23151–1
456 Serenata
   Matrix C 23151–2 *Destroyed*
457 Scordame
   Matrix B 23152

Victor. *Camden*, Thursday, January 29, 1920. Pasternack, conductor. 75.00 RPM.
458 Love me or not
   Matrix C 23713–1 *Destroyed*
459 Love me or not
   Matrix C 23713–2 *Destroyed*
460 Love me or not
   Matrix C 23713–3 *Destroyed*
461 Love me or not
   Matrix C 23713–4
462 *Serse*: Ombra mai fu ('Largo')
   Matrix C 23714–1 Accompanied by Lapitino, harp *Destroyed*
463 *Serse*: Ombra mai fu ('Largo')
   Matrix C 23714–2 Accompanied by Lapitino, harp *Destroyed*
464 *Serse*: Ombra mai fu ('Largo')
   Matrix C 23714–3 Accompanied by Lapitino, harp *Destroyed*
465 *Serse*: Ombra mai fu ('Largo')
   Matrix C 23714–4 Accompanied by Lapitino, harp *Destroyed*
466 *Serse*: Ombra mai fu ('Largo')
   Matrix C 23714–5 Accompanied by Lapitino, harp
   Matrix 2B 3571–1 Re-recorded with organ.

Victor.   *Camden*, Tuesday, September 14, 1920. Pasternack, conductor.   75.00 RPM.
  467 Noche felíz
      Matrix B 24460–1 *Destroyed*
  468 Noche felíz
      Matrix B 24460–2 *Held*
  469 Noche felíz
      Matrix B 24460–3 *Destroyed*
  470 Noche felíz
      Matrix B 24460–4
  471 *La Juive*: Rachel, quand du seigneur
      Matrix C 24461–1 *Destroyed*
  472 *La Juive*: Rachel, quand du seigneur
      Matrix C 24461–2
  473 I'm'arricordo 'e Napule
      Matrix C 24462–1 *Destroyed*
  474 I'm'arricordo 'e Napule
      Matrix C 24462–2

Victor.   *Camden*, Wednesday, September 15, 1920. Pasternack, conductor.   75.00 RPM.
  475 Noche felíz
      Matrix B 24460–5 *Destroyed*
  476 Noche felíz
      Matrix B 24460–6 *Destroyed*
  477 Vaghissima sembianza
      Matrix B 24463–1 *Destroyed*
  478 Vaghissima sembianza
      Matrix B 24463–2 *Destroyed*
  479 Vaghissima sembianza
      Matrix B 24463–3 *Destroyed*
  480 Vaghissima sembianza
      Matrix B 24463–4
      Matrix OB 6070–2 Re-recorded with symphony orchestra.
  481 *L'Africana*: Deh, ch'io ritorni alla mia nave
      Matrix C 24464–1 *Destroyed*
  482 *L'Africana*: Deh, ch'io ritorni alla mia nave
      Matrix C 24464–2 *Destroyed*
  483 *L'Africana*: Deh, ch'io ritorni alla mia nave
      Matrix C 24464–3 *Destroyed*
  484 *Amadis de Gaule*: Bois épais, redouble ton ombre
      Matrix B 24465–1 *Destroyed*
  485 *Amadis de Gaule*: Bois épais, redouble ton ombre
      Matrix B 24465–2 *Destroyed*
  486 *Amadis de Gaule*: Bois épais, redouble ton ombre
      Matrix B 24465–3 *Destroyed*
  487 *Amadis de Gaule*: Bois épais, redouble ton ombre
      Matrix B 24465–4 *Destroyed*
  488 A Dream
      Matrix B 24466–1 *Destroyed*

Victor.   *Camden*, Thursday, September 16, 1920. Pasternack, conductor.   75.00 RPM.
  489 *L'Africana*: Deh, ch'io ritorni alla mia nave
      Matrix B 24464–4 *Held*
  490 *L'Africana*: Deh, ch'io ritorni alla mia nave
      Matrix B 24464–5
  491 *Amadis de Gaule*: Bois épais, redouble ton ombre
      Matrix B 24465–5 *Destroyed*
  492 *Amadis de Gaule*: Bois épais, redouble ton ombre
      Matrix B 24465–6

493 A Dream
    Matrix B 24466–2 *Held*
494 A Dream
    Matrix B 24466–3
    Matrix BS 71799–1 Re-recorded with symphony orchestra; Shilkret, conductor,
    December 3, 1932. (3 takes)
495 *Petite Messe Solennelle*: Domine Deus
    Matrix C 24473–1 *Held*
496 *Petite Messe Solennelle*: Domine Deus
    Matrix C 24473–2
497 *Petite Messe Solennelle*: Crucifixus
    Matrix B 24474–1
498 *Petite Messe Solennelle*: Crucifixus
    Matrix B 24474–2 *Destroyed*

Restorations of Caruso Records on Long-Playing Records

The Complete Caruso: RCA Victor Records:
Volumes 1 through 3 will not be published until early 1988. They will contain the recordings
from 1902–1905, as well as some items not released in the previously published albums,
including:

1,	2,	3,	4,	5,	6,	7,	8,	9,	10,
11,	12,	13,	14,	15,	16,	17,	18,	19,	20,
21,	22,	23,	24,	25,	26,	27,	28,	29,	30,
31,	32,	33,	34,	35,	36,	37,	38,	40,	41,
42,	43,	44,	45,	46,	47,	48,	359,	364,	366.

Volume 4: '1906–1907' Notes by Francis Robinson   ARM1–2766
| Side A: | 52, | 49, | 50, | 51, | 53, | 55, | 54, | 56 | |
| Side B: | 59, | 60, | 61, | 63, | 64, | 62, | 68, | 66 | |

Volume 5: '1908–1909' Notes by Harvey Philips   ARM1–2767
| Side A: | 71, | 72, | 73, | 82, | 80, | 85, | 84 | | |
| Side B: | 89, | 91, | 88, | 90, | 92, | 94, | 104, | 109 | 108 |

Volume 6: '1909–1910' Notes by Martin L. Sokol   ARM1–3373
| Side A: | 106, | 107, | 117, | 111, | 112, | 114, | 113 | |
| Side B: | 115, | 119, | 121, | 129, | 133, | 122, | 124 | |

Volume 7: '1910' Notes by George Jellinek   ARM1–3374
| Side A: | 126, | 128, | 132, | 135, | 137, | 138, | 139, | |
| Side B: | 140, | 141, | 142, | 143, | 146, | 148, | 149, | 151 |

Volume 8: '1910–1911' Notes by John R. Bolig   ARM1–3570
| Side A: | 155, | 153, | 152, | 156, | 157, | 159, | 161 | |
| Side B: | 160, | 164, | 163, | 172, | 166, | 165 | | |

Volume 9: '1911–1912' Notes by Irving Kolodin   ARM1–3571
| Side A: | 169, | 170, | 174, | 178, | 175, | 177 | | |
| Side B: | 186, | 180, | 181, | 182, | 184, | 185, | 193 | |

Volume 10: '1912–1913' Notes by Gerald Fitzgerald   ARM1–4046
| Side A: | 190, | 196, | 195, | 207, | 208, | 211, | 213 | |
| Side B: | 215, | 216, | 218, | 220, | 222, | 223 | | |

Volume 11: '1913–1914' Notes by Tom Villella   ARM1–4047
| Side A: | 224, | 225, | 226, | 229, | 233, | 235, | 237 | |
| Side B: | 239, | 240, | 243, | 245, | 247, | 252 | | |

Volume 12: '1914–1915' Notes by Michael Scott   ARM1–4684
| Side A: | 253, | 255, | 257, | 258, | 262, | 263, | 265, | 266 |
| Side B: | 269, | 271, | 276, | 277, | 281, | 289, | 292, | 294 |

Volume 13: '1915–1916' Notes by Aida Favia-Artsay   ARM1–4686
 Side A: 293, 297, 301, 304, 306, 309, 311, 314
 Side B: 315, 317, 319, 324, 325, 328, 334, 336

Volume 14: '1916–1918' Notes by Aida Favia-Artsay   ARM1–4914
 Side A: 337, 340, 341, 343, 344, 345, 349, 351
 Side B: 354, 357, 49, 361, 363, 365, 367, 369

Volume 15: '1918–1919' Notes by John Ardoin   ARM1–4915
 Side A: 371, 376, 380, 385, 393, 396, 399, 401
 Side B: 403, 411, 417, 421, 424, 427, 430, 434, 437

Volume 16: '1919–1920' Notes by Ted Fagan   ARM1–7008
 Side A: 443, 447, 451, 453, 455, 457, 461, 466, 470
 Side B: 472, 474, 480, 490, 492, 494, 496, 497

Note: In ARM1–4914, the 1906 version of 'Marta: M'apparì tutt'amor' (number 49) was erroneously used instead of the 1917 version (number 359). Mrs Favia-Artsay's notes describe the later version.

Stanford University Archives released a 33 RPM record containing a fragment of *Rigoletto*: 'Bella figlia dell'amore' (number 352).   STaRS 1000

PART THREE

Notes

CHAPTER I 1873–1894

1 There is some doubt as to whether he was born on February 25 or 27. The earlier date was accepted until he corrected it himself – see the (New York) *Sun* and *New York Herald*, February 26, 1920. However, according to Greenfeld's *Caruso*, Enrico Caruso Jnr., his son, thinks the earlier date more likely, and that he was baptized on the 27th.
2 Pierre V. R. Key, *Caruso, a Biography*, 11.
3 *Ibid.*, 13.
4 But did he in fact leave the Meuricoffre company? *Musical America* and the (New York) *World* both print stories, allegedly written by him, which make that claim, but Key in his biography states that Caruso continued working for it until his conscription.
5 *Musical America*, February 20, 1918.
6 Adolfo Narcisso, *Varietà del ottocento*, 244.
7 *The Boston Post*, April 21, 1918.
8 *The Boston Post*, April 21, 1918.
9 Key, *Caruso*, 40.
10 Quoted in Bruno Zirato's manuscript Draft Biography.
11 *Everybody's Magazine*, November 11, 1950.
12 *The London World*, May 28, 1890.
13 Franco Onorati, 'Libiamo, Libiamo. . .', 83 *et seq.*

CHAPTER II 1895–1897

1 *Il Pungolo parlamentare*, March 16/17, 1895.
2 *Don Marzio*, March 17/18, 1895.
3 *Il Vespero*, April 4, 1895.
4 *Ibid.*, May 2, 1895.
5 *The New York Times*, December 3, 1921.
6 Arthur Rubinstein, *My Many Years*, 40.
7 Key, *Caruso*, 54/55.
8 *Corriere di Napoli*, December 8, 1895.
9 Emma Calvé, *My Life*, 164.
10 *Gazzetta dei teatri*, January 30, 1896.
11 Quoted in Zirato's Draft Biography.
12 Key, *Caruso*, 67.
13 *L'Eco*, September 11, 1896.
14 *La Frusta*, September 26/27, 1896.
15 *L'Eco*, November 23, 1896.
16 Key, *Caruso*, 71.
17 *La Frusta*, November 24/25, 1896.
18 Key, *Caruso*, 78.

CHAPTER III 1897–1898

1 *Gazzetta dei teatri*, June 3, 1897.
2 Rosa Ponselle and James Drake, *Ponselle*, 102.
3 Zirato, Draft Biography.
4 *Gazzetta livornese*, August 16/17, 1897.
5 Key, *Caruso*, 90.
6 *Gazzetta dei teatri*, November 4, 1897.
7 *Ibid.*, December 2, 1897.
8 Nicola Daspuro, *Enrico Caruso*, 22.
9 Author's conversations with Giovanni Martinelli.
10 *Rivista teatrale melodrammatica*, March 15, 1898.

11 *The* (New York) *World*, February 28, 1918.
12 *Revista teatrale melodrammatica*, April 8, 1898.
13 *Gazzetta dei teatri*, November 10, 1898.
14 Gemma Bellincioni, *Io e il palcoscenico*, 125/126.
15 *Ibid.*, 132.
16 Mario Morini, *Umberto Giordano*, 29.
17 *Gazzetta dei teatri*, November 24, 1898.
18 Key, *Caruso*, 101.

CHAPTER IV 1898–1900

1 Fred Gaisberg, *The Music Goes Round*, 50.
2 Key, *Caruso*, 104.
3 *Gazzetta dei teatri*, June 8, 1899.
4 Zirato, Draft Biography.
5 Key, *Caruso*, 66.
6 *The* (New York) *World*, April 23, 1918.
7 *Popolo romano*, November 5, 1899.
8 *Il Messaggero*, November 5, 1899.
9 *La Voce della verità*, November 5, 1899.
10 *Fanfulla*, November 13, 1899.
11 Augusto Carelli, *Emma Carelli*, 49.
12 *La Rassegna melodrammatica*, January 7, 1900.
13 Zirato, Draft Biography.
14 *Ibid.*
15 *Il Mondo artistico*, November 11, 1900.

CHAPTER V 1900–1902

1 *L'Alba*, December 27, 1900.
2 Carelli, *Emma Carelli*, 74.
3 *Ibid.*, 75/76.
4 *Gazzetta dei teatri*, January 24, 1901.
5 Giulio Gatti-Casazza, *Memories of the Opera*, 103.
6 *Ibid.*, 105.
7 *Gazzetta dei teatri*, February 21, 1901.
8 Gatti-Casazza, *Memories of the Opera*, 118.
9 *Gazzetta dei teatri*, March 20, 1901.
10 Zirato, Draft Biography.
11 *Il Trovatore*, June 15, 1901.
12 *The* (New York) *Morning Telegraph*, February 16, 1906.
13 Geraldine Farrar, *Such Sweet Compulsion*, 69.
14 *Il Resto del Carlino*, December 1, 1901.
15 Zirato, Draft Biography.
16 Key, *Caruso*, 151.
17 *Don Marzio*, December 29–30, 1901.
18 *Il Pungolo parlamentare*, December 31, 1901.
19 *Corriere di Napoli*, January 3, 1902.
20 *Il Pungolo parlamentare*, January 3, 1902.
21 *Ibid.*, January 17–18, 1902.
22 Daspuro, *Enrico Caruso*, 29.
23 *Le Journal de Monaco*, February 4, 1902.
24 *Ibid.*, February 18, 1902.
25 Nellie Melba, *Melodies and Memories*, 130.

CHAPTER VI 1902–1903

1 Gaisberg, *The Music Goes Round*, 48.

2 In *The Antique Phonograph Monthly*, Vol. V, No. 4, in an article entitled 'The "Pre-Victor" recordings of Enrico Caruso', Martin Sokol explains how these ten recordings were in fact the very first Caruso made.
3 Sydney Homer, *My Wife and I*, 191.
4 *The* (New York) *Sun*, August 3, 1921.
5 Aida Favia-Artsay, *Caruso on Records*, 184.
6 E. F. Benson, *Final Edition*, 57.
7 (London) *Daily Telegraph*, May 15, 1902.
8 (London) *Sunday Times*, May 18, 1902.
9 (London) *Daily News*, May 15, 1902.
10 Félia Litvinne, *Ma Vie et mon art*, 159/160.
11 Richard Barthélemy, *Memories of Caruso*, 2.
12 Frances Alda, *Men, Women and Tenors*, 67.
13 Dorothy Caruso, *Enrico Caruso*, 101.
14 *Gazzetta dei teatri*, November 13, 1902.
15 Key, *Caruso*, 166.
16 *Indipendente*, December 11, 1902.
17 From a letter of Vittorio Gui written in 1972 and printed in *Omaggio a Enrico Caruso* by the Associazione Museo Enrico Caruso, Milan.
18 *Cronache musicale e drammatiche*, February 3, 1903.
19 *Le Journal de Monaco*, March 29, 1903.
20 *Le Courrier de la Plata*, May 20, 1903.
21 Carelli, *Emma Carelli*, 98.

CHAPTER VII 1903–1904

1 Clara Leiser, *Jean de Reszke and the Great Days of Opera*, 208.
2 Montrose J. Moses, *Heinrich Conried*, 172.
3 *The* (New York) *Sun*, January 19, 1935.
4 *The New York Times*, November 24, 1903.
5 *The* (New York) *Sun*, November 24, 1903.
6 *New York Daily Tribune*, November 24, 1903.
7 *The New York Times*, December 1, 1903.
8 *The* (New York) *Sun*, December 1, 1903.
9 *New York Daily Tribune*, December 1, 1903.
10 *The* (New York) *Evening Post*, December 3, 1903.
11 *New York Daily Tribune*, December 3, 1903.
12 *The New York Times*, December 3, 1903.
13 *The* (New York) *Sun*, December 3, 1903.
14 *The New York Times*, December 7, 1903.
15 *The* (New York) *Sun*, December 7, 1903.
16 *The* (New York) *Evening Post*, December 10, 1903.
17 *The* (New York) *Sun*, January 9, 1904.
18 *The New York Times*, January 25, 1904.
19 *Le Journal de Monaco*, March 8, 1904.
20 *Il Trovatore*, March 9, 1904.
21 'Geraldine Farrar to sing here soon', the *Montgomery Advertiser*, October 24, 1920.
22 Key, *Caruso*, 192.
23 Gabriel Astruc, *La Carrière d'Enrico Caruso à Paris*, unpublished manuscript.
24 *Il Trovatore*, April 9, 1904.
25 *La Publicidad*, April 24, 1904.
26 Key, *Caruso*, 197.
27 Ludwig Hartmann, 'Italian opera in Dresden', the *Dresdner Neueste Nachtrichten*, May 10, 1904.
28 *Manchester Guardian*, May 18, 1904.
29 *Pall Mall Gazette*, May 20, 1904.
30 Barthélemy, *Memories of Caruso*, 2.
31 *Daily Telegraph*, June 21, 1904.

CHAPTER VIII 1904–1905

1 Rawlins L. Cottenet, 'Enrico Caruso – why he is the greatest of all tenors', *The* (New York) *World*, March 6, 1919.
2 Maurice Halperson, 'My visit to Bellosguardo, Caruso's famous villa', *Musical America*, February 3, 1917.
3 Henry Russell, *The Passing Show*, 113/115.
4 *Pall Mall Gazette*, October 15, 1904.
5 Leiser, *Jean de Reszke*, 263.
6 *The* (London) *Times*, April 6, 1925.
7 L. A. G. Strong, *John McCormack*, 112.
8 Henry Wood, *My Life of Music*, 322.
9 Michael Scott, *The Record of Singing, Vol. 1*, 34.
10 Henry Lahee, *The Grand Opera Singers of Today*, 39.
11 *The New York Times*, November 22, 1904.
12 *Ibid.*, December 6, 1904.
13 *Chicago Tribune*, March 21, 1905.
14 *Kansas City Star*, April 2, 1905.
15 *San Francisco Chronicle*, April 7, 1905.
16 Key, *Caruso*, 204.
17 *Ibid.*, 210.
18 *Le Matin*, May 15, 1905.
19 Thomas Burke, *Nights in London*, 245–247.
20 A letter from George Bernard Shaw to *The Times*, July 3, 1905.
21 *Pall Mall Gazette*, July 3, 1905.
22 A letter from Tito Ricordi to Caruso in Zirato.
23 *Le Carillon*, August 5/6, 1905.
24 *Le Saison d'Ostende*, August 9, 1905.

CHAPTER IX 1905–1906

1 *The* (New York) *Sun*, November 21, 1905.
2 *The Philadelphia Inquirer*, December 6, 1905.
3 *The New York Times*, December 15, 1905.
4 *The* (Baltimore) *Sun*, March 20, 1906.
5 *The Pittsburgh Press*, March 28, 1906.
6 *The Chicago Tribune*, April 6, 1906.
7 Mary Cushing, *The Rainbow Bridge*, 94.
8 Herman Klein, *The Golden Age of Opera*, 247.
9 *The* (London) *Sketch*, May 20, 1906.
10 Key, *Caruso*, 227/228.
11 *The* (New York) *Morning Telegraph*, October 26, 1912.
12 *Pall Mall Gazette*, May 16, 1906.
13 Titta Ruffo, *La mia parabola*, 283.
14 *The* (New York) *World*, November 17, 1906.
15 *Ibid.*, November 18, 1906.
16 *New York American*, November 30, 1906.
17 *Ibid.*

CHAPTER X 1906–1908

1 *The New York Herald*, November 29, 1906.
2 *The* (New York) *Globe and Commercial Advertiser*, November 29, 1906.
3 John Frederick Cone, *Oscar Hammerstein's Manhattan Opera Company*, 3.
4 *The New York Times*, December 4, 1906.
5 *The Philadelphia Inquirer*, March 8, 1907.
6 *Ibid.*
7 *The Chicago Tribune*, April 9, 1907.
8 *Ibid.*
9 *The Kansas City Times*, April 21, 1907.

NOTES

10 *The Minneapolis Journal*, April 27, 1907.
11 *The Nashville Banner*, April 29, 1919.
12 *The (New York) Morning Telegraph*, June 12, 1907.
13 *Ibid.*, July 4, 1907.
14 *Musical Courier*, August 7, 1907.
15 *Musical America*, August 10, 1907.
16 Key, *Caruso*, 243/244.
17 *Neues Wiener Tagblatt*, October 5, 1907.
18 Bruno Walter, *Theme and Variations*, 107.
19 *Leipziger Neueste Nachrichten*, October 14, 1907.
20 Frieda Hempel, *Mein Leben dem Gesang*, 43.
21 Emil Ledner, *Erinnerungen an Caruso*, 63.
22 *The (London) World*, July 13, 1907.
23 *The (New York) Sun*, February 27, 1908.
24 Henry Edward Krehbiel, *Chapters of Opera*, 392–393.
25 *The New York Times*, January 19, 1908.
26 *The (New York) Sun*, February 27, 1908.
27 Farrar, *Such Sweet Compulsion*, 111.
28 Key, *Caruso*, 251.
29 *The (New York) World*, August 20, 1919.
30 *Le Figaro*, June 12, 1908.
31 *Musical Courier*, September 27, 1908.
32 *Musical America*, November 7, 1908.
33 *Ibid.*, October 31, 1908.

CHAPTER XI 1908–1910

1 *The New York Times*, November 18, 1908.
2 Farrar, *Such Sweet Compulsion*, 118.
3 *Ibid.*, 121.
4 Victor Sheean, *Oscar Hammerstein I*, 164.
5 Gatti-Casazza, *Memories of the Opera*, 162.
6 *Ibid.*
7 *The (New York) Morning Telegraph*, January 29, 1909.
8 *The Memphis Commercial*, January 29, 1909.
9 *The New York Times*, October 28, 1928.
10 *Corriere della sera*, July 15, 1909.
11 *Musical America*, August 7, 1909.
12 *The Irish Times*, August 21, 1909.
13 Landon Ronald, *Variations on a Personal Theme*, 146.
14 Lotte Lehmann, *Midway in My Song*, 44.
15 Favia-Artsay, *Caruso on Records*, 94.
16 *The (New York) Sun*, November 16, 1909.
17 *Ibid.*
18 Mary Jane Matz, *The Many Lives of Otto Kahn*, 91.
19 Astruc, *La Carrière d'Enrico Caruso à Paris*, unpublished manuscript.
20 Frances Alda, *Men, Women and Tenors*, 157.
21 *L'Etoile Belge*, September 28, 1910.
22 *Münchner Zeitung*, October 10, 1910.
23 Otto Klemperer, *Minor Recollections*, 67.
24 Key, *Caruso*, 281.
25 Ledner, *Erinnerungen an Caruso*, 50.
26 *The (New York) World*, December 18, 1910.
27 *The (New York) Sun*, November 15, 1910.
28 Cushing, *The Rainbow Bridge*, 198.
29 *The New York Times*, December 11, 1910.
30 Robert Tuggle, *The Golden Age of Opera*, 71.
31 *Musical America*, January 7, 1911.

32 *Chicago Tribune*, January 15, 1911.
33 *The New York Herald*, April 6, 1911.
34 *Musical Courier*, April 10, 1911.

CHAPTER XII 1911–1913

1 Key, *Caruso*, 293.
2 *The* (New York) *Morning Telegraph*, November 6, 1908.
3 *The Chicago Morning Telegraph*, January 17, 1911.
4 *The* (New York) *World*, November 8, 1911.
5 *Boston Evening Transcript*, August 23, 1912.
6 *Musical America*, October 21, 1911.
7 *Orfeo*, November 2, 1911.
8 *The* (New York) *Morning Telegraph*, November 3, 1911.
9 Irving Kolodin, *The Metropolitan Opera, 1883–1966*, 230.
10 *Le Guide musical*, May 21, 1912.
11 *Ibid.*
12 *The New York Times*, October 27, 1912.
13 *Ibid.*
14 D. Caruso, *Enrico Caruso*, 39.
15 *New York Daily Tribune*, Nov. 12, 1912.
16 *The* (New York) *Sun*, December 28, 1912.
17 *Boston Evening Transcript*, March 19, 1913.
18 *The* (London) *Times*, May 21, 1913.
19 Gaisberg, *The Music Goes Round*, 126.
20 Osbert Sitwell, *Good Morning*, 134.
21 *Münchner Post*, October 2, 1913.
22 *The* (New York) *Sun*, February 18, 1918.
23 *Musical America*, November 29, 1913.
24 Giuseppe Valdengo, *Scusi, conosce Toscanini?*, 37/38.
25 *Il Giornale d'Italia*, October 21, 1914.
26 'Caruso, Gold Medals and South America', *Musical Courier*, February 1918.
27 Key, *Caruso*, 281.
28 Parker, *Eighth Notes*, 62/63.

CHAPTER XIII 1914–1916

1 *The* (New York) *Sun*, February 27, 1914.
2 Farrar, *Such Sweet Compulsion*, 132.
3 D. Caruso, *Enrico Caruso*, 45.
4 *The* (New York) *Evening Post*, June 8, 1914.
5 *Pall Mall Gazette*, May 15, 1914.
6 *The* (London) *Evening Star*, June 30, 1914.
7 Harvey Sachs, *Toscanini*, 129.
8 *The New York Herald*, November 17, 1914.
9 *The New York Press*, November 17, 1914.
10 *The* (New York) *Sun*, November 20, 1914.
11 *The New York Press*, December 25, 1914.
12 *New York Daily Tribune*, December 25, 1914.
13 *The* (New York) *Evening Mail*, January 2, 1915.
14 Zirato, Draft Biography.
15 *Le Petit Monégasque*, March 14, 1915.
16 Litvinne, *Ma Vie et mon art*, 42.
17 *Le Journal de Monaco*, March 21, 1915.
18 Zirato, Draft Biography.
19 Key, *Caruso*, 309.
20 *Ibid.*, 311.
21 From a letter by Florentine V. Sanguinetti printed in *Ayer y hoy de la Opera*, Ano III, Núm. 3, Sep.–Oct. 1979.

22 *Corriere della sera*, September 25, 1915.
23 *New York American*, October 20, 1915.
24 Key, *Caruso*, 313/314.
25 *The New York Herald*, November 16, 1915.
26 *New York Daily Tribune*, November 16, 1915.
27 Mary Fitch Watkins, *Behind the Scenes at the Opera*, 98/99.
28 *Musical America*, January 15, 1916.
29 *Ibid.*, February 10, 1916.
30 *New York Daily Tribune*, December 12, 1915.
31 *Ibid.*, February 10, 1916.
32 Gatti-Casazza, *Memories of the Opera*, 190.
33 *The (New York) Sun*, February 8, 1917.
34 *New York Daily Tribune*, February 8, 1917.
35 *The New York Times*, February 8, 1917.
36 Alda, *Men, Women and Tenors*, 215.
37 Kolodin, *The Metropolitan Opera*, 262.
38 *The New York Press*, February 26, 1916.

CHAPTER XIV 1916–1918

1 *Boston Daily Globe*, April 8, 1916.
2 *Ibid.*
3 *Ibid.*
4 *Ibid.*, April 13, 1916.
5 *Atlanta Post*, April 25, 1916.
6 *The New York Times*, November 14, 1916.
7 *The (New York) Morning Telegraph*, November 15, 1916.
8 *New York Daily Tribune*, December 31, 1916.
9 *The (New York) World*, December 31, 1916.
10 Compare reviews in *New York Daily Tribune*, *The New York Herald* and *The Sun* all of December 31, 1916.
11 *The (New York) Globe and Commercial Advertiser*, January 11, 1917.
12 *New York Daily Tribune*, December 5, 1916.
13 *The (New York) Sun*, February 13, 1917.
14 *The (New York) Evening Sun*, March 24, 1917.
15 From a letter of John T. McGovern of the Dutch Treat Club to Francis Robinson. Francis Robinson Collection, University of Nashville.
16 Francis Robinson: *Caruso, His Life in Pictures*, 191.
18 *The Toledo Times*, May 1, 1917.
19 'Caruso, Gold Medals and South America', *Musical Courier*, February 1918.
20 *Ibid.*
21 *Ibid.*
22 *The Buenos Aires Standard*, June 27, 1917.
23 'Caruso, Gold Medals and South America', *Musical Courier*, February 1918.
24 *The New York Herald*, November 5, 1917.
25 *New York American*, November 13, 1917.
26 *The (New York) Globe and Commercial Advertiser*, November 13, 1917.
27 *The (New York) World*, November 14, 1917.
28 *The (New York) Evening Mail*. November 13, 1917.
29 *Musical America*, November 17, 1917.
30 *The (New York) Sun*, November 16, 1917.
31 *New York American*, November 16, 1917.
32 *The (New York) World*, November 22, 1917.
33 *Musical Courier*, November 29, 1917.
34 *The Philadelphia Record*, November 28, 1917.
35 *The (Philadelphia) Press*, November 28, 1917.
36 *The (New York) Evening Telegram*, November 11, 1917.
37 *The New York Times*, January 13, 1918.

38 *New York American*, January 13, 1918.
39 *New York Daily Tribune*, January 13, 1918.
40 *The* (New York) *Sun*, January 13, 1918.
41 *The* (New York) *World*, January 27, 1918.
42 *The* (New York) *Sun*, February 8, 1918.
43 *The New York Times*, February 8, 1918.
44 *New York American*, February 8, 1918.
45 *Musical Courier*, February 14, 1918.
46 *Musical America*, February 16, 1918.
47 *New York American*, March 15, 1918.
48 *Plays and Players*, March 15, 1918.
49 *New York Daily Tribune*, March 15, 1918.

CHAPTER XV 1918–1919

1 Dorothy Caruso and Mrs Goddard, *Wings of Song*, 15/16.
2 *Ibid.*, 50.
3 Dorothy Caruso, *Enrico Caruso*, 12.
4 *The New York Times*, November 12, 1918.
5 *Ibid.*, November 16, 1918.
6 *New York Daily Tribune*, November, 1918.
7 *The* (New York) *Evening Sun*, November 16, 1918.
8 *The New York Herald*, November 24, 1918.
9 *The* (New York) *Evening Sun*, November 25, 1918.
10 *The* (Philadelphia) *Press*, December 11, 1918.
11 *The* (New York) *Evening Journal*, December 26, 1918.
12 D. Caruso, *Enrico Caruso*, 66.
13 *Ibid.*, 67.
14 *The* (New York) *World*, Jan 27, 1918.
15 *The* (New York) *Morning Telegraph*, January 7, 1919.
16 D. Caruso and Mrs Goddard, *Wings of Song*, 85.
17 *The New York Times*, March 23, 1919.
18 *The* (Philadelphia) *Public Ledger*, March 12, 1919.
19 Herman Klein, *An Essay on Bel Canto*, 20.
20 Pier Francesco Tosi, *Observations on the Florid Song*, 13.

CHAPTER XVI 1919–1920

1 Bruno Zirato, 'My boss, my friend', *Opera News*, Caruso Centenary Edition, February 1973.
2 *The Atlanta Journal*, April 26, 1919.
3 *The Kansas City Times*, May 6, 1919.
4 D. Caruso, *Enrico Caruso*, 35–8.
5 *The* (New York) *Morning Telegraph*, September 4, 1919.
6 José Mojica, *I, a Sinner*, 204.
7 D. Caruso, *Enrico Caruso*, 96.
8 *The New York Herald*, October 26, 1919.
9 Rubinstein, *My Many Years*, 63.
10 *New York Daily Tribune*, November 2, 1919.
11 D. Caruso, *Enrico Caruso*, 117.
12 *El Democrata*, October 10, 1919.
13 *Le Courrier du Mexique*, October 18, 1919.
14 Key, *Caruso*, 376.
15 D. Caruso, *Enrico Caruso*, 94.
16 Key, *Caruso*, 343–4.
17 *The* (New York) *Sun*, November 23, 1919.
18 *New York Daily Tribune*, November 23, 1919.
19 D. Caruso and Mrs Goddard, *Wings of Song*, 93–4.
20 D. Caruso, *Enrico Caruso*, 161.

21 *Ibid.*, 170.
22 *Ibid.*, 178/179.
23 *Ibid.*, 181.
24 *Ibid.*, 184.
25 *Ibid.*, 186.
26 *Ibid.*, 187.
27 *Ibid.*, 202/203.
28 Rubinstein, *My Many Years*, 96.

CHAPTER XVII 1920–1921

1 *New York Daily Tribune*, October 8, 1920.
2 D. Caruso, *Enrico Caruso*, 195.
3 *New York American*, June 15, 1920.
4 *The Kansas City Star*, June 27, 1920.
5 *The New York Times*, June 20, 1920.
6 *The New Orleans Times-Picayune*, June 27, 1920.
7 Stanley Jackson, *Caruso*, 260.
8 Manuel Garcia, *L'Art du chant*, Chapter V, Section 4.
9 D. Caruso and Mrs Goddard, *Wings of Song*, 224.
10 *The Toronto Evening Telegram*, October 1, 1920.
11 *Chicago News*, October 4, 1920.
12 *Chicago Record*, October 4, 1920.
13 Key, *Caruso*, 360.
14 *The New York Times*, November 28, 1920.
15 (New York) *Evening Post*, November 16, 1920.
16 *New York Daily Tribune*, November 16, 1920.
17 *The* (New York) *Evening Telegram*, November 16, 1920.
18 *The New York Times*, November 28, 1920.
19 *Ibid.*
20 Key, *Caruso*, 364.
21 *The New York Times*, November 28, 1920.
22 *The* (New York) *World*, November 28, 1920.
23 Key, *Caruso*, 380.
24 Gatti-Casazza, *Memories of the Opera*, 231.
27 (New York) *Sun*, December 14, 1920.
26 Gatti-Casazza, *Memories of the Opera*, 232.
27 *The* (New York) *Sun*, December 25, 1920.
28 D. Caruso and Mrs Goddard, *Wings of Song*, 228.
29 From a letter to Giovanni Caruso by Enrico Caruso, dated February 1, 1921, included in Zirato's manuscript.
30 D. Caruso, *Enrico Caruso*, 247.
31 Robert W. Prichard, 'The Death of Enrico Caruso', *Surgery, Gynecology and Obstetrics*, July 1959, 118.
32 D. Caruso, *Enrico Caruso*, 248.
33 D. Caruso and Mrs Goddard, *Wings of Song*, 237/238.
34 *Ibid.*, 243.
35 *Ibid.*, 244.
36 Prichard, 'The Death of Enrico Caruso', *Surgery, Gynecology and Obstetrics*, July 1959, 118.
37 *Ibid.*
38 D. Caruso, *Enrico Caruso*, 264.
39 *Ibid.*, 265.
40 *New York American*, October 31, 1921.
41 From a letter of Raffaele Bastianelli to Dr Prichard dated October 5, 1959.
42 *New York American*, October 31, 1921.
43 D. Caruso, *Enrico Caruso*, 272.
44 D. Caruso and Mrs Goddard, *Wings of Song*, 255.

45 *New York American*, Otober 31, 1921.
46 Prichard, 'The Death of Enrico Caruso', *Surgery, Gynecology and Obstetrics*, July 1959, 118.
47 *Ibid.*
48 *Ibid.*
49 *The* (London) *Star*, January 23, 1889.
50 *Brooklyn Junior Eagle*, December 31, 1916.

BIBLIOGRAPHY

BOOKS

Alda, Frances. *Men, Women and Tenors*. Boston: Houghton Mifflin Co., 1937.

Aldrich, Richard. *Concert Life in New York*. New York: G. P. Putnam's Sons, 1941.

Armstrong, William. *The Romantic World of Music*. New York: Dutton, 1922.

Associazione Museo Enrico Caruso. *Omaggio a Enrico Caruso*. Milan: Centro Studi Carusiani, 1978.

Barthélemy, Richard. *Memories of Caruso*. Trans. by Constance S. Camner. Plainsboro, N.J.: La Scala Autographs, 1979.

Battaglia, Fernando. *L'arte del canto in Romagna*. Bologna: Edizioni Bongiovanni, 1979.

Bauer, Robert. *Historical Records, (1898–1908/9)*. London: Sidgwick and Jackson, 1947.

Beetz, Wilhelm. *Das Wiener Opernhaus 1869–1945*. Vienna: Amaltea Verlag, 1952.

Bellincioni, Gemma. *Io e il palcoscenico*. Rome: Quintieri, 1921.

Benson, E. F. *Final Edition*. London: Longmans, Green and Co., 1940.

Blumenthal, George, and Arthur H. Menkin. *My Sixty Years in Show Business*. New York: Frederick C. Osberg, 1936.

Bracale, Adolfo. *Mis memorias*. Caracas: Editorial Elite, 1931.

Burke, Thomas. *Nights in London*. London: Allen and Unwin Ltd., 1918.

Caamaño, Roberto. *La historia del Teatro Colón, 1908–1968*. Buenos Aires: Editorial Cinetea, 1969.

Caccini, Giulio. *Le Nuove musiche*. Florence, 1602.

Calvé, Emma. *My Life*. Trans. by Rosamund Gilder. New York: D. Appleton and Co., 1922.

Carelli, Augusto. *Emma Carelli*. Rome: Editrice Maglione, 1932.

Carré, Albert. *Souvenirs de Théâtre*. Paris: Librairie Plon, 1950.

Caruso, Dorothy. *Enrico Caruso*. London: T. Werner Laurie Ltd., 1946.

——, and Mrs Torrance Goddard. *Wings of Song*. London: Hutchinson & Co., 1929.

Castellan, Joelle. *Special Monte-Carlo centenaire de la Salle Garnier (1879–1979)*. Paris: Opéra International, 1979.

Cavalieri, Lina. *Le mie verità*. Rome: Edizione Maglione, 1932.

Celletti, Rodolfo. *Le Grandi voci*. Rome: Istituto per la collaborazione culturale, 1914.

Cerquera, Paulo de O. C. *Um secolo de Opera em São Paulo*. São Paulo: Empresa Grafica Editora Guia Fiscal, 1954.

Chaliapin, Feodor. *Man and Mask*. Trans. by Phyllis Mégroz. London: Victor Gollancz Ltd., 1932.

Ciotti, Ignazio. *La vita artistico del Teatro Massimo di Palermo*. Palermo: Tipolitografia Priulla, 1984.

Cone, John Frederick. *Oscar Hammerstein's Manhattan Opera Company*. Oklahoma, Oklahoma University Press, 1964.

Cushing, Mary Watkins. *The Rainbow Bridge*. New York: G. P. Putnam's Sons, 1954.

Daspuro, Nicola. *Enrico Caruso*. Mexico City: Ediciones Coli, 1943.

Davis, Ronald. *Opera in Chicago*. New York: Appleton-Century, 1966.

Dawson, Peter. *Fifty Years of Song*. London: Hutchinson & Co., 1951.

De Angelis, Alberto. *Dizionario dei musicisti*. Rome: Ausonia, 1922.

De Brito Chaves Jr., Edgard. *Memorias e Glorias de um Teatro*. Rio de Janeiro: Companhia Editora Americana, 1971.

De Hegermann-Lindencrone, L. *The Sunny Side of Diplomatic Life*. New York: Harper's, 1914.

Domanski, Piotr Jerzy. *Repertuar Teatrow Warszawskich*. Warsaw: Instytut Sztuki Polskiej Akademii Nauk, 1976.

Downes, Olin. *Olin Downes on Music*. New York: Simon and Schuster, 1957.

Duey, Philip A. *Bel Canto in its Golden Age*. New York: King's Crown Press, 1951.

Eames, Emma. *Some Memories and Reflections*. New York: D. Appleton and Co., 1927.

BIBLIOGRAPHY

Eaton, Quaintance. *Boston Opera*. New York: Appleton-Century, 1965.
——*Opera Caravan*. New York: Farrar, Straus and Cudahy, 1957.
Farkas, Andrew, ed. *Titta Ruffo, An Anthology*. Westport, Conn.: Greenwood Press, 1984.
Farrar, Geraldine. *Such Sweet Compulsion*. New York: The Greystone Press, 1938.
Favia-Artsay, Aida. *Caruso on Records*. Valhalla, N.Y.: The Historic Record, 1965.
Filippis, F. de, and Arnese, R. *Cronache del Teatro di San Carlo*. Naples: Edizione Politica Popolare, 1961.
Finck, Henry T. *Musical Progress*. Philadelphia: Theodore Presser, 1923.
——*My Adventures in the Golden Age of Music*. New York: Funk and Wagnalls Co., 1926.
——*Success in Music and How It Is Won*. New York: Charles Scribner's Sons, 1913.
Flint, Mary H. *Impressions of Caruso and His Art*. Privately printed. New York, 1917.
Frajese, Vittorio. *Dal Constanzi all'Opera*. Rome: Edizioni Capitolium, 1978.
Franko, Sam. *Chords and Dischords*. New York: The Viking Press, 1938.
Frassoni, Edilio. *Due secoli di lirica a Genova*. Genoa: Cassa di Risparmia di Genova e Imperia, 1980.
Gadotti, Adonide. *Carmen Melis*. Rome: Bardi Editore, 1985.
Gaisberg, Fred. *The Music Goes Round*. New York: Macmillan, 1942.
Gara, Eugenio. *Caruso storia di un emigrante*. Milan: Cisalpino-Goliardica, 1947.
García, Manuel. *L'Art du chant*. Paris, 1847.
Gatti, Carlo. *Il Teatro alla Scala*. 2 vols. Milan: Recordi, 1964.
Gatti-Casazza, Giulio. *Memories of the Opera*. New York: Charles Scribner's Sons, 1941.
Gelatt, Roland. *The Fabulous Phonograph*. Philadelphia: J. B. Lippincott, 1955.
Gerhardt, Elena. *Recital*. London: Methuen, 1953.
Gigli, Beniamino. *The Memoirs of Beniamino Gigli*. London: Cassell, 1957.
Glackens, Ira. *Yankee Diva*. New York: Coleridge Press, 1963.
Greenfeld, Howard. *Caruso*. New York: G. P. Putnam's Sons, 1983.
Gunsbourg, Raoul. *Cent Ans de souvenirs . . . ou presque*. Monaco: Editions du Rocher, 1959.
Hanslick, Edouard. *Music Criticisms 1846–1899*. Edited and trans. by Henry Pleasants. London: Pelican books, 1951.
Hempel, Frieda. *Mein Leben dem Gesang*. Berlin: Argon Verlag, 1955.
Henderson, W. J. *The Art of Singing*. New York: The Dial Press, 1938.
Hetherington, John. *Melba*. London: Faber and Faber, 1967.
Heylbut, Rose, and Aimé Gerber. *Backstage at the Opera*. New York: Thomas Y. Crowell Co., 1937.
Homer, Sydney. *My Wife and I*. New York: Macmillan, 1939.
Huneker, James. *Bedouins*. New York: Charles Scribner's Sons, 1920.
——*Steeplejack*. New York: Charles Scribner's Sons, 1921.
Jackson, Stanley. *Caruso*. New York: Stein and Day, 1972.
Kapp, Julius. *185 Jahre Staatsoper*. Berlin: Atlantic-Verlag, 1928.
Key, Pierre V. R., with Bruno Zirato. *Caruso, a Biography*. Boston: Little, Brown, and Co., 1922.
Klein, Herman. *An Essay on Bel Canto*. London: Oxford Univ. Press, 1923.
——*The Golden Age of Opera*. London: Routledge & Sons, Ltd., 1933.
——*Great Women Singers of My Time*. London: Routledge & Sons, Ltd., 1931.
——*Musicians and Mummers*. London: Cassell, 1925.
——*The Reign of Patti*. New York: Century, 1920.
——*Thirty Years of Musical Life in London 1870–1900*. London: William Heinemann, 1903.
Klemperer, Otto. *Minor Recollections*. London: Dennis Donson, 1964.
Kolodin, Irving. *The Metropolitan Opera 1883–1966*. New York: Alfred A. Knopf, 1966.
Krehbiel, Henry Edward. *Chapters of Opera*. New York: Holt and Co., 1908.
——*More Chapters of Opera*. New York: Holt and Co., 1919.
Kutsch, K. J. and Leo Riemens. *Unvergängliche Stimmen, Sängerlexicon*. Berne: Francke, 1983.
Lahee, Henry C. *The Grand Opera Singers of Today*. Boston: L. C. Page and Co., 1912.
Lauri-Volpi, Giacomo. *Equivoco*. Milan: Edizione Corbaccio, 1939.
——*A viso aperto*. Milan: Edizione Corbaccio, 1953.
——*Voce parallele*. Bologna: Edizione Bongiovanni, 1977.
Lawton, Mary. *Schumann-Heink, The Last of the Titans*. New York: Macmillan, 1928.
Ledbetter, Gordon. *The Great Irish Tenor*. London: Duckworth, 1977.

BIBLIOGRAPHY

Ledner, Emil. *Erinnerungen an Caruso*. Hanover: P. Steegemann, 1922.

Lehmann, Lilli. *My Path Through Life*. Trans. by Alice Benedict Seligman. New York: G. P. Putnam's Sons, 1914.

Lehmann, Lotte. *Midway in My Song*. New York: Bobbs-Merrill, 1938.

Lehrmann, Johannes. *Caruso singt!* Berlin: Lehrmann, 1940.

Leiser, Clara. *Jean de Reszke and the Great Days of Opera*. London: Gerald Howe, 1933.

Litvinne, Félia. *Ma Vie et mon art*. Paris: Librairie Plon, 1933.

Lochner, Louis P. *Fritz Kreisler*. New York: Macmillan, 1950.

Lumley, Benjamin. *Reminiscences of the Opera*. London: Hurst and Blackett, 1864.

Mackenzie, Barbara and Findlay. *Singers of Australia from Melba to Sutherland*. London: Newnes Books, 1968.

Mackinley, Sterling. *Garcia: the Cententarian and His Times*. London: W. Blackwood & Sons, 1908.

Mancini, Giambattista. *Pensieri, e riflessioni pratiche sopra il canto figurato*. Vienna, 1774.

Mapleson, James Henry. *The Mapleson Memoirs, 1848–1888*. 2 Vols. London: Remington, 1888.

Marchesi, Blanche. *A Singer's Pilgrimage*. London: Grant Richards, 1923.

Marchesi, Mathilde. *Marchesi and Music*. New York: Harper, 1898.

Marinelli Roscioni, Carlo. *Cronologia del Teatro Comunale*. Treviso: Longo & Zoppelli, 1977.

Marone, Silvio. *Caruso: aspectos de sua personalidade psico-dinâmica, suas atividades em São Paulo*. São Paulo: Grafica Gentlemen, 1973.

Massenet, Jules. *My Recollections*. Trans. by H. Villiers Barnett. Boston: Small, Maynard and Co., 1919.

Matz, Mary Jane. *The Many Lives of Otto Kahn*. New York: Macmillan, 1963.

McCormack, Lily. *I Hear You Calling Me*. Milwaukee: The Bruce Publishing Co., 1949.

Melba, Nellie. *Melodies and Memories*. London: Thornton Butterworth, Ltd., 1925.

Mohr, Albert Richard. *Das Frankfurter Opernhaus 1880–1980*. Frankfurt: Waldemar Kramer, 1980.

Mojica, José. *I, a Sinner*. Chicago: Franciscan Herald Press, 1963.

Monteux, Doris. *It's All in the Music*. London: William Kimber, 1956.

Moore, Edward C. *Forty Years of Opera in Chicago*. New York: Horace Liveright, 1930.

Morini, Mario. *Pietro Mascagni*. Milan: Sonzogno, 1964.

——*Umberto Giordano*. Milan: Sonzogno, 1968.

Moses, Montrose J. *The Life of Heinrich Conried*. New York: Thomas Y. Crowell Co., 1916.

Mouchon, Jean-Pierre. *Enrico Caruso, His Life and Voice*. Gap, France: Editions Ophrys, 1974.

Narcisso, Adolfo. *Varietà del ottocento*. Naples, Adriana, 1944.

Noel, Edouard and Edmond Stoullig. *Les Annales du théâtre et de la musique*. Paris, 1875–1916.

Nice, L'Opéra de. *D'Un Siècle à l'autre – L'Opéra de Nice 1885–1985*. Nice: L'Opéra de Nice, 1985.

O'Connell, Charles. *The Other Side of the Record*. Westport Conn.: Greenwood Press, 1970.

Olavarria y Ferrari, Enrique. *Resena Historica del Teatro en Mexico*. Mexico City: Biblioteca Porrua, 1961.

Onorati, Franco. *Libiamo! Libiamo!* Rome: Il Ventaglio, 1987.

Parker, H. T. *Eighth Notes: Voices and Figures of Music and Dance*. New York: Dodd Mead, 1922.

Pituello, Luciano. *Caruso a Milano*. Milan: Associazione amici del Museo Teatrale alla Scala, 1971.

Pleasants, Henry. *The Great Singers*. New York: Simon and Schuster, 1961.

Ponselle, Rosa and James A. Drake. *Ponselle: A Singer's Life*. New York: Doubleday, 1982.

Read, O., and W. L. Welch. *From Tin Foil to Stereo*. Indianapolis: Howard W. Sams & Co. Inc., 1959.

Robinson, Francis. *Caruso, His Life in Pictures*. New York: Bramhall House, 1957.

Ronald, Landon. *Variations on a Personal Theme*. London: Hodder & Stoughton 1922.

Rosenthal, Harold. *Two Centuries of Opera at Covent Garden*. London: Putnam, 1958.

Rubinstein, Arthur. *My Many Years*. New York: Alfred A. Knopf, 1980.

——*My Young Years*. New York: Alfred A. Knopf, 1973.

Ruffo, Titta. *La mia parabola*. Rome: Staderini, 1977.

Russell, Henry. *The Passing Show*. London: Thornton Butterworth, Ltd., 1926.

BIBLIOGRAPHY

Sachs, Harvey. *Toscanini*. London: Weidenfeld and Nicolson, 1978.
Salgado, Susana. *Breve Historia de la Musica Culta en el Uruguay*. Montevideo: Aemus, 1971.
Schoen-Rene, Anna Eugenie. *America's Musical Inheritance*. New York: Putnam, 1941.
Scott, Michael. *The Record of Singing to 1914*. London: Duckworth, 1977.
Seltsam, William. *Metropolitan Opera Annals*. New York: H. H. Wilson, 1947.
Shaw, Bernard. *Shaw's Music 1876–1950*, 3 Vols. London: Bodley Head, 1981.
Sheean, Vincent. *First and Last Love*. New York: Random House, 1956.
——*Oscar Hammerstein I*. New York: Simon and Schuster, 1956.
Sitwell, Osbert. *Good Morning*. London: Macmillan, 1948.
Spalding, Albert. *Rise to Follow*. New York: Henry Holt & Co., 1946.
Strong, L. A. G. *John McCormack*. New York: Macmillan, 1941.
Tetrazzini, Luisa. *My Life of Song*. Philadelphia: Dorrance and Co., Inc., 1922.
Thompson, Oscar. *The American Singer*. New York: The Dial Press, 1937.
——, ed. *The International Cyclopedia of Music and Musicians*. New York: Dodd, Mead, 1956.
Tosi, Pier Francesco. *Observations on the Florid Song*. Trans. by J. E. Gaillard. London, 1742.
Trezzini, Lamberto. *Due secoli di vita musicale*. Bologna: Edizione Alfa, 1966.
Tuggle, Robert. *The Golden Age of Opera*. New York: Holt, Rinehart and Winston, 1983.
Valdengo, Giuseppe. *Scusi, conosce Toscanini?* Aosta: Musumeci, 1984.
Van Vechten, Carl. *Interpreters and Interpretations*. New York: Alfred A. Knopf, 1917.
——*In the Garret*. New York: Alfred A. Knopf, 1920.
——*The Merry-Go-Round*. New York: Alfred A. Knopf, 1918.
Wagner, Charles L. *Seeing Stars*. New York: Putnam, 1940.
Wagner, Hans. *200 Jahr Münchner Theaterchronik 1750–1950*. Munich: Wissenschaftlicher Verlag Robert Lerche, 1958.
Walsh, T. J. *Monte Carlo Opera*. Dublin: Gill and Macmillan, 1975.
Walter, Bruno. *Theme and Variations*. New York: Alfred A. Knopf, 1944.
Watkins, Mary Fitch. *Behind the Scenes at the Opera*. New York: Frederick A. Stokes, 1925.
Wenzel, Joseph E. *Geschichte der Hamburger Oper 1678–1978*. Hamburg: Hamburgischen Staatsoper, 1978.
Wolf, Stephane. *L'Opéra au Palais Garnier, 1875–1962*. Paris: L'Entr'acte, 1963.
Wood, Henry J. *My Life of Music*. London: Victor Gollancz, 1938.
Ybarra, T. R. *Caruso, the Man of Naples and the Voice of Gold*. New York: Harcourt, Brace, 1953.

Manuscripts and Letters

Astruc, Gabriel. *La Carrière d'Enrico Caruso à Paris*. Manuscript in the Francis Robinson Collection, Vanderbilt University, Nashville, Tennessee.
Robinson, Francis. Letters and other memorabilia relating to Caruso, contained in Francis Robinson Collection, Vanderbilt University, Nashville, Tennessee.
Zirato, Bruno. Original draft for biography of Caruso; some of it – but not all – was later used by Key. Francis Robinson Collection, Vanderbilt University, Nashville, Tennessee.

Operas – Caruso's
First (Or Only) Appearances

* known world premiere

*I Briganti nel giardino di Don Raffaele, Campanelli & Fasanaro, 1887, Naples,
  Bronzetti school
*L'Amico Francesco, Morelli, March 15, 1895, Naples, Nuovo
Faust, Gounod, March 28, 1895, Caserta, Cimarosa
Cavalleria rusticana, Mascagni, April 28, 1895, Caserta, Cimarosa
Camoëns, Musone, as above, Caserta, Cimarosa
Rigoletto, Verdi, July 21, 1895, Naples, Bellini
La Traviata, Verdi, July 25, 1895, Naples, Bellini
La Gioconda, Ponchielli, October 1895, Cairo, Ezbekieh Gardens
Manon Lescaut, Puccini, October 1895, Cairo, Ezbekieh Gardens
I Capuleti ed I Montecchi, Bellini, December 7, 1895, Naples, Mercadante
Lucia di Lammermoor, Donizetti, February 15, 1896, Trapani, Garibaldi
Malia, Frontini, March 21, 1896, Trapani, Garibaldi
La Sonnambula, Bellini, March 24, 1896, Trapani, Garibaldi
Mariedda, Bucceri, June 23, 1896, Naples, Bellini
I Puritani, Bellini, September 10, 1896, Salerno, Municipale
La Favorita, Donizetti, November 22, 1896, Salerno, Municipale
A San Francisco, Sebastiani, November 23, 1896, Salerno, Municipale
Pagliacci, Leoncavallo, November 1896, Salerno, Municipale
Carmen, Bizet, December 6, 1896, Salerno, Municipale
Un Dramma in vendemmia, February 1, 1897, Naples, Mercadante
*Celeste, Lamonica & Biondi, March 6, 1897, Naples, Mercadante
Il Profeta velato, Napoletano, April 8, 1897, Salerno, Municipale
La Bohème, Puccini, August 14, 1897, Leghorn, Goldoni
La Navarrese, Massenet, November 3, 1897, Milan, Lirico
Il Voto, Giordano, November 10, 1897, Milan, Lirico
*L'Arlesiana, Cilea, November 27, 1897, Milan, Lirico
La Bohème, Leoncavallo, March 8, 1898, Genoa, Carlo Felice
I Pescatori di perle, Bizet, February 3, 1898, Genoa, Carlo Felice

OPERAS

Hedda, Le Borne, April 2, 1898, Milan, Lirico
Mefistofele, Boito, May 4, 1898, Fiume, Comunale
Saffo, Massenet, June 4, 1898, Trento, Sociale
Fedora, Giordano, November 17, 1898, Milan, Lirico
Iris, Mascagni, June 22, 1899, Buenos Aires, de la Opera
La Regina di Saba, Goldmark, July 4, 1899, Buenos Aires, de la Opera
Yupanki, Berutti, July 25, 1899, Buenos Aires, de la Opera
Aida, Verdi, January 3, 1900, St Petersburg, Grand Théâtre du Conservatoire
Un Ballo in maschera, Verdi, January 11, 1900, St Petersburg, Grand Théâtre du Conservatoire
La Resurrezione di Lazaro, Perosi, February 13, 1900, St Petersburg, Grand Théâtre du Conservatoire
Stabat Mater, Rossini, as above, St Petersburg, Grand Théâtre du Conservatoire
Maria di Rohan, Donizetti, March 2, 1900, St Petersburg, Grand Théâtre du Conservatoire
Manon, Massenet, July 28, 1900, Buenos Aires, de la Opera
Tosca, Puccini, October 23, 1900, Treviso, Sociale
Le Maschere, Mascagni, January 17, 1901, Milan, La Scala
L'Elisir d'amore, Donizetti, February 17, 1901, Milan, La Scala
Lohengrin, Wagner, July 7, 1901, Buenos Aires, de la Opera
Germania, Franchetti, March 11, 1902, Milan, La Scala
Don Giovanni, Mozart, July 19, 1902, London, Covent Garden
Adriana Lecouvreur, Cilea, November 6, 1902, Milan, Lirico
Lucrezia Borgia, Donizetti, March 10, 1903, Lisbon, São Carlos
Gli Ugonotti, Meyerbeer, February 3, 1905, New York, Metropolitan
Madama Butterfly, Puccini, May 26, 1906, London, Covent Garden
Marta, Flotow, December 3, 1906, New York, Metropolitan
L'Africana, Meyerbeer, January 11, 1907, New York, Metropolitan
Andrea Chénier, Giordano, July 20, 1907, London, Covent Garden
Il Trovatore, Verdi, February 26, 1908, New York, Metropolitan
Armide, Gluck, November 14, 1910, New York, Metropolitan
La Fanciulla del West, Puccini, December 10, 1910, New York, Metropolitan
Julien, Charpentier, February 26, 1914, New York, Metropolitan
Samson et Dalila, Saint-Saëns, November 15, 1915, New York, Metropolitan
Lodoletta, Mascagni, July 29, 1917, Buenos Aires, Colón
Le Prophète, Meyerbeer, February 7, 1918, New York, Metropolitan
L'Amore dei tre re, Montemezzi, March 14, 1918, New York, Metropolitan
La Forza del destino, Verdi, November 15, 1918, New York, Metropolitan
La Juive, Halévy, November 22, 1919, New York, Metropolitan

Index

INDEX